British Imperial Strategy
and the Origins of the
Cold War 1944–49

British Imperial Strategy and the Origins of the Cold War 1944–49

John Kent

Leicester University Press
Leicester, London and New York

Distributed exclusively in the USA and Canada by St. Martin's Press

Leicester University Press
(a division of Pinter Publishers Ltd)
25 Floral Street, Covent Garden, London, WC2E 9DS

First published in Great Britain in 1993

Distributed exclusively in the USA and Canada by St. Martin's Press, Inc., Room 400, 175 Fifth Avenue, New York, NY 10010, USA

John Kent is hereby identified as the author of this work as provided under Section 77 of the Copyright, Designs and Patents Act 1988.

British Library Cataloguing in Publication Data

A CIP catalogue record for this book is available from the British Library

ISBN 0 7185 1330 4

Library of Congress Cataloging-in-Publication Data

Kent, John, 1949–
    British imperial strategy and the origins of the Cold War /John Kent.
        p.   cm.
    Includes bibliographical references and index.
    ISBN 0-7185-1330-4
    1. Great Britain—foreign relations—1945–.   2. Great Britain—Colonies—History—20th century.   3. Imperialism—History—20th century.   4. World politics—1945–.   5. Cold War.   I. Title.
DA588.K46   1993
327.41′009′044—dc20   93–5048
                                                                              CIP

Typeset by Florencetype Ltd, Kewstoke, Avon
Printed and bound in Great Britain by
Biddles Ltd, Guildford and King's Lynn

Contents

Abbreviations

ACA	Armistice Terms and Civil Administration Committee
ADM	Admiralty
CAB	Cabinet Office
CC	Cabinet Conclusions
CEDC	Colonial Economic Development Council
CFM	Council of Foreign Ministers
CM	Cabinet Minutes
CO	Colonial Office
COS	Chiefs of Staff
CP	Cabinet Paper
CRO	Commonwealth Relations Office
DBPO	Documents on British Policy Overseas
DEFE	Defence Department
DO	Dominions Office
EPC	Economic Policy Committee
FO	Foreign Office
FRUS	Foreign Relations of the United States
JP	Joint Planners
MEP	Ministerial Committee on Economic Policy
PREM	Prime Minister's Papers
PUSC	Permanent Undersecretary Committee
SC	Suez Canal Committee
WO	War Office
WP	War Cabinet Paper

Note on sources

The aim of the research of this book has not been to track down every paper, public and private, in every archive in order to attempt a descriptive analysis of British policy as allegedly represented in a variety of minutes and memoranda; it has been to try and illustrate the conflicting views with and between departments concerned with the economic, military and foreign policy aspects of imperial strategy. By so doing, the reader can then judge the extent to which policy was coordinated and refined by senior officials and ministers conversant with the conflicting views on strategy, or whether it was made in a more ad hoc, ill-defined manner. More particularly, the reader can answer whether policy was implemented because of considered assessments of specific and clearly quantifiable issues or because of more general, emotive considerations.

The starting point, and most important and well-organized series was FO 371, Foreign Office general correspondence, which contains a selection of papers from Cabinet committees, the service Ministers, the Dominion and Colonial Offices, and records of interdepartmental meetings. The minutes of the full Cabinet papers presented to it, CAB 128 and CAB 129 respectively, are important for a guide to the information determining Cabinet decisions, and PREM 4 and PREM 8 reveal the Prime Minister's papers. For the war period, Cabinet meetings and memoranda are in CAB 65 and CAB 66. Useful material from the Cabinet Office records can be found in CAB 134, Standing Committees of the Cabinet, CAB 21, General Registered files, CAB 131, Minutes and memoranda of the Defence Committee, CAB 104, Supplementary registered files originally retained as sensitive. CAB 105 War Cabinet Telegrams, CAB 95 and CAB 87, Ad Hoc Cabinet Committee papers on the Suez Canal and Reconstruction Committee, and CAB 127, Private Collections of ministers' and officials' papers.

Colonial Office files of interest centre on CO 537, which until 1951 contained all secret files. CO 852 is a large series covering colonial economic affairs, and CO 936 and CO 968 refer to International Relations and Defence. DO 35 is the main source of Dominion Office files, but material on the broader issues, e.g.

Commonwealth meetings, can be found in FO 371. Treasury papers have been extracted from T 234, Home and Overseas Planning and T 236, the Overseas Finance Division. It is a difficult series to deal with but covers many of the issues dealt with by the equivalent Board of Trade section whose files are in BT 11. In essence, the Treasury tended to respond to the financial aspects of other departmental policies rather than to produce policy initiatives.

The most important defence files are in CAB 79 and 80, minutes and memoranda of the Chiefs of Staff up to the end of 1946, and DEFE 4 and 5 for the period after 1947. The Joint Planners memoranda are in CAB 84 and DEFE 6 and the Post Hostilities Planning Committee's meetings and memoranda in CAB 81. The Secretariat files of the Joint Planning Staff are in CAB 119 and the Air Ministry's Director of Plans papers in AIR 9. DEFE 11 contains the Chief of Staff Secretariat files and ADM 116 the Admiralty and Secretariat files, while DEFE 32 covers the Chiefs of Staff Secretariat files containing sensitive material excluded from the minutes of the Chiefs of Staff Committee.

Finally, Ernest Bevin's papers have been consulted in FO 800, the Chiefs of the Imperial General Staff's papers in WO 216, along with Lord Swinton's papers at Churchill College, Cambridge.

Preface

When Winston Churchill became Prime Minister of the wartime coalition government he did so with a determination not to preside over the dissolution of the
British Empire.[1] This famous commitment to a future imperial role for Britain was
to a large extent shared by the post-war Labour government. There were of course
differences between the Labour leaders and the former Prime Minister over the
means to be employed to achieve this, and differences within the Attlee administration over Britain's imperial strategy. In part these reflected the numerous and
varied concepts of what the Empire, or Commonwealth as it was increasingly to be
known, essentially involved. For some imperial advocates the Empire was an
emotive but vague concept. (Churchill himself always preferred the term Empire
and was never fully reconciled to the idea of Commonwealth.)[2] For others the
Empire was centred on a particular region – the Middle East, the Cape–Cairo line,
or the Indian Ocean. Others were more concerned to define the Commonwealth
by the nature of the political and constitutional ties, formal and informal, between
the various territories and the mother country. But for all policy makers involved in
wartime and post-war planning for the Empire's future, the ultimate aim was to
maximise Britain's influence on a global basis.

Much time has been spent on the sterile debate over whether Britain refused to
face up to its weakened world position following the enormous post-war shifts in
the global balance of power. In fact policy makers were fully aware of the decline in
British power produced by the war, but believed that such a decline could be
reversed.[3] It was fully expected that Britain would regain its economic strength
and international influence, and therefore it was a question of finding the means to
achieve such ends. This was the rationale behind an imperial strategy which is best
analysed in terms of the economic and military factors deemed essential for the
Empire's maintenance as a global power bloc, and in terms of the links between
the British Empire and other powerful nations which were seen as necessary to
maintain Britain's status and influence in the first rank of global powers.

Adopting such an approach is radically different from an examination of imperial stategy which focuses on the ending of formal colonial rule (decolonisation) as the central feature of Britain's changing global position. While the replacing of colonial rule by a relationship which was expected to preserve influence through informal means does form a part of the changing nature of the Empire, it will not be given much coverage here. In part this is because of a need to make a broad, wide ranging topic more manageable. Yet it is also because attitudes to the eventual ending of direct British rule in the late 1940s, and indeed in the 1950s, were not seen as part of managing Britain's imperial decline in the sense of projecting less power and influence in the world, but as part of the attempts to rebuild the British Empire as a global system on somewhat different lines. By focusing on these military, economic and foreign policy factors, which were seen as much more important than the constitutional relations within the Empire, the aim is to get away from the idea that progress towards the ending of colonial rule was part of an organised retreat from power. For example, if the abandonment of formal controls over parts of Asia had any effect on imperial policy it was to strengthen British desires to reassert their power and influence in other areas, most notably the Middle East, rather than to be 'deliberately and regularly bending'[4] in that very important area of informal Empire.

It is the key areas of Empire, defined in terms of what was vital for Britain's great-power status, and for the economic and military strategies deemed necessary to regain it, which provide one focus for this study. The other is the relations between the British Empire on the one hand and the United States, Western Europe and the Soviet Union on the other; this affected the position of the Empire and the kind of imperial role that foreign policy makers in particular expected Britain to play.

No one book can provide a detailed and comprehensive account of the issues arising from or relevant to the attempts to define and implement an imperial strategy based on such lines. This book certainly does not claim to provide such a coverage, and there remains scope for further studies on particular issues which may reach different conclusions to the ones drawn here. The purpose of this study is to attempt to link imperial economic policy and military strategy with foreign policy in a framework based on the overriding importance of the British Empire's position as a world system and its relations to the United States, the Soviet Union and the countries of Western Europe. It also aims to place the British Empire at the heart of the global power struggle which developed following the defeat of the Axis powers. Although essentially based on primary sources, it is less a thorough and definitive research monograph than an attempt to use a wide variety of different sources, some of which already feature in secondary literature, to produce some new ideas and interpretations of British strategy during the collapse of the wartime alliance between 1945 and 1947, and then of British policy during the initial years of the Cold War.

The fundamental assumption in the first half of the book is that while the Cold War has eventually to be defined in terms of a Soviet–American conflict, Britain played a major role in the development of Allied tensions that culminated in the effective breakdown of tripartite cooperation at the end of 1947. Far from reacting to Soviet imperialism and Stalin's attempts to project Russian power and influence, the British also had an imperial strategy and played an active role in the breakdown of Allied cooperation. And this role was not based on alerting the

United States to the dangers of Soviet expansion because of essentially European concerns, but on the policies which Britain attempted to implement in order to achieve a particular position of global standing relative to the United States and the Soviet Union. Thus the essential issue is the clash between rival imperialisms and the British attitude to a possible accommodation with the Soviet Empire.

The fact that this clash developed in the Eastern Mediterranean and the Middle East is one reason for the focus on that region and the relatively small coverage given to Asia. In addition the Middle East, having been the scene of Britain's most successful military campaigns, continued after the war to assume more importance in the eyes of the military strategists than any other region until 1950. Preserving paramount influence in the Middle East and Eastern Mediterranean was the essential element of that part of Britain's imperial strategy designed to prevent any further erosion of great-power status. The strategy for rebuilding this power and status was seen to depend on new links between Europe and the colonial Empires in Africa, and the efforts to achieve these are described in the second half of the book. The British aim was to regain a position of equality with the United States and the Soviet Union, but the means employed to do this within Europe and the Empire produced the problems and conflicts which eventually undermined Britain's imperial strategy in 1949.

Research for this book was conducted in the Public Record Office at Kew over the last ten years and I am deeply in debt to the staff there. Material from the Public Record Office is reproduced here by kind permission of the Controller of Her Majesty's Stationery Office. The research provided pleasant and frequently amusing interludes. I have benefited from discussions with John Hargreaves, Helen Mercer, Jim Tomlinson and many others including students at the London School of Economics who have helped me articulate ideas on Empire and Cold War. A special debt is owed to John Young whose ideas and advice, as well as his presence in London bars, have had an important influence on parts of this book. I alone, of course, am responsible for the ideas expressed here and the errors and omissions that may surround them. The manuscript was typed by Janet Smith, Celine Silve and Jenny Berry with help from Pat Christopher and Brenda Kent. My parents have again enabled me to work in pleasant surroundings away from the horrors of London. Gill Haigh, Jerry Jolly, Jane Royale and Mick Stuart have continued to provide support. My wife Brenda and my children Nicola, Gary and Lindsey are still putting up with my absences and I have no hesitation in acknowledging that their love and our involvement with swimming, walking and the fortunes of Aberdeen Football Club have proved more rewarding and meaningful than the writing of history books.

Notes

1. The Prime Minister stated firmly in a Mansion House speech that he had 'not become the King's First Minister in order to preside over the liquidation of the British Empire'. Winston S. Churchill *The End of the Beginning: War Speeches* (London 1943) p. 268.
2. CAB 128/28 CM (55) 28th 5.4.55.
3. A. Adamthwaite 'Britain and the World, 1945–49: the View from the Foreign Office' *International Affairs* 61, 2 (1985).
4. D. A. Low 'The End of the British Empire in Africa' in Wm Roger Louis and Prosser Gifford (eds.) *Decolonisation and African Independence* (London 1988) p. 39.

Chapter 1
Britain's wartime allies, post-war planning and the future of the empire

The period between the fall of Singapore in 1942 and the commencement in earnest of planning for the post-war future of the British Empire was a remarkably short one. The most traumatic experience in imperial history was almost immediately followed by attempts to provide general guidelines and specific policies for the Empire's future. Security pacts, regional cooperation in defence and colonial policy and creating a post-war international order for the benefit of imperial trading and financial interests were all to be given consideration over the next three years. Enlisting adequate support for imperial defence, an eventual but not immediate return to multilateral trade and international cooperation under the auspices of a successor to the League of Nations were important goals. To some extent they reflected the growing worldwide commitment to internationalism, but for the vast majority of Britain's political and official elites such measures would be adopted to strengthen and preserve, rather than replace or undermine the British Empire by the establishment of international organisations.

At the outset it was believed that in the post-war world Britain must either have some powerful ally (or allies) or cease to be a world power; the Empire in short could only be a world force as part of some wider organisation of international cooperation. To some extent this was to provide the rationale for the commitment to the United Nations and the maintenance of wartime cooperation after the conclusion of hostilities. At the same time it was to justify attempts to link the Empire more closely with France and the other Western European powers. More specifically, as Gladwyn Jebb the head of the Foreign Office's Economic and Reconstruction Department noted, the main objectives of British post-war policy were the restoration of export trade in order to maintain the necessary imports; the restricting of German and Japanese power; the maintenance of armed forces to *inspire confidence* and contribute to collective security; the maintenance of British power in *those parts of the world where it had hitherto been exercised* and where it represented a civilising and educational force, and the promotion of world trade and peace by means of international cooperation.[1] Clearly there was no commitment to a retreat from power, but the maintenance of Britain's position would depend on a variety of unpredictable factors. In individual territories and regions it would have to rely on policies which were acceptable to the native inhabitants of British territories and of those foreign countries in which Britain hoped to exercise influence; on a global scale it would hinge on the relationships among the British Empire, the United States, the Soviet Union and Western Europe.

The nature and relative importance of the relationships among these four areas of the globe was a question considered carefully by British elites whose views sometimes revealed important differences of emphasis. Subsequently historians have not all agreed on which relationships at which time were considered most significant by British policy makers. Churchill, with his close American connections, was so concerned to focus on the Anglo-American relationship that an appreciation of the practical difficulties and eventual consequences of associating the United States with the British Empire tended to escape him. His 1943 proposal of a common citizenship for the United States and the Commonwealth reflected Churchill's passionate commitment to an Anglo-American alliance; it was a commitment which rarely considered the considerable divergence of views in London and Washington over the future of the British Empire. Anthony Eden, Foreign Secretary since 1941, believed firmly in the value of good Anglo-American relations but was less sanguine about achieving them, and less inclined to put all Britain's eggs in what, during the war, was a decidedly anti-imperial American basket. Eden, preferred to look to France and Europe, along with the Empire, to give Britain more authority amongst the great powers. Similar views were later put forward by Ernest Bevin, who as Foreign Secretary in the post-war Labour government, was to be the architect of Britain's imperial strategy. Bevin looked to an alliance with the European states bordering on the Atlantic to be combined with those bordering on the Mediterranean, although he acknowledged that possible Russian reactions would have to be carefully considered.[2] In 1944, however, Eden and his officials were as concerned with American reactions to British policy as they were with Soviet susceptibilities and were increasingly dubious about the prospects of securing benefits from closer Anglo-American relations.[3]

Throughout the twentieth century periods of close Anglo-American relations and the pursuit of common interests have been accompanied by elements of competition and rivalry as the United States replaced Britain as the dominant global power. The position of the British Empire had always figured prominently in those Anglo-American conflicts. In 1928 Baldwin believed that 'American money power' was 'trying to get hold of the natural resources of the Empire'.[4] Roosevelt on the other hand feared that Chamberlain was attempting to engineer an Anglo-German agreement which would exclude American trade and finance from Europe, Africa and Latin America.[5]

Once the war began, the American President's concerns were centred on an Anglo-French imperial trading bloc which would exclude the United States. The importance of access to overseas markets dramatically increased for American policy makers during a war which doubled the capacity of industrial plant in the United States. As a result it was believed that new markets were required to preserve wartime prosperity. By 1945 the Director of War Mobilisation and Reconversion was telling the House Ways and Means Committee that post-war exports would have to be double the pre-war level if prosperity and full employment were to be attained.[6] Traditional American anti-colonialism, embodied in the Atlantic Charter of 1941, which promised all peoples the right to choose their own government, was thus accompanied by an anti-imperialist drive for equal access to overseas markets born out of what was believed to be economic necessity. Given these considerations it is understandable that in the wake of Singapore American Undersecretary of State Sumner Welles, a close confidant of Roosevelt until 1943, was referring to the end of imperialism.[7]

In Britain there were different ideas in the early years of the war on future relations between the United States and the British Empire. Gladwyn Jebb, keenly conscious of the broad issues at stake, believed Britain would have to go a long way towards meeting American requirements in Britain's Far Eastern Empire in order to secure United States involvement in European security.[8] This embodied an imperial strategy which required cooperation with the United States for which a price would have to be paid. As head of the Economic and Reconstruction Department Jebb was committed to the rebuilding of Britain's overseas export trade. Any concessions which would weaken imperial economic ties were therefore likely to prove highly undesirable; more scope seemed to be offered for concessions on colonial policy, especially as the loss of the Asian colonies to the Japanese revealed that the benefits of British rule were not regarded by native subjects as worth fighting to preserve. Moreover the British Embassy in Washington reported that the British were increasingly seen in the United States as 'bungling imperialists'. This stemmed from a view that 'British colonial policy has been oppressive, stupid, inefficient and insulting to the natives, with the result that the Malays and the Burmese have been conspicuously disloyal in contrast to the loyalty of the Filipinos'.[9]

In the summer of 1942, when the impact of Singapore had sunk in, officials in the Foreign Office and the Colonial Office were busy drafting papers on post-war policy in the region. The Far Eastern Department of the Foreign Office, aware of Roosevelt's statement that it would be impossible for Britain to return to its old position in Malaya, had long since believed that there could be no question of Burma, Malaya or Hong Kong being handed back to Britain to be governed as before; even if Britain retook them there would be pressures for international control. Nigel Ronald went even further in stating that the Americans would decide what to do with Britain's former colonies without even consulting London.[10] The head of the North American Department was quite prepared to abandon Hong Kong because it would 'show the United States we are going to be liberal to their beloved Chinese'. There were those in the Foreign Office therefore who were proposing the surrender of British territory in order to win American support for the defence of Britain's remaining Far Eastern Empire, although Undersecretary Sir Maurice Peterson disagreed. Even more astonishing was the Colonial Office's draft paper on Hong Kong and Malaya. Not only did the draft paper propose the return of Hong Kong, but officials envisaged a United Nations Council for the Pacific to which all countries in the area would be 'responsive' and which would provide for security and economic development; within this broad framework of apparent international accountability Malaya would be regarded as a British sphere of influence. This was too much for the Conservative Secretary of State, Lord Cranborne, to swallow, and he instructed his officials to abandon the idea of including Malaya in such a scheme. Some officials in the Foreign Office disagreed with this line because they felt economic incentives would not be sufficient to secure a defence commitment from the United States in the region; the latter could only be obtained by giving the Americans a political say in the running of the territories.[11] This was very much in line with the general thinking in the State Department, whose Advisory Committee on Post-War foreign policy was considering the future of the British colonies in the summer of 1942. Chaired by Sumner Welles, the Committee 'made sweeping recommendations about changes of sovereignty' and expressed a belief 'in trusteeship as a transition to independence'. Cordell Hull, the American Secretary of State, hoped to use the recommendations as a basis for a set of principles which would be universally accepted by the colonial powers in a joint declaration on future policy.[12]

The Colonial Secretary was appalled by such an idea and equally opposed to the views of the Foreign Office on Britain's Far Eastern colonies. Believing British colonialism had nothing to be ashamed about he wrote what Eden called a 'cheerfully robust' letter to the Foreign Secretary arguing that Britain should not allow itself to be manoeuvred into standing in a white sheet. Cranborne believed that the divergent views in the Foreign and Colonial Offices stemmed from 'a great degree of ignorance and a serious atrophy of our power to think "imperially". An essential basis for establishing our leadership depends therefore on promoting new awareness at home of the problems involved and on arousing the nation to a sense of having a mission to continue and fulfil in the world at large, particularly in our colonial Empire.' This would clearly not be achieved by sacrificing British rights to administer its Far Eastern colonies for the involvement of the United States in regional security schemes. The Colonial Secretary had strong support from Amery in pushing for the maintenance of British imperial authority. Amery felt that the war against Hitler was only a means to the essential end of preserving the British Empire and all it stood for in the world. If this were not achieved the fact that Hitler had been 'replaced by Stalin, Chiang Kai-shek or even an American President' would provide 'no consolation'.[13] Thus any Anglo-American cooperation should not involve concessions on Britain's part which would handicap its ability to play an undiminished imperial role. Nevertheless there were clearly those who assumed in 1942 that Anglo-American cooperation was so important that imperial sacrifices should be made to achieve it. If these were ruled out then it boiled down to ensuring that the Americans approached cooperation with the British Empire in the right sort of way.

The question of foreign economic policy seemed of particular importance for gauging whether American policy was likely to complement or conflict with British imperial interests. Could the determined American attempts to develop new markets be reconciled with the future development of the sterling area? In the early years of the war there tended to be an assumption that there would be some form of economic cooperation between the United States and the British Empire and in 1941 a Cabinet Committee had been established on Post-War External Economic Problems and Anglo-American Cooperation; but by the following year there were signs that such cooperation could not be taken for granted. There was no doubt in the North American Department that the United States would pursue an expansionist foreign economic policy after the war; the uncertainty was over whether this would 'take place on internationally planned lines', or whether it would develop 'as the purely arbitrary and unilateral pursuit of the selfish aims of Big Business'.[14] British concerns focused therefore on the attitudes of the American administration to the broad questions of imperial preferences, economic development of the non-European territories, the role of the sterling area, and also on the attitudes of American businessmen and the policies of wartime bodies, such as the Board of Economic Warfare and the Office of Lend Lease Administration, who had a direct role in the organisation of wartime trade and the provision of American goods.

Cordell Hull, Secretary of State until 1944, was firmly convinced that international conflicts originated from the economic rivalries engendered by protectionist and discriminatory trade policies. Getting rid of such policies was a particularly important post-war goal, given the difficulties of removing congressional support for some degree of American protectionism. Non-discrimination in commercial relations and the availability of raw materials to all nations on equal terms were essential elements of Hull's foreign economic policy. The implication was that American economic interests would have much greater involvement within the British Empire. Indications of this were increasingly evident by 1943, and reactions were largely conditioned by the extent to which the region involved was regarded as an exclusive British preserve. In the Middle East, US economic interest in the region was apparent during the phoney war and 'United States exporters worked feverishly to cash in on the elimination of their German, French and Italian competitors from the Middle East'. In 1941 when the constraints of the Neutrality Act of 1939, which banned American shipping from the Red Sea and the Gulf, were removed, American exports to the Middle East outstripped British exports. The establishment of the Anglo-American Middle East Supply Centre was an attempt to prevent competition seriously damaging British economic interests, and it enabled government control to be exerted over American commercial and Lend Lease exports to the Middle East for civilian use.[15]

The Middle East, unlike Black Africa and the Indian sub-continent, was an area where nominally independent states predominated. In the latter two regions the increasing involvement of American commercial interests had political implications which threatened the continuing preservation of British administrative authority. In India, Roosevelt was using American missions, and in particular his personal representative Louis Johnson, to facilitate a settlement between the Cripps Mission and the Congress Party.[16] The Viceroy, Lord Linlithgow, was perturbed by these 'machinations' and by the superfluously large mission the Americans were assembling in Delhi. He suspected 'that they were making ground where they could with a view to strengthening the United States' post-war position in Indian markets at British expense'.[17] In West Africa, the British Resident Minister, Lord Swinton, was primarily concerned with the political impact of the United States' wartime presence. One member of the Office of War Administration claimed to have orders to explain to Africans the meaning of Roosevelt's 'Four Freedoms'. More significantly there were various rumours circulating about a future American takeover in the Gold Coast: the British had been given two years to leave; the United States had received the territory on a 99-year lease; or the Americans were to receive Ashanti and the Northern Territories leaving Britain with the colony. In addition certain individual GIs engaged in activities which were likely to arouse native resentment: excessive joyriding, refusing to pay ferry tolls and the gatecrashing of rest houses were frowned upon by the Gold Coast government along with a more serious incident in which several Africans were mown down by a US army lorry. Swinton concluded that 'although the abuse of natives and exhibitionism with native prostitutes makes Africans compare the United States unfavourably with Britain, the ultimate result is to foment colour feeling and increase Britain's racial problems'. But there were also signs, as elsewhere, of increasing American economic interest, and that certain American army officers, acting on the instructions of US Intelligence, were attempting to obtain information on communications, industries, ports, labour supply and power plants in West Africa.[18]

In London the position was considered serious enough for a Colonial Office paper on 'American Influence in West Africa' to be considered by the Cabinet, as American business interests there 'might acquire a position that would seriously undermine British authority and hamper the task of British administration'. Desmond Morton, Churchill's Intelligence adviser and a close wartime confidant of the Prime Minister, saw in the activities of American business representatives in French and British West Africa another sign of the tendency of some United States agencies or interests to aim at world economic dictatorship. Moreover the region, unlike the Far East, was not one where American assistance to meet defence requirements was seen as necessary. In an area of influence regarded as exclusively British there was a tendency throughout Whitehall to see Anglo-American cooperation as less desirable. The Colonial Secretary, Oliver Stanley, was therefore quick to thwart any prospect of the British authorities providing information of commercial value to American personnel. As he informed Swinton, 'there would clearly be objections to supplying information of the above character when disclosure might affect a future interest of existing British commercial concerns'.[19]

More generally the degree of cooperation, as opposed to competition with American interests, would depend not just on the greater or lesser need to preserve exclusive British influence and administrative authority, but on the aims and attitudes of particular American individuals and organisations. In the Foreign Office those Americans who were opposed to economic cooperation with the British Empire were referred to as 'economic imperialists'. It was believed that their ranks had been strengthened by those previously isolationist elements who now advocated the assumption of world leadership by the United States and who attacked economic planning as a plot to create an 'un-American collectivist state'. Such individuals would be the flag bearers in what Morton feared could prove to be American economic dictatorship in the post-war world. On the other hand there were advocates of American economic expansionism who seemed prepared to adopt a more cooperative approach to foreign economic cooperation and the British Empire. Hull referred to British colonial possessions in a speech on American war aims in July 1942, arguing that colonial development had a role to play in creating a new economic internationalism; it was through international investment that natural resources and productive capacity would be developed in the more backward areas of the globe. John Foster Dulles had been more explicit in a conversation with Lord Cranborne in the same month. Speaking on the subject of American distrust of the British Empire, Dulles suggested that the only way to remove such deep seated prejudices in the United States would be to invite

American cooperation in post-war colonial development; if this could be done, especially in Africa, then a solid foundation for worldwide cooperation would be laid.[20]

In 1943, however, there were clearly fears in London that the economic imperialists, bent on American domination of the British Empire would win out over the economic expansionists prepared to cooperate with Britain. Such was the concern that Graham Spry was sent as a temporary employee of the Foreign Office to assess the general nature of American opinion on the British Empire, and his report, drawn up after his return in 1943, was to pay particular attention to American views on future commercial policy. In the meantime the State Department was made aware of British worries about American traders in the undeveloped world in an *aide-mémoire* delivered in July. The submission on Latin America referred to a British 'impression, however false, that there may be some desire on the American side to supplant British traders in their established and traditional markets, not only for the war period, but permanently thereafter'.[21]

In the Foreign Office Graham Spry had returned from the United States in November 1943 and was preparing his report for submission in 1944. The report was to be submitted to the Law Committee on American opinion and the British Empire established two years earlier under the chairmanship of Richard Law, Minister of State in the Foreign Office. It was at the centre of an organised attempt to assess American views on the Empire, and to conduct a propaganda campaign through the Washington Embassy, which had a colonial attaché, and the British Information Service in the United States; it was a campaign designed to 'educate' American public opinion on the nature, development and ultimate value of Britain's colonial Empire. Spry outlined four trends in United States commercial policy and the various groups who supported them. The New Deal International Planners were the group perhaps most favourably inclined to an international arrangement accommodating both American and British interests. Supported by Henry Wallace the group also had some backing in business circles and one Philadelphia businessman with strong Wall Street connections believed that the United States

needed to cooperate with Britain in meeting British needs and allowing for British export growth and shipping shortages. Otherwise the British system of free enterprise will not continue. They will rigidify their system on a narrow Empire basis. This foreshadows bilateral trade agreements. It would mean greater government control of credit and investment, especially in the colonies.

Opposed to these Eastern progressive elements were the traditional protectionists of the Midwest who looked to the development of a strong internal market behind a high tariff which would protect American industries.

More important, from the Empire point of view, were those who believed that the American market would not suffice to absorb the dramatic wartime increases in production. On the one hand were Cordell Hull and the free traders who were supported by the major exporting interests including tobacco firms, cotton producers and the oil industry, along with the New York banking houses and the larger and older businesses; these were clearly seen by Spry as the more moderate members of the expansionist lobby. On the other hand there were the 'economic imperialists' who had ambitious anticipations of profits and American expansion. They contained new interests such as aircraft manufacturers, aviation companies and the engineering, electrical and plastics industries which relied on new technology. Advocating foreign investment to encourage American exports of capital equipment they believed that Britain should accept a role as the junior partner of the United States. Within the administration there was strong support in the State Department for Hull's policies of joint agreements on accepted principles of non-discriminatory multilateral trade between independent nations. The more aggressive elements seeking to oust the British by fair means or foul were believed by Spry to be strong within the Foreign Economic Administration.[22]

The Foreign Economic Administration had been established in September 1943 to take over all Washington-based activities affecting export controls, licensing and import requirements. Its creation stemmed from the State Department's desire to exercise more control over the representatives of some government agencies, notably the Office of Lend Lease Administration and the Board of Economic Warfare. Its first head, Leo T. Crowley, asserted that he would ensure American business interests in foreign areas were adequately protected and promoted.[23] For those in the Foreign Office who were optimistic about accommodating American expansionism, as opposed to having to deal with American imperialism of the more extreme kind, this was not necessarily a bad thing. A. A. Dudley, a junior official in the North American Department, urged that Britain should cooperate with the United States in foreign economic policy and avoid stressing Anglo-American rivalries. Colonial development seemed a particularly promising area for Anglo-American cooperation to Dudley, who suggested that 'if we are genuinely interested in promoting development and the good of the local communities in the colonies, if we want Americans to take the right sort of interest in the Empire, and if we are short of capital for such investments, [as the Treasury was arguing in 1943] it seems to me that we ought to pursue the idea of encouraging the investment of American resources in Empire countries'.[24] Other officials were more sceptical about involving the Americans. Sir R. I. Campbell, a minister in the Washington Embassy, believed that 'in the name of benefiting the backward populations and improving standards of life, we shall get a combination of Wallace up-lift and National Association of Manufacturers export drive, much to the detriment of the nations who will be forced to run before they have learnt to walk'.[25]

In the Colonial Office a departmental study was underway at the end of 1943 on relations between the United States and the colonial Empire. Presumably convinced that government-financed development would emerge as the exclusive preserve of the Colonial Office, Sir William MacLean's report concentrated on the prospects for American trade and business interests in the colonies. It noted that there was some possibility of increased United States participation in trading operations, particularly in West Africa, but this was not seen as significant. American producers were felt to be generally incapable of understanding and producing for African requirements. There was therefore neither a threat from American business interests nor much point in encouraging their activities.[26] Even for those with less sanguine views, American economic involvement with British colonies was but one part of a much more important whole – the creation of a stable and prosperous post-war economic order. If American businessmen and government agencies were behaving in threatening and unreasonable ways in the colonies, was this a sign of more general difficulties in the way of Anglo-American cooperation? The role of American business in colonial development was certainly not the only question concerning those seeking to deal with the broader issues of British global influence, the relationship between the sterling area and the dollar zone and the preservation of exclusive administrative authority in the colonies.

The year 1944 was to see major progress towards defining the nature of the post-war international economic order with the Bretton Woods Conference establishing the International Bank for Reconstruction and Development and the International Monetary Fund. Dominated by the United States, because American finance underwrote their operations, these new bodies were nevertheless symbols of international cooperation in easing the transition to multilateral trade and convertible currencies. At the government level there were signs of economic cooperation to overshadow the anti-British activities of certain US firms and organisations, although at the start of the year Sir Orme Sargent, Deputy Undersecretary in the Foreign Office, enquired rather seriously, 'are we sure that there may not be forces in the United States (big business and naval circles) who will work for a system of close collaboration between the United States and Russia in which there would be small or no part for Great Britain?'[27] It was the first indication of a British fear, linked in this case to economic concerns, which was to dominate imperial strategy in 1944 and 1945.

To some extent it was grounded in a British defeat over the future conduct of military operations discussed and implemented by the Allies before and after the meeting of the Big Three leaders at Tehran in November and December 1943. Not only did the Americans give much greater priority than the British to Far Eastern campaigns designed to bolster Chiang Kai-shek, but they sided with the Russians over the conduct of the war in Europe. Amphibious campaigns in the Eastern Mediterranean were ruled out and Churchill's much vaunted Italian strategy was given less priority than the invasion of southern France (Operation Anvil) in support of the Normandy landings. Thus the war effort was not to be geared to Britain's imperial interests in the Far East, or, much more importantly, in the Mediterranean.[28] Churchill, always concerned with both the Empire's position and Britain's prestige, urged Ismay (Chief Staff Officer to the Prime Minister) to make sure the Americans were aware that Britain had been ill treated and was furious.[29]

Undoubtedly relations between the two Anglo-Saxon allies deteriorated in 1944 just as the correspondence between Roosevelt and Churchill had become more formal.[30] But the Prime Minister's silences, like his outbursts, were essentially expressions of annoyance at the way the Americans were dealing with Britain and its Empire; the Americans could arouse anger and resentment, but they were never seen as universally threatening in any sinister sense. The Foreign Secretary also gave vent to his annoyance, claiming that American anti-colonialism was designed to make the non-self-governing territories economically and politically dependent on the United States;[31] this too, was irritation over the aims and attitudes of some Americans who were jeopardising the establishment of what was seen by the British as a mutually advantageous relationship between the Empire and the United States. The element of fear was generally lacking: however badly the Americans were behaving they were still behaving as friends; and while friendships could be weakened and damaged the behaviour of friends would always be fundamentally different from the behaviour of enemies or potential enemies.

The remarkable thing, and a highly significant one in terms of Britain's relationship with her other wartime ally, was that despite the evidence that the United States could well present a threat to the maintenance of colonial authority and the reestablishment of imperial trade, there was never any suggestion in London that cooperation per se was undesirable. However disturbing American behaviour became there were always those prepared to play down its effects. Equally there were always those who believed that American behaviour could be modified in the light of superior British experience and know how in world affairs; thus the belief that cooperation with the United States would ultimately be secured on terms beneficial to Britain's imperial interests was always present despite the doubters who saw more problems than advantages as the war drew to a close. As one official wrote:

It must not be our purpose to balance our power against that of America, but to make use of American power for the purposes which we regard as good . . . If we go about our business in the right way we can help steer this great unwieldy barge, the United States of America, into the right harbour. If we don't, it is likely to continue to wallow in the ocean, an isolated menace to navigation.[32]

Given the maritime traditions of British imperial power the metaphor was a significant one. Despite the active wartime interest in the political and economic aspects of the British Empire the United States could still be portrayed as 'wallowing in isolation'.

To some extent, particularly in economic terms, the British were making a virtue out of necessity when they talked of a satisfactory modus vivendi with their Atlantic ally. Battered and bruised by a war which had drained the nation's wealth, Britain was in no position to police the high seas. Its overseas trading potential was drastically reduced, its overseas assets had been cashed in and it was left with an industrial base geared primarily to the manufacture of armaments rather than consumer goods. Britain could not therefore isolate itself from the world's richest nation without an appalling period of austerity. Moreover, as a major trading nation dependent on imports for survival, it was in Britain's interest, as much as America's, to establish an international order based on an expanding system of multilateral trade. Thus the controversial Article VII of the Lend Lease agreement, which committed the signatories to do everything possible to promote the expansion of trade, the elimination of all forms of discriminatory treatment of international commerce and the reduction of tariffs, was for the British a statement of principle in keeping with their long-term aims as a major trading nation. Similarly Anglo-American cooperation was a necessity in the Far East where it was clear that Britain would have to rely on the United States to prevent a revival of Japanese aggression and to fulfil the main role of regional policeman. Imperial strategy was based therefore on cooperation with the United States being both necessary and desirable in economic and defence terms. But in order to preserve British power and influence it remained important to ensure that British authority was not undermined in those areas where colonial rule and informal influence appeared most likely to endure for a considerable time. With this in mind there is no doubt that British elites had, by 1944, recovered from the shock of Singapore and rediscovered the will to think imperially. At the same time it was clear that in so doing they were coming into conflict with the United States. Whether this would be a serious problem at the end of the war would depend on whether those with influence in Washington were more or less opposed to the continuation of an essentially unreconstructed British Empire; their attitudes would to a large extent determine the extent to which cooperation or conflict would dominate the Anglo-American relationship.

From the British point of view, however, despite the reservation about success-fully establishing cooperation on a basis of equality which would not undermine the British Empire, the fundamental point was that the United States had already been judged as a friendly power with whom the wartime partnership should be preserved. Instead of seeing the Empire as an instrument which would give Britain the power to outface the United States, American power was seen as necessary in the aftermath of war to preserve the Commonwealth and Empire. The Soviet Union, on the other hand was judged much more negatively; cooperation was deemed desirable, but certainly not seen as necessary and was dependent on the Soviet Union convincing British elites that it was an essentially friendly power.

During the war the Soviet Union had not been acting as an anti-imperial power in the same way as the United States. There had been no conflicts over economic policy or colonial declarations and the Soviets had not threatened Britain's overseas markets. As a communist state isolated from the capitalist world there was no question of the Soviets either competing or cooperating with Britain's imperial economic policy. The Soviet Union had of course been a traditional rival of the British Empire from the Himalayas to the Mediterranean, and this clearly meant that a careful eye would have to be kept on Soviet actions and intentions. The Soviets might be prepared, as an ally with whom Britain hoped to cooperate in the post-war years, to accept the British Empire, or they might attempt to undermine it. It was this uncertainty about Soviet behaviour which dominated British policy in the period of post-war planning between 1942 and 1944. But there was a crucial difference in the nature of the assumptions made by British elites about Soviet and American behaviour. In part this resulted from the geographical positions of the three wartime Allies. The Far East and the Pacific Ocean were areas in which American power was clearly dominant and in which the former basis of British rule had been destroyed by the Japanese. It was therefore natural that Britain should expect the United States rather than the Soviet Union to help pick up the pieces. Moreover the latter was not seen as a major force in the region, and the Far Eastern department concluded that Russian aims in the Far East were not likely to conflict with Britain's strategic interests.[33] In the Middle East and Eastern Mediterranean however, Soviet power was much closer and Soviet influence likely to grow as a result of the advance of Soviet armies. The Middle East was an area of greater strategic importance to the Empire than the Far East and it was an area in which the war years had seen a build up of British military power as opposed to its defeat. In addition there was the inevitable increase of Soviet power in Europe to consider from a British standpoint that did not give the Russians the same kind of blessing accorded to the United States as an essentially friendly power.

If judgements were going to be made about the friendliness of Soviet behaviour, an obvious point of focus was that region of Europe which Soviet troops would need to pass through and occupy in order to defeat Nazi Germany and its allies. Hungary and Romania had joined Germany in their assault on the Soviet Union in 1941, whereas Bulgaria between 1941 and 1944 was at war with Britain and the Allies, but not with the Soviet Union. The nomenclature of this geographic area between Germany and the Soviet Union is often confusingly referred to in the historiography. 'Central Europe', 'Eastern Europe', 'Southeastern Europe' are vague concepts which may or may not be applied to certain countries. The question for historians is to determine what particular countries were associated with particular areas and what priority, if any, each was accorded in terms of British interests and Soviet behaviour. If, as has been argued, the Moscow Foreign Ministers' Conference of 1943 marked the surrender of Eastern Europe, did that mean the whole of Europe east of the German border?[34] Were there different perceptions by Britain, and indeed by the Soviet Union, of the relative importance of the various states? Did Poland in northern Europe matter more than Yugoslavia in the south or Romania in the east or Hungary in central Europe?

In Britain, apart from the Foreign Office itself, important ministerial and official committees were considering the issues arising from the Soviet advance towards Germany in 1944. The balance of power in Europe, Britain's interests in the wider world, especially the Eastern Mediterranean, the occupation of enemy territories and the strategic implications of Germany's defeat had all to be considered in an atmosphere of uncertainty about Soviet intentions. A ministerial committee on Armistice Terms and Civil Administration was established and succeeded by the Armistice and Post-War Committee (APW), chaired by the Deputy Prime Minister and including the Foreign Secretary, Anthony Eden, and his eventual successor Ernest Bevin. The APW's brief was to consider questions affecting armistice terms and their execution, along with the administration of territories liberated or conquered, and general political and military questions in the post-war period. It was linked to the Foreign Office by the head of the Economic and Reconstruction Department who also conducted liaison between the Foreign Office and the Post-Hostilities Planning Committee. The latter succeeded the military Sub-Committee in 1943, and as a sub-committee of the Chiefs of Staff Committee had a responsibility to report to the military chiefs as well as to the APW and the Foreign Office. It was to put forward solutions to problems arising from the occupation of enemy territory in so far as such problems were connected with the administration of instruments of surrender or with questions of general political-strategic importance, and to advise the Foreign Office on the military and strategic aspects of these political and administrative questions.[35] It was within this framework that evaluations about the Soviet role in Europe and the implications for British policy were made.

For the historian, the main interest of the post-war planners' ideas in 1943 and 1944 lies not in the assumptions they reveal about the Soviet Union or communism. However much British ruling elites may have regarded the Soviet system with fear and loathing there was an important veneer of respect combined with the oft expressed hope that wartime cooperation would continue. Nor did the ideas of the planners define the nature of post-war policy; inevitably such policy was made and implemented in the rapidly changing circumstances of a return to peace. What is of prime interest is the light the planners' ideas shed on expectations of Soviet behaviour. Or, more precisely, given the prevailing uncertainty, what Soviet actions would be deemed compatible with British interests and the continuation of cooperation; in other words, what Soviet requirements in the post-war world could be reconciled with a stable Europe and the continued maintenance of British global power and influence?

An early assessment came from the British Ambassador in Moscow, Sir Archibald Clark Kerr, in November 1942. The Soviets, he believed, would require Eastern Poland, Bessarabia and the Baltic states to secure their frontiers, but how much further they would go in terms of frontiers and spheres of influence would depend on the conditions at the end of the war and the actions of Allies.[36] The issue of spheres of influence was one that was to be discussed and considered at conferences and in briefings for the next few years and its significance has been debated by historians ever since. Did a sphere of influence mean an exclusive one? Did it mean simply the control over the foreign policy of the states within it, or did it mean the control of domestic policy as well?[37] At the highest levels in the Foreign Office there appeared to be few illusions about what Stalin desired. Yet a junior official, who in many of his minutes was optimistic about future Anglo-Soviet relations and less ready to regard the Soviets as inherently unreasonable, believed that Stalin would not require tightly controlled and disciplined communist regimes in Eastern Europe. He saw the Russians as favouring broad Popular Front governments and saw no evidence of a desire to apply elsewhere detailed models of the communist economic system. His undersecretary was in fact horrified by such a prospect. If broad popular front governments were based on a parliamentary system and comprised 'flabby democratic socialists' and generally speaking resembled the Blum government in France before the war then, said Sargent, 'heaven help us – it will mean corruption, inefficiency and Civil War'. However, Sargent did not believe that Stalin would find such a prospect any more appealing than he did. The Soviet leader, he argued, wanted a strong and dictatorial government in those territories in which Russia would be the dominant influence. Such states would therefore have autocratic rulers administering a system of state socialism and following a pro-Russia policy.[38]

As traditional imperial powers with controls over large areas of the globe, Britain and the Soviet Union could well have a mutual interest in the post-war development of spheres of influence. On the other hand, in areas conquered by the Allies or liberated from the Germans there could well be advantages from the British point of view in denouncing them, particularly as the United States was known to be hostile to such manifestations of power politics. As a question of principle, it could well prove desirable for internationalist reasons to avoid them; as a question of self-interest it would certainly be desirable to denounce them in those areas where there was very little chance of exercising any real influence. This had been the rationale for Britain's inter-war attempts to create a zone between Germany and the Soviet Union which was not within the sphere of influence of the two more powerful states to the east and the west. For whatever reason, Eden decided at the Moscow Conference in October 1943 to propose the renunciation of European spheres of influence; the rejection of the proposal by Molotov prompted Orme Sargent to conclude that Russia was contemplating exclusive spheres of influence in Eastern Europe (although no particular countries were specified).[39]

At the highest level in the Foreign Office, where an overall view of post-war

Europe had to be discerned and defined, such a prospect did not arouse the kind of concern that was eventually to become apparent. Some nine months later, a Foreign Office paper submitted to the full Cabinet entitled 'Soviet Policy in Europe' assumed that the Soviet Union would not want to antagonise the West by undue interference in European countries, (again no particular states were mentioned) and therefore Britain should be able to maintain influence in most, if not all, European countries. The foundation of Britain's European policy, it continued, must be an Anglo-Soviet alliance to restrain Germany.[40] This assumption can only have been made on the basis of an overall assessment of the European situation together with the idea that Europe west and south of Germany would not be of concern to the Soviets. In addition it was linked to a vital distinction between different areas of Europe east of Germany in terms of British assessments of Soviet behaviour in Europe and the prospect of Anglo-Soviet cooperation. The paper on Europe made no reference to the Balkans which had been dealt with in great detail in an earlier Cabinet Paper submitted in June.[41] In part this reflected a departmental distinction between the Central and Northern Departments, who were assessing Soviet behaviour in terms of a stable European system which could contain the German threat, and the Southern Department who was steeped in the nineteenth-century traditions of containing Russia's power in the Balkans. For the Central and Northern Departments, a strong Soviet Union, which was inevitable at the end of the war, offered the inherent advantage of containing a German revival. Moreover, as will become clear, the Foreign Office did not see *vital* British interests at stake in that part of Eastern Europe north of the Balkan states. However any increase in Soviet power also threatened an increase of Soviet influence in the Balkan states, which would threaten Britain's influence in the Eastern Mediterranean and the Middle East which was of vital interest to Britain's imperial strategists.

In 1944 there was thus a difference of approach in British assessments of Soviet actions and behaviour, dependent on whether they affected the general balance of power in Europe or the specific dominance of British power in the Eastern Mediterranean and Middle East. In the case of the latter, post-war planners, in keeping with traditional strategic and power-political interests, saw the countries of Greece and Turkey as particularly important. Each bordered on the Aegean Sea which was strategically significant for the maintenance of British naval dominance in the Eastern Mediterranean. Moreover, Turkish territory was bisected by the Straits of the Dardanelles and the Bosporus, an important maritime link connecting two seas in the same way as the Suez and Panama Canals, and like the Suez Canal subject to an international convention. The Straits Convention signed at Montreux in 1936 was, from the British viewpoint, designed to nullify the threat presented to imperial communications in the Mediterranean by the Soviet navy. The position of Greece and Turkey was the crux of the problem presented by wartime Soviet expansion in the eyes of British policy makers; and second in importance were Bulgaria and Yugoslavia because of their geographical position in relation to Greece, Turkey and the Aegean and Black Seas. Soviet behaviour in these territories would therefore be assessed differently from the Soviet actions in the rest of the area between the Adriatic and the Baltic.

The significance of Greece and Turkey in comparison to that central area of Europe between Germany and the Soviet Union has not been emphasised by historians of Britain and the Cold War. Moreover, the Mediterranean and its shoreline has often been overshadowed by Germany and Poland as a cause of Allied disagreements. Looked at from a long term perspective there is no doubt that Germany's future position in Europe was crucial and that it became a source of conflict and suspicion in Anglo-Soviet relations. Yet in 1944 the German issue was the one on which the Foreign Office assumed that agreement with the Russians was most likely. Moreover as the German question never became the focus of attention in the discussions of the peace makers until 1947, its role as an early source of Anglo-Soviet conflict has to be questioned. Poland was in fact much more of an issue in 1944 and 1945 and has rarely been ignored as an important factor in the breakdown of tripartite Allied cooperation. Yet in 1944 much British effort was devoted to ensuring that the Poles fell in with Russian wishes, notably over the eastern Polish frontier with the Soviet Union. A certain amount of Russian influence over Poland was seen as not only inevitable but desirable in the context of a general European settlement.[42] No amount of Russian influence over Turkey, Greece or the Eastern Mediterranean was ever contemplated with anything but horror.

Nowhere was this more so than in the Southern Department where Pierson Dixon was a leading member of the campaign to alert the Foreign Office to the dangers presented by Soviet power. Dixon was later to play a key post-war role along with another virulent Russophobe, Sir Orme Sargent, as Ernest Bevin's Private and Permanent Undersecretaries respectively. During the war Sargent was the supervising undersecretary for both the Northern and Southern Departments between 1942 and 1945. The departmental structure of the Foreign Office is not without significance in producing views on the Soviet position and Europe. In 1943 and 1944, the Northern Department covered the Soviet Union, the Baltic States and Scandinavia, the Central Department was responsible for Austria, Benelux, Germany, Hungary, Czechoslovakia, Poland, Portugal, and Spain; which as France had its own department left Albania, Bulgaria, Greece, Italy, Romania, Turkey and Yugoslavia for the Southern Department. As early as 1942, the Southern Department, seemingly unaware that the Soviet Union could have any interest in the defeat of Germany, saw the Russians as poised for an invasion of the Balkans; if Hitler's ally Romania was defeated, far from providing a boost to the resistance movements in the Balkans, the Southern Department view was that Greece, Yugoslavia and Bulgaria would be in an unenviable position. Dixon maintained that it was in Britain's interest to lay plans to counter the expansionist moves on the part of the Soviet Union, but realised the threat this posed to the maintenance of good Anglo-Soviet relations. As British policy was predicated on not impairing good relations with the Soviets, how were Britain's interests to be maintained? It was a dilemma that was to resurface continually over the ensuing months. Lord Hood was, meanwhile, in no doubt of the consequences facing the British Empire if the Balkans were effectively welded into the Soviet Union; this, he minuted, would present a menace more serious than Germany.[43]

These fears were partially reflected in a February 1944 paper, circulated in Whitehall by the Foreign Office, which assessed 'Probable Post-War Tendencies in Soviet Foreign Policy as Affecting British Interests'. It focused not on Poland, Germany or the central sector of Eastern Europe, but on Turkey, Bulgaria and the Straits. In a passage significant for its rather sanguine prediction of limited Soviet aims, the memorandum asserted that physical control of the Straits was unlikely to be demanded by any Soviet statesman. However, this, according to the paper, would be largely immaterial as any foreign air force in control of Bulgarian airfields would control the Straits and thereby dominate Turkey. For Turkey therefore, Soviet designs on Bulgaria were now, according to the Foreign Office, as crucial as Soviet designs on the Straits. For their part the Soviets would be equally concerned about a hostile Turkey as it threatened Russia's vital Black Sea communications and the security of the Caucasian oilfields. This was seen as particularly significant because of the Turkish alliance with Britain which would make Turkey less manageable in Soviet eyes. Russia, it was concluded, would therefore take a close interest in the Middle East, and this feature of the post-war years would be accentuated if Russia became suspicious of British intentions or found that cooperation with Western nations did not pay. The Foreign Office had therefore identified a possible source of conflict between Soviet aims and Britain's imperial position in the Middle East due to the inevitable Russian interest in Turkey, Bulgaria and the Straits and the strategic implications of air power.[44]

Their assessment was similar but not identical to that being reached by the post-war military planners, and indicated the way ideas about future Soviet behaviour were being related to specific British interests. There was agreement on what these interests were, but differences over what the implications would be if Soviet power was to impinge upon them. As far as the Straits were concerned, the Post Hostilities Planners sub-committee had been asked to examine the issue of Russia's post-war position there in early 1943, because of the likelihood that the Soviets would demand unrestricted access to a warm water port.[45] The role of the Post Hostilities Planning Committee (PHP), later the Post Hostilities Planning Staff, has been given much attention by Julian Lewis, and its reports cited by many leading historians, but in a recent article Richard Aldrich and Michael Coleman have questioned its importance in determining the parameters of Britain's post-war strategy, even to the extent of referring to it as a 'low level body'.[46] Thus the controversy engendered by the PHP's work, which later produced a rift with the Foreign Office, has now been extended to the historiography. It is certainly worth noting, as is evident from Lewis's book, that the PHP was not the only military body assessing the implications for Britain's strategic interests of the rise of Soviet power. The PHP's reports were filtered through the Joint Planning Staff and had to be approved by the Chiefs of Staff, and like all wartime planning bodies they were disbanded at or before the war's end. Subsequently some of their plans and assumptions were changed to meet new circumstances and requirements. In addition the PHP's role was never defined as planning the whole basis for Britain's defence strategy in the context of technical advances, foreign policy requirements and resource allocation. But in the context of defining Britain's strategic interests and how these would be affected by Soviet policy it clearly had a significant if not definitive role. The Chiefs of Staff agreed in early 1944 that PHP papers on Bulgaria should be used to guide the UK representatives on the European Advisory Commission; when issues were raised at the Yalta Conference which warranted military views, the Chiefs of Staff turned to the PHP to make an assessment. Finally it should be noted that despite the PHP's anti-Soviet reputation, in some aspects of its analysis of the Soviet threat, as will be shown below, it was much less concerned by the possible strengthening of the Soviet position in the Straits and much less hardline than the Chiefs of Staff or even, by 1945, some officials in the Foreign Office.

In the case of the Straits and the implications of Russian demands for unrestricted access to a warm water port, the PHP assessment was completed in August 1943. It was dominated by the increased threat from Russian air power if the Soviets secured control of the Dardanelles. This would enable broad zones to be developed on both sides of the Straits in which a large air force could be deployed; the whole of the Suez Canal area was within 800 miles of the Straits and the distance to the North African coast between Benghazi and Alexandria a mere 600 miles. In addition Soviet land forces in the Straits would force the Turkish army to deploy there as well as on the eastern Turkish frontier with the Soviet Union; this would facilitate an advance through Syria towards Egypt, while any deployment in the Straits would make it easier for an invasion of Greece to be mounted. Therefore, from the British point of view, if relations with the Soviets deteriorated, British forces in the Eastern Mediterranean and the Middle East would have to be strengthened. The Soviet naval threat was not seen as so significant because a Russian fleet entering the Aegean and the Mediterranean would be faced by the Royal Navy operating from a large array of British bases. The PHP therefore proposed a revision of Montreux to allow Russian ships unrestricted passage when the Soviet Union was not at war with Turkey.[47] Similar views were being expressed at exactly the same time by the Prime Minister. Churchill, recalling the fact that Constantinople had been offered to the Russians early in the First World War, was therefore certain that Soviet demands for alterations in the regime at the Straits would be forthcoming. At Tehran in November 1943 Churchill had proved sympathetic to Stalin's desire for a revision of Montreux. He told the Soviet leader that there were 'no obstacles' to Russia having a warm water port. 'Russia would sail the ocean with her Navy and merchant ships and we would welcome her ships'. The Russian grievance would be met because the future government of the world must be entrusted to satisfied nations, who wished nothing more for themselves than what they had.[48]

The Joint Planners and the Chiefs of Staff had a rather different view about Soviet grievances on the passage of Russian ships through the Straits. Pointing out that a similar air threat would exist from Bulgarian airfields as from the Straits, and therefore in a sense Soviet air bases next to the Dardanelles were not of any great significance, the Joint Planners came out against giving the Russians unrestricted rights of passage.[49] This in fact was the view endorsed by the Chiefs of Staff. If Russia could move freely through the Straits they would be well placed to seize, as their opening moves against Greece and Turkey, vital ports and airfields in the northern Aegean, and Britain's naval superiority could be significantly threatened by Soviet submarines. A further reason for not revising Montreux was that it provided Britain with an acceptable reason for maintaining full diplomatic and military support of Turkey which 'must always be of the greatest importance as long as there is a threat to the Middle East from any European power'. Unless therefore there was evidence of Soviet intentions to move through the Caucasus to the Persian Gulf, as an alternative warm water location, then unrestricted Soviet rights of passage should be opposed. In other words unless there was an even more important threat to Britain's imperial position arising from Soviet desires for free access to a warm water port, Britain's Eastern Mediterranean dominance should not be undermined by the revision of Montreux. It was a question of balancing one imperial strategic interest against another, and this led the Directors of Plans to consider studying, along with the PHP, the whole strategic position of the British Empire vis-à-vis the Soviet Union.[50]

Meanwhile the importance the Joint Planners, the Chiefs of Staff and the Foreign Office gave to Bulgaria because of its air bases, was endorsed by the PHP in February 1944 in a paper which proposed that British forces should occupy the country.[51] The main aim, which the Southern Department supported, was to prevent Bulgaria falling under Soviet domination, and one British division was suggested. In the spring of 1944 it was difficult to see how this could be justified in terms of force allocation, especially as Turkey was not yet in the war and no state of hostilities existed between the Soviet Union and Bulgaria. But the issue came before the Armistice Terms and Civil Administration Committee, with the Foreign Office pointing out that Russia was likely to claim a large share in the occupation of southeastern Europe and British interests lay in preventing the extension of Soviet influence towards the Straits and the Mediterranean. At one point the Foreign Office was proposing the despatch of 47,000 troops to Bulgaria, such was the significance of the perceived threat to British interests, and the issue remained unresolved until August 1944 when Attlee in his capacity as Chairman of the APW quashed all ideas of involving British troops in the occupation of Bulgaria.[52]

Thus before the PHP reported on the impact of Soviet policy on British strategic interests as a whole, there were already specific areas identified where a hostile Soviet Union would pose a threat, namely the Straits, Turkey, Greece and Bulgaria, and suggestions were being made as to how these should be countered. It was assumed that whatever Anglo-Soviet cooperation could be achieved the Soviet Union, unlike the United States, *could* prove to be a hostile power and was situated in a geographic region where any such power *would* pose a threat to vital British interests. These views were confirmed by the global PHP study, a draft version of which appeared in May, and the final version of which was endorsed by the Chiefs of Staff on 15 June 1944. Britain's strategic interests were defined as the security of the Commonwealth and Empire and of its vital communications and the security of oil supplies from the Middle East. The vital interests which might be threatened by the USSR were therefore oil, Mediterranean communications by way of Turkey and, if the Soviet Union become a first-rank naval power, Britain's sea communications. In reaching these conclusions the PHP made a startling assumption about the post-war situation in Europe as a whole. The military planners in effect assumed that the Soviets would dominate Eastern Europe, and unlike many references to that geographic region defined what countries were contained within it. Soviet influence would be dominant in Poland, powerful in Czechoslovakia and predominant in Hungary; the Russians were expected to occupy Romania, have a close interest in Bulgaria and great influence in Yugoslavia. Given this position the PHP initially took no account of the fact that the Soviet Union might profit from its position in Eastern Europe to extend its influence over Western Europe. The assumption was that a stable Europe would be assured. Such views were an extension of the belief of the Chief of the Imperial General Staff, Alanbrooke, that if Russia got part of Poland, part of the Baltic states and perhaps concessions in the Balkans it would be anxious to assist Britain in maintaining the peace in Europe.[53]

In the drafting of the PHP paper the assumption about no Soviet expansion into Western Europe had caused some concern in the Foreign Office. With the Soviets dominant in the East they would be faced with nothing but a vacuum in the West, and Gladwyn Jebb, supported by Frank Roberts, believed attention should be given to this fact. In their view the temptation facing the Soviet Union would be great because there would be little to prevent the Russians organising the whole of Europe, East and West, into a Soviet led bloc. France and de Gaulle could certainly not be trusted to reject a pro-Soviet orientation, and therefore Britain, and what were termed its 'natural associates' in Western Europe, should establish a high level of armaments to prevent a Soviet dominated Europe. The Northern Department's head, Christopher Warner, was less enamoured with the idea of suggesting this to any military representatives; he did not want to plant the idea of a Western bloc in opposition to the Soviet Union in the minds of military leaders. On the other hand, as Warner acknowledged, as long as British armaments were ostensibly directed against Germany they would appear to be highly respectable. Thus, as early as April 1944, the idea of a Western bloc directed against the Soviet Union was present within the Foreign Office.[54] It was accompanied by an acceptance of Russian domination of Eastern Europe excluding the Balkans (although precisely what this entailed was still a matter of debate in 1944), and this in turn was linked to the maintenance of Anglo-Soviet cooperation, with the future of Germany perceived as the most likely basis of that cooperation. The Foreign Office were convinced that the Soviets were ready to give cooperation with Britain a try, and therefore the value of a highly armed group of Western European states would be to limit Soviet dominance to Eastern Europe and reassure those in the West who feared that there would be an unlimited expansion of Russian influence.[55]

This sanguine acceptance of Soviet dominance over areas of Eastern Europe excluding the Balkans was accompanied by uncertainty about how the Soviets would approach the latter region, which for Britain was the key European area because of its proximity to British imperial interests in the Eastern Mediterranean and the Middle East. In the face of this uncertainty Soviet behaviour would be judged not so much in Poland, Romania, Hungary or Czechoslovakia, but in those countries from which it was possible to threaten British strategic interests and influence. To suggest therefore that British policy became concerned in 1944 with the prospect of Soviet domination of Eastern Europe is to be geographically imprecise and to ignore the fact that certain countries were perceived to be of greater importance than others. Moreover, military planners had produced papers in which Soviet dominance over the countries of Hungary, Poland, Czechoslovakia and Romania was seen as the inevitable outcome of the Russian defeat of Germany; this fact also aroused no great concern in the Foreign Office where it appeared to be taken for granted if Western Europe could be protected. There were not, however, unanimous views on the nature of Soviet domination or indeed any thorough examination of what this would mean for the domestic governments of the states concerned. Clearly there was both an optimistic view that democratic popular front states open to British influence would survive and a more pessimistic one which associated Soviet dominance with an autocratic system of government running a tightly controlled communist economy. These views in 1944 are vital to an understanding of what aroused British concerns from the end of 1944 onwards.

The fact that Soviet expansionism was foreseen and accepted in Eastern Europe excluding the Balkans is difficult to reconcile with explanations of the Cold War based on reactions to post-war Soviet expansionism in Eastern Europe (defined in terms of the countries listed above). It is also worth pointing out that no Soviet expansion took place *after* the war, as is often assumed, because the Soviet position in Europe was established, as the British acknowledged, as a direct consequence of the military defeat of Germany.[56] In 1944 the British were more concerned that the Soviet Union would not expand and would perhaps become less committed to the struggle against Germany once Soviet territory had been regained. Churchill was even afraid that Stalin would secretly let it be known to the Germans that they could safely remove troops from the eastern front in order to deal with the British and Americans in the west.[57] What worried British policy makers was not Soviet dominance in Eastern Europe but Soviet influence in Western Europe and the Eastern Mediterranean.

The position of the Balkan countries of Bulgaria, Yugoslavia and Greece was still uncertain. Papers produced in 1944 were equivocal about Russian dominance of Yugoslavia, and there remained a strong view within the Foreign Office in 1944 that Soviet control of Bulgaria should be avoided. Whether this could be achieved was always seen as doubtful even before the Red Army crossed the Bulgarian border. There was, however, a general belief that British control over Greece could and should be established at the end of the war. Regarding southeastern Europe and the Straits, not only had it been admitted that to defend certain British interests was likely to disturb the Soviet Union, but some policy makers believed that the understandable need for the Soviet Union to change the status quo at the Straits would threaten Britain's position. Similarly an increase in Soviet influence in Greece, Bulgaria and Yugoslavia would be equally damaging to Britain's imperial position. During 1944 events in these countries made it more urgent to ensure that this was avoided without any damage to Anglo-Soviet relations. Churchill's visit to Moscow in October 1944 has therefore to be seen in this light more than in the light of general balance of power considerations in Europe.

Notes

1. Sir L. Woodward *British Foreign Policy in the Second World War* Vol. 5 (London 1976) pp. 3–4; memorandum by Gladwyn Jebb 5.10.42 (emphasis added).
2. See Ch. 4.
3. CO323/1877/6 Eden to Stanley 27.12.43; R. M. Hathaway *Ambiguous Partnership: Britain and America 1944–47* (New York 1981) p. 46.
4. T. Jones *A Whitehall Diary* 8.3.28 cited in D. Cameron Watt. *Succeeding John Bull* (Cambridge 1984) p. 60.
5. Watt op. cit. p. 81.
6. Hathaway op. cit. pp. 18–19.
7. J. E. Williams 'The Joint Declaration on the Colonies: an Issue in Anglo-American Relations 1942–44' *British Journal of International Studies* 2, 3 (1976) p. 274.
8. FO371/31777 minute by G. Jebb 28.8.42.
9. FO371/30652 F. Hoyer Miller to N. Butler 6.7.42 enclosing memorandum on 'Things which Americans hold against the British'.
10. Ibid.; minute by P. Broad and N. Ronald 24.5.42.
11. FO371/31777 minutes by N. Ronald 28.8.42 and 3.9.42; minute by Ashley Clarke

27.8.24; minute by Sir J. Brennan 25.8.42. This file contains the draft papers on post-war Far Eastern policy. Eventually the Colonial Office paper sent to the Foreign Office on 18 August 1942 was incorporated into a joint memorandum which stated that discussions on giving up Hong Kong sovereignty were not to be precluded.

12. Wm Roger Louis *Imperialism at Bay 1941–45* (Oxford, 1977) p. 147.
13. FO371/37177 Cranborne to Eden and Eden note 19.8.42.
14. FO371/34136 minute by J. G. Tahourdin 7.1.43.
15. M. W. Wilmington *The Middle East Supply Centre* (London 1971) pp. 30, 73–5.
16. Kenton J. Clymer 'Franklin D. Roosevelt, Louis Johnson, India, and Anti-colonialism: Another Look' *Pacific Historical Review* 1988 p. 267.
17. J. Glendevon *The Viceroy at Bay* (London 1971) p. 269.
18. Churchill College Cambridge, Swinton Papers 270/5/8; Swinton to Secretary of State 18.12.42; 174/3/3 Swinton to Sir E. Bridges 6.11.43; R. W. Graham 'American Imperial Interests in West Africa During the Second World War', paper presented to SOAS Conference on Africa and the Second World War (May 1984).
19. CAB 66/32 WP(42)601 22.12.42; CO852/509/4 minute by G. Creasy 29.7.43; FO371/34141 Secretary of State to Resident Minister (Achimota) 15.4.43.
20. FO371/34136 minute by J. G. Tahourdin 12.5.43; G. Kolko, *The Politics of War: the World and United States Foreign Policy 1943–45* (New York 1968) p. 251; H. Macmillan *The Blast of War 1939–45* (London 1984) pp. 179–80, recording a conversation between Lord Cranborne and J. F. Dulles in July 1942.
21. *FRUS 1943* Vol. 3 p. 62.
22. FO371/38523 report by G. Spry on 'United States Relations with the British Empire' 1.5.44.
23. FO371/34140 'Post-War Trends in the United States' report no. 8 16.10.43.
24. FO371/34137 minute by A. A. Dudley 13.8.43; FO371/34142 minute by A. A. Dudley 1.12.43.
25. Hathaway op. cit. p. 46 citing FO371/38547 minute by Sir R. I. Campbell 12.8.44; E. Barker 'Problems of the Alliance: Misconceptions and Misunderstandings' in W. Deakin, E. Barker and J. Chadwick (eds.) *British Political and Military Strategy in Central, Eastern and Southern Europe, 1944* (Basingstoke 1988).
26. FO371/38522 Colonial Office memorandum 'Relations between the United States and the Colonial Empire', (January 1944).
27. FO371/43335 minute by Sir Orme Sargent 31.1.44.
28. For details on the disagreements over military strategy see C. Thorne *Allies of a Kind* (Oxford 1978) and K. Sainsbury *The Turning Point, The Moscow, Cairo and Teheran Conferences* (Oxford 1985).
29. Fraser J. Harbutt *The Iron Curtain, Churchill, America and the Origins of the Cold War* (New York 1986) p. 64 citing PREM 3/271/9 6.7.44.
30. See W. Kimball (ed.) *Churchill and Roosevelt: the Complete Correspondence* 2 Vols (Princeton 1984).
31. Lord Avon *The Eden Memoirs: The Reckoning* (London 1965) p. 513.
32. FO371/38523 memorandum by A. A. Dudley 21.3.44. An earlier draft is in FO371/38522.
33. FO371/43384 minute by Ashley Clarke 7.3.44.
34. This is the argument of Sainsbury op. cit.
35. CAB 87/66; J. Lewis, *Changing Direction, British Military Planning for Post-war Strategic Defence, 1942–47* (London 1988) pp. 52–54.
36. G. Ross *The Foreign Office and the Kremlin: British Documents on Anglo-Soviet Relations, 1941–1945* (Cambridge 1984) p. 115. Document 6 Clark Kerr to Eden 25.11.42.
37. For a discussion of American perceptions on this see E. Mark 'American Policy Towards Eastern Europe, 1941–1946 and the Origins of the Cold War' *Journal of*

American History 68 (1981).
38. FO371/43335 minute by G. M. Wilson 11.6.44; minute by Sir O. Sargent 11.6.44.
39. Ross op. cit. p. 144 (doc. 22: Extracts from Proceedings of Moscow Conference) and p. 39.
40. CAB 66/53 WP (44) 436 9.8.44.
41. CAB 66/51 WP (44) 304 7.6.44 annex.
42. On wartime British attitudes to the Poles see V. Rothwell, *Britain and the Cold War, 1941–47* (London 1982) pp. 151–80.
43. Ibid, pp. 194–210 for the views of the Southern Department on which this account is based. FO371/40733 has interesting minutes including that of Lord Hood on 11.3.44.
44. ADM 116/5118. FO Paper on 'Soviet Foreign Policy Tendencies and Affecting British Interests' February 1944.
45. Lewis op. cit. p. 55.
46. R. Aldrich and M. Coleman 'Britain and the Strategic Air Offensive against the Soviet Union, The Question of South Asian Air-Bases, 1945–9' *History* (74) 242 p. 403.
47. CAB 81/41 PHP (43)5 final 16.8.43.
48. M. Gilbert *Road to Victory: Winston Churchill 1941–45* (London 1986) pp. 464–5, 585 citing CAB 120/714 and 120/113.
49. Lewis op. cit. citing CAB 84/55; JP (43) 294 final 20.9.43.
50. CAB 80/75 COS (43) 569 (0) 22.9.43; Lewis op. cit. pp. 58–9.
51. FO371/40733 PHP (43) 36 final 10.2.44.
52. Ibid. ACA (44) 23 14.4.44; memorandum by the Minister of State 'British Interests in SE Europe'. Rothwell, op. cit. p. 212.
53. CAB 81/45 PHP (43) 1 (0) final 1.5.44; PHP (44) 13 (0) final 6.6.44; CAB 79/76 COS (44) 195th meeting 15.6.44.
54. FO371/43384 minute by G. Jebb 7.4.44.
55. Ibid.; FO371/43335 FO Memorandum 'Possible Tendencies in Soviet Policy' 29.4.44.
56. I am indebted to Helen Mercer of the University of Leeds for making this point to me so forcefully.
57. Rothwell op. cit. p. 125.

Chapter 2
The Empire and global strategy: imperial needs defined
April 1944–August 1945

When the Prime Minister and his urbane if unstable Foreign Secretary went to Moscow in October 1944, they were faced with the tiresome problem of the London Poles and the Soviet–Polish boundary. Indeed this issue took up more time during the meetings than anything else. Churchill had been exerting great pressure on Mikolacjczyk to accept the Curzon line, but time was now running out for the London Poles. Stalin, although the British were reluctant to acknowledge this, had refrained from advancing on Warsaw in the summer of 1944 in order to let the Germans smash the internal resistance movement in the Polish capital which was not well disposed to the Soviet Union. Moreover Soviet support for the London Poles appeared to be finally ruled out with the establishment of the Lublin Committee as the government in Warsaw in September 1944; this also made it more difficult to get an agreement between Stalin and Churchill over the future Polish government. As a result the time devoted to the Polish issue was perhaps more a reflection of the thorny nature of the problem than of its importance to Britain; or at least to British officials who would not have to explain the abandonment of the London Poles to parliament which was a major concern of the Prime Minister's. Much more important was the general question of Soviet intentions in those areas which might jeopardise Britain's strategic position in the Eastern Mediterranean and Middle East, and Churchill's aim at Moscow was undoubtedly, as Elizabeth Barker maintains, to protect vital British interests by setting a limit on Soviet expansion. More precisely it was to delimit the areas of Soviet influence by making sure that Greece was established unequivocally in the British sphere. The timing of Churchill's visit was conditioned by the development of the military campaign on the eastern front and internal developments in Greece and Bulgaria which made it imperative to remove some of the uncertainty about Soviet aims which affected British interests.

The spring of 1944 marked a change in the attitudes of Churchill and Eden to the rise of Russian power. Always preferring to try and secure a joint Anglo-American approach to post-war problems in general, and to the Russians in particular, the Prime Minister had failed to secure that at Tehran in 1943. Churchill then rapidly became nervous and uncertain as the British felt more isolated and increasingly impotent compared to the greater power of the Americans and the Russians, which now seemed to be directed towards common military goals without due regard for British interests. But the significant development in the spring was what the British undoubtedly regarded as Soviet interference in their Mediterranean sphere of influence. From this point on there were frequent records of Churchillian outbursts on the subject of the westward Soviet advance, which, while often intermingled with pro-Soviet statements, indicated the extent of the Prime Minister's fears and suspicions about Russian intentions and 'behaviour'.

Soviet 'interference' occurred almost simultaneously in Greece and Italy. In the latter country the Russians supported the broadening of the Italian government of Badoglio, a policy which had been urged on Churchill by the Americans in March. The Prime Minister had, however, successfully resisted Roosevelt's requests on the grounds that any changes should wait until Rome was captured. The Soviets were, as Eden noted, seeking to establish what in effect would be a broad based popular front government under Badoglio that included the communists. Eden was furious, believing that the communists would swallow up the other left-wing parties and then Badoglio himself. He demanded to know why the Russians were gatecrashing in Italy, adding that 'all this has been planned while Mr Macmillan drifts complacently around the Mediterranean'.[1] In the same month of April 1944 the Soviets, also for the first time, began to criticise British policy in Greece, and to come out openly in support of the EAM, the National Liberation Front, which although supported by many non-communists, was largely controlled by the Greek Communist Party.

At the start of the month Churchill had made what became the standard 1944 assessment of Soviet territorial aims: the Russians were resolved to seize the Baltic states and take what they wanted from Poland and Romania. The Prime Minister was, however, worried that what he termed a second series of demands might follow further Russian military victories.[2] Clearly, as he noted a few days later, Churchill was unable to trust the communists.[3] On 2 April the Red Army entered Romania and Churchill's private secretary recorded that the Prime Minister was full of gloomy foreboding about future Russian policy to Europe and the world. Eden too was worried and uncertain about Soviet intentions, recording his apprehension that 'Russia has vast aims and that these may include the domination of Eastern Europe and *even* the Mediterranean and the "communizing" of much that remains'.[4]

The prime concern was not Russian dominance over Poland, Hungary, Czechoslovakia or Romania, (and in Churchill's case Bulgaria), but whether such dominance would be used to undermine British interests in the Mediterranean. More precisely the British were worried, and increasingly so, that in Greece the military campaigns for the liberation of the country would not enable them to establish the kind of friendly government deemed necessary to preserve their Mediterranean dominance. Despite the leading British role in Greece there was a danger that the Soviets, as in Italy, would attempt to get in on what was an exclusive Anglo-American Mediterranean act. In April therefore, Eden approached the Soviet Ambassador in London, Gousev, to express his concern about Soviet attitudes to Greece. The British Foreign Secretary suggested that Greece, for the purpose of military operations, should be a British concern and Romania a Soviet one, and urged the Russians to back British policy on Greece. The Ambassador agreed provided American support could be secured.[5] In the meantime the Prime Minister became more agitated about Russian interest in the countries of the Northern Mediterranean, commenting that 'evidently we are approaching a showdown with the Russians about their communist intrigues in Italy, Yugoslavia and Greece'. The alternative seemed to be, as Churchill suggested to Eden, British acceptance of the communisation of the Balkans and perhaps Italy.[6]

Showdown or not there were problems creating an exclusive British sphere of influence in Greece, which was the main point of the Moscow exercise. Throughout the early years of the war Churchill had supported the exiled Greek monarchy which was opposed by the democratic EAM and their rivals the EDES (National Republican Hellenic League). British encouragement of the former, more radical body, which was not tainted by collaboration with the Germans, was much more likely to promote effective anti-German resistance. But the Ambassador in Greece, Sir Reginald Leeper, argued at the end of 1943 that the British should attempt to dissolve the whole Greek guerrilla movement. Churchill was already itching to send in British troops to take over after the withdrawal of the Germans, but it was decided that the guerrilla movement would have to be sustained in order to maintain the morale of the Greeks and that the King would have to accept that his return could only be conditional on the approval of the majority of the Greek people.[7] As armed clashes developed between the rival factions within Greece, disturbing news came in April 1944 from Cairo where the official Greek armed forces mutinied. It was tempting to blame the Russians but there was no evidence of any such involvement. The British response was to approach George Papandreou, an opponent of the EAM, and then to urge him to bring EAM representatives into his government on a minority basis. Churchill was unashamed of British interference and, as in 1943, more than prepared to contemplate a military solution. As he told Eden, 'you cannot be too stiff in handling this situation and making them feel that the "fairy godmother" is capable of giving any of them a good smack over the head.'[8] Unfortunately a political solution would also be required, but this could only be achieved on terms favourable to the British if a national government under Papandreou effectively controlled the EAM. Eden's approach to Gousev was aimed at getting open Russian support for the establishment of a coalition under Papandreou. This seemed more likely when the leaders of the most important political groups in Greece met in the Lebanon from 17 to 20 May, and agreed in principle to set up a broad coalition government. Guerrilla bands would be unified under the orders of the government and the Greek armed forces would be reorganised. Despite this, both the Greek Communist Party and the EAM refused to join the coalition.[9] It therefore seemed that military methods might be necessary for the suppression of the EAM. At the end of May, the Special Operations Executive Commander in Greece, pointing to the dangers inherent in Russia's impending Balkan offensive, suggested a way of ensuring the defeat of the EAM and preventing a Russian dominated Greece. The idea was attractive because it did not involve lowering Greek morale and turning opinion against Britain by overt opposition to the military operations of the resistance movement. It was suggested that support for the guerrilla operations should be continued until the liberation and then all political support should be withdrawn; this could perhaps overcome the conflict between supporting the guerrillas and ensuring their political defeat. But such a policy, it was argued, could only be successfully implemented if Britain had effective military control of Greece, and therefore it was important for the Soviets to allow the British army a free hand. Such views were reinforced by the military in London who emphasised the strategic importance of Greece and its islands, and suggested that 'politically, if Russian influence, as is possible, predominates in Romania, Hungary, Bulgaria and Yugoslavia, it is even more important that Greece should not be Russian dominated'. If Greece was abandoned, the Joint Planners concluded, Britain would be seen as surrendering to Russia in the Balkans.[10]

Churchill might look with horror at the prospect of the *communisation* of the Balkans, but for the Foreign Office, as well as the military, the issue in 1944, was essentially a *power-political* one between two states seeking imperial domination through the creation of subservient governments. In its paper submitted to the Cabinet in June, the Foreign Office made a clear distinction between the spread of communism and the spread of Russian influence. The partisans might spread communist theories, but the Foreign Office believed there was no central organi- sation out to communise the Balkans, and that the Russians could not be accused of organising the spread of communist ideology. The spread of Russian influence was a different thing, and this concerned the Foreign Office because they believed the Soviets were out for a predominant position in southeastern Europe by forming governments subservient to Russia. Assuming however that the Russians would accept a deal with Britain, the Foreign Office considered what arrangement would best enable them to encourage Greek resistance without creating the conditions for a communist-dominated government. The option of an Anglo- Soviet self-denying ordinance in Greece, Yugoslavia and Albania was definitely ruled out. Even if the Soviets agreed it would, so the Foreign Office believed, be unacceptable for Britain not to continue 'to play an active part' in the internal affairs of Greece and Yugoslavia and not to have a say regarding Bulgaria when the time came.[11] A wartime spheres of influence deal with the Soviets would, however, enable Britain to install a well disposed government in Greece and thereby secure its Mediterranean position. Whatever the implications of the earlier efforts at Tehran to commit the Soviets to a liberal and democratic Southern and Eastern Europe, by the summer of 1944, it was deemed much more important to ensure that British troops had a free hand to install a non-communist government in Greece. It was for that reason that Churchill expressed extreme annoyance in June when he discovered that American opposition to spheres of influence had fright- ened off the Russians (who wanted a permanent agreement) and no wartime arrangements for Greece and Romania could be finalised. The Prime Minister could see no prospect of countering Russian influence in Romania and was horrified that the 'pedantic interference' of the United States would lead to a regime of triangular telegrams with the British and the Americans interfering in Romania and the Russians boosting the EAM in Greece. Fortunately from Britain's point of view, after renewed efforts, the State Department accepted a three-month trial arrangement of what amounted to an exclusive role for Britain and the Soviet Union in military operations in Greece and Romania respectively. Stalin finally approved this on 5 July 1944.[12]

This agreement apparently gave the British a temporary breathing space, but the situation remained fraught with danger. On July 26th a Soviet military mission under Colonel Grigori Popov reached ELAS headquarters unannounced amidst British consternation at what appeared to be Soviet interference. The EAM was still refusing to participate in the government except on its own terms, but within days of the mission's arrival the EAM agreed to join the Papandreou government in exile on the terms it had been rejecting for two months. If, as seems likely, the mission was sent specifically to persuade the EAM to enter the government, then Stalin was in fact assisting in the political demise of the Greek communist movement; this could only mean that the Soviets were keen to honour the three-months spheres of influence agreement and ensure that British policy was implemented along the lines proposed by Eden to Gousev.

The British remained on edge however, because they did not believe that the national government could successfully be established without the presence of British troops. After some debate in which the British military proved extremely reluctant to undertake operations in Greece, on 9 August 1944, following Eden's statement that the 'traditional connection' between Britain and Greece was indispensable to Britain's strategic position in the Balkans and Eastern Mediterranean, the War Cabinet approved the despatch of a British force to Greece the moment the Germans had withdrawn; its overriding object would be to ensure that a 'friendly' government was installed in Athens.[13]

On 23 August the pro-German Romanian government of Antonescu was overthrown by a coup which brought back King Michael, undermined the German position and threatened to bring Soviet forces to the Greek frontier sooner than was expected. The Russian military victories of August 1944 in Moldavia and Bessarabia marked the triumph of the last of the three great eastern front offensives begun in June. Suspicions therefore remained that Soviet military power would enable them to dominate the Balkans to the extent that British influence in Greece, and to a bigger extent Yugoslavia and Bulgaria, would be destroyed. One historian, who has consulted Soviet and Bulgarian sources, concludes that there is no evidence that the Soviet offensive in the Balkans was organised at short notice or for political reasons, or because of unexpected opportunities to advance Soviet interests, which had not been foreseen in general terms by Stalin.[14] But with the unexpectedly rapid Soviet advance the danger increased that a sudden German defeat or retreat would enable the Greek communists to assert control before the British had time to establish the national government, as military operations at short notice could prove difficult in Greece.

In September, concern over their position in Greece led the British to give more attention to Bulgaria. The British were still uncertain as to whether the Soviets would pursue policies directly threatening British influence: in particular whether they would support Bulgarian claims for an outlet on the Aegean; this rather than a fear of communism was the prime influence on British policy. In August, Sargent, a key official supporter of the showdown with the Soviet line, had suggested that Britain should insist on a showdown over Bulgaria before it was too late.[15] No doubt Sargent was then still hoping that with the Soviet Union not yet at war with Bulgaria, Britain could secure an important voice in the armistice and occupation arrangements. On 25 August the Bulgarian government, no longer controlled by pro-German elements, had declared its neutrality and asked the Western Allies for their terms of withdrawal from the war. Eleven days later the Soviet Union declared war on Bulgaria, and on 8 September the Red Army crossed the frontier. There were important military reasons for the Soviet action: neutralising Bulgaria and outflanking the retreating German army was vital; there was a need to secure the flank of the second Ukrainian front as Soviet forces advanced through Romania into Southern Hungary, linking up with the Yugoslav partisans and cutting off the retreat of the 12th German Army from Greece. However, on 9 September the Fatherland Front government, a coalition controlled by a communist dominated National Committee, seized power.[16] With the Red Army advancing through Bulgaria as well as Romania its capacity to influence events in Greece was much greater. As Eden pointed out there was now an entirely new situation in the Balkans because even if the Red Army did not enter German occupied Greek territory its presence to the north in Yugoslavia and Bulgaria was bound to have political repercussions. It was therefore vital that, unless British influence in the region was to suffer, British troops should enter Greece as soon as possible[17] There was a more concrete danger stemming from the wartime Bulgarian occupation of parts of Greek territory, notably Thrace and Macedonia. The Bulgarian communists took the initiative in declaring that they had liberated these areas, and ministers of the Fatherland Front toured them, apparently assuming they would be retained by Bulgaria, and proclaiming their support for the EAM.[18] With no British presence in Greece this was a major challenge to Britain's prestige and influence and further increased the urgency of despatching a military force and getting Soviet agreement to British military operations aimed, if necessary, at strengthening Greece against any territorial claims by the new Bulgarian government; this of course was still accompanied by the need to install the Papandreou government and contain the opposing forces in Greece's internal conflict. On 23 September Stalin gave his consent to British military operations, and on 1 October British troops landed on the western coast of the Peloponnese. As a result, six days later, the German High Command ordered the evacuation of the whole of Greece enabling British troops, surprisingly unopposed by the EAM, to enter Athens and install the Papendreou government on 18 October.[19] The Germans believed that when the retreat came the British restrained from attacking them in order to give full attention to preventing the communists from controlling Greece.[20] Certainly the British, unlike the Soviets in Romania and Bulgaria, could provide no military rationale, in terms of defeating Germany, for their campaign in Greece.

In Bulgaria British influence could now only be sustained if the Soviets thought it desirable. Eden, not surprisingly, given the importance attached to Bulgaria by the Southern Department, was annoyed by some aspects of Soviet policy; but he recognised that the USSR had the 'right to take the lead' provided they recognised that Britain had the same right in Greece.[21] Thus the original issue of a straight Anglo-Soviet deal over Romania and Greece which would last for the war period and enable each power to install suitably favourable governments had been overtaken by events. With the Soviets effectively dictating military operations in Bulgaria and no British troops for operations outside Greece, no further pairings of spheres of influence could conveniently be made on a wartime basis of military occupation. Moreover the Soviet occupation of Bulgaria had political implications, which, especially in the face of Bulgarian occupation of Greek territory, could not be nullified by the British on the basis of a Greek–Romanian deal with Moscow. In order that the main British aim of freedom to interfere in Greece's internal affairs could be secured, there was therefore a case for extending the scope and the duration of the initial three-month agreement, irrespective of the general strategic importance of Bulgaria for Britain's Mediterranean and Middle Eastern position.

Whether this was a practical proposition or not seemed to be a matter of dispute between those like Churchill, who sometimes took a very pessimistic line, and those in the Foreign Office who were more optimistic about the prospects of preserving some British influence in the Balkans outside Greece. The June cabinet paper on the region, while arguing for a temporary deal on Greece and Romania in order to secure Britain's position in the former territory, had suggested that Britain's best long-term policy was to consolidate its position in Greece and Turkey but, whilst avoiding any direct challenge to Russian influence in Yugoslavia, Albania, Romania and Bulgaria, to take every opportunity to spread British influence there. Yet as has been seen, by the autumn of 1944, new circumstances posed new threats to Britain's position in Greece; this meant that on a longer term basis it was now vital to commence military operations designed to secure this, and to ensure that the Soviet position in Bulgaria did not endanger such operations. It was therefore more a question of securing British control in Greece than preserving British influence in the rest of the Balkans. Churchill, more so than the Foreign Office, was disposed to see the position primarily in this light, as indeed was the man on the spot in the Mediterranean, Harold Macmillan, who noted in October that 'all the rest of the Balkans are gone. This [Greece] is our last chance of avoiding the establishment of a communist society'.[22]

Churchill's road to Moscow in October 1944, was therefore mapped out in the spring and summer of 1944 when Russian statements on Greece and Italy initially aroused fears that the Soviets might be preparing to challenge Britain's exclusive Eastern Mediterranean predominance. By the autumn the military situation had made action to prevent this urgent. The two most important elements of Britain's position were seen as Greece and Turkey, and given the uncertainty and instability of the Greek situation, it was this that attracted most British concern in 1944. The Foreign Office realised that the problem was of such magnitude that an Anglo-Soviet self-denying ordinance on external intervention would not be sufficient to secure British interests. Initially, hopes centred on a wartime spheres of influence deal to enable the two imperialist powers to take whatever action was necessary for the creation of puppet governments in Greece and Romania. But the military campaign against Germany in the east produced an extremely rapid Russian advance which in turn created more uncertainty about the future of Britain's position within Greece and within the Balkans in general. Even though Stalin honoured the three-month deal and sanctioned British military operations designed to prevent the communists taking power, by September the presence of Soviet troops in Bulgaria was distinctly unsettling for the British who had seen significant strategic disadvantages in this. Even more disturbing was the fact that Bulgarian troops were, at the beginning of October, still occupying Greek territory. When attending the Quebec Conference in September 1944 Churchill was still uncertain as to Russian intentions, and it was for this reason that the Prime Minister was keen for the Allied armies to get to Vienna first.[23]

With the Balkan and Mediterranean position deemed more important by Britain than events in areas of Central and Eastern Europe to the north, the continuing uncertainty about the impact of Soviet military actions required fresh efforts to remove it and to extend the initial deal over Greece and Romania. This was the background to a conference designed to protect Britain's vital interests in the Mediterranean which had become an urgent issue in 1944; the unstated belief, founded in military and Foreign Office assessments, was that the British position in the Mediterranean should be supported by the Russians as Soviet dominance over Eastern and Central Europe from Romania though Hungary, Czechoslovakia, Poland and eastern Germany had already been recognised as a vital Soviet interest.

When Churchill first met Stalin on the evening of 9 October the agreement on Greece and Romania had just six days to run. It was at this first meeting that Churchill produced the now famous piece of paper suggesting the various per-centages which would signify British and Soviet influence in the Balkan states.[24] The paper pushed across the table by Churchill, on which Stalin made a large blue pencil tick, contained the following proposal. Romania: Russia 90 per cent; the others 10 per cent. Greece: Great Britain (in accord with USA) 90 per cent; Russia 10 per cent. Yugoslavia: 50–50 per cent. Hungary: 50–50 per cent. Bulgaria: Russia 75 per cent; the others 25 per cent. Discussion then centred on Bulgaria where Churchill argued that, unlike Romania, Britain had to be a little more than a spectator. The Prime Minister had no love for the Bulgarians, recalling that in the last war they had cruelly attacked the Romanians and had done the same in the present war to the Greeks and the Yugoslavs. Britain, he affirmed, had been much offended by Bulgaria, and this may have distracted Churchill's attention from the strategic importance of the country. The conversation then moved to the Straits with Churchill repeating his Tehran pledge that he would support free access to the Mediterranean for Russian merchant ships and ships of war. The next day Eden was to question the wisdom of such a concession. His protests were based on a forceful minute by Sir Orme Sargent that added political arguments to the strategic considerations of the Chiefs of Staff. Sargent acknowl-edged that Montreux was unsatisfactory, but believed there were grave objections to revision. Russian aims were described as 'far reaching' and defined as limiting Turkey's power to close the Straits, rights of egress in war or participation in the administration of the Straits. Any of these would endanger Turkish neutrality in war and its integrity and sovereignty in general. Sargent linked the issue to the weak position Britain found itself in because of recent events in southeast Europe. Consequently any bargaining counters should strenuously be preserved, and two of these were the Anglo-Turkish alliance and Britain's age old opposition to Russia in the Straits; the former in particular was seen by Sargent as an asset in the struggle to maintain Britain's position in south-east Europe. In the eyes of the supervising undersecretary of the Southern Department, British imperial strategy should, in this instance, attempt to use a neutral ally against one committed to defeating the Germans. Otherwise if Britain proved willing even to discuss Montreux this would lead to proposals, which while they might have to be accepted, should form part of the general Anglo-Soviet bargain at the end of the war. Churchill, who had been intensely irritated by the Turkish commitment to neutrality, was not, however, moved by Eden's protests, made in any event after the horse had bolted from the stable. The Prime Minister replied that Britain had 'no need to fear the movement of a Russian fleet through the Straits . . . All Russian ships who are on the sea, warships or merchant, are hostages to the stronger naval Power. On the other hand, I think it is like breeding pestilence to try to keep a nation like Russia from free access to broad waters.'[25]

Having therefore supported the Soviet position in two areas where official policy makers in London were keen to limit Russian influence, Churchill then raised another question which may have been more important for him. Italy, obviously a significant Mediterranean state, had been at the forefront of British minds since the signs of Soviet interference in April, and contained a sizeable communist party. The British leader therefore urged Stalin to refrain from encouraging the Italian communists. Stalin, in reply, for the first time put forward his own proposals. Possibly perceiving that Churchill was asking for a British position in Italy equivalent to that in Greece, Stalin suggested that the figures for Bulgaria should be revised, perhaps with a view to an Italian–Bulgarian deal equivalent to the one on Greece and Romania. Churchill's only comment was to indicate that such details should be left for Eden and Molotov to go into.[26]

Churchill was at pains to point out, apparently for the benefit of the Americans and his Cabinet colleagues, that the agreements did not amount to spheres of influence, although this is difficult to reconcile with the position the British expected for themselves in Greece. His biographer presents them as something much less than formal spheres of influence arrangements, citing Churchill's reference, in a draft letter to Stalin, to his belief that no ideology should be imposed on any small country. Let them work out their own fortunes, Churchill argued, free from an aggressive, proselytising communism. Churchill's view, as expressed in the letter, was that the percentages were 'no more than a method by which in our thoughts we can see how near we are together, and then decide the necessary steps to bring us into full agreement'. Thus the final Eden/Molotov agreement in which the Russians were given 80/20 in Hungary and Bulgaria appears to assume little significance. However, the letter expressing Churchill's interpretation of the agreement was never sent to Stalin for the somewhat odd reason, according to Gilbert, that Averell Harriman, US Ambassador in Moscow, recalling the event some years later, had informed the British that Roosevelt would repudiate the agreements.[27] In the context of why the letter was never sent no opinion was apparently expressed, then or later, on the Soviet leader's likely reaction to a proposal that his wartime enemies in Romania should be allowed to work out their own future after the Soviets had conceded the British right to intervene militarily in the internal affairs of Greece.

Gilbert's account portrays a settlement short of spheres of influence in which British aims were directed to securing guidelines and allowing the peoples of southeastern Europe to choose their own future; he does not refer to Stalin agreeing at Churchill's insistence on 9 October that Britain must be the leading Mediterranean power: a strange omission given the British desire in 1944 for an arrangement with the Soviets which would at least protect their position in Greece.

Warren F. Kimball is, however, convinced that the most pressing issue for the British in Moscow was maintaining their Mediterranean dominance.[28] This interpretation is in line with the analysis of the events in Greece and the Balkans which influenced Churchill's decision to go to Moscow. If true it makes the idea that in 1944 Britain seriously expected Stalin to accept the principle of all the peoples of southeastern Europe choosing their own government difficult to believe, except as a very long-term goal. The latter would in effect be contrary to previous British assessments of the Balkan situation. If it is to be believed that Churchill expected to preserve Britain's Mediterranean dominance on the basis of not allowing the Russians to control Romania, not only does this involve an extraordinary lack of realism on the Prime Minister's part, but again it flies in the face of earlier British assessments. The most that could, and may have been, expected by the British was that Bulgaria would not be subject to the same form of great power control as Romania and Greece. Given some earlier attitudes even this is stretching a point, and it seems more likely that the initial Foreign Office aim in Bulgaria was to ensure Russian dominance there did not directly impinge on British dominance in Greece. If this was indeed the goal then it was certainly successful, for by the end of October the Soviets had put pressure on the Bulgarians to withdraw their forces of occupation from the disputed Greek territory.[29]

One argument against this idea of the Moscow Conference being directed towards the achievement of important and precise British goals centres on the apparent vagueness of the agreements. Eden did in fact inform the Foreign Office that the arrangements were not meant to apply to the number of representatives on the Allied Control Commissions which would have to be established in the occupied ex-enemy territories.[30] It is easy to interpret this as another example of Churchillian vagueness and eccentricity: an exercise divorced from the main thrust of British post-war strategy. Given the events of 1944 and the growing British concern over the impact of developments in the Balkans on Britain's vital imperial interests in the Mediterranean and Middle East, this is clearly not the case. The Moscow Conference was the logical result of these concerns which were related, not to Soviet domination of Eastern Europe, north of Greece, Bulgaria and Yugoslavia, never an area of vital British interest, but to the uncertainty about Soviet intentions after this inevitable outcome of the war against Germany.

In the Far East, from which the threat to Britain's imperial position was most acute during the earlier wartime years, as the war drew to a close Russian aims were not seen in the Foreign Office as likely to conflict with Britain's strategic interests. Even the military planners, while concerned that a large Russian fleet in the Far East could constitute a potential threat to Britain's strategic interests, were generally unconcerned about Russian acquisition of warm water ports and bases because Britain's interests would not be adversely affected provided Russian policy was primarily defensive. Given that this was likely to be so, there was no real likelihood of Anglo-Soviet rivalry in the Far East.[31]

This was clearly not the case in the Middle East and the Eastern Mediterranean where there was a clash of strategic interests and spheres of influence in an area where Russian policy was not likely to be defensive in nature. What was needed therefore was some form of reassurance that British interests would be protected: some sign that Soviet 'behaviour' was likely to be based on respect for these interests. Earlier in the year uncertainty focused almost exclusively on Russian interference in the internal affairs of Greece and Italy which would prevent the British ensuring that favourable governments were eventually installed and given popular approval. As the military campaign gathered momentum the question became a much broader one of growing Russian influence, given its proximity to Greece and its general dominance in Romania and Bulgaria. Churchill, perhaps without grasping all the implications of the complicated Balkan situation, at least seemed to have safely secured Greece within a British sphere of influence where military operations against those who had fought the Germans were now being supported by the Russians. Yet while the Soviets' 'behaviour' in this respect may well have been interpreted as favourable, their presence in Bulgaria and their advance through Yugoslavia were signs that Soviet power would unavoidably be impinging on Britain's vital interests.

While the meetings in Moscow were taking place, back in London an important committee was considering another area of vital British concern; its deliberations were soon to produce divisions within the government over the kind of imperial strategy to be followed. At the same time, divisions in Whitehall over another issue which was to be central to Britain's future imperial strategy were finally shelved if not resolved. The first issue was Britain's future role in the Suez Canal Zone, the second the nature of the proposed Western bloc initially conceived to enhance Britain's post-war security.

The Suez Canal had played a central role in the history of the British Empire and was to continue to do so in the future. Sometimes described as the jugular vein of the British Empire, its strategic importance had been eroded by the development of air power which had effectively closed the Mediterranean as a major supply route during the Second World War. It was, however, of enormous symbolic significance, and of considerable economic importance to the British Empire in peacetime. The British presence there, in a vital area of imperial communications, was also deemed necessary for air staging facilities if the links to the Far East and the antipodean Dominions were to be preserved. From a long-term British imperial perspective, the situation at Suez was far from satisfactory. The Canal Company's concession was due to expire in 1968 when the Canal would revert to Egyptian control leaving the British government with nothing but the right to safeguard the international waterway; even this assumed that such a right, granted in the Anglo-Egyptian treaty of 1936, would be renewed on the expiry of that treaty in 1956.

A Cabinet committee was established to consider the Suez Canal question, chaired by the Deputy Prime Minister and containing Oliver Stanley (Colonial Secretary), A. V. Alexander (First Lord of the Admiralty), Lord Leathers (Minister of Transport) and Ralph Assheton (Financial Secretary to the Treasury). At its first meeting the committee considered a paper by the Foreign Secretary advocating that responsibility for the defence of the Canal should remain British in perpetuity and that dues should be fixed at the lowest possible rate compatible with efficient administration and a reasonable return for shareholders. Attlee immediately questioned such a policy and suggested that the defence aspects should be considered by the Chiefs of Staff, but Assheton had different ideas. Going much further than Eden, Assheton suggested that Britain should acquire the Canal Zone in return for the transfer of the whole or part of Cyrenaica to Egypt. It was then pointed out that the Canal Zone was not defensible in isolation from Egypt because it needed water and supplies from outside, while Cyrenaica was not Britain's to give away. Agreement was however easier on the future of the Canal

Company, where the general consensus was that it should become a public utility. Unfortunately agreement on whether it should be under British or Anglo-Egyptian control or whether the concession should be given to an international body was more difficult. For Stanley the question had three aspects: ownership, control and responsibility for the defence of the Canal, the last of which he felt was most important and should be secured through an international agreement; British interests, he argued, would be best protected under the cloak of international control.[32]

It was an argument which Stanley had developed in response to international critics of the Empire, and which he embodied in his proposals for regional commissions in Asia, Africa and the Caribbean which were designed to replace the mandates. The Colonial Secretary's thinking was geared to the creation of some powerless institutions under international auspices which would help conceal the fact that real responsibility was preserved by the British authorities. Other members of the committee were later to see snags because the United States and Russia would require a share in the control of the Canal if the concession was given to an international organisation. The main focus should therefore be on a permanent defence agreement, endorsed by the UN, enabling Britain to station troops in Egypt; if that was secured it would not matter whether the Egyptians received the Canal lock, stock and barrel. But both the Labour members of the committee favoured an internationalist approach to the defence of the Canal: Attlee because he believed that the cost of policing the waters of the world should not continue to fall on the British taxpayer, and therefore other nations, notably the United States, should take a share; Alexander because he was interested in using such arrangements to exclude the Soviet Union, which he felt was possible as the Russians were anxious to revise the Montreux agreement, and if Britain went along with that, concessions on the Suez Canal might be made by Moscow.

The idea of some Anglo-Soviet deal was endorsed by Stanley who did not accept the views of his Conservative colleagues that internationalisation of the Suez Canal Company and securing British responsibility for the defence of the area through an international agreement would necessarily mean Soviet involvement. The Colonial Secretary explained that the idea was not that every nation should have a say in policing every area of the world. Each country should be allocated its exclusive sphere of influence and the Suez Canal should be Britain's responsibility.[33] This in its initial and rather vague form was the outline of an Anglo-Soviet deal to delimit areas of imperial influence. Such arrangements were to be central to the development of Britain's imperial strategy over the next 12 months. For some imperial thinkers, however, international arrangements were a very repugnant cloak for exclusive British responsibilities. Killearn, whose wartime experience in Egypt had distinguished him as a great supporter of an active British role there, felt that any international mandate for British actions in Egypt would inevitably give the Russians a direct say in the country which might later be exploited to Britain's disadvantage. British strategy should not be to protect its vital imperial position in Egypt through some kind of international arrangements, but to get American support for pressure on the Egyptians to grant whatever Britain required. There was another key idea, that of American backing for the maintenance of Britain's imperial position, which was to figure in the discussions of Britain's Middle Eastern and Mediterranean strategy in 1945 and long after.[34]

As regards Western Europe, significant developments had occurred in British thinking since the original Foreign Office ideas of a security organisation directed against Germany, and the later concerns in 1944 about the implications for Western Europe of Soviet dominance in the East.[35] These were to produce a major conflict of views between the Foreign Office and service representatives on an issue which was to be central to British foreign policy over the next few years. The controversy has been discussed by Julian Lewis in enormous detail, but he has failed to highlight the essential differences of approach within Whitehall. Much of his analysis centres on a portrayal of an essentially Russophile Foreign Office reluctant to allow the Chiefs of Staff and their subordinates in the PHP and Joint Planning Staff to consider the implications of a potentially hostile Soviet Union. This is not an accurate portrayal of Foreign Office assessments of the Soviets or its strategy for dealing with the potential threat to British interests. In May 1944 the Foreign Office had been hoping to create a loose organisation of states to deal with the European problem, which would include the Soviet Union and, if possible, the United States. Officials were only too aware of the danger of a weak divided Europe being exploited by the Soviet Union. In addition to this proposed grouping, established as some form of United Nations Commission, the Foreign Office proposed a scheme for Western Europe defence designed to keep Germany in order. They were, however, ready to acknowledge the Chiefs of Staffs' point that the Soviet Union might not cooperate with any international organisation after the end of the war. Consequently it was necessary to base strategic appreciations on the fact that British forces might be required, in association with the United States, to form a Western European group capable of resisting Soviet attempts to dominate the Continent, and, more significantly, to cause the Russians to think twice before attempting any policy of expansion in the Middle East or Eastern Mediterranean. The Foreign Office was, however, concerned that this might encourage what Warner regarded as the fear of Bolshevism amongst the 'rabidly anti-Soviet Services' and lead to too great an emphasis being placed on the Soviet Union as a potential enemy. If the latter was the case, which was what Sargent concluded after seeing the June 1944 draft of the PHP paper on 'The Effect of Soviet Policy on British Strategic Interests', the military might then assume that Britain had to take steps 'to deter the Soviet Government by force of arms from advancing their own interests at our expense'.[36]

In fact this was a relatively unimportant difference, because although Foreign Office policy was not yet based on this supposition, such an eventuality was clearly being considered.[37] Moreover, as the military planners pointed out, purely strategic planning and the need for military preparations to support it should not be unduly influenced by political considerations.[38] The really significant development, which produced the rift that came to a head between August and October 1944, was the Chiefs of Staffs' reactions to the generally accepted idea that a Western bloc could be useful against Germany and a potentially hostile Soviet Union. This emerged in July 1944 in response to a Foreign Office request for the Chiefs' views on a Western bloc, and on the PHP paper of 20 July, 1944. What concerned the Chiefs was the assumption that a Western bloc containing Britain, France and the lesser Western European states would provide a solution to the problem of United Kingdom defence. Britain's military leaders saw such a

Western European grouping as merely the first step towards a system, which, if British security was to be assured, must include part if not the whole of Germany. The time might come, they argued, when Britain would have to rely on Germany against Russia. As the CIGS noted in his diary on 27 July, Russia has now replaced Germany as the dominating European power, and therefore Germany needed to be gradually built up and brought into a federation of Western Europe. Or as the Chiefs of Staffs' reply to the Foreign Office put it rather more diplomatically, as the 'possibility of a hostile Russia making use of the resources of Germany must not be lost sight of . . . any measures which we now take should be tested by whether or not they help to prevent that contingency ever arising'.[39]

This was clearly the advocacy of *political* action to incorporate Germany into a Western bloc, and naturally aroused the wrath of the Foreign Office. As Sargent pointed out, the idea that any diplomatic measures Britain should now take had to be tested against their preventing Russia using German resources sounded like a policy of winning Germany over to Britain's side and preserving German resources for use against Britain's ally of the next 20 years. Sargent was convinced that such thinking was not confined to a small number of military figures or indeed to the PHP. The latter had in fact been redrafting papers in line with their superiors' wishes. But the main Foreign Office concern was that instead of pointing to the potential military threat of a hostile Soviet Union and advocating military measures to deal with it, the British military were in fact urging that *political* steps should now be taken to deal with the potential Soviet menace.[40]

In addition the Foreign Office had considerable evidence that the military were not seeing the Soviet Union merely as *potentially* hostile, but positively assuming that it would be. Indeed one military paper actually began with the words 'Since a hostile Russia is one of our basic assumptions . . .'.[41] What was worse, the military were talking to journalists on the lines of the Western bloc being considered from the point of view of war with the Soviet Union, and Sargent feared the next thing would be that the Americans would get to hear of it. The Deputy Undersecretary wanted all planning based on the idea of the Soviet threat to be kept highly secret and limited to a very small circle.[42] The whole controversy indicated the extent of the anti-Soviet feeling at senior levels in the British services, which existed as early as the summer of 1944, and which favoured a policy of building up Britain's prime enemy in order to assist in any future conflict with one of its major allies. As those attitudes were now becoming public knowledge, and therefore available to the Russian Embassy, the chances of Soviet suspicions developing would naturally increase. Thus not only were the military trespassing upon the Foreign Office's territory by suggesting political measures to deal with Germany, their ideas were threatening to undermine one of the main British hopes for the post-war world, namely that cooperation with the United States and the Soviet Union would continue; this was precisely the point made by Eden when he met the Chiefs of Staff in October. The differences could not be resolved but were reduced by agreement to keep secret any views on the Soviet threat, and by both sides accepting that the PHP would now be strictly limited to considering *military* questions and would not therefore require a Foreign Office representative.[43]

The affair revealed the Foreign Office view that the Soviet Union's hostility or friendliness was something on which no definite judgements could yet be made. Unlike the United States the Soviets were, however, potentially hostile, and therefore the idea of a Western bloc was to be welcomed because it could be directed both against Germany and the Soviet Union.[44] Further than that the Foreign Office was not prepared to go, especially if it involved rebuilding Germany or ensuring that parts of a dismembered Germany were integrated into a Western bloc. Such policies had to be avoided at all costs because it was believed, crucially, that once Soviet suspicions were aroused their interest in the Middle East would grow, and talk of a revived Germany was, more than anything else, certain to advance such suspicions. The British Empire therefore had a particular reason to avoid giving offence to the Soviets on Germany.[45] In the event the whole idea of a Western bloc with or without Germany was shelved for the lifetime of the wartime coalition government because of the attitude of the Prime Minister. Churchill could not understand how the idea of a Western bloc had got round in the Foreign Office and other influential circles. Until a really strong French army was rebuilt he saw nothing in the Western European countries but 'hopeless weakness'. Their leaders would inevitably ask for a British military commitment to defend them, and as Churchill could not imagine that Britain could afford to maintain an army of 50 or 60 divisions, which would be necessary to play the continental war game, he deemed it imprudent for Britain to undertake to defend the countries of Western Europe.[46]

British policy makers were therefore left to concentrate on the one area they regarded as more significant than Western Europe for their future security and global influence – the Middle East and the Eastern Mediterranean. In Greece a new crisis was brewing in the wake of the EAM's refusal to accept the demobilisation of their armed forces. An agreement had been signed with the Papandreou government in October 1944 which stipulated that all 'volunteer bodies' of the Greek armed forces, would be disbanded. The communists argued that the whole of the armed forces, including those in the Middle East, were volunteers and that the agreement therefore meant universal demobilisation. With the national government unable to accept this interpretation the country drifted towards civil war. On 3 December a number of EAM supporters were shot dead as they demonstrated against the government in Athens, and the following day the EAM leaders proclaimed Papandreou's government illegal. The armed struggle for Greece had begun, and the British were thus forced to commit more and more troops to ensure that the communist dominated EAM did not emerge triumphant.[47]

The actions of the British soon provoked criticism at home and abroad, especially in the United States. As in April 1944 the problems of Italy and Greece coincided. At the end of November the Italian government collapsed and the British let it be known that they could not support any new government in which Count Carlo Sforza was either Prime Minister or Foreign Secretary. Based on Churchill's dislike of Sforza this policy of internal intervention in the affairs of another nation was soon criticised in the United States. The criticism began to mount with the British intervention in Greece, and the new American Secretary of State, Stettinius, felt bound to exert his authority by disassociating the State Department from British policy in both Greece and Italy. An official statement on 5 December made it clear that the Italians should be allowed to work out their problems 'without influence from the outside' and concluded that 'this policy would apply to an even more pronounced degree with regard to governments of the United Nations in their liberated territories'. It was a clear reference to

Greece, which incensed the British Prime Minister, although Churchill could take some comfort from the fact that the White House was not inclined to join in the public condemnation of British actions. Roosevelt, as was the case in Eastern Europe, was not inclined to oppose spheres of influence and external intervention provided his domestic position was not weakened by any direct association of the United States with such arrangements.[48] American congressional hostility to the general thrust of British imperialism was, however, to cast a temporary cloud over Anglo-American relations. British actions in Greece provided the springboard for more criticism of the British Empire. Representative Celler regarded them as 'imperialism run riot'. When the United States was bearing the brunt of the battle in France, British troops were killing Greek patriots. The British Prime Minister was contributing to the eradication of fascism and the implementation of the Atlantic Charter by 'buttering up Franco and leaving Nehru in jail'.[49]

Stalin on the other hand was quite content to leave British imperialism to run its course in Greece. It was another illustration of the apparent compatibility of Soviet and British power-political interests in contrast to the anti-imperialism of those in the State Department who hoped to found a new world order based on the universal acceptance of American ideals. Churchill was able to draw much support from the attitude of the Russians which allowed him to pursue such an uncompromising Greek policy. Having paid what the Prime Minister regarded as a high price to secure British freedom of action in Greece, there should be no hesitation about the use of force. In order to keep his side of the Anglo-Soviet bargain Churchill slapped down complaints from the British military mission in Romania about the lack of Soviet consultation; it was a country in which the British were little more than spectators, he remarked. In return Stalin was uttering no criticism of British actions in Greece, and as Churchill himself recorded, Russia was giving Britain better treatment there than the United States.[50]

Thus as preparations began at the beginning of 1945 for the holding of the next meeting of the Big Three leaders, there were good indications that an Anglo-Soviet 'modus vivendi' had been secured. Indeed it has been suggested that Stalin welcomed British actions in Greece 'since it established a convenient precedent for ruthless Soviet intervention in the internal affairs of Eastern Europe'.[51] The original idea of a Greek/Romania exclusive Anglo-Soviet arrangement was holding firm. Regarding the Straits, although there had been some military fears about the revision of Montreux this was not universally accepted in military circles, and in December the Joint Intelligence Committee concluded that Russia would have no strategic interests in controlling sea routes in and through the Mediterranean which could not be secured without large commitments. Black Sea domination was deemed to be the Soviet aim, and therefore only freedom of passage through the Straits would be required. Full control of the Straits would require Turkish territory, and intelligence estimates concluded that the Soviets would not go so far. More ominously, given Foreign Office attitudes, the JIC believed that Russia would wish for the end of the Anglo-Turkish alliance and expect to stand on an equal footing with the other great powers in the Middle East. These views on Soviet aims and intentions in an area vital to the British were linked to a JIC assessment of Russian requirements in Eastern Europe. The Soviet Union, so it was assumed, would have a protective screen of Finland, Poland, Czechoslovakia, Hungary, Romania and to a lesser extent Yugoslavia. In the Balkans Russia would exercise less control over Bulgaria than Romania which would only be nominally independent. This was confirmation of earlier British assessments which assumed Soviet control over much of Eastern and Central Europe. Similar views were expressed in the Foreign Office by Gladwyn Jebb. Jebb did not expect the Soviets to seek domination over the whole of the European continent and assumed therefore that Russian influence would not go beyond a certain line; that line would be such as to leave the Soviets 'paramount' in Poland, Czechoslovakia, Romania, Hungary and Bulgaria and possibly in Yugoslavia and Austria also. At the end of 1944 both the military and the Foreign Office were clearly accepting Soviet dominance of all of Eastern and Central, Europe and probably of all the Balkans excluding Greece.[52]

The question must again be asked what exactly the British meant by Soviet dominance or what internal arrangements would be necessary to secure a Soviet protective screen. Jebb believed the Soviet satellites would look to Russia for armaments and follow the Soviet line in foreign affairs. The JIC view was that the Soviets would want a position in those countries similar to that enjoyed by the British in Egypt. In other words independence would be granted, presumably after some influence had been exerted over the formation of the government, as long as the Soviets could ensure that the states in the security zone pursued policies that protected their strategic interests.[53] The question of what sort of governments would do this, given the longstanding hostility of Poles and Romanians to the Soviet Union, was not, as far as our limited knowledge enables us to tell, addressed by the JIC. The Foreign Office had, as has been seen, addressed the issue, with one official believing that the Russians would favour broad based popular front governments, while the Deputy Undersecretary was sure that Stalin would require strong dictatorial governments administering a system of state socialism and following a pro-Russian policy; this, in his view would be preferable to inefficient popular front regimes.[54] Here was a reason for supporting the imposition of firm Soviet controls in the Russian sphere of influence. The problem was of course that Poland would clearly be within that sphere, and with so many Poles fighting alongside British servicemen, the coalition government had an obligation to consider Polish aspirations or face serious criticism in parliament. Churchill therefore, despite his longstanding irritation with the leaders of the London Poles, decided to make public statements supporting the reestablishment of Poland as a fully sovereign and independent state free to model its institutions along any non-fascist lines. This was to become a major problem and to be entangled in the subsequent Anglo-Soviet disputes over influence in the Balkans.

Another problem was Britain's general position in southeast Europe which, apart from Greece, seemed to have to be abandoned in the same way as her position in the rest of Central and Eastern Europe. The position of the Red Army in the East, in comparison to that of the Anglo-American forces in the West, was even stronger by December 1944 due to problems on the Western front. De facto control of all of Eastern and Central Europe seemed even more certain as the British believed the battle west of the Rhine was not going to prove decisive and the Germans would be difficult to finish off.[55] In December the initially successful German counter offensive in the Ardennes made the general European situation look even more gloomy from the British point of view. What was at stake of course was not only the general European balance of power, which in any case was bound -

to be irrevocably changed, but the British position relative to the Soviet Union. The more that Britain was excluded from the military campaign from Germany to the Balkans the less say it was likely to have in the general settlement and the more its post-war position as a great power would be eroded.

The issue at the beginning of 1945 was, therefore, very much a power-political one linked to the strength of the British and Soviet Empires and their ability to project power and influence on a global basis. Churchill, however, who may not have been so aware of the subtle Foreign Office distinction between the spread of communism and the extension of Russian influence, often portrayed this pre-Yalta situation in ideological terms.

In November 1944 he explained to Eden that the Moscow agreement had been designed to forestall Soviet influence in the Adriatic and Mediterranean which lay beyond the reach of the Red Army. Every country liberated was seething with communism and only Britain's influence with Russia prevented Stalin from encouraging communist movements. In December Britain was having increasing trouble in maintaining cooperation with Tito and Churchill was even more pessimistic. Communist influence, he noted, was likely to establish itself under Russian patronage throughout the Balkan peninsula save possibly in Greece, even without specific action by Russia. The following month the situation appeared even worse, and the Prime Minister commented, as Russian troops reached the Oder, 'make no mistake, all the Balkans except Greece are going to be Bolshevised and there is nothing I can do to prevent it. There is nothing I can do for poor Poland either.'[56] Despite Churchill's confusing Soviet power with communist influence, the growth of Soviet strength, combined with the increasingly evident, but long recognised American military and economic power, were weighing heavily on him and casting shadows over Britain's increasingly subordinate global position. Soviet military successes were raising the price which Britain would have to pay to preserve its special position in the Eastern Mediterranean. In addition, by reducing British influence in Central, Eastern and southeastern Europe, Soviet military successes were diminishing Britain's post-war great power status; this appeared inevitable irrespective of the nature of the regime in Moscow. As the Prime Minister set out for Yalta his mood was clearly not one of optimism. He was conscious of Britain's lack of bargaining power and aware of the enormous responsibilities hanging on the three Allied leaders as they sought agreement on the broad outlines of the post-war settlement and the amicable resolution of differences.

The Yalta conference has continued to arouse controversy almost from the very day that its deliberations were concluded. Despite the Russians and Americans publishing their official records, and despite the now well known protocols setting out the signed agreements, a variety of conflicting interpretations of the conference remain. Speculation about the health of the American president remains a key and irresolvable issue. Roosevelt's health was undoubtedly failing, but whether this affected his handling of the issues remains a matter of conjecture. Inevitably some historians will continue to see Soviet–American cooperation as a sign of Roosevelt's weakness and folly irrespective of whether this was induced by poor heath.

Alongside those who take such views are historians who imply that Roosevelt

manipulated the conference in order to satisfy Stalin's power-political requirements in Eastern Europe and the Far East. The President was required to do this,
they argue, for the sake of great power cooperation, but at the same time he had to
satisfy domestic opinion; and therefore such arrangements had to be concealed
behind a cloak of rhetoric that portrayed the conference as a triumph of American
idealism and the banishment of spheres of influence and all forms of totalitarian
government. Only by so doing could the President gain public acceptance of a
major American role in the future world organisation which was necessary for the
maintenance of peace and great power cooperation. Other more simplistic, and
fundamentally inaccurate approaches, have simply stigmatised Yalta as a cynical
great power agreement to carve up the post-war world.[57] In fact the British
analysis of Yalta in February 1945 and in the months immediately following saw it
as something quite the reverse, because for the Foreign Office it provided some
hope of an eventual abandonment of a spheres of influence arrangement, originally
seen as the best way to protect British vital interests, but now seen as more
problematic. From the British perspective the most astonishing and welcome
aspect of the conference was Stalin's apparent acceptance of the right of the
British and the Americans to influence the process by which provisional and then
permanent governments would be established in Poland and other areas of vital
interest to the Soviets and which were covered by the Declaration on Liberated
Europe. With spheres of influence much less likely to fulfil all Britain's imperial
requirements by February 1945, Stalin's attitude appeared to offer the welcome
possibility that British influence in Europe could be extended outside Greece and
thus enhance Britain's post-war international standing.

In general terms Stalin approached the conference with much greater confidence than either Churchill or Roosevelt. The Russian leader did not have public
opinion to consider, and the Soviet victories in the east had given him some very
strong cards to play. While in January the Allies in the west, to some extent helped
by the Russian offensives in the east, had reversed the temporary German
successes and were pushing on towards the Rhine, by the time the conference
ended the Red Army was only 36 miles from Berlin. Although agreement had
already been reached on German zones of occupation it did not seem likely that
either of the Western Allies would be able to stand on a par with the Russians as
conquerors of Germany. There are no signs from the British records however that
Stalin attempted to exploit to the full the strong position the military situation gave
him, preferring instead to concentrate on securing great power cooperation as the
best means of protecting Russian interests by preventing the emergence of any
future German threat. For Stalin the German question was the most important
issue at Yalta but he was prepared to accept the American proposals for the voting
formula in the proposed United Nations' Security Council. The latter, and
agreement on the membership of the United Nations, were the priorities of the
American President who, in keeping with his penchant for personal diplomacy,
was determined to provide a framework within which tripartite cooperation could
effectively create and preserve post-war stability. If this was done he believed there
was no reason why he, along with Churchill and Stalin, could not successfully
overcome post-war difficulties.

Stalin had no such priorities. Having secured de facto control over all Eastern
and Central Europe, with the exception of Greece and possibly Yugoslavia, the

Russian leader had no pressing concerns apart from what would ultimately be the most important issue of all – the treatment of a defeated Germany. But as long as Germany was still fighting this issue was not yet urgent, and indeed virtually all decisions on the future of Germany were postponed. Roosevelt suggested a definite plan should be drawn up on German dismemberment, in the knowledge that Stalin was extremely keen to secure the dismantlement of the German Reich and that the British Prime Minister had in the past referred to plans for the creation of separate German states.

Churchill however was no longer so keen on taking such measures before the unconditional surrender of Germany, and was successful in ensuring that the issue be postponed. In the meantime a committee would study the procedure for German dismemberment in so far as it was deemed necessary for peace and security. Despite the apparent affinity of Soviet and American views the British had got their way. A similar situation was produced by the issue of German reparations. Stalin and Roosevelt were keen to impose reparations whereas Churchill had distinct reservations. Again the issue was to be discussed by a commission, which was to meet in Moscow, and to take as a basis for its deliberations the Soviet proposals on reparations, although the British refused to agree that any definite figures should be mentioned. Nor was any decision made on the boundary between Germany and Poland which would certainly have been crucial had the main intention been to divide Europe into spheres of influence.[58]

In many respects Stalin's approach to the Yalta meeting reflected, on the surface at least, an extraordinary amount of complacency and incompetence which may have been an indication of overconfidence because of the Russian position in Central and Eastern Europe and the Balkans. Not taken at face value it reflects an equally extraordinary degree of cynicism, and a lack of concern over the future conflict between the making of tripartite agreements and their implementation. Before the Declarations on Liberated Europe and Poland the great statement of principle on the nature of the post-war world was the Atlantic Charter. Churchill's virulent denouncement of the Charter as having no validity within the boundaries of the British Empire, and his lengthy tirade against any future interference with the running of Britain's overseas possessions seems to have struck nothing more than a chord of wry amusement in the Soviet leader. The fact that the British leader was then to support the application of the Atlantic Charter principles to areas of Europe of great concern to the Soviets and to try and ensure that British and American representatives had a role in their implementation appeared to leave Stalin equally unmoved. The debate on these principles was in fact to be conducted with reference to Poland and other areas under Soviet control, as opposed to those areas of the world which were under British control. Small wonder that Churchill, having realised by the sixth plenary meeting (out of eight) that Britain's vital interests were not going to be challenged, could remark that for him the most important issue at Yalta was Poland.

Much of the conference was dominated by discussions on Poland and on the principles to be applied in the treatment of liberated Europe. As such it concentrated on areas where Soviet interests and control would be subjected to Allied cooperation and joint policies. Thus the British were able to avoid discussions on the Straits, the Italian peace treaty, Greece, Romania and Bulgaria where there were important British interests or a spheres of influence arrangement. As a result it would be easier to avoid concessions which in Moscow Eden had already seen Churchill make on the Straits. Stalin did mention the Straits and Greece, but in the latter case only to emphasise that he was in no way intending to influence British policy, but merely desired to be kept informed of what was happening.

Much of the Polish discussion centred on the nature of the provisional government to be established there because it was soon agreed that the eastern frontier should be the Curzon Line and that substantial compensation should be given to Poland in the west. Russian recognition of the Lublin Committee as the provisional government of Poland was obviously a blow to British hopes that the exiled Polish government in London would be able to play a major role in the immediate post-war period. Churchill clearly wanted therefore to broaden the representative nature of the provisional Polish government, which, if based on the Lublin Committee would simply consist of pro-Russian communists. If this was going to prove difficult then it was important for free elections to be held in which all democratic anti-fascist parties would have the right to participate. Churchill eventually accepted that Britain would be satisfied if this could be agreed along with some 'reorganisation' of the Lublin government. Stalin was extraordinarily agreeable, although of course the dominance of the pro-Russian Poles was not going to be effectively challenged in the short term. He did refer to France, where the provisional government had been recognised, without any Soviet objections, but did not suggest that de Gaulle's pro-British provisional government should be 'reorganised' to include more communist representatives who had been prominent in the struggle against the Germans.

Poland may have been considered by Stalin to be in an equivalent position to France, which makes it even harder to understand why he agreed to the French being represented on the Allied Control Commission for Germany. In addition Stalin, speaking informally, suggested that free elections would be held in Poland within a month. That the Soviet leader, who had refused to refer to an independent Polish state at Tehran, as opposed to respect for the Polish language and culture, should promise free elections in the Western sense is bizarre; that he should have promised them within a month when there was no likelihood of such elections in France or Greece where there were conflicts between communist and non-communist elements in the population is quite extraordinary. Moreover, Stalin extended these apparent concessions to most of the area which official policy makers, who did not have to face the likely parliamentary and public reaction to complaints from dissatisfied non-communist Poles, had already marked down for Soviet dominance. The Declaration on Liberated Europe signed by all three leaders stated:

The establishment of order in Europe and the re-building of national economic life must be achieved by processes which will enable the liberated peoples to destroy the last vestiges of Nazism and Fascism and to create democratic institutions of their own choice. This is a principle of the Atlantic Charter – the right of all peoples to choose the form of government under which they will live – the restoration of sovereign rights and self-government to those peoples who have been forcibly deprived of them by the aggressor nations.

To foster the conditions in which the liberated peoples may exercise these rights, the three governments will jointly assist the people in any European liberated state or former Axis satellite state in Europe where in their judgement conditions require (a) to establish conditions of internal peace; (b) to carry out emergency measures for the relief of distressed peoples; (c) to form interim governmental authorities broadly representative of all democratic elements in the population and pledged to the earliest possible establishment through free elections of governments responsive to the will of the people; and (d) to facilitate where necessary the holding of such elections.

The final text of the agreement on Poland stated:

A new situation has been created in Poland as a result of her complete liberation by the Red Army. This calls for the establishment of a Polish Provisional Government which can be more broadly based than was possible before the recent liberation of Western Poland. The Provisional Government which is now functioning in Poland should therefore be reorganised on a broader democratic basis with the inclusion of democratic leaders from Poland itself and from Poles abroad. This new government should then be called the Polish Provisional Government of National Unity. M. Molotov, Mr Harriman and Sir A. Clark Kerr are authorized as a Commission to consult in the first instance in Moscow with members of the present Provisional Government and with other Polish democratic leaders from within Poland and from abroad, with a view to the reorganization of the present government along the above lines. This Polish Provisional Government of National Unity shall be pledged to the holding of free and unfettered elections as soon as possible on the basis of universal suffrage and secret ballot. In these elections all democratic and anti-Nazi parties shall have the right to take part and to put forward candidates.

In the circumstances there has been surprisingly little discussion on the state of Stalin's health at Yalta. What then is the explanation for Stalin's behaviour, which is definitely the most neglected and most interesting aspect of the Yalta Conference? Did he expect to curry favour with the British and the Americans and to display his willingness to cooperate, by accepting policies that would please Anglo-American opinion? Did Stalin expect that he could safely manipulate the agreements to suit his requirements by, for example, arguing that all anti-Russian parties were either fascist or undemocratic? Did he expect that such declarations would not be taken seriously and that 'free' elections in Poland would not be demanded in the immediate future by the British who were using military force against their ideological opponents to prepare the ground for elections when such opponents would be weaker? Did Stalin believe that, as had been the case in Italy, the military commanders would, in the short term, assume real authority for the government of the country. Was it simply a cynical acceptance of decadent bourgeois democratic views when neither Britain nor the United States was in any position to impose its ideas? Did Stalin simply regard the issues of Eastern Europe as insignificant in comparison to the German problem, or was he simply unaware of the implications of the agreement?

From the text of his speech at Yalta, it seems that Stalin may well have believed that with the destruction of the wartime resistance in Warsaw, the Poles would have no alternative focus for their anti-German sentiments than the pro-Russian leaders now forming the Lublin Government. Stalin certainly informed Churchill and Roosevelt at the fifth plenary session that the liberation of Poland by the Red Army had changed the attitude of the Polish people towards Russia; the old resentment had, he claimed, disappeared, and good will had taken its place. This of course could have been an exercise in disseminating misleading propaganda, but it could also indicate that Stalin himself had been misled about the extent of support for the Lublin government within Poland. A genuine misperception in Moscow about the nature of the pro-Lublin support is, however, difficult to reconcile with the Russian determination not to have Anglo-American involvement with the Polish elections except in so much as the principle of non-involvement in Greece and Italy had been accepted by Stalin. It is difficult, even with the benefit of hindsight and a vast amount of secondary literature to find a totally convincing explanation of Stalin's behaviour in any of these analyses. Nor it is clear whether the British and the Americans ever expected him to implement the agreements or whether it became important, for reasons of domestic opinion or international standing, for them later to insist on their implementation.

In the British case, whatever the expectations built up by Yalta (and the evidence suggests they were considerable), it is clear, that, with the possible exception of Poland, the British in 1944, did not expect such concessions from the Soviets in what was regarded as an area of vital interest. In short, the British had gone to the Crimea in a pessimistic state of mind, concerned that their sphere of influence in Greece and the Eastern Mediterranean would be in jeopardy despite the guarantees gained at Moscow. At the same time they believed that the speed of the Soviet advance in the east and the lack of Anglo-American progress in the west meant that Britain could well be excluded from any future role in Central and Eastern Europe apart from Greece. In such circumstances any extension of the spheres of influence approach was bound to favour the Soviets. Yet Stalin had apparently moved away from this and accepted the principle of representative government, which could include leaders favourably disposed to non-communist political and economic systems. He had in fact opened the door to an arrangement enabling British influence to be maintained where Britain had no real interests except in preserving the appearance of a major world power concerned with, to a greater or lesser degree, all areas of Europe. In addition the status quo in areas where Britain did have vital interests had not effectively been challenged.

There were of course no means for the British or the Americans effectively to ensure that Stalin carried out the agreements on liberated Europe, and one of the few concessions made by Churchill and Roosevelt was to accept that their Ambassadors in Poland would not be directly involved in the organisation and supervision of the elections. Time would tell whether Stalin would sacrifice the kind of control over Eastern and Central Europe which Sir Orme Sargent quite explicitly, and many others implicitly, had expected him to impose in 1944.

Even with this important reservation, British ministers and officials not surprisingly returned from Yalta in a more optimistic frame of mind and expressing unanimous approval of the conference's achievements. The War Cabinet sent congratulations to Churchill 'on the most satisfactory result you have achieved' and Colville noted in his diary that 'we seem to have won most of our points'. Small wonder that Cadogan claimed 'I have never known the Russians so easy and accommodating'.[59] The British could claim that Churchill had done something for 'poor Poland' and that as Stalin had expressed his desire not to interfere in Greece, at worst the British would only have to acquiesce in their exclusion from Romania; the Declaration of Liberated Europe could conveniently supersede the percentages agreement except perhaps on the basic trade off between Greece and Romania. Not everybody in the Foreign Office was so naive as to assume that suddenly Yalta had changed everything, especially as there was no guarantee that the London Poles would be satisfied even if Stalin honoured the agreements. Moreover in those areas which, unlike Poland, were closer to Britain's vital interests, Sargent believed that, in the aftermath of Yalta and despite the Declaration on Liberated Europe, Britain would have to accept that Romania, Bulgaria and probably Yugoslavia would have Soviet dominated governments.

In addition to these concerns there were two fears that were to develop from the Yalta meeting. The first was that the United States would not continue to maintain the unique form of cooperation with Britain which had developed during the war. Roosevelt had of course refused to meet Churchill prior to the conference in order to avoid any impression of a common Anglo-American strategy. The second, and interconnected fear, was that the Russians and the Americans might be prepared to cooperate without due consideration for British interests, with the result that Britain's international standing as one of the three first-rank powers would be irretrievably damaged. Such scenarios were to worry British policy makers more and more between the Yalta and Potsdam Conferences. The Crimean meeting had, ominously, produced several instances of Soviet–American agreement in the face of British opposition. This threat to Britain's position was, however, compensated for by the apparent Soviet willingness to meet British wishes and acknowledge the possibility of British influence in areas of Eastern and Central Europe which post-war civilian and military planners had previously regarded as areas of Soviet dominance. In the wake of Yalta, the Soviet willingness to accept this was to be one yardstick of Soviet 'behaviour', along with the more important requirement of Soviet acceptance of exclusive British influence in the Eastern Mediterranean and the Middle East. In short, a spheres of influence deal to protect Greece was now seen as insufficient to prevent the erosion of Britain's general position and its appearance as the junior partner, but the prospect of preserving influence in most of Eastern and Central Europe, apart from Romania, appeared, thanks to Stalin's apparent eagerness to cooperate, as a lifeline. The successful preservation of Britain's position would therefore depend on developments in what was regarded as a new situation in Eastern and Central Europe as well as on the maintenance of vital imperial interests which were linked to European problems by Greece and, to a lesser extent, the remainder of the Balkans.

Churchill, while disliking what the Soviets were doing in Romania, and being prepared to let Stalin know of British views on this, pointed out that Romania and Bulgaria had been Britain's enemies and the same risks could not be run for them as for Greece and Poland. If the Polish situation was going to be troublesome then the Prime Minister did not want to be accused of breaking the Anglo-Russian understanding on Greece and Romania by interfering in the affairs of the latter country. It was more important to prevent Soviet involvement in Greece, where, in the spring of 1945 the British removed the Plastiras government and installed a more conservative regime under Voulgaris, a naval admiral involved in the suppression of the 1944 armed forces mutinies. In March 1945 the British also refused to support American proposals for a tripartite economic mission to Greece, arguing that the Soviets should be excluded; it was a clear indication of their perception of the spheres of influence arrangement as a means of preventing Soviet involvement in Greece.[60] On the other hand on 6 March, Churchill told the Cabinet 'it would be for consideration whether the Yalta Declaration on Liberated

Territories could be construed as superseding arrangements such as that in respect of Romania and Greece'. Abandoning them entirely left the problem of Greece, for as Churchill told Roosevelt, although Stalin was trampling down the principles of Yalta in Romania he was anxious to avoid the Soviet leader saying 'I did not interfere with your action in Greece, why do you not give me the same latitude in Romania?'[61]

There is some evidence that Churchill began to perceive the acceptance of Soviet dominance in Bulgaria as a way of compensating for the broadening of the Lublin government and the denial of Soviet dominance in Poland. That certainly seemed a desirable option as it became clear in March that Stalin had no immediate intention of implementing the Yalta agreement on Poland. If accepted it would of course be a marriage of the spheres of influence agreement with the Yalta Declaration that allowed for the power shift in favour of the Soviets in the Balkans. The Foreign Office had always had more concern for Bulgaria than the Prime Minister and had no doubt that the Soviets wanted a paramount position in the Balkans despite their 'wholly correct attitude' to the Greek embroglio. Given Foreign Office concern with Britain's position in the Mediterranean could it therefore accept the idea that the Soviets would impose their will in Romania *and* Bulgaria but that Britain would have its say in Poland?[62]

Later in the month the British Ambassador in Moscow addressed this issue of Poland, Romania and Bulgaria in the context of Britain's vital interests. It was an important despatch because it confirmed the general Whitehall perception of Britain's vital interests, and because it shed light on the Soviet attitude to the Yalta agreements. Clark Kerr explained that whenever mention was made of Russian actions in Romania it was pointed out that British arguments were at odds with the statutes agreed upon for the Allied Control Commission; this Clark Kerr interpreted as indicating that the Soviets treated the Yalta Declaration as little more than a sedative. The Ambassador also pointed out that the word 'cooperation', like the word 'democracy', had a different meaning in Moscow. For the Soviets it meant something like the division of the world into spheres with no partner hampering or criticising the other in their sphere. It would therefore be a mistake to believe that the Kremlin had turned away from cooperation with the West. The Soviets, he believed, had a unique opportunity to control internal developments in Romania, Bulgaria and Poland, but these were limited objectives none of which immediately endangered any essential British interests. Clark Kerr acknowledged that, although not a vital British interest, Poland was a question of utmost importance because on it rested a great part of British hopes for a cordial understanding with the Soviets. Poland could therefore become a test case of Soviet behaviour. But it should not, he concluded, become an issue which need prevent the maintenance of an alliance, and Britain would certainly be better served by avoiding fruitless arguments over Romania and Bulgaria and concentrating on standing up for its vital interests in Greece, Persia and Turkey. In these areas the Ambassador was encouraged by Soviet behaviour, which he characterised as showing extreme moderation in Greece. The Kremlin had also refrained from demands for oil concessions in Persia because, he believed, Soviet leaders realised Persia was a matter of vital concern for Britain. Clark Kerr even saw little to worry about in the recent Soviet denunciation of the Soviet–Turkish treaty because he saw no evidence that the Russians were doing any more than prepare the ground for the revision of Montreux. Overall, therefore, Britain should not be unduly discouraged by the post-Yalta events because none of them impinged upon vital British interests.[63]

The question of the revision of Montreux, raised by Stalin at Yalta, had prompted Eden to request the Chiefs of Staff to provide yet another assessment of the strategic implications for Britain. The Chiefs had given the task to the PHP whose report was completed three days after Clark Kerr's despatch. They pointed out that the Soviets could seize the Straits in war anyway, and argued that the significance of Montreux lay in its peacetime provisions and in the opening stages of a war. If the Soviets had unrestricted passage, they could develop a submarine force in the Eastern Mediterranean immediately, and also develop a surface fleet there in the early stages of a conflict. To that extent, to allow the Soviets unrestricted passage would be against Britain's strategic interests. However they would require air bases and possibly naval bases in Greece or Turkey before such a threat became serious. The planners believed British bases in Crete and the Dodecanese would limit the Soviet naval threat and their main fear was that the revision of Montreux would weaken the political standing of Greece and Turkey relative to the Soviet Union. Noting that the Chiefs of Staff had tentatively accepted the idea that there should be no opposition to reasonable Soviet demands where there was no conflict with vital strategic interests, the PHP concluded that it would be better to accept the Soviet desire for unrestricted passage.[64] Thus despite Sargent's reservations it seemed that the revision of Montreux was unlikely to provoke an Anglo-Soviet clash if the British were merely to insist, as Clark Kerr suggested, on standing up for their vital interests.

However, would the defence of vital interests, which would also involve accepting the Soviet right to defend its vital interests, be enough to maintain Britain's global position in the post-war world? It was a question now addressed in some detail by Sir Orme Sargent, who was more concerned to focus on this than on the related questions of whether a world based on spheres of influence would be acceptable to the United States or desirable in principle. Sargent's memorandum was prompted by the dramatic improvement in the Anglo-American military position as a result of the European successes achieved by the armed forces in March 1945. On 8 March Colville noted in his diary that the 'war goes better and better' with the Americans crossing the Rhine north of Koblenz after an unexpected bridge seizure. In the Foreign Office, Sargent had previously assumed that the Russian armies would occupy the heart of Germany before the British and the Americans had penetrated German defences in the west, and establish a military predominance in the heart of Europe which it would be foolish to ignore. However the change in the war situation led Sargent to suggest in early April a change in the nature of Britain's diplomatic approach to the Soviets.

The Undersecretary's new proposals were linked to his view, not yet universally accepted in the Foreign Office, that spheres of influence would not serve to maintain Britain's status in the first rank of world powers. In effect he was arguing for a more aggressive diplomatic posture by Britain. When the military situation had been so unfavourable, especially in the late summer and autumn of 1944, it only made sense to propitiate the Russians, even though in Sargent's view the policy had produced few results. Now that the Western Allies were going to meet the Soviets on equal terms in Germany the situation had radically changed.

Sargent believed the Russians were aware of this and were therefore being more truculent and less cooperative, in contrast to their behaviour at Yalta. They were now giving nothing away because with the new military situation the Russians would need all the bargaining cards they could lay their hands on. Yet the British and American forces, Sargent believed, would be able to make their influence felt in Poland, Czechoslovakia, Austria and Hungary.

There was however a danger that the Soviets might decide to consolidate their *cordon sanitaire* out of a fear that Britain and the United States would rehabilitate Germany in the same way they had undertaken to rehabilitate Italy to save it from communism. In order to prevent this, Sargent proposed a diplomatic showdown with Stalin. Britain should speak plainly to the Soviet leader and formulate what the Foreign Office considered to be British rights, for if Britain continued to propitiate the Russians when Britain's military position was much stronger this would be interpreted by Stalin as a cunning manoeuvre intended to put him off his ground. If there was no implementation of the Polish agreement made at Yalta there should be the 'plainest of plain speaking' on the question of the future treatment of Germany and Austria and the Soviet *cordon sanitaire*. Initially Sargent had believed the Soviets had no firm plans for defining and consolidating their sphere of influence in the area between Germany and the Soviet Union. Now he believed their policy was taking shape in Poland, Romania and Bulgaria. For him the question was whether the Soviets would extend this to Yugoslavia, Hungary, Austria, Czechoslovakia, and possibly Turkey. Acknowledging that a spheres of influence agreement could easily prevent this, with Britain 'saving' Czechoslovakia, Yugoslavia, Austria and Turkey at the expense of Poland, Romania, and Bulgaria, Sargent rejected any such deal as inconceivable. It would be a cynical abandonment of the small nations and '*represent the abdication of our right as a great power to be concerned with the affairs of the whole of Europe and not just areas in which we have a special interest*'. That in effect ruled out a spheres of influence agreement, and Sargent concluded that if Britain could not found its policy of cooperation towards the Soviet Union on exclusive spheres of influence it was important to make it clear to the Kremlin that Anglo-Soviet cooperation must apply in Central and southeastern Europe as well as in the rest of the world.[65]

But there was a major snag in such cooperation with the Soviets because it meant collaboration in those areas of the world which were of vital interest to Britain, and at the highest level in the Foreign Office this was not seen as at all desirable. The Suez Canal Committee had presented its report to the Cabinet just over a week before Sargent's call for a change in Britain's approach to relations with the Soviets. Given Attlee's belief in the value of international responsibility for the defence of the Canal, which would have provided an opportunity for Anglo-Soviet cooperation, and the opposition of the Conservative members to such an idea, the Cabinet was requested to decide whether responsibility for the defence of the Canal should be vested in HMG in perpetuity and whether Britain should continue to play the predominant role in the defence of the Middle East. The PHP had responded to Attlee's support for internationalism in the Middle East as early as April 1945. They pointed out that if the UN became responsible for the defence and security of the Middle East Britain would be deprived of its predominant role in the defence of the region and this would be unacceptable. The Middle East could only be declared a UN concern if effective control of the region's defence policy remained in UK hands; Britain could accept assistance from the United States, France and the Middle Eastern states but for 'strategic reasons' Soviet help should be limited as far as possible.[66]

In response to the Suez Canal Committee's request Eden submitted a paper to the Cabinet arguing most strongly against any moves to compromise Britain's position in the Suez Canal Zone or the Middle East. The Foreign Secretary argued that the Middle East was one of the most important strategic areas of the world

an area the defence of which is a matter of life and death to the British Empire . . . Consequently, we are bound to give the Middle East an extremely high priority when allotting our available resources to the areas where we have responsibilities. For this reason alone, we cannot afford to resign our special position in the area (even though in an emergency we may be able to accept the help of others in defending it) and allow our position to become dependent on arrangements of an international character.

Eden went on to argue that the future World Organisation should give each of the Great Powers special defence responsibilities in its particular area or areas, and the United States and the Soviet Union had areas of responsibility which were as vital to their interests as the Middle East was to Britain's. Thus 'the position of the United States in relation to the Panama Canal is identical with our own in relation to the Suez Canal, as is the position of Russia with regard to certain areas of Eastern Europe'. Britain should therefore secure its position in the Middle East by its own means, and this would not be 'out of harmony with the general international background'. This interestingly, implied acceptance of an imperial trade off based on vital spheres of interest rather than its rejection as incompatible with Britain's global status.

Eden's views were strengthened by the views of the Resident Minister in the Middle East, which were approved by the Middle East Defence Committee before being circulated to the Cabinet at the beginning of July. The Minister, Sir Edward Grigg, defined the Empire as a 'cooperative commonwealth of widely separated peoples', whose 'life and strength' depended upon the freedom of its communications. It would not survive as a cooperative system, he claimed, if its communications were liable to severance by some foreign power, and Middle Eastern communications, along with the oilfields in Iraq and Persia, were 'absolutely indispensable' to the Empire's 'cohesion and security'. Using the same dramatic terminology as the Foreign Secretary, Grigg defined the Middle East as 'a region of life and death consequence for the British Empire' because of its oil and communications *and* because it was essential for Britain's 'status and influence as a major Power'. It was a region in which the 'British political method must make good if the British way of life is to survive'.[67]

The references to the Middle East as a 'matter of life and death for the British Empire' were clearly signs of the increasingly pivotal role the region was to play in Britain's imperial strategy, despite a PHP paper in June, which, while emphasising the Soviet threat, attached greater strategic importance to the Indian Ocean than the Middle East. Certainly in the early months of 1945 it was regarded by both Eden and his officials as an area, unlike the Far East, where Britain's commitments were under threat and had to be maintained. The initial idea of thinking imperially had been born out of the possible abandonment of part of Britain's formal Empire in the Far East. In 1945 the imperial thinkers became much more concerned with informal Empire than the role of colonies in general or the Far Eastern situation in particular. The Colonial Secretary's idea of using regional commissions to placate the internationalists while strengthening Britain's exclusive administrative responsibilities by the abolition of the mandates was effectively ended at Yalta. Neither Churchill nor Eden was keen to support the idea once it became clear that the new concept of trusteeship would only apply to the former mandates and the colonies of the defeated Axis powers.

In the Foreign Office, officials of the Far Eastern Department were much better disposed to the Soviet Union than their counterparts in the Southern Department and more prepared to countenance a retreat from power. One official took exception to the idea that the British and the Americans should have a sphere of influence in the Pacific which would exclude the Soviet Union. Others pointed to the 'necessity of cutting our coat according to our cloth' and regretted the general tendency within the Foreign Office to urge the maintenance of 'commitments far beyond our manpower or our future financial and material resources'.

Certainly the maintenance of an elaborate system of Far Eastern bases in the 1950s was opposed at the official level.[68] The Far East, unlike the Middle East, was not seen as an area where Britain's informal position had to be maintained, or an area which, because of its significance in terms of spheres of influence and its relation to the changing balance of power in Europe, would have a major impact on Anglo-Soviet relations and Britain's global position.

The Foreign Secretary's assessment of the position in the Middle East had significant implications for Anglo-Soviet relations and Sargent's suggested new approach. If Britain had to have an exclusive role in the Suez Canal Zone, comparable to that of the Soviets in part of Eastern Europe, how could the British expect the Soviets not to maintain such a position in their areas of vital interest? Clearly there would be problems if the spheres of influence approach had to be completely abandoned in order to avoid the erosion of Britain's status associated with its exclusion from parts of Europe. It was hardly surprising therefore that Sargent's proposed new approach did not win acceptance within the Foreign Office. G. M. Wilson, acknowledging the unpleasant nature of Soviet behaviour in Bulgaria, Romania and Poland, thought it too much to expect that a stable situation could be produced in the latter country with or without an active British role. He pointed out that the Poles and the Russians had been unable to settle their differences for hundreds of years, while Britain's nineteenth-century interventions on behalf of the Poles had done them no good whatsoever. Moreover, the Russians, according to Wilson, had every reason to believe that Britain regarded Romania and Bulgaria as within their sphere of influence, and that all aspects of Russian policy to which the British were objecting in the spring of 1945 were within the Soviet sphere. The position of Poland seemed to be rather ambivalent as clearly many of the objections of the Prime Minister and others concerned Poland, which Wilson appeared not to put as completely in the Soviet sphere as Romania and Bulgaria. Nevertheless Wilson's general conclusion was clearly to support the line of the Ambassador in Moscow in favour of Anglo-Soviet cooperation based on live and let live with no interference in each other's vital interests.[69]

Support for the spheres of influence idea also came from Frank Roberts, who was later to play an important role as Bevin's private secretary. Roberts argued that despite the post-Yalta disappointments there was still the prospect of preserving a useful relationship with the Soviet Union provided Britain 'took a leaf out of the Russian book' and approached every problem in a tough and realistic manner. It was vital to show that the British were determined and strong enough to defend their own interests in the same way that the Soviets were pursuing their interests by consolidating their zone of influence in countries recently liberated by the Red Army. Unlike Sargent, Roberts acknowledged, however, that Britain, while protecting its interests, must expect to be excluded from Poland, Czechoslovakia, Bulgaria, Romania and even Yugoslavia. If Europe was going to be divided it would be better for Britain to concentrate its efforts on the western half.[70]

This idea of a western bloc was inevitably to become more appealing as difficulties with the Soviets increased. April 1945 was not a good month for Anglo-Soviet relations and was made all the more disquieting for the British by the uncertainties following the death of Roosevelt. Churchill had made great efforts in March and early April to get the President to take a tough stance, alongside the British, over Poland. The Americans were, however, reluctant to take such a line in Poland and wanted to avoid any ultimatums in the hope that the Soviets could be persuaded to follow more liberal policies.[71] This was at odds with the growing belief in Whitehall that a tough position should be taken irrespective of whether it was geared to the establishment of spheres of influence or the insistence on Western involvement in those areas which the Soviets felt were their exclusive zones. In Washington the Joint Staff Mission sent reports indicating the military's acceptance of the idea that Britain and the United States could afford to be tougher in their dealing with the Soviets. In London, in addition to Roberts and Sargent, Bruce Lockhart, a Soviet expert in the Foreign Office, also believed that there was a need for 'bolder but still friendly diplomatic action' by Britain and the United States while Anglo-American strength was at its peak.[72]

The permanent head of the Foreign Office attempted to assess the way ahead in the light of Sargent's radical suggestion of a tough policy aimed at ending spheres of influence in line with the Yalta agreements. Cadogan was not clear as to the form or object of Sargent's proposed showdown; for him the test case was Poland, but Sargent appeared to be suggesting a showdown even if the Russians satisfactorily implemented the Yalta accords. Cadogan would only endorse this if there was no Russian action in Poland along the agreed lines. He had after all expressed the view that Britain was fighting to secure liberty and a decent existence for the peoples of Europe. The question whether British policy was based on this, and the corollary that Soviet 'behaviour' would be judged friendly or unfriendly in terms of liberty for the people of Eastern Europe, or whether there were other influences on Britain's policy linked to its vital interests and to its position as a first rank global imperial power, is a key one in terms of understanding the origins of the Cold War and the development of an imperial strategy in London. Did the British simply react to unpleasant Soviet behaviour in Europe, or were their policies defined by the need to ensure that developments in Europe, the Eastern Mediterranean and the Middle East did not undermine their position as a great imperial power?

By the spring of 1945 there were, as has been seen, good indications of what priorities British policy makers had in terms of the rapidly evolving post-war situation. There were also signs of a growing consensus that Britain should adopt a tougher line with the Soviets, yet there were clearly disagreements about what such a line should aim to achieve.[73] Between April and July, Britain's imperial strategy and attitudes to the Soviet Union were to become much clearer and better defined.

The Prime Minister did not accept that Britain was fighting to secure liberty and a decent existence for the people of Eastern Europe. 'Not a bit of it', he told Cadogan, 'we are fighting to secure the proper respect for the British people'. This of course would be linked to the kind of great power role Britain would play in the post-war world. In April the British became aware of one State Department view on this embodied in a memorandum that referred to Britain's consciousness of its junior position and a concern to buttress this position vis-à-vis the United States and the Soviet Union by exerting leadership over Western Europe and knitting the Commonwealth closer together.[74]

For Churchill, the idea of Britain becoming a junior partner was disturbing. Concerned about misinterpretations of Yalta, the Soviet's attitude to Poland and their overwhelming influence in the Balkans outside Greece, Churchill, in May, believed the fate of the world was at stake, not just the European balance of power. What the Prime Minister wanted was a three-power meeting of equals to sort out the post-Yalta difficulties.[75] Instead Truman sent Harry Hopkins to Moscow to resolve the Polish problem which had developed in the wake of the Russian refusal to implement the Yalta accords. Thus there appeared the prospect of Soviet–American rather than tripartite cooperation. Hopkins told Stalin that Poland was the symbol of the Allies' ability to work out problems, and in the event an agreement was reached on the 'reorganisation' of the Polish Lublin government, as laid down at Yalta, by which four non-Lublin Poles would be incorporated into the government.[76] It did not of course fulfil Stalin's Yalta promise to hold elections within a month, but it clearly meant that the Polish question was no longer such an acute problem as it had been in the early spring. June also saw progress in other areas, with agreement on the use of the veto at the proposed United Nations, and on the execution of the original wartime decision on Allied occupation zones in Germany.

This improvement in the prospects for cooperation in Europe was not, however, seen to bode well for Britain's future position in the world, largely because it was based on Soviet–American cooperation. In an election speech in June Churchill told the British people that 'without our influence on other nations now so high, we should lose the confidence we have won during the war from the self-governing Dominions of our Empire and Commonwealth. In a short space of time we might then by our own folly fall to the rank of a secondary Power'. The Moscow Embassy also feared the effect of the Soviet–American rapprochement, even though the Ambassador acknowledged that the Hopkins mission had led to a general improvement in the international situation. Clark Kerr interpreted it as more than a temporary flirtation, because he saw the Soviets and the Americans attempting to establish a direct relationship which would avoid an Anglo-American or an Anglo-Soviet bloc. Consequently he warned that Britain might find itself playing a more modest role in the future than it deserved.[77]

This development which threatened Britain's general world status was accompanied by growing concerns about Soviet ambitions. The original Foreign Office view in 1943 that policy should be primarily directed to the future containment of Germany had now changed. In a minute by Oliver Harvey, endorsed by the Permanent Undersecretary, the view was that 'our immediate anxiety is lest the Soviets should extend their influence and control not only over the Eastern European and Balkan states but beyond into Persia, the Levant, Greece, Italy, Germany and the Western democracies – either by force of arms or by Moscow controlled communist infiltration. Our next anxiety, though less immediate than the above is to prevent the recovery of a militarist Germany.'

Concerns about the extension of Soviet influence beyond Eastern Europe had been aroused by two events in June that had grave implications for Britain's vital interests. The Soviets raised the question of their involvement in the negotiations on the future international administration of Tangier and made it clear to the Turkish government that they would like to have Soviet bases in the Straits. The question of Soviet bases was by far the most important issue for the British because it destroyed the previous assumption of the strategic planners and the Foreign Office that the Soviets would not require bases on Turkish territory. Moreover, the strategic implications for Britain's military position would be quite serious. The base question arose from a June 1945 conversation between Molotov and the Turkish Ambassador in Moscow who mentioned granting bases to the Soviets in certain wartime conditions.[78] However, it was accompanied by growing Soviet pressure for territorial concessions by the Turks. The Turkish government had raised the question of a new treaty with the Kremlin following the Soviet denunciation of the existing treaty in March 1945. Molotov's reply was that before any such treaty could be signed the Soviets would require the return of the provinces of Kars and Ardahan that had once belonged to the Russian Empire. The Foreign Office instructed Clark Kerr to complain to the Soviets that the questions of the Straits and any territorial claims were not exclusively Turkish–Soviet matters and required consultation with other members of the United Nations and the signatories of the Montreux Convention.[79]

The Ambassador saw the Soviet attitude to Turkey and Greece as the most disquieting feature of the situation in early July 1945. The Soviet press was now criticising the Greek government and encouraging Yugoslavian and Bulgarian territorial ambitions, while the demands made on Turkey suggested a threat to Britain's position in the Middle East. Clark Kerr felt that the undermining of the British position had not yet made much progress and the Russians were being careful not to embarrass Britain in the Levant. There was therefore, he claimed, still time to show the Soviets that Britain was not prepared to abandon Greece and Turkey nor to contemplate a general encroachment on its vital interests through-out the Middle East. It appeared to the Ambassador from the Soviets' raising of the Tangier question that the Kremlin was still unsure about how far Britain was prepared to stand up for its principles and vital interests. He suggested therefore that what would serve Britain best would be 'a progressive, forthright and clear cut policy aimed at those areas for which we have long been responsible – our colonial Empire and the Middle East – and above all where our new responsibilities lie in the British zones in Germany and Austria'. In the latter territories it would be necessary not to fall short of the Soviets in uprooting fascism and punishing war criminals.[80]

This was another call for an imperial strategy, and a policy towards the Soviets, based on the protection of vital interests, rather than making efforts to ensure a British voice was heard in those areas, notably Poland and Romania, where there were no vital British interests at stake. One possible interpretation of the events between April and July is that by professing concern and dissatisfaction with Soviet behaviour in Poland, Romania and Bulgaria, Britain had encouraged the Russians to criticise British policy in Greece and to seek to influence events in Turkey in favour of the Soviet Union. This was certainly seen as possible by Gladwyn Jebb, now a counsellor in the Foreign Office, but long concerned with post-war planning. Jebb felt Soviet actions over Greece and Turkey might be a kind of 'defensive offensive' in reaction to British attempts 'to keep an end up' in Romania, Bulgaria and Yugoslavia, where, in the latter country, Churchill had insisted on a strong line against Tito.[81] On the other hand, the demands made on Turkey might simply have stemmed from Stalin's evident keenness to reestablish the territorial boundaries of the Russian Empire, and such imperialism may have been unconnected with British policy towards Central and Eastern Europe.

Whatever the explanation the fact was that between April and July there developed for the first time a Soviet challenge to Britain's vital interests along with more signs that Britain was being perceived and treated as a junior partner in the wartime alliance. This was the essence of the problem confronted by Sir Orme Sargent when he wrote his now famous memorandum 'Stocktaking on VE Day' in the week before the Potsdam Conference began. Sargent began by reiterating his long held belief in the value of an assertive policy, as neither the United States nor the Soviet Union would be 'likely to consider British interests overmuch if they interfere with their own and unless we assert ourselves'. Unfortunately, as the Foreign Office was increasingly realising, 'in the minds of our big partners, especially in that of the United States, there is a feeling that Great Britain is now a secondary power and can be treated as such, and that in the long run all will be well if they – the United States and the Soviet Union – as the two supreme World Powers of the future understand one another. It is this misconception which it must be our policy to combat.'

Sargent, typically, saw the Foreign Office's 'diplomatic experience' and Britain's 'political maturity' as important cards to play, but he believed that Britain should also increase its strength in the economic and military spheres. 'This clearly can best be done', claimed Sargent, 'by enrolling France and the lesser Western European Powers, and, of course, also the Dominions, as collaborators with us in this tripartite system. Only so shall we be able, in the long run, to compel our two big partners to treat us as an equal.' In the short term, Europe in particular was faced by an economic crisis which could be exploited by the Soviet Union and therefore Britain would have 'to obtain the wholehearted cooperation of the United States, who alone have the material means of coping with it'. It was deemed perfectly possible for Britain to hold the Soviets at bay in Europe and to cooperate with the Americans, although 'the process of inducing the United States to support a British resistance to Russian penetration in Europe will be a tricky one'. What concerned Sargent was that the reason he had put forward for challenging the Soviets in Europe, namely the need to be involved with the affairs of most of the European states in order to be seen as a Great Power, would not be acceptable to the Americans. Britain therefore 'had to continue to demonstrate to the

American public that our challenge is based on upholding the liberal idea in Europe and not upon selfish apprehensions as to our own position as a Great Power'. How the Soviets would be convinced that Britain had no selfish apprehensions, and that they should continue to cooperate with the British in Europe and the wider world, as part of a tripartite system, was not explained.

In the Far East Sargent rejected the thesis of some junior officials who had played down the importance of the region, but sought to maintain tripartite cooperation:

for in isolation we should be in a weaker position even than in Europe. For the same reason we shall probably find it useful to organise under our leadership the lesser colonial powers who have a stake in the Far East; in other words, France, the Netherlands and Australia. But unless we take a more active interest in the Far East and bestir ourselves to reestablish our influence there, there will be little question of such cooperation. We and the lesser colonial Powers will be ignored by both Russia and the United States in Far Eastern matters, and the smaller powers will gravitate to the United States. We are perhaps in danger of regarding ourselves as a European Power and tend to overlook the fact that we are still the centre of an Empire. If we cease to regard ourselves as a World Power we shall gradually cease to be one.

The importance attached to maintaining a position as a world power in Europe and the Far East and avoiding becoming a junior partner of the Russians and the Americans was clear. But Sargent had also considered the more important problem of Britain's informal Empire in the Eastern Mediterranean and its crucial connection to Britain's European policy. He noted that

it must be an essential feature of our European policy to maintain close and friendly relations with Italy, Greece and Turkey, so as to secure our strategic position in the Eastern Mediterranean, especially now that Russia, stretching down from the North is once again exerting pressure on this all important link between Great Britain on the one hand, and India, Malaya, Australia, New Zealand and our Persian and Iraq oil supplies on the other.

Italy, Greece and Turkey would have to be built up as 'bastions of "liberalism" even though this may involve us in responsibilities and commitments of which we otherwise would be only too glad to be rid. It will be all the more important to do so if Russia remains in control of Bulgaria and acquires physical control of the Straits.' The Soviet 'pressure' which had aroused the concern of Clark Kerr had also affected Sargent, and in one respect changed his approach from that outlined in the early spring. Britain should continue to take a tough stand against the Soviets in most of the European countries in which Russian influence was strong, but the countries that might have to be abandoned to Soviet domination had now changed. Sargent believed that as Britain's military strength in Europe would decline quicker than Russian strength, 'we must take a stand in the immediate future if we are to prevent the situation crystallising to our permanent detriment'. But whereas before he had believed Britain might have to accept Soviet dominated governments in Romania, Bulgaria and possibly Yugoslavia, now Britain must maintain its 'interest in Finland, Poland, Czechoslovakia, Austria, Yugoslavia and Bulgaria, even though we may have to acquiesce in Russian domination in Romania and Hungary'.[82]

Bulgaria, positioned much closer to the Straits, and therefore important for Britain's strategic position, could not be abandoned to the Soviets while Hungary, along with Romania, could form part of an exclusive Soviet sphere, even though free elections were to be held in Hungary later in 1945. The policy was not predicated on a concern for liberty in the countries of Eastern or Central Europe, and indeed in July 1945, one official, whose attention had been drawn to the behaviour of the Soviets in Eastern Europe, minuted that the Northern Department 'does not collect information about atrocities against indigenous civilians in East Europe'. It was only concerned with evidence of Russian maltreatment of former British POWS.[83] For the Foreign Office it was a question of devising a European policy that did not damage Britain's general position as one of the Big Three powers and which did not threaten its specific interests in the Eastern Mediterranean.

How this should be done had been a source of difficulty since the percentages agreement, which had complicated matters by committing Britain to accept the loss of Romania in return for removing the threat to Greece. Exclusive spheres of influence, if accepted at all, would have to be small enough in Europe to be reconciled with the maintenance of Britain's general European position. Unfortunately this would then be difficult to reconcile with Britain's large exclusive sphere of influence in the Eastern Mediterranean and the Middle East. Similarly with the preservation of the latter, it would be much harder to secure the large scale abandonment of exclusive European spheres of influence which would have been beneficial to Britain's general global position. As it was, the post-Yalta attempt to secure what would in effect have been the best of both British worlds was being seen in the Foreign Office as a possible reason for Soviet interference in Britain's sphere of influence in the Mediterranean and Middle East. Indeed it was beginning to look as if an imperial bird in the hand, which was very much the pre-Yalta policy, was being jeopardised by the attempt to secure two in the bush by reducing the Soviet sphere of influence in Central and Eastern Europe. As one official lamented, 'we were before Yalta prepared to allow Russian predominance in ex-satellite Balkan countries to which we agreed last October in Moscow, but it proved impossible to convince Russia that the Yalta Declaration on Liberated Territories altered this and obliged and entitled us to interest ourselves in what the Russians were doing'.[84]

The same official also addressed the issue of what the Russians were doing in what he termed simply Eastern Europe. He was not convinced that the Russians were about to 'remodel' countries there by installing completely pro-Russian governments, because although this had been done in Romania where, he believed, there was a large amount of German secret service activity, in Hungary they had put in power a comparatively bourgeois government not under complete communist control.[85] This of course was the country which the Deputy Undersecretary felt should be handed over to communist domination, in order, in effect, to try and limit Soviet influence in Bulgaria. Another official expressed similar views when noting that the Russians 'genuinely interpret the Yalta Declaration differently' with complaints arising from their failure to accord the British the cooperation to which they felt entitled.

It is important to be clear on the attitudes of officials to these questions of Eastern Europe in order to understand their role in influencing the definition of

Britain's imperial strategy, in relation to the Soviet Union, which emerged in the summer of 1945. British assessments of the relationship between their influence in Eastern Europe and Soviet influence in the Eastern Mediterranean affected the tactics to be employed by British ministers in their dealings with the Soviets. Given the official views already outlined, it is easy to see why the Permanent Undersecretary suggested to the Prime Minister that at Potsdam Britain should not at an early stage give away any cards in its hand, and even if Soviet requests were reasonable Britain should not grant them unless the Soviets agreed to reasonable British requests.[86]

When Churchill and Eden went to Potsdam in July 1945 for the meeting with Stalin and the new American President Harry Truman, the Polish question was no longer the thorny issue it had been in the spring. The issue had not been resolved, but the Hopkins mission in May 1945 had certainly taken the heat out of it. Moreover, when Truman, as president of the first plenary meeting on 17 July, was proposing items for the agenda and included the failure to implement the Declaration on Liberated Europe, the statement he read out contained no reference to Poland. What the United States wanted to secure was the reorganisation of the governments in Romania and Bulgaria. Churchill of course was keen to discuss Poland, although not with the emphasis, as Stalin wanted, on the winding up of the Polish emigré government. The first item the Russian leader suggested for discussion was the question of territories to be placed under trusteeship, indicating that the Soviet Union would like some territories of the defeated states. Stalin also wanted to discuss the question of Tangier and those of Syria and Lebanon. Thus there was now the danger of attention being focused on parts of the world in which Britain regarded itself as the predominant power.[87]

The proposed agenda produced a sharp reaction from Eden once the meeting was over. He told Churchill that the Russians had no direct interest in such matters as Tangier and the Levant nor in the countries to be placed under trusteeship which he claimed was a matter for the United Nations rather than the Potsdam Conference. 'The truth is', he continued, 'that on any and every point, Russia tries to seize all that she can'. The Foreign Secretary was now prepared to allow the Soviets free access to the Mediterranean, but he was opposed to raising the issue of Montreux revision at the conference. The reason lay in the Soviet 'behaviour' of the summer, which he saw not as a reaction to Britain claiming a right to be interested in the affairs of Soviet occupied territories in Europe, but in response to Britain's expressed support for the revision of the Straits agreement. Such generous British behaviour was deemed to be responsible for the further demands made on Turkey during the summer, and therefore Eden concluded that making concessions to the Soviet view merely produced more demands.[88]

The Deputy Prime Minister, who was also present at the first plenary meeting, had a very different reaction. Attlee agreed on the need to counter Russian pressure on Turkey, but believed there was a danger of getting into a position where Britain and the Soviet Union, as rival Great Powers, were confronting each other at a number of points of strategic importance. He did not believe that Britain should claim a special interest in the Mediterranean because 'we ought to confront the Russians with the requirements of a world organisation for peace, not with the needs of the defence of the British Empire'. Accepting exclusive responsibilities for imperial interests would also involve a heavy burden of defence expenditure which for Attlee provided a second important reason for placing strategic areas in the Mediterranean under the control of the United Nations.[89]

The Potsdam Conference, like the meeting at Yalta earlier in the year, was to postpone many of the contentious issues for discussion at a later date. With the agreement to establish a Council of Foreign Ministers to draw up the peace treaties with Germany and its allies, this meant that discussions would recommence in London later in the year with the Italian treaty the first to be drawn up. Questions affecting the Mediterranean would therefore assume immediate importance, given that no agreement had been reached on them at Potsdam. Unlike at Yalta, there had been significant discussions of areas where the British, rather than the Soviets, were the leading power, as well as on the problem of Germany and the German/Polish frontier. This latter question aroused some heated debates, as did the question of recognising the provisional governments of Romania and Bulgaria, which the British and the Americans adamantly refused to do, on the grounds that they were not sufficiently representative of the democratic parties. The British expressed firm views on this, as they did on other contentious questions concerning Yugoslavia, the admission of defeated powers to the United Nations, German reparations and the economic administration of Germany. On some questions concerning the Mediterranean they were not, however, keen to have discussions, and their sensitivity to Soviet interest and involvement was only too apparent. In effect the British were demanding a major voice, in line with US policy, in the discussions on the Romanian and Bulgarian governments, a question of great concern to the Soviets, while hoping to deny the Soviets a voice on questions of great concern to Britain.

The question of trusteeship was discussed at the sixth plenary meeting on 22 July 1945. Molotov proposed to discuss Italy's colonies in the Mediterranean and Africa first, either at the plenary meeting or at the Foreign Ministers' meeting the following day. The British brief for Potsdam (Terminal), even supposing Churchill had read it, offered no specific ideas on the future of the Italian colonies, merely pointing out the need to ensure they did not come under the control of a potential enemy state, and that Cyrenaica, the eastern part of Libya, might be classified as a strategic area. For whatever reason Churchill was reluctant to discuss the trusteeship of the Italian colonies, arguing that the matter was in the hands of the World Organisation, but Truman stated that it was just as appropriate to discuss the trusteeship question as it was to discuss Poland or anything else. The Americans in fact could hardly support Churchill's view that the matter was in the hands of the United Nations when they had previously informed the Soviets that discussing specific trusteeship territories was outside the scope of the San Francisco Conference called to establish the new World Organisation. The State Department had, moreover, encouraged the Soviets to involve themselves in the trusteeship question by telling them they 'would be happy to support in principle the Soviet proposals as to the eligibility of your government as a potential administering authority'.[90]

The Russians were clearly concerned by Eden's House of Commons statement that Italy had lost its colonies once and for all. The two American records of the Potsdam discussions on this contain conflicting views on whether Stalin or Molotov was expressing the Soviet viewpoint. The Russian record, however, claims it was Stalin who demanded to know who had decided that Italy had lost its colonies, and if that was so who had found them. Churchill replied by pointing to the suffering of the British army which, he claimed, alone had conquered Italy's colonies. When Stalin noted that Berlin had been conquered by the Red Army, Churchill conceded that Eden's statement did not rule out the peace conference restoring Italy's colonies to it, but the Prime Minister also stated that Britain had great interests in the Mediterranean and any marked alteration in the status quo would need long and careful examination. In response Stalin expressed a willingness to postpone any decisions on whether Italy would lose its colonies or to whom they should be transferred. As Churchill openly commented at the time, he had never seriously considered the possibility of the Soviets desiring a large tract of African shoreline which would clearly have enormous implications for the future position of the British Empire.[91]

It soon appeared that Soviet aims were not going to be set so high, for at the Foreign Ministers' meeting the next day, Molotov suggested a joint tripartite trusteeship, but accepted Eden's view that the question should be considered in connection with the settlement of an Italian peace treaty and be the first item on the agenda of the Council of Foreign Ministers. This kind of international administration could therefore be a further extension of the principle already being applied in the Western Mediterranean to Tangier, where it was agreed to welcome Soviet participation in the preliminary discussions on the future international administration of Tangier to be held in Moscow.

The tripartite international cooperation in the Western Mediterranean was likely to influence the approach to the issue of the Straits raised at the seventh plenary meeting. Stalin, for the first time, discussed in detail the Russian demands. Claiming that Turkey was too weak to guarantee free passage through the Straits, the Russian leader insisted that they should be 'defended by force' in the same way as the Panama and Suez Canals. If, however, Russian bases in the Straits were going to be unacceptable to the Turks then let the Soviets be given some other base which could be used for repair and refuelling and from where, in cooperation with their Allies, the Soviets could protect the Straits. This was coming dangerously close to a system of international cooperation in the Eastern Mediterranean which Eden and others had already rejected as a threat to the very existence of the British Empire. On the 23rd this particular question did not receive lengthy attention because Truman presented a paper on the free navigation of inland waterways, although Churchill expressed the view that unrestricted Soviet passage through the Straits should be guaranteed by all.[92]

The issue resurfaced at the next plenary meeting on 24 July when Stalin pointed out that Truman's paper did not deal with the Black Sea Straits which the Soviets were primarily concerned with. The Russians wanted Soviet bases with Turkey and the Soviet Union alone determining the nature of the regime to ensure freedom of commercial navigation in the Straits. Churchill did not like the idea of bases nor of an exclusive Soviet–Turkish relationship, and repeated his proposal that freedom of passage through the Straits should be guaranteed by the international community which he felt would be more than a 'substitute for the fortification of the Straits'. The question of international arrangements for strategic areas, rather than exclusive bases, had of course already been considered by Attlee and the Suez Canal Committee, so Churchill's proposals for the Straits clearly had important implications for British policy. The Soviets too were quick to realise their significance, and the following exchange is worth quoting in full. If international arrangements were to be a substitute for bases in the Straits, Molotov asked 'if the Suez Canal were under the same principle. Churchill replied that it was open in war and peace to all. Molotov enquired if it were under the same international control as was proposed for the Black Sea Straits. Churchill said that this question had not been raised. Molotov said that he was asking. If it was such a good rule why not apply it to the Suez? Churchill said that they had an arrangement with which they were satisfied and that this arrangement had operated for some years with no complaints. Molotov said there had been a lot of complaints. They should ask Egypt. Eden said that Egypt had signed the treaty with them. Stalin said that the British asserted that international control was better.'[93]

This latter assertion of course was perfectly true as regards the Straits, but completely the opposite with regard to Suez, where the predominant British view was in favour of maintaining exclusive influence. In the Foreign Office Gladwyn Jebb realised that issues of the greatest importance were being raised which affected Britain's entire foreign policy. Jebb was aware that it was clearly illogical for Britain to have a base at Suez while opposing Soviet bases in the Straits, but he also believed that other questions complicated this fundamental point. One possible escape from the British dilemma would be a trade off between an exclusive British sphere of influence in the Eastern Mediterranean and Middle East and an exclusive Soviet sphere in Eastern Europe, which could perhaps be realised if Britain changed the post-Yalta policy of keeping its end up in Romania, Bulgaria and Yugoslavia.

However, Jebb concluded that Russias' objectives in the Eastern Mediterranean would remain even if it ceased actively pursuing them. These involved physical control of the Straits and the political control of Greece and Turkey, which for Jebb meant the kind of governments that had been installed in Romania, Bulgaria and Yugoslavia. Jebb believed that the achievement of either objective would lead to the other being secured, and therefore Soviet bases in the Straits could not be accepted for political reasons. The resulting pro-Soviet regimes in Greece and Turkey would, according to Jebb, have an unfavourable effect on Britain's whole position in the Middle East and the world. The only solutions therefore were either the abandonment of Soviet claims in the Straits, or getting the Americans to oppose Soviet ambitions in the Straits by force.

But there was a more general issue arising from the clash of rival imperialisms in the Eastern Mediterranean, to which Sargent had already drawn attention in terms of Britain's European policy, namely the impact of any concessions to the Soviets on Britain's general world position. If Britain was going to be increasingly seen as a junior partner then not only would its vital interests in the Eastern Mediterranean and the Middle East have to be protected, but it would have to oppose any extension of Soviet influence which would affect perceptions of British power and status. Therefore, Jebb concluded (in order, in effect, to remain on equal terms with its wartime allies), for Britain 'to yield to *any* Russian demand would clearly mean we are not prepared to play the part of a Great Power which has been allocated to us in the present World Organization'.[94] It was an extension of Sargent's policy of pursuing a strong line in Europe in order to maintain Britain's international status.

Here were two embryonic strands of a negative British strategy emerging by the time of the Potsdam Conference. Defend Britain's general global standing by a policy of no concessions to Russian wishes, whether they affected Britain's vital interests or not, and if necessary encourage US support for the defence of those interests where they were threatened by the Soviet Union. The positive aspect being suggested was to enrol France and the Western European powers as collaborators with the British Empire in order to ensure that Britain's global position as one of the Big Three would be rebuilt in terms of economic and military resources.

In the summer of 1945 policy makers like Jebb and Sargent, who were formulating these goals of Great Power status, had to convince their ministerial bosses of their attainability and deal with the threats to them. The Potsdam Conference meant that, with regard to Britain's Mediterranean position, the questions of the Straits and the Italian colonies would have to be immediately addressed and specific policies formulated; these might well be done in line with the firm policy of opposing the Soviets which Jebb and Sargent were advocating. The snag, as Jebb had already pointed out, was that as far as the Straits were concerned, Britain's position in Egypt made such a policy illogical. The problem was made worse by the Chiefs' opposition, not only to concessions to Soviet demands for bases, but to any revision of Montreux which even Churchill had long since favoured. A further difficulty was the expressed Egyptian desire to seek a revision of the 1936 treaty by which 10,000 British troops were entitled to remain in Egypt. Given this situation the Foreign Office sought the Chiefs of Staffs' views in August, but requested they should be given 'having regard to the overriding political considerations'.

The political considerations of Soviet ambitions in Turkey and the Straits had earlier been defined by the Foreign Office as a potential source of Anglo-Soviet conflict. The situation was now increasingly perceived as a battle to incorporate Turkey into either the British or the Russian sphere of influence. The Anglo-Turkish treaty was, it was believed, causing dissatisfaction in Moscow because of the view there that countries bordering the Soviet Union should not ally themselves with any third power, but in the Foreign Office it was desired to keep Turkey and Greece in 'our orbit'. At least there was no question of Soviet opposition to democracy clouding the issue as in Europe, for Turkey was described by the Foreign Office as a democratic 'facade'.[95]

It was in August that news reached the Foreign Office confirming the importance of Turkey for Britain's relations with the Arab world. Nuri Said, one of Britain's leading friends in Iraq, and indeed throughout the Middle East, spoke about Russian expansion and called for a firm British policy in Greece, Turkey and Iran as politically conscious Arabs were looking to see how strong a Middle Eastern shield Britain would be.[96] There was also the question of Egypt and the military base there, which formed an important link between British policy in Turkey and the Straits and Britain's position in the Middle East. A firm policy in Turkey was becoming more and more necessary yet, as Jebb had already pointed out, clearly illogical if it denied the Soviet bases while Britain continued to have a military presence in Egypt, to which some leading Egyptians were already raising objections.

The Foreign Office saw three possible options for Britain. The first was conceding to the Soviet demand for bases which, apart from the undesirable principle of concessions to the Russians, was seen as leading to the collapse of Britain's Middle East position. The second alternative of revising Montreux to give all Russian ships right of passage at all times, while refusing to accept Soviet bases, could only be carried through with American support. The third involved some form of internationalisation which would have implications for Britain's position at Suez, and the Foreign Office had therefore examined what this might mean in practice. It could mean demilitarisation under international supervision, an international commission, or international bases for use by all the Great Powers. The latter would almost certainly mean the presence of Soviet troops in the Suez base, but surprisingly some officials in the Foreign Office did not regard this as too alarming. Any such development would be going towards the kind of internationalism which Eden deemed incompatible with the continuance of the British Empire. On the other hand it would avoid conceding to the Soviet demand for bases, and also perhaps reduce Soviet pressure on Turkey and Greece. Of the three, however, the idea of an international commission appeared to be the least disturbing provided it had supervisory rather than executive functions.

The Chiefs of Staff accepted this idea as a possible solution only with extreme reluctance. They preferred the status quo, or if that was not possible, they were now prepared to revise Montreux to give the Soviets unrestricted passage. Bases, joint or shared, were ruled out, because that would give the Russians a predominant position in Turkey, while demilitarisation would weaken the Turks, relative to the Soviets, and provide an unfortunate analogy for Suez. An international commission, the Chiefs realised, would also have dangerous implications for Suez and Gibraltar, and should only be considered if it was simply to advise the Turks on the defence of the Straits and report to the governments of those states who were represented on it.

The military leaders were now very conscious of the political requirements of an imperial power needing to maintain its predominant influence in the Middle East and the Eastern Mediterranean in the face of the Soviet challenge. This concern was unlikely to have been produced solely by the Foreign Office letter and was to remain a key element in future military considerations of British policy in the region. The Russian proposals for bases, so the Chiefs argued, would be the first step in the Soviet domination of Greece and Turkey; they believed that Soviet political infiltration was more likely in those two countries if bases were established, and not less likely as one voice in the Foreign Office, in opposition to Jebb, was suggesting. In addition, conceding to the Soviet requests was seen as bringing Russian influence to the borders of the Middle East. Finally, and perhaps most importantly, the Chiefs argued 'we should appear to be giving ground to Russia which would lower our prestige throughout the whole Middle East'. Here was a view echoing that of Gladwyn Jebb and based on the principle that any concessions to the Soviets would be damaging to the maintenance of British prestige and status.[97] It was a view confirming the hardline stance, as opposed to the idea also being floated of some very limited form of internationalism which might maintain and promote Anglo-Soviet cooperation.

The second important issue emerging from the Potsdam Conference, that stemmed from the Soviet desire to gain a position in the Mediterranean, was the future of the Italian colony of Libya, divided into its two main regions of

Tripolitania in the west and Cyrenaica in the east. As with the Straits, British perceptions reflected fears of Soviet influence in a predominantly British imperial region. Now that the Russians were mounting a challenge there, they were invariably seen more as potential enemies than potential friends. In short, their behaviour in the Balkans, Turkey and the Mediterranean was not the sort of behaviour which indicated an acceptance of the British Empire's exclusive area of influence in the Eastern Mediterranean and the Middle East. Consequently imperial rivalry required that any state in the Mediterranean area, including Italy, had to be won over to the British rather than the Russian side. In addition there were the strategic implications of the future of Libya, and the position of Italy in any Western European bloc linked to the British Empire in line with the requirements of Sargent's 'stocktaking' memorandum; this in turn was connected to the need to remain an equal member of the wartime alliance which was still prosecuting the war against Japan and attempting to fashion a new post-war international order.

Ideas on the future of Libya had been floated in the Foreign Office throughout 1945, where interest, as with the military, centred on Cyrenaica. They included the idea of a nominally independent Arab emirate bound to Britain by treaty, a British mandate and an Egyptian mandate. Cyrenaica was the area deemed by the British to be of major strategic importance. It was seen as necessary for the protection of British air routes, and air bases there would provide a useful supplement to Britain's defence and transport system. In addition it possessed the harbours of Tobruk and Benghazi and offered an exceptionally promising training area for British armoured units. Finally, facilities in Cyrenaica would be useful if the Egyptian treaty could not be revised in ways favoured by the British military. The 1936 Egyptian treaty had provided for the stationing of 10,000 troops to protect the Canal Zone, but by the end of the war there were ten times that number of men in what had become the largest military base in the world. If the Middle East was to continue to be the main British HQ for any future campaigns in a major conflict more than 10,000 troops would be required. If the Egyptians, as seemed likely, would not accept this, then facilities to station troops in Cyrenaica would be vitally important.[98] As with the Straits, however, these particular strategic concerns were to be increasingly overshadowed by the general need to maintain Britain's predominant position in the Mediterranean.

It was realised that Cyrenaica, dominated by the Senussi whose leader, Sayid Idris, had organised resistance to the Italians, could not stand alone because of its hopeless economic weakness. Equally the Senussi, who had been encouraged and supported by the British, could not be handed back to the Italians without going against a wartime British commitment to preserve them from Italian rule. Given the Senussi minority in Tripolitania, that could mean the whole of Libya, if not independent, would have to be given to some non-Italian power to administer, or be placed under some form of international control. Britain, given American attitudes, had to be wary of attempting to enlarge the British Empire; to try and gain effective control over Tripolitania as well as Cyrenaica would therefore be very problematic, even though Sayid Idris desired to rule over a single kingdom. If this was to be ruled out the Foreign Office favoured an Italian administration of Tripolitania with Britain responsible for Cyrenaica. The Foreign Office, because of Italy's position as a Mediterranean power, were keen to ensure that the Italian peace treaty was not a harsh one in order to encourage Italy to 'look West rather than East'. They realised however that the return of Tripolitania to Italy would not only be opposed by Sayid Idris, but would be strongly opposed by the Arabs, and might have adverse repercussions on British prestige in the Middle East because Britain would be seen as betraying the Arabs in North Africa. The difficulties inherent in this situation meant that the issue had not been resolved in the Foreign Office by the time of the Potsdam Conference.[99]

The fact that the Russians were seen as more than potentially hostile because of their desire for a presence in the Mediterranean made the maintenance of Britain's position there all the more vital. The idea, first proposed by Bevin, of leaving it to the UN to decide on the trustees for the various Italian colonies was therefore problematic. Minutes and memoranda circulating in the Foreign Office and the service departments at this time refer constantly to how maintaining and strengthening Britain's position in the Middle East must be a cardinal feature of policy, and to the necessity of preserving Britain's prominent position there.

This was the position outlined by Bevin and the Colonial Secretary, George Hall, in their joint memorandum for the Overseas Reconstruction Committee that argued for Tripolitania becoming an Italian trust territory with Britain securing the trusteeship of the designated strategic area of Cyrenaica. Because the maintenance of Britain's Middle Eastern position was defined as a cardinal feature of policy, Bevin and Hall believed that Britain should be prepared to undertake the commitments and expenditure inherent in the maintenance of that position. It was this overall political consideration that was deemed by one official to be more important than particular strategic requirements. There was as yet no global or regional strategic plan linked to any operational concept, partly because the impact of the atomic bomb had not yet been fully assessed, and also because, as was blatantly obvious, the advent of air power made control of maritime communications, on which British strategic thinking had previously been based, extremely difficult and not vital to the success of military operations. The importance of political considerations was formalised at the beginning of September when Bevin summoned a conference of British Middle Eastern representatives to consider whether Britain should maintain its political predominance in the Middle East and its overriding responsibility for its defence, or whether the extensive assistance of other powers should be sought.[100]

In response to this fundamental question which was most immediately affected by the future of the Italian colonies, the Prime Minister submitted a memorandum to the Cabinet which was at odds with views of the imperialist thinkers in the Foreign Office and the Service Ministries. Attlee began by expressing his dissatisfaction with Bevin and Hall's memorandum which ultimately he saw as concerning the defence of the British Empire and the importance of retaining control of strategic areas in the Middle East. For Attlee, the Colonial and Foreign Secretaries were thinking in terms of an imperial strategy which had been rendered useless by the advent of air power. In these new circumstances 'the British Empire can only be defended by its membership of the United Nations Organisation. If we do not accept, this, we had better say so. If we do accept this we should seek to make it effective and not at the same time act on outworn conceptions.' More specifically the Prime Minister believed that Cyrenaica would saddle Britain with additional expenses it could ill afford, and suggested that the

United States or some Scandinavian power should take responsibility for the region; he even suggested that it would be to Britain's advantage to give up British Somaliland, apart from 'the sentimental objection to giving up a piece of the Empire', and replace colonial rule there by some form of international administration.[101]

An early response to such a radical failure to think imperially was formulated within the Foreign Office by a relatively junior official, whose views were however endorsed by the Acting Undersecretary, Sir R. Campbell. The minute by Lord Hood argued that Britain still had to be concerned with imperial communications, both by sea and by air, for the sake of future food supplies and war materials. It stated that there had to be an element of reinsurance in terms of Britain's attitude to the United Nations based on a strong position in the Middle East, and supported the idea of a world organisation in which each of the Great Powers would be primarily responsible for organising security arrangements in different regions of the world. Therefore Britain should organise security arrangements in the Middle East, and this, if in line with the general Whitehall consensus, would mean organising them in order to exclude the Soviet Union.[102] Once again, this brought up the question of who should organise security arrangements in other regions, notably Europe and the Far East, and whether Britain could accept its exclusion from them if the Soviet Union was to be the power responsible for all or part of such regions. This in turn would have to be considered in the context of British efforts to stand, as a Great Power, on equal terms with its wartime allies.

This latter issue was to arouse greater concern after Potsdam because of information from the Washington Embassy suggesting that in the United States 'in recent months a view has steadily gained ground that Great Britain has come to occupy a position on the world stage which in terms of power and influence is inferior to that of the Soviet Union and the United States'. The reasons for this were said to be first, the behaviour of the Australian Foreign Minister, Evatt, whose independent and abrasive personality had frequently aroused British resentment, and which demonstrated that Britain could not always count on the steady support of all the Commonwealth countries; this of course implied a weakening of the imperial partnership with the Dominions. Second, there was the perceived threat to Britain's imperial communications inherent in the Soviet interest in Tangier and the Dardanelles combined with growing Arab nationalism. Third, the belief that Soviet relations with the United States were the key to future world peace. There was of course evidence of considerable support in the United States for a strong and prosperous Britain which would be beneficial for American interests, but such pro-British elements, the Embassy believed, were careful to distinguish Britain from the British Empire. Moreover, Americans were concerned that in areas of Europe and the Middle East adjacent to the Soviet orbit of power, British foreign policy makers were liable to embark on ill-advised courses of action that might constitute a threat to US security. Even more ominously, but ironically in view of the developments at the end of the decade, the Embassy assessment was that the United States was groping its way towards a new order in which Britain, while important for West European security, and the focal point of a far-flung American oceanic system, would be a junior partner in an orbit of power under United States aegis. Comments by one US general that 'Britain is nowadays of no more significance than Costa Rica' could of course be reconciled with such an analysis of the new world order that some in the United States were apparently groping for.[103]

The issues raised by the despatch from Washington were clearly related to how Anglo-Soviet arrangements in Europe, the Eastern Mediterranean and the Middle East would affect Britain's international standing. They were also related to other measures raised in Sargent's stocktaking memorandum, concerned with the rebuilding of British global power and influence through the enrolling of the Western European powers as collaborators with the British Empire. It was to be several weeks before the information from Washington was digested at the highest official levels in the Foreign Office, a fact no doubt related to the demands of the forthcoming London Council of Foreign Ministers. However, as early as August the new Foreign Secretary was looking at the possibility of developing close ties with the countries of Western Europe in line with Sargent's ideas and the general support in the Foreign Office and service departments for some form of Western bloc. At a meeting with officials on 13 August 1945 Bevin expressed his desire for the eventual creation of some type of organisation embracing not only the countries of Western Europe, but eventually those in Scandinavia and the Iberian peninsula which were on the Atlantic fringes of Europe.[104]

The most important country in any future Western European grouping would of course be France, and the first and most important stage in establishing such a group would be to secure closer Anglo-French relations. Unfortunately in the summer of 1945, Britain's relations with France were going through a particularly difficult period. The leader of the French government, General de Gaulle, had had a peculiar love/hate relationship with the British during the war. For de Gaulle the need for Free French cooperation with London was tempered by an unconcealed rage over what he frequently regarded as a British refusal to consider French interests; this he attributed to an Anglo-Saxon desire to further their imperial ambitions at France's expense. These tensions culminated in the Levant crisis of the summer of 1945 when British troops were used to prevent French forces acting against Syrian leaders who were asserting an independence which had, to all intents and purposes, been promised to them during the war. In addition there was the fact that, as in the past, Britain and France had different views on the future treatment of Germany, with the French insisting on German dismemberment to prevent future German aggression. Consequently there were major hurdles to be overcome in terms of Anglo-French relations before a Western bloc could be established. At the same time the possibility of any such grouping being seen to be directed against the Soviet Union had to be avoided if tripartite cooperation was to be extended into the post-war years. Both these circumstances contributed to Bevin's decision to concentrate on economic cooperation, rather than alliances or military treaties, as a way of cementing West European links once the removal of the Anglo-French bone of contention in the Levant had been achieved and a general improvement in Anglo-French relations secured.

Bevin had given a clear indication of his long-term goals for strengthening Britain's international position through taking the lead in the formation of a Western European grouping. The shorter-term problem was the implementation of an imperial strategy in which the maintenance of the British position was bound to affect Anglo-Soviet relations. It was also a more difficult problem because of the differences of view at the official level within the Foreign Office and the Moscow Embassy. Defining a single Foreign Office position on interdepartmental questions of high policy related to Britain's global strategy is an impossible task for the historian. Consequently the implementation of policy, rather than the expression of attitudes, is the key element, although the position and promotion of officials is an important guide to which views were carrying most weight. In the particular circumstances of the summer of 1945 the new Foreign Secretary was not in a position to accept or reject a particular Foreign Office view; in reality he had to decide between a number of different alternatives in terms of British goals and the tactics that should be adopted to secure them. However, the difference of view at the official level should not be overstated: often it was more a problem of determining what exactly the policy implications of a particular minute were. Also, in the crucial period between Churchill's visit to Moscow and the end of the Second World War in September 1945, it is possible to discern more generally held views, and to detect some important shifts in the Foreign Office's overall approach to Anglo-Soviet relations, along with the definition of an imperial strategy which might or might not win the approval of the Prime Minister.

When Churchill was sufficiently concerned about Britain's post-war position, relative to the Soviet Union, to discuss Europe and the Eastern Mediterranean with Stalin, the Foreign Office view on future British policy towards Central and Eastern Europe was based on a distinction between those areas in which Britain had a vital interest and those in which much less was at stake. North of the Balkans, it was both recognised and accepted that the Soviet Union would emerge as the controlling power because of its inevitable defeat of the German armies; this would enable the Russians to dominate most of Germany as well as the territories stretching eastward to a new Polish–Soviet boundary established to provide for Soviet expansion westwards. Anglo-Soviet cooperation would be maintained because both had an interest in the defeat and subsequent containment of Germany. What exactly Soviet control or domination of the areas east of Germany would involve produced some disagreement in the Foreign Office; nor was it always clear which particular territories were being referred to. However, there is no evidence in the summer of 1944 that the fate that large areas of Eastern and Central Europe were likely to suffer at the hands of Stalin and his supporters was a matter of concern to officials. Moreover in the Foreign Office and the service departments this extension of Soviet power was accepted with resignation and indifference, rather than apprehension, because of both the expected disposition of military forces and the lack of any clash of vital Soviet and British interests.

Then as the military campaigns on the eastern front moved closer to the Balkans Britain's future position in Greece in particular, and the Eastern Mediterranean in general, was seen to be endangered. Churchill aimed to secure Britain's position in Greece, vital for its future dominance of the Mediterranean and the Middle East, by agreeing on the de facto exclusive British and Soviet spheres of influence in Greece and Romania. The problems inherent in extending the spheres of influence deal were never resolved but the issues became increasingly important. Disagreements appeared within Whitehall on how vital Bulgaria was to Britain's strategic position in the Eastern Mediterranean. Could it safely be abandoned to Soviet control? Would acceptance of Soviet domination there be regarded as entitling Britain to influence what went on in Poland once the fate of the Poles became a source of political embarrassment? Would the Russians see their control over Bulgaria as equivalent to the Anglo-American control over Italy? How could any general Anglo-Soviet spheres of influence deal be reconciled with American attitudes to the post-war international order?

Such problems arose as the implications of any revision of Montreux were also arousing disagreement in London. Stalin's evident determination to replace the 1936 Convention had implications in an area which was of vital concern to Britain. By the end of 1944 there was a growing fear that the inevitable extension of Soviet power could affect vital British interests. Such fears only emerged in the form they did because the Soviets were regarded as a potential enemy, unlike the United States, even though American economic policies in particular were perceived as a possible threat to vital imperial interests. Anti-Soviet feelings were most in evidence amongst British military elites, some of whom were pressing for immediate political and diplomatic action to be taken against the Soviet Union. The Foreign Office remained wedded in late 1944 to the goal of Anglo-Soviet cooperation, but like the Prime Minister, was soon to show concern over Soviet 'behaviour' which did not give total recognition to Britain's exclusive interests in certain regions; it was also concerned about the more general implications for Britain's international status as one of the Big Three powers.

The question of whether this could best be preserved by spheres of influence deals in Europe, the Eastern Mediterranean and the Middle East was favourably affected from the British point of view by the Yalta Conference in early 1945. For reasons which must remain obscure Stalin offered the possibility of European arrangements which would not involve the imposition of Soviet domination over areas in Eastern and Central Europe which British officials had previously assigned to the Soviet sphere. At the same time, apart from the issue of the revision of Montreux, there were no indications at Yalta that the Soviets would be expecting to exert an influence in the predominantly British sphere of influence in the Mediterranean that was deemed vital to the Empire's position. So important was this region that there were many voices raised in the spring and summer months emphasising the necessity of excluding any international arrangements which by their very nature would undermine the exclusive nature of British imperialism.

Shortly after Yalta, unexpected military victories on the western front in Europe offered the possibility, in Sargent's view, of enabling Britain to take a much firmer line by insisting on a right to be involved in the affairs of most, if not all, the states of vital concern to the Soviets. Indeed this was to become increasingly important as fears grew that the Americans and the Russians were tending to regard the British as a distinctly junior partner. Conceding that Britain had no right to be involved with the affairs of most of the European states, even those in which it had no real interests, could only reinforce such damaging perceptions. This new British assertiveness could however be justified, and American support encouraged, by the clear Soviet failure to carry out Stalin's extraordinary promises in Poland and in some other areas of Europe controlled by the Red Army.

No sooner had the Polish problem apparently been resolved, by some insignificant concession from Stalin which could be reconciled with part of the Yalta agreement, than the Russians began to show an interest in extending their influence, not just in Bulgaria, which had previously concerned the British, but in

Turkey which, along with Greece, was most vital for Britain's Mediterranean and Middle Eastern dominance. The strategic implications of these imperialistic ambitions were given great attention by British military and civilian elites, but the political implications of the Soviet moves were deemed to be of overriding importance. The effect of such moves, while initially increasing British dislike of Soviet behaviour, implied a power-political clash between rival imperial states in which British prestige and status could be damaged; this would be the case even if the sting were taken out of such rivalries by incorporating them into international arrangements designed to enhance security and preserve the cooperation embodied in the wartime alliance. United Nations involvement was therefore felt to be unacceptable, except by Clement Attlee, who was to question the desirability of preserving what he regarded as an unaffordable and outmoded imperial position in the Mediterranean and Middle East.

By the summer of 1945, Foreign Office officials were therefore faced with a Soviet challenge to specific and vital British interests in the Middle East and Mediterranean, but also with the more general threat to Britain's status presented by the rise of Soviet power in Europe. The extent of the former had been dramatically increased by the end of the Potsdam Conference. It became evident that the Soviets were seeking not just a revision of Montreux but bases in the Straits which they felt would be equivalent to the British base at Suez, ostensibly in existence to protect another important international waterway; and in addition to bases at the eastern end of the Mediterranean the Soviets were, it emerged, also seeking a position of influence in Libya through the acquisition of a trusteeship over Tripolitania. This kind of challenge to the British Empire was perceived to be much more threatening than the American challenge, either to the economic aspects of the British Empire or to the political and administrative aspects of British colonialism. The Soviets were regarded as the next enemy by many of the military and the only potential enemy by the Foreign Office. The threat they presented in the Mediterranean and Middle East was more menacing because of its strategic implications and because of the region's perceived 'life or death' importance. Most significantly of all, because bases and other symbols of imperial influence were in dispute, questions of prestige and status were more openly at issue.

It was suggested in the Foreign Office that these Soviet attempts to extend their influence could have emerged in response to British efforts to insist on not being excluded from areas of Central, Eastern and Southern Europe. Therefore one possible solution to the British dilemma would be to abandon such a policy and accept exclusive Soviet spheres of influence in these areas in return for exclusive British spheres of influence in the Middle East and Mediterranean. This would remove the specific threat to vital British interests but not the general threat to Britain's global standing perceived to be inherent in the exclusion of British influence from significant areas of Europe. No wonder one official lamented the Russian refusal to accept that Yalta required the Soviets to renounce exclusive spheres of influence where they were the leading Allied power, but to accept exclusive spheres of influence where the leading Allied power was the British Empire. This led another official to advocate a policy of refusing any concessions to the Soviets because of the detrimental effect this would have on Britain's international standing; even though, in the specific context of the Middle East and

Mediterranean, it was acknowledged that such a position was illogical and dependent on American support. The importance of getting the United States to support Britain's imperial interests, in the face of the Soviet challenge, while British economic strength was rebuilt, had already been referred to within the Foreign Office and in the PHP's overall assessment of the Soviet threat to the British Empire; it was seen as essential if Britain was to regain its position in the first rank of global powers. It would inevitably become more important if a hardline approach to cooperation with the Soviets was to be adopted. The extreme position of no concessions, whatever the circumstances, was not the only stance being advocated within the office in the summer of 1945. Other officials, and members of the service ministries, were still discussing the desirability of concessions to the Soviets, especially meeting the least significant Soviet demand for the revision of Montreux to allow unrestricted passage for all Soviet ships. There was also the tactical ploy being considered of making concessions to the Soviets provided they agreed to accept equivalent British demands; and the possibility of international arrangements on both Suez and the Straits had resurfaced, despite vehement earlier opposition, as perhaps the least damaging means of maintaining British status and influence. What position was adopted by the British government would be dependent to a large degree on the views of the Foreign Secretary, Ernest Bevin, not only because he was the ultimate arbiter of different official views, but because, as the British representative in the forthcoming Allied discussions on the peace treaties with the ex-enemy states, he would be in a key position to decide both the general strategic aims and, in the light of assessments of Soviet policy, the tactics to be employed to secure them. His stance would soon be tested when the London Council of Foreign Ministers convened on 11 September 1945.

Notes

1. FO371/43304 minute by Eden 3.4.44.
2. FO371/38508 minute by Churchill 31.3.44.
3. FO371/43304 minute by Churchill 1.4.44.
4. John Colville *The Fringes of Power: Downing Street Diaries 1939–55* (London 1985) p. 484; FO371/43304 minute by Eden 3.4.44; D. Dilks (ed.) *The Diaries of Sir Alexander Cadogan 1938–45* (London 1971) p. 614.
5. FO371/43636 Eden to Sir A. Clark Kerr 18.4.44; G.M. Alexander *The Prelude to the Truman Doctrine, British Policy in Greece 1944–47* (Oxford 1982) pp. 28–9.
6. FO371/43636 minute by Churchill 4.5.44.
7. P. Papastratis *British Policy Towards Greece during the Second World War 1941–44* (Cambridge 1984) pp. 152–4; Lawrence S. Wittner *American Intervention in Greece 1943–49* (New York 1982) pp. 4–5.
8. Wittner op. cit. p. 6; Papastratis op. cit. p. 187 citing FO371/43731 Churchill minute 28.5.44.
9. S. G. Xydis *Greece and the Great Powers 1944–7* (Thessaloniki 1963) p. 36; Papastratis op. cit. pp. 177–200; Alexander op. cit. pp. 28–9.
10. L. Baerentzen, 'British Strategy Towards Greece in 1944' in Barker, Deakin and Chadwick, op. cit. (see Ch. 1, n. 25) p. 132.
11. CAB 66/51 WP (44) 304 7.6.44.
12. FO371/43636 minute by Churchill 10.4.44; minute by Sir Orme Sargent 6.7.44; note by Eden on Churchill's minute n.d.; Xydis op. cit. p. 48; Alexander op. cit. p. 42.
13. Xydis op. cit. p. 49 and pp. 197, 202; Alexander op. cit. p. 48.

14. M. Mackintosh 'Soviet Policy on the Balkans in 1944: A British View' in Deakin, Barker and Chadwick op. cit. p. 238.
15. E. Barker 'Bulgaria in August 1944: A British View' in Deakin, Barker and Chadwick op. cit. p. 205.
16. Mackintosh op. cit. p. 247.
17. Papastratis op. cit. p. 210 citing FO371/43716 12 and 13 September 1944.
18. C. M. Woodhouse *The Struggle for Greece* (London, 1976) p. 90.
19. Papastratis op. cit. pp. 211–16; Xydis op. cit. pp. 54–5.
20. Baerentzen op. cit. pp. 141–2.
21. K. Sainsbury 'Central and Eastern Europe at the Quebec Conference' in Deakin, Barker and Chadwick. op. cit. p. 63.
22. Wittner op, cit. p. 10 citing American record 5.10.44
23. *FRUS: The Conference at Quebec 1944* p. 314.
24. The literature on the percentages agreement is now of considerable proportions. It includes articles by J. M. Siracusa 'The Meaning of Tolstoy: Churchill, Stalin and the Balkans: Moscow 1944' *Diplomatic History* 3, 4 (1979) which reprints some of the official records, P. G. H. Holdich 'A Policy of Percentages? British Policy and the Balkans after the Moscow Conference of October 1944' *International History Review* 9.1 (1987), A. Resis 'The Churchill–Stalin Secret "Percentages Agreement"' *American Historical Review* 83 (1978), K. G. M. Ross 'The Moscow Conference of October 1944 (Tolstoy)' in Deakin, Barker and Chadwick op. cit. and by far the most stimulating Warren F. Kimball 'Naked Reverse Right: Roosevelt, Churchill, and Eastern Europe from Tolstoy to Yalta – and a Little Beyond' *Diplomatic History* 9, 1 (1985). In addition detailed accounts can be found in B. R. Kuniholm *The Origins of the Cold War in the Near East* (Princeton 1980), which has details in diagram form, and Gilbert op. cit. (see Ch. 1, n. 48), which has details of a passage omitted from the official secret record of the conversation.
25. FO371/44165 minute by Sir Orme Sargent 6.10.44; minute by Eden 10.10.44; minute by Churchill 12.10.44. Gilbert op. cit. p. 1002.
26. Gilbert op. cit. pp. 992–5.
27. Ibid. pp. 999–1001.
28. Kimball op. cit. p. 5.
29. Xydis, op. cit. p. 58.
30. FO371/43647 Tolstoy to FO; Eden to Sir O. Sargent 12.10.44.
31. Lewis op. cit. (see Ch. 1, n. 35) p. 144 quoting JP (44) 278, 1.1.45. SC (M) 44 1st; FO371/43384 minute by Ashley Clarke 7.3.44. Such views were endorsed by Churchill who instructed that Britain should not be hostile to the restoration of the Soviet position in the Far East. Gilbert op. cit. p. 1059.
32. CAB 95/18 1st Suez Canal Committee Meeting 11.10.44.
33. Ibid. SC (M) (45) 2 Memorandum by the Financial Secretary to the Treasury 1.2.45; SC (M) 45 1st meeting 13.3.45. For Stanley's ideas on regional commissions see Louis, op. cit. (see Ch. 1. n. 12); J. Kent 'Anglo-French Colonial Cooperation 1939–49' *Journal of Imperial and Commonwealth History* 17, 1 (1988).
34. CAB 95/18 Lord Killearn to FO 5.4.45.
35. See below (p. 19).
36. CAB 21/1614 FO memorandum 'British Policy Towards Europe', 22.5.44; Lewis, op. cit. pp. 100–4 quoting Sargent's minute in FO371/40740.
37. See below. (pp. 36–7).
38. Lewis op. cit. p. 105.
39. CAB 21/1614 COS (44) 248th 26.7.44 annex. This document is reprinted in full in Lewis op. cit.; FO371/40741 A Secretary of Chiefs of Staff Committee to FO 27.7.44, which also appears in *DBPO* Series I Vol. I Doc. 119. Alanbrooke's diary

is quoted by A. Bryant, *The Alanbrooke Diaries: Triumph in the West* (London 1959) p. 242.
40. FO371/43006 minute by Sir Orme Sargent 18.8.44.
41. Ibid. Draft letter to the Prime Minister Oct. 1944. Lewis actually quotes this document PHP (44) 23 (0) of 16.9.44 but without comment. To be fair it is not entirely clear whether this was a general assumption or one specific to the paper. The Foreign Office, evidently aware of military attitudes, took it to be the former.
42. FO371/43006 minutes by G. M. Wilson 24.9.44 and Sir Orme Sargent 18.8.44.
43. FO371/43336 record of a meeting in the Secretary of State's room 4.10.44.
44. These were the exact views of the head of the Northern Department who had been critical of the anti-Soviet views of the military. Lewis's limited understanding of the objections of the Foreign Office is revealed by his description of Warner's minute as 'uncharacteristic' and 'difficult to reconcile' with his opposition to the approach of the Chiefs of Staff. Lewis op. cit., pp. 138–9.
45. FO371/43335 FO memorandum 'Probable Tendencies in Soviet Foreign Policy' 29.4.44.
46. Gilbert op. cit. p. 1070, quoting a Churchill minute of 25.11.44.
47. Alexander op. cit. pp. 64–79.
48. Hathaway op. cit. (see Ch. 1, n. 3) pp. 90–3; Kimball op. cit. pp. 4, 8–9; Wittner op. cit. p. 25.
49. Hathaway op. cit. p. 104.
50. Gilbert op. cit. pp. 1055–6, 1095.
51. Alexander op. cit. p. 80.
52. FO371/40741 B minute by G. Jebb 18.12.44.
53. FO371/47860 JIC (44) 467 (O) F, 18.12.44; FO371/40741 B minute by G. Jebb, 18.12.44.
54. See p. 13.
55. Dilks op. cit. p. 682; Gilbert op. cit., pp. 1107–8.
56. Colville op. cit. p. 555; Gilbert op. cit. p. 1090.
57. The number of books dealing with the Yalta Conference are as numerous as the subsequent newspaper articles referring to the event in passing. The American records are in *FRUS, 1945; The Conferences of Malta and Yalta.* The Soviet account in *The Teheran, Yalta and Potsdam Conferences: Documents* (Moscow 1969) and the British version in FO371/50839. The secondary work of D. S. Clemens *Yalta* (New York 1970) remains a useful account providing good background information. The distinction between Roosevelt's public idealism and private *realpolitik* is referred to in D. Yergin *The Shattered Peace* (Boston, 1977) and Kuniholm op. cit.
58. *FRUS 1945* op. cit. pp. 975–980; Clemens op. cit. pp. 142–4. Gilbert op. cit. pp. 1178–9.
59. *FRUS 1945* op. cit. pp. 973–7; Gilbert op. cit. pp. 1205–7; Colville op. cit. p. 560; Dilks op. cit. p. 708.
60. Gilbert op. cit. pp. 1240–1; Wittner, op. cit. p. 30.
61. Harbutt, op. cit. (see Ch. 1, n. 29) p. 94; Churchill to Roosevelt 8.3.45 cited in Kimball 'Naked Reverse Right' p. 19.
62. FO371/47860 WP. (45) 156 12.3.45; Gilbert op. cit. p. 1238.
63. FO371/47941 Sir A. Clark Kerr to Eden 27.3.45. Also reprinted in Ross op. cit. doc. 34.
64. CAB 79/31 PHP (45) 9 (0) final 30.3.45.
65. FO371/47888 memorandum by Sir O. Sargent 2.4.45. Printed in Ross op. cit. doc. 35, emphasis added.
66. CAB 66/63 WP (45) 197 20.3.45; CAB 81/46 PHP (45) 13 (0) final 18.4.45.
67. CAB 66/65 WP (45) 256 13.4.45; FO371/45270 CP (45) 55 2.7.45 memorandum by Minister Resident in the Middle East.

68. CAB 81/46 PHP (45) 29 (0) final 29.6.45 'The Security of the British Empire'; FO371/50774 minutes by L. H. Foulds, R. Allen and V. Cavendish Bentinck 14.2.45 and 3.3.45.
69. FO371/47941 minute by G. M. Wilson 19.4.45.
70. FO371/47882 F. K. Roberts to C. F. A. Warner 25.4.45.
71. Kimball 'Naked Reverse Right' p. 20.
72. CAB 105/188 Field Marshal Wilson to COS 21.4.45; FO371/47860 minute by Bruce Lockhart 11.4.45.
73. FO371/47888 minute by Sir A. Cadogan 4.4.45; Dilks op. cit. p. 711
74. Dilks op. cit. pp. 727–8.
75. Gilbert *Never Despair: Winston S. Churchill, 1945–65* (London 1988) pp. 24–5.
76. Harbutt op. cit. p. 106.
77. Gilbert *Never Despair* p. 52; FO371/47883 Sir A. Clark Kerr to Eden 10.7.45. Reprinted in Ross op. cit. doc. 41.
78. CAB 119/126 FO to Washington (copy of telegram sent to Istanbul); FO371/49068 minute by O. Harvey 26.6.45.
79. FO371/48773 Istanbul to FO 21.6.45; FO to Moscow 5.7.45.
80. Ibid. Clark Kerr to Eden 10.7.45.
81. (*DBPO*) Series I Vol. I 1945 doc. 459 memorandum by G. Jebb 29.7.45.
82. FO371/50912 memorandum by Sir O. Sargent 11.7.45. A shorter version of the memorandum can be found in PREM 4 31/5 and *DBPO* Series I Vol. I doc. 102. The longer version provides a more detailed and interesting expression of Sargent's views.
83. FO371/51066 minute by T. Brimelow 25.7.45.
84. FO371/47883 minute by D. L. Stewart 12.7.45.
85. Ibid.
86. FO371/47964 minute by V. G. Lawford 20.7.45; R. Smith 'Ernest Bevin, British Officials and British Soviet Policy, 1945–47' in A. Deighton (ed.) *Britain and the First Cold War* (Basingstoke 1990) p. 35. citing FO800/416 Cadogan to Churchill 2.7.45.
87. *FRUS: The Conference of Berlin* Vol. II, pp. 52–9, 643–4.
88. *DBPO* Series I Vol. I 1945 doc. 176 Eden to Churchill 17.7.45.
89. Ibid. doc. 179 Attlee to Eden 18.7.45.
90. *FRUS: The Conference of Berlin* Vol. II, pp. 234, 252–3, 264.
91. Ibid. pp. 365–6. *The Teheran, Yalta and Postdam Conferences: Documents* p. 225. The British records are in FO371/50867 and reproduced in *DBPO* Series I Vol. I.
92. *FRUS: The Conference of Berlin* Vol. II pp. 281–2, 285–6, 302–4.
93. Ibid. pp. 365–6. The British records in *DBPO* Series I Vol. I p. 652 omit the second Soviet reference to applying the same international principles to Suez as to the Straits. They also have the final comment being made by Molotov not Stalin.
94. *DBPO* Series I Vol. I 1945. Doc. 459. Memorandum by G. Jebb, 29.7.45 (emphasis in original).
95. FO371/48774 Sir M. Peterson to Bevin 11.8.45; minute by G. L. McDermott 16.8.45; FO371/45924 Cairo to FO 1.9.45, referring to Nokrashi Pasha wanting every British soldier out of Egypt.
96. FO371/48774 minute by H. Beeley 26.8.45.
97. CAB 80/97 COS (45) 551 (0) Sir O. Sargent to Secretary Chiefs of Staff Committee 28.8.45 and annex; COS (45) 573 (0) 11.9.45; annexes I and II. For other views on the implications of Soviet troops in Egypt see FO371/48775 minute by R. Allen 1.9.45. and the marginal note saying 'this would finish our position in Egypt'.
98. FO371/50792 minute by Lord Hood 3.9.45; FO memorandum on Cyrenaica 5.8.45.
99. FO371/50791 minute by P. Scrivener 15.7.45; FO371/50790 minute by F. R. Hoyer Millar 7.7.45; FO371/50792 minute by G. L. Goodwin 3.9.45; FO371/50790 minute by Lord Hood, 22.6.45; FO371/50792 joint FO/CO memorandum for the

Overseas Reconstruction Committee 25.8.45, reproduced in *DBPO* Series I Vol. II doc.12; FO371/50790 brief for Terminal (Potsdam) n.d.; FO371/50791 minute by G. L. Goodwin 11.9.45.
100. FO371/50792 record of Overseas Reconstruction Committee Meeting 30.8.45; joint FO/CO memorandum 25.8.45; minute by Lord Hood 3.9.45 reproduced in *DBPO* Series I Vol. II Doc. 20; CAB 84/75 JP (45) 252 14.9.45; FO371/48775 minute by R. Allen 1.9.45; CAB 129/1 CP (45) 130 28.8.45.
101. CAB 129/1 CP (45) 144 1.9.45, *DBPO* Series I Vol. II Doc. 18.
102. FO371/50792 minute by Lord Hood 3.9.45.
103. FO371/44557 Halifax to Bevin 9.8.45. Drafted by J. Balfour.
104. FO371/49069 record of FO meeting 13.8.45.

Chapter 3
Empire and global strategy, 1944–46: implementing an imperial strategy and the breakdown of Allied cooperation, September 1945–December 1946

Ernest Bevin was born in Somerset, the son of a domestic help. His father is unknown and he was brought up in great poverty by his mother with little or no schooling. His rise to the top of the political hierarchy was a remarkable success story that bore witness to a strong and determined personality capable of transcending social and educational barriers and overcoming material obstacles. It was achieved through the medium of the Trade Union movement in which Bevin gained high office as an untrained, unskilled and self-educated member before rising to become General Secretary of the Transport and General Workers Union. His success in the Trade Union movement made him an important figure in the Labour Party before he turned politician and was drafted into the wartime coalition government by Churchill with whom he developed a good relationship based on the mutual respect of two uniquely forceful personalities.[1]

Bevin was flung into the post-war debate on imperial strategy possessing an imperial instinct similar to that of Britain's wartime leader. His lifelong concern for the British working class, towards whom he had an undying sense of loyalty and admiration, naturally translated into an earthy and forceful patriotism. This was linked to the protection of ordinary British people in terms of material benefits and of the prestige and status associated with an effective voice on the international stage which would represent their uniquely British qualities and values. In terms of the material issues, Bevin's interest in the Empire had first appeared through his involvement with the Colonial Development and Welfare Act under the Labour government of 1929. The Act was conceived in order to promote colonial development through schemes which would stimulate British industry and thus alleviate some of the burdens imposed on the British working classes by the economic difficulties of the inter-war years. It was an interest that Bevin was to develop further on becoming Foreign Secretary, albeit within a generally accepted view of imperial economics that assumed, however unjustifiably, that colonial development could and would bring benefits to British consumers and to colonial producers. During the 1930s the terrible economic problems again led Bevin to look for salvation in the Empire, and he was one of the leading members of the Labour Party prepared to abandon the long established commitment to free trade in order to move more towards an autarkic imperial trading bloc.[2]

In terms of Britain's role on the world stage, Bevin's experience of wartime government indicated an inflated conception of the influence Britain could exercise, and a determination, similar to Churchill's, to maintain Britain's position in Greece by any military and diplomatic means. During the war, Bevin was convinced Britain would emerge as the leader of Western Europe with even de Gaulle looking to Britain for leadership, while in the Balkans he believed Bulgaria would also look to Britain rather than the Soviet Union.[3] In 1944, at the Labour Party Conference, he had staunchly defended the government's interventionist policy in Greece, on the grounds that it was a necessary part of maintaining Britain's position in the Mediterranean.[4] These imperial instincts led one historian to refer to him as more Churchillian than Churchill on imperial questions, a view which is well borne out by a close examination of his views on the maintenance of Britain's global standing, and his ideas on forging strong links with the Empire in order to gain economic and power-political benefits.[5]

Bevin's essentially nineteenth-century, traditional views on Britain's world position were accompanied by two other distinctive beliefs important in the context of imperial strategy. In terms of the long-run goals for the Empire, Bevin, like many socialists, believed imperialism was the result of the exploitative actions of uncontrolled capitalist enterprises. If these could be taken in hand by a progressive socialist government then exploitation would cease, and, over time, closer economic relations between the metropolitan and peripheral areas of formal and informal Empire would produce greater prosperity for both. As regards the short-term necessity of maintaining status and influence between Britain's two apparently more powerful Allies, Bevin's reactions to the Soviet challenge were undoubtedly conditioned by a dislike of communism acquired from dealing with inflexible, dogmatic and obstructive communist leaders within the Trade Union movement. Given that his private secretary, Pierson Dixon, had developed extremely Russophobe views from his time in the Southern Department, it is not difficult to see how Bevin would have been encouraged to transfer his dislike of Trade Union communists on to Soviet communists.

The new Foreign Secretary inherited a department which, while not united on all aspects of policy towards the Soviets, was growing increasingly worried about imperialist Soviet ambitions now that, between June and August, these presented a definite threat to British imperialism. Officials were also worried about Britain's military and economic strength relative to the United States and the Soviet Union. But there was a general conviction, first discerned by Anthony Adamthwaite, that the decline of British power was a temporary rather than a permanent phenomenon.[6] Officials like the Deputy Undersecretary, Sir Orme Sargent, who were concerned with reversing the decline, had to face the difficult task of adapting long-term planning to the more immediate tasks of responding to the everyday concerns increasingly dominated by the question of the peace treaties. The London Council, for example, which opened on 11 September, coincided with the meeting of Middle Eastern diplomatic representatives summoned by the Foreign Secretary. The latter began on 5 September and Bevin explained his desire to broaden the base of British influence in the region by promoting economic development; he was assuming that British political domination and responsibility for Middle Eastern defence would continue, and that economic development 'would help counteract nationalist tendencies'.[7] Bevin was not going to stay his hand to await the outcome of the London Council or to ensure that he had the support of the Prime Minister on such matters.

Several developments before the Council opened are worth noting in order to understand the background of official opinion against which Bevin had to deal with the Russians. On 6 September the Ambassador in Moscow reported better news on Eastern Europe. Some elements in Romania, who did not look exclusively to Moscow, had regained power without provoking any Soviet reaction. It looked therefore as if the Soviets might allow British representatives on the Control Commission greater freedom of movement and access to information, and might even agree to reconstruct the Romanian government. Soviet actions could either have been an attempt to make meaningful concessions before the opening of the Council or part of a charade designed to persuade the Allies that the Soviet policy of exclusive control over Romania was going to change. Whatever the true explanation, the Ambassador took the opportunity to reemphasise his previously stated conviction that the real danger spots in Anglo-Soviet relations remained in the Near and Middle East.[8]

Back in London the Chiefs of Staff were faced with disturbing news from Egypt where, on 2 September, the Consultative Committee of 18 politicians decided that the time had come to begin discussions about revising the Anglo-Egyptian treaty on the basis of British withdrawal from Egypt; a move that was seen as bringing nearer a formal government request for renegotiation.[9] It may have been why, on 6 September, Admiral Cunningham, Chief of the Naval Staff, argued that it was very important not to give the Russians what they wanted, in case it turned out that they would not support Britain in the base negotiations with Egypt. Therefore in terms of the Straits, particularly the bases question, while the issue had been postponed at Potsdam to allow discussions between the Big Three and Turkey, it was also being suggested that any British support for the resolution of the problem should await the settling of the Anglo-Egyptian treaty question. At the same Chiefs of Staff meeting the primacy of the political question was again confirmed when the CIGS remarked that on *military* grounds he could see no reason for opposing Soviet bases in the Straits as there was nothing to prevent them seizing the Straits in war anyway.[10] On the day the London Council first met, the Chiefs then endorsed a policy of not agreeing to any revision of the Montreux Convention outside the United Nations, unless the Russians agreed to support Britain in their renegotiations with Egypt.[11] This was bound to appear illogical to the Soviets who would be asked to support the British in imposing a base agreement on reluctant Egyptians, not in return for the British supporting Soviet imposition of a base agreement on reluctant Turks, but simply for the revision of the Montreux Convention to allow unrestricted passage for Soviet vessels.

On the other key Mediterranean question, the disposal of the Italian colonies, the Foreign Office view was embodied in a memorandum of 10 September, which was important because it was approved by Bevin and submitted to the Cabinet as a counter to Attlee's views on the question. Since the original Hall/Bevin paper which had sparked off the controversy, Field Marshal Smuts had expressed strong views on the importance of keeping the Soviets out of the Mediterranean and

Africa, and the United States had indicated it was prepared to leave the Italians with all their colonies under trusteeship. Bevin was opposed to the latter because it 'would surely scandalize a large section of opinion in this and other countries', and because 'it would seriously damage our prestige in the Middle East'. The Foreign Secretary also argued that because the security of the route through the Mediterranean was vital to the safety of the British Empire, Britain should retain primary responsibility for it 'which we should firmly refuse to share with the USSR'. Unlike Attlee he dismissed the possibility of air power changing the strategic situation and argued that Britain must have the trusteeship of Cyrenaica; the future of Tripolitania could be left open, although Bevin believed that in practice there would be no alternative to Italy.[12]

The question was discussed by the Cabinet the following day because a decision on the line the Foreign Secretary should take at the Council had to be taken. Bevin explained that the American proposal would damage Britain's prestige in the Middle East and portrayed the Soviet position as each trustee having the right to establish bases in Tripolitania and Cyrenaica which would lead to conflict between the two powers.[13] The implication was that the Soviets desired military bases in Tripolitania to match the proposed British military bases in Cyrenaica. But there is no evidence from the Potsdam Conference of any Soviet claim for military bases in Tripolitania; nor, as will be seen, was any such claim made during the London Council of Foreign Ministers. Bevin could have been acting on assessments or information provided by the Embassy, or he could simply have been mistaken. Alternatively he could have been exaggerating the threat presented by the Soviet position to win Cabinet support for a firm line at the Council in order to maintain British prestige in the Middle East and a predominant position there.

The question of prestige and status also applied to the Far East, although, as has been seen, the area was not arousing the same degree of concern as the Middle East. Yet like Eastern Europe, where Britain had even smaller vital interests, the post-war arrangements for ex-enemy states were seen to be relevant to Britain's global standing. In August the American government had proposed the establishment of a Far Eastern Advisory Commission which would discuss the control machinery for Japan. The British proposed the establishment of a Control Commission, on the lines of those set up in the former ex-enemy states in Europe, which would formulate the policy to be applied by the Supreme Commander. In response to the British suggestion, the Americans explained that they did not envisage the establishment of a Control Commission to assist the Supreme US Commander. The Foreign Office was convinced that the Americans were departing from the principle of collective governmental responsibility for policy making and was opposed to any such departure because it believed Britain was entitled to have a real voice in the control of Japan. 'At the very least,' it was claimed, 'it seems important that we should not play a lesser part in the control of Japan than Russia and China, as otherwise our prestige and standing as one of the Big Four powers might suffer damage.'[14]

The London Council of Foreign Ministers was obliged, under the terms of the Potsdam agreement, to first consider the terms of the Italian peace treaty. Thus the question of the Italian colonies and the Mediterranean would be at the centre of the initial test of post-war great power cooperation. The way in which the Council was to conduct its business was also laid down by the Potsdam agreement which stated that for the discharging of its tasks of drawing up the peace treaties 'the Council will be composed of the members representing those states which were signatories to the terms of surrender imposed upon the enemy concerned', with France being regarded as a signatory to the Italian surrender. In other words, of the five powers present, those not involved with the armistice arrangements would be excluded from the meetings except for those occasions 'when matters directly concerning them' were under discussion. States not directly involved should be invited to send representatives when questions of direct interest to them were being considered.[15] At the first meeting Bevin requested a procedural change which would alter the arrangements stipulated by the Potsdam agreement. Already committed to better Anglo-French relations, the Foreign Secretary was evidently attempting to prevent further French resentment at being excluded from meetings of the Big Three; such resentment was inevitable given the well-known French feelings over their exclusion from the Yalta and Potsdam Conferences. Bevin proposed that all five members should attend the meetings and take a full part in the discussions, but that the representatives of those states who had not signed the particular armistice agreement would be excluded from voting. It was a clear departure from the Potsdam agreement but one which won general acceptance.

The question of the subsequent items on the agenda proved more controversial but indicative of great power attitudes to areas of the world where each felt it should play a predominant role. Molotov expressed surprise that the proposed agenda, circulated by the British delegation, did not include Japan as the British had previously indicated that it might come up for discussion. The explanation lay in a meeting between British and American representatives on the proposed agenda in which the latter made it clear that they were determined to discourage the discussion of Far Eastern questions. Japan of course was the area in which the United States hoped to effectively control post-war developments. Romania was one of the areas in which the Soviets expected to enjoy similar domination, and Molotov, having agreed to an item on the political situation there, was keen to discuss Japan, and also requested that the Council discuss the political situation in Greece. If the British were determined to be involved with the arrangements in Romania then it seemed the Soviets would expect a quid pro quo in Greece.[16] The British of course were not at all keen on such developments.

The first discussion of the Italian colonies took place on 14 September on the basis of an American memorandum which reflected a change of position. No longer arguing for Italian trusteeships, Byrnes proposed that for the next 10 years, prior to independence, the whole of Libya should be under the trusteeship of the United Nations. This would involve the appointment of an administrator with full executive powers who would be responsible to the United Nations Trusteeship Council. Attached to the administrator would be an Advisory Committee of seven members from Britain, the US, the USSR, France, Italy and a Libyan and a European representative to be decided upon by the five powers. Bevin immediately disputed the idea of Libya being treated as a single territory, arguing that Tripolitania and Cyrenaica should be referred to separately, and, while accepting the principle of trusteeship, referred to the British pledge not to put the Senussi back under Italian rule. This issue of Libya's division enabled Molotov, while not rejecting the US proposal, to suggest that individual trusteeships would be preferable, and that the Soviet Union should be the trustee for Tripolitania. For their part the French doubted the wisdom of depriving Italy of its colonies. Thus the issues of whether Italy should lose Libya, whether there should be a trusteeship agreement and whether the colonies should be administered by individual states or jointly on behalf of the UN, and if the former, by whom, were all deemed matters for further discussion.[17]

The Joint Planners in London immediately came out against the American proposals. They disliked the idea that Russians would be brought into Libya, albeit in an advisory capacity, and objected to the vagueness of Byrnes's proposals which left open the key question of the provision of defence forces. Most importantly Britain would be prevented from acquiring bases in an area of great strategic importance.[18] The following day the Chiefs of Staff confirmed that the American proposals, and of course the Soviet proposals, were unacceptable. They believed that Russian infiltration into the Mediterranean would lower Britain's prestige in the Middle East and produce Arab unrest which would prove expensive for the British. It was not clear to the Chiefs why the Russians were claiming Tripolitania, but they were sure that an international administration would be better than a Soviet trusteeship. The Joint Planners argued that a Soviet trusteeship in Tripolitania would give the Russians control of an area from which they could cut Mediterranean communications; it would also strengthen the case for Soviet bases in the Straits and might even produce demands for Aegean bases in order to maintain sea communications. The disadvantage of the American proposals, apart from the undesirability of bringing the Russians into Libya in an advisory capacity, would be simply to prevent Britain obtaining bases in an area of great strategic importance. In order to avoid the latter eventuality the Chiefs suggested that British interests should be allowed to predominate in the Mediterranean in return for the British recognition, already given, they claimed, of Russian interests in the states on its western borders.[19] It was a return to the old, straightforward spheres of influence approach.

Bevin immediately seized on the Chief's views and put them to the Cabinet meeting held on the same day as the next session of the Council. It provides an early example of how Bevin's views often coincided with those of the military, rather than with those of the Prime Minister, or indeed his Cabinet colleagues, when questions affecting the Empire were at stake. Yet it was not clear to what part of Eastern Europe the Chiefs were referring. Did they mean Romania and Bulgaria, or Poland or other areas east of Germany? In Cabinet the Foreign Secretary claimed there were indications that the Russians were anxious to establish themselves on the African continent even though they had successfully established themselves in those territorial areas which interested them in Europe and the Far East. Again the crucial point was as yet unclear. Did Bevin believe that because Russia had made territorial gains in those areas it should have no further interest in the Mediterranean, either through bases in the Straits, or a trusteeship of Tripolitania; or did it mean that he felt Britain had accepted a Soviet sphere in much of Eastern and Central and even Southern Europe, and therefore the Soviets should cease to interest themselves in the British sphere in the Mediterranean and Middle East? Nye Bevan took a rather different line and argued that collective trusteeship would prevent any individual power establishing bases and would therefore meet the essential requirement of denying Cyrenaica to any potentially hostile power.[20] Whatever the explanation, on the specific point of the American proposals, and perhaps fearing that his hands might be tied, Bevin suggested that the best British tactics would be not to take too firm a line but to play for time.

The only submission on the Italian colonies by the British government to the Council suggested that Italy should accept the loss of its colonies and the right of the powers to administer them pending their final disposal. At the fifth session of the Council Bevin argued that this proposal was made on the same basis as Russian claims in Eastern Europe, namely security. He was therefore surprised that the Soviets were now claiming a trusteeship in North Africa where Britain had vital interests, as Britain had supported Soviet claims for adjustments of its western frontier, and accepted the Soviet position in other settlements which had since been made. Yet the British, he continued, were fully prepared to accept the US proposals on Libya and agreed they should be studied by the Foreign Ministers' deputies.[21] It was a concession (but significantly not to the Soviets) which, like the idea of revising the Straits agreement, the British military were not keen on. In addition to Cabinet pressure, Bevin's change of mind may well have been caused by the attraction of a common Anglo-American approach to Mediterranean issues, reflected in his privately expressed aim of getting the USA brought into Mediterranean arrangements within six months. It did not, however lead Molotov to abandon his claims to Tripolitania. The Soviet Foreign Minister did not see why Britain should have a monopoly of communications in the Mediterranean because Russia needed bases for its merchant fleet with no military facilities; this could be done, he claimed, without restricting in any way the facilities available to the British Commonwealth for maintaining communications with all parts of the world.[22]

The next four days were largely taken up discussing other aspects of the Italian treaty on which none of the participants had firm proposals or well defined objectives, except on the future of the Dodecanese Islands which Britain wanted ceded to Greece. The Soviets, perhaps playing for the time which Bevin had initially proposed as a British tactic on Libya, asked for more time to study the question. Then on 20th September the Council's attention shifted from the area of British vital interests to that of the Soviets when the Finnish treaty was discussed on the basis of Soviet and British papers. Bevin objected to the Soviets not being prepared to restrict the Finnish peacetime military establishments in the treaty because similar provisions had been proposed in the Italian treaty. In the face of this impasse Molotov proposed an Anglo-Soviet Commission to study the question, but that afternoon the French objected. Bevin of course had no desire to exclude the French or to restrict further the Powers entitled to air their views on the peace treaties. He was also under strong pressure from the Dominions, particularly South Africa, who wanted a larger voice in the drawing up of the Italian peace treaty.[23] Policy was in fact being geared to the sensibilities of the Dominions and other future collaborators with the British Empire. This increasingly meant that Anglo-Soviet cooperation was at best becoming more problematic.

Thus in the first half of the Conference, Soviet demands in both its own and Britain's areas of interest had been opposed by Bevin, and Britain's proposals for the Dodecanese blocked by Molotov, while there appeared to be a common Anglo-American policy for Libya. The second half of the Conference began with discussions on Romania. This was to provide a major argument stemming from the American refusal to recognise the Romanian government as sufficiently representative of democratic elements; and therefore free and fair elections under such a government would, in the American view, be impossible. The American claim, made by Secretary of State Byrnes, was that the Allies had agreed at Yalta to take specific measures to promote democratic governments in the liberated countries, and as a result Molotov's point that the United States recognised fascist governments in Spain and Argentina was irrelevant. The main Soviet complaint was that the British were suppressing democratic elements in Greece prior to holding elections, which therefore made it odd that in Romania the Americans were insisting on elections before recognition.[24]

The British stance on the Romanian question was obviously crucial in relation to the Anglo-Soviet spheres of influence deal on that country, and also significant for any future spheres of influence arrangements. Sargent called the American attack 'clumsy', but did not believe that should prevent Britain supporting it, which in essence was what Bevin and George Bidault, the French Foreign Minister, decided to do at the time.[25] The day after being confronted by a common Anglo-American position, and by calls for a Commission of Inquiry into the harsh Soviet controls imposed on Romania, Molotov declined to attend the Council and summoned a special meeting with Byrnes, Bevin and their advisers. He claimed progress had been far too slow (an indisputable point) and urged that France should be excluded from discussing Balkan questions and that the Council's procedure should revert to that stipulated in the Potsdam agreement. If this were not accepted Molotov gave notice he would no longer be able to attend the Council. Bevin immediately rejected both propositions, and wrote to Attlee to explain his decision and obtain Prime Ministerial support.[26] To accept Molotov's proposals, he claimed, would be to give mortal offence to France and open Britain to criticism from the Dominions and other allies who regarded even a Council of five members as too restricted. Bevin believed that by standing firm there was a risk the Russians would walk out, but he regarded that as the lesser of two evils. Whether the other was seen as the creation of French and Dominion resentment or the disastrous effect on Britain's international standing of making any concessions to the Soviets was not explicit.[27]

As the Council reached this deadlock, on what was technically a procedural point, a post-mortem began in the Foreign Office along with an assessment of Soviet aims and tactics. Clearly, in terms of the Foreign Office analysis the Soviets were in some difficulty. Leaving aside Soviet claims in the Mediterranean, the Americans were firmly committed to the independence of Romania and Bulgaria and to applying the Declaration of Liberated Europe. It was not surprising because Byrnes had been at Yalta for part of the proceedings and, carefully stage-managed by Roosevelt, had been sent home early in order to provide, with genuine conviction based on ignorance, an interpretation of Yalta as a triumph of American idealism.[28] Faced with American attempts to undermine their control over puppet states in Eastern Europe, the Soviets were also faced with the possibility of a Western grouping or bloc based on Anglo-French cooperation, the concept of which was being attacked in the communist press (although Soviet opposition to an Anglo-French treaty was denied by Molotov in a conversation with Bevin).[29] The possibility of a spheres of influence deal with the British based on a trade off between parts of Europe and the Middle East, even if acceptable to London, could not be implemented because of American opposition to Soviet control in Romania and Bulgaria. Yet the renunciation of spheres of influence would be equally problematic because the Soviets were now aware of Bevin's determination to exclude them from the Mediterranean.

Then there was the question of Japan which Molotov took up with Byrnes on the same day as he raised the procedural question. The Soviet Foreign Minister insisted that the debate on Japan now be opened and demanded an Allied Control Commission. Byrnes refused to discuss it, and almost immediately began to put pressure on the British to reject a Japanese Control Commission, even hinting that the prospects of an American loan would be adversely affected if the British did not comply.[30] Molotov was therefore faced with British and American pressure to deny the Soviets exclusive control over Romania and Bulgaria with the Americans apparently determined to control Japan so exclusively that even a Control Commission was unacceptable, and with the British determined to exclude the Soviets from the Mediterranean. American control over Japan could, as in Greece, offer the prospect of democracy once sufficient measures had been taken to ensure free elections would produce the right result; but in Romania and also in Poland deep rooted fear and hatred of Russia meant the Soviets would be unable to manage things in the same way. Was the claim for a trusteeship in North Africa therefore put forward as a bargaining counter to win acceptance of Soviet domination in Romania and Bulgaria? Did the Soviets conclude in London that it was now time to assert complete domination in their sphere because of attempts to exclude them from Japan and the Mediterranean?[31]

Sargent interpreted Russian tactics as designed to undermine British attempts to associate the French with a Western bloc because he believed this was the most likely way of dividing Britain and the United States. The Americans would dislike a Western bloc for the same reason that they disliked the sterling area, and in any case Sargent believed the United States wanted France as their client.[32] Thus emerged a theme which was to be developed in the coming months and which had its origins in the 'Stocktaking' memorandum. Britain needed to join with the United States to resist the immediate Soviet challenge, despite the element of competition inherent in the Anglo-American relationship, while aiming for closer relations with France and the Empire.

In minutes noted by the Foreign Secretary, both Pierson Dixon and the Permanent Undersecretary agreed with Sargent's assessment that the Soviets were out to undermine the Western bloc idea by alienating the French from the British. Dixon felt the procedural issue was carefully chosen because if Britain accepted the Soviet view it would be discredited in the eyes of France and the smaller nations. The Russians could quite easily say they were not perturbed by the idea of a Western bloc because if the manoeuvre succeeded Britain would not be able to form one anyway. For Dixon, the most hardline of all the officials, this Soviet threat to Britain's imperial strategy was made worse by his belief that the main Russian objective was a base in the Mediterranean which made the Mediterranean 'the real Russian challenge' at the London Council. Policy should therefore be based on a refusal to meet Russian demands over the Straits or Tripolitania. Dixon was later to record in his diary that although the Council apparently broke down on a procedural issue, the real reason, which he persuaded Bevin not to reveal to parliament, 'was our refusal to meet Russian ambitions in the Mediterranean'. Dixon also believed that on these imperial questions Britain was less likely to get American support because of the United States phobia about the British Empire.[33]

Neither Sargent nor Cadogan fully agreed with Dixon's interpretation of Soviet aims and tactics. Sargent rejected the idea that a Mediterranean base was the main Russian objective, arguing that they could not have really hoped to obtain Tripolitania which was claimed in order to strengthen their bargaining position. Cadogan went further by suggesting that Russian claims could be a response to Anglo-American attempts to interfere in Russian interests nearer at home in the Balkans; he agreed that a Soviet trusteeship of Tripolitania should be resisted, but doubted if Britain could refuse to consider any revision of Montreux. All three officials were in favour of resisting the exclusion of the French, even though Cadogan insisted they were not on good legal ground, and this unanimous view was formally adopted by Attlee in a letter to Stalin rejecting the idea that the Council's decisions on procedure could be reversed.[34]

From this point the Council was effectively doomed. There was, however, time for the Soviets to propose an Allied Control Council for Japan and for the Americans to resurrect their ideas on international control of inland waterways without any agreement being reached. There was also time for two exchanges between Bevin and Molotov on their imperial rivalries in the Mediterranean. On 23 September, after Bevin had emphasised that the Western bloc was not to be directed against the Soviet Union, and Molotov had stressed that Anglo-Soviet relations must be based upon the principle of equality, the conversation focused on the Mediterranean. Molotov argued that now France and Italy had ceased to be Great Powers Britain could not expect to monopolise the region; he could not understand why there was no corner for the Soviet merchant fleet. Then there was the question of bases in the Straits where Molotov accused the British of wanting the Turks to hold the Russians by the throat. Bevin replied that he would study the Straits question which he had been unable to mention to the Chiefs of Staff, but expressed fears of anything happening in North Africa which 'might, so to speak, cut the Empire in half'. He had supported the American position which did not coincide with selfish British interests that lay in the trusteeship of Cyrenaica, with Italy becoming the administering authority in Tripolitania. It is impossible to tell whether the Soviet stance reflected genuine attempts to cooperate with Britain in the Mediterranean through Soviet bases in the Straits and facilities for the Russian merchant fleet in Tripolitania. What can be said is that there was an unequivocal British determination to exclude the Russians from the Mediterranean and to gear policy to the rebuilding of British power and status in Europe and the Middle East.[35]

In a sense Italy had as important a role as France to play in the process. The French had been expelled from the Levant in order to preserve good Anglo-Arab relations, which ruled out a joint Anglo-French Middle Eastern policy and created difficulties for Anglo-French relations in Europe. If the Italians were not expelled from Libya it would, according to the British Ambassador in Rome, bring them 'joyfully' into the 'British orbit' and keep the Russians out of the Mediterranean altogether. As time went on this idea was to gain ground and lead the British away from a common Anglo-American approach to Libya. For the moment Bevin was still willing to deny to Molotov that Britain wanted Cyrenaica, or even, as he put it, 'an inch of territory'. He was pretending that as Britain wanted nothing the Soviets should be equally self-denying and should stop complaining, as Molotov was doing, that the British 'did not want to give the Russians anything'; or put another way, were unprepared to make any concessions to them. The Foreign Secretary even went so far as to deny that the Mediterranean dispute was 'a question of power politics'. British policy, he maintained, was influenced by security and the need to calm public fears because 'it would cause a great upset in this country if any new military power were to get across the lifeline of the British Empire'.[36]

Molotov, however, was not only displeased with the British, he was also furious with the Americans because of their position on Japan and their international waterway scheme. As a British despatch from Moscow put it, the Soviets feared that foreign machinations would deprive them of the place in the world to which they were entitled. They were not of course the only ones with such fears. While Molotov complained to Bevin about the Anglo-American refusal to treat the Soviet Union as an equal, Bevin, in turn, complained that Britain was not being treated as an equal by the Russians and the Americans. Moreover, according to Dixon, British officials shared other perceptions with their Soviet counterparts in Moscow. The latter saw Britain as a possible leader of a group stretching from Iraq and Egypt along both shores of the Mediterranean and up the Atlantic seaboard to Scandinavia, which was very much part of Britain's imperial strategy. It was acknowledged in the Foreign Office that such a force would be a threat to Russian security, but it was already clear that British imperial strategy was being geared to the creation of such a grouping. In that sense conflict was bound to follow from Anglo-Soviet attempts to attain what each saw as its rightful imperial place in the world.[37]

Officials still tended to believe, however, that the Soviets were committed to collaboration. The problem was getting them to accept a basis for cooperation which did not threaten British interests. The proposed line from the Embassy in Moscow was based on a firm stand (given that the Soviets were still seeking cooperation) that set out Britain's vital interests so that the Russians knew how far they could go. It was a concept grounded in a specific form of *realpolitik*, which the Embassy had associated with Soviet policy makers in the past, as opposed to discussions on general principles. Roberts believed such an approach would prevent the Russians trying to split Britain from the United States, but the snag was that Britain would have to recognise Soviet vital interests in the Balkans and elsewhere. Then with remarkable obtuseness the despatch suggested that Britain's vital interests should not be presented simply as British requirements, but as part of a wider world system to which the United States could subscribe. The futility of attempting to have a spheres of influence cake and eat it with American principles was soon spotted in the Foreign Office where it was noted 'as has been pointed out before, it would be very hard to prevent a discussion with the Russians on the basis of respecting each other's vital interests not to result in an agreement on spheres of interest'.[38] In early October Bevin and the Foreign Office were not inclined to support a spheres of influence arrangement, not only because of the impact on Britain's world position of being excluded from large areas of Europe, but because the Council of Foreign Ministers clearly indicated the American intention to have a say in the affairs of Romania and Bulgaria. Bevin also appeared to rule out a deal with the Soviets over the Straits and Cyrenaica. Molotov, referring to control of the Straits as a means of strangling the Soviet Union, produced a response from Bevin emphasising the importance of Cyrenaica to the security of the British Empire which he feared could be cut in half in the Mediterranean. 'Let us agree', replied the Russian Foreign Minister, clearly implying that a deal could easily be made between Soviet requirements in the Straits and British requirements in Cyrenaica. This would have been a significant concession to the Russians and Bevin chose to change the subject.[39]

At the official level the idea of a spheres of influence deal had been given renewed consideration after the Moscow Embassy's suggestion that Britain should discuss its 'vital interests' with the Russians and be prepared to recognise Soviet 'vital interests' in the Balkans. In an official draft Britain's choice was defined as either a deal in which Russia effectively gained control of Eastern and Central Europe in return for not impinging on British or American interests in other areas of the world; or the repudiation of spheres of influence deals, with Britain demanding a say in Eastern Europe in return for allowing Russia to play its full part in security arrangements in all parts of the world.[40] The alternative was seen by officials as giving Britain the worst of both worlds yet Bevin appeared disinclined to take up a spheres of influence deal. This was confirmed on October when Warner recorded the Secretary of State's view that the Russians 'should be left alone' and that Britain's vital interests should not be discussed with them.

It was not easy to see, if spheres of influence arrangements were to be ruled out, and if no concessions were to be made to the Soviets, how Britain's exclusive position in the Mediterranean and the Middle East could be justified. Yet for Bevin, keen to rebuild British power, this was deemed essential for the preservation of Britain's imperial position. As he lamented in October, with the Russians 'driving in on us through peace treaty negotiations' and the Americans demanding bases, 'if we are not careful our victory in the war may lead to us being plucked by our Allies'.[41]

Some signs of how the Foreign Secretary conceived the respective British and Soviet positions can be detected at the London Council of Foreign Ministers; they were to be made much clearer as a result of a memorandum by Smuts received by Bevin on the same day as his rejection of an Anglo-Soviet deal on spheres of influence and which he requested officials to send to Byrnes because it represented his own views. The South African leader argued that Britain should be rewarded in Africa and the Mediterranean for its wartime sacrifices because the Soviets had been rewarded in Europe. Smuts was not, however, thinking of any spheres of influence arrangements along the lines made by Churchill; he believed that Soviet rewards stemmed from the territorial gains it had secured at Yalta, largely at the expense of Poland and the Baltic republics. It was precisely because of British good will in satisfying Russian claims at the expense of others, rather than at the expense of the British Empire or Britain's general international status and influence, that, according to Bevin, the Soviets were making demands in the Mediterranean; British good will in agreeing to their territorial gains in Europe had only succeeded in whetting their appetites. Britain's position in the Mediterranean and the Middle East had now to be maintained by a firm no concessions line and justified on the basis that the Soviets had received the reward of territorial gains in Eastern Europe.

In a sense this was linked to Eden's view of the Soviets which assumed that British concessions would produce more Soviet demands. For Smuts and Bevin the Russians were hard bargainers prepared to haggle over questions of procedure in order to achieve their aims, and who were not prepared to lay all their cards on the table. Consequently, having secured their territorial concessions, they were proceeding to fight hard over other points which particularly interested the Allies. In response the tactics advocated by Smuts and Bevin were to make no single concessions until all the relevant matters had been tabled, discussed and disposed of as a whole. Otherwise the situation that had arisen when the Dalmatian Islands were granted to Yugoslavia but the Dodecanese not ceded to Greece might be repeated. What was at stake was the imperial position of Britain in the African continent, a position compared by Smuts to the Soviet Empire in Europe.

Thus there was still no acceptance of an absolute policy of no concessions but a refusal to make any piecemeal concessions or to accept Soviet involvement in the Mediterranean. It was an approach well suited to bilateral negotiations but which was much more problematic in the context of tripartite talks when, at the final denouement it would be much more difficult to thrash out suitable compromises. Moreover, because of the rejection of any concessions on single issues the process of negotiating was bound to be a lengthy and more complex one, unless of course the Soviet Union accepted British aims and requirements. Nevertheless the Smuts/Bevin strategy was proposed on the basis that with hard bargainers like the Soviets, great power unity was more likely to be achieved by such tactics than by making piecemeal concessions. After all, it was claimed, the future of the world would depend on the present territorial arrangements and safeguarding the communications of a scattered maritime group like the British Commonwealth.[42]

The aim was clearly to stand firm until the Soviet Union, rather than attempting to advance its influence through further encroachments, came to accept that changes in the status quo would involve concessions on all sides and adopted a policy of compromise and cooperation on that basis. In the meantime, and until the Soviets made concessions, it would be important to obtain the backing of the United States in order to hold the line. Here again Bevin was pursuing the policies suggested by Sir Orme Sargent, who believed the Soviets were attempting to isolate Britain on Mediterranean questions. Russian pressure on the United States might result in the Americans ceasing to support Britain's fight to reestablish France as a great power and to exclude the Russians from the Mediterranean.[43] More importantly, in Bevin's view the situation had become a test of Anglo-American firmness in which the Soviets would exploit any weakness to avoid having to make concessions to meet the British and the Americans halfway.[44] In a sense foreign policy was revolving around essentially primitive attempts at 'squaring up' in the hope that the other side would back down first and thereby prevent any loss of status, prestige or imperial influence.

As a consequence there was a danger that long-term cooperation would be threatened by the short-term confrontation that was being sought by British imperial strategists. Recognising this, Roberts pointed out that it was not simply an Anglo-Soviet clash over Russian exclusion from the Mediterranean, but a Soviet–American clash over Russian exclusion from Japan. It was felt in Moscow, after a conversation between Stalin and Harriman, that the Russian leader genuinely believed the Western Allies had been given the same treatment in the Balkans as the Russians had received in Italy, and that the Soviets had made concessions over Berlin. Moreover, Stalin made it clear that if the Americans preferred to keep the Russians out of Japan, well and good. Each of the victors would run its sphere in its own way.[45] This would be all the more likely if the Russians were excluded from the Mediterranean as well. Thus the British perception of a trade off between territorial concessions in Poland and the maintenance of an exclusive British sphere of influence in the Mediterranean was not likely to be accepted by the Soviets. Consequently, the short-term policy of confrontation was likely to lead to a long-term consolidation of spheres of influence. And while the Soviets might have abandoned their imperialist ambitions in the Mediterranean and the Far East, they were hardly likely to do so in return for greater British involvement in Bulgaria, Romania or Poland. No one in the Foreign Office seems to have considered these points, perhaps because the obvious alternative policy was bound to involve the undermining of the British position in the Mediterranean and the erosion of Britain's status as a great world power.

In Washington, Soviet–American tensions over Asia, Europe east of Germany, and atomic questions were seen as more dangerous to the Grand Alliance than in London. Byrnes, in the view of one historian, concluded that a grand gesture was necessary to preserve Allied cooperation, and therefore on 23 November the US Secretary of State recommended a Moscow Conference to Molotov in the hope that the problems of the autumn could be resolved and international cooperation over atomic energy secured. Bevin was furious when informed about Byrnes's approach to Molotov two days later, and the Foreign Secretary initially refused to attend the Conference.[46] It was intended that the meeting should be a tripartite one, which itself was a concession to the Russians, and which threatened Anglo-French cooperation, a key element in British strategy, by ignoring the French who were desperate to retain a seat at the great power table. More importantly, the Conference threatened to undermine a firm Anglo-American stance against the Soviets, even though the Americans appeared committed to their stand on Romania and Bulgaria, and it reintroduced the spectre of Soviet–American cooperation at the expense of British imperial interests. On the other hand the latter would be more likely if the British boycotted the Conference and made no attempt to prevent Soviet-American cooperation materialising. In addition, the Ambassador in Moscow, regretting Bevin's disinclination to attend, pointed to a growing Soviet tendency to see Britain, and Bevin in particular, as hostile to the Soviet Union, and therefore argued that the Conference presented an opportunity to dissipate the notion that Bevin 'was a big, bad wolf'.[47] Yet Clark Kerr also realised the danger that Byrnes might attempt to 'secure a Far Eastern settlement satisfactory to the Americans leaving undiscussed the questions in Europe and the Near and Middle East of more immediate concern to us'. Therefore for Clark Kerr it was important to ensure the Conference was held as a forum for a general survey of Anglo-Soviet relations.[48]

On 7 December the British agreed to send a delegation to Moscow, and the Foreign Office began the task of preparing briefs. Drawing on views expressed in October, one brief opposed the Ambassador's line by arguing that a broad survey would crystallise into a discussion of spheres of influence, and that general discussions would encourage Molotov to try and put Britain on the defensive 'with the object of extracting undertakings from us on specific points without giving anything in return. These considerations apply particularly to the Middle East and the Mediterranean'.[49] In itself this shed interesting light on British attitudes, as the Foreign Office did not see an opportunity to put the Soviets on the defensive by extracting undertakings from them without a quid pro quo. A more comprehensive brief suggested a new British approach to achieving power-political goals, while also providing an analysis of the main thrust of British policy over the last 12 months or so. It pointed out that

the policy of His Majesty's Government in the Russian dominated areas of South Eastern Europe has hitherto been based upon the principle that we must do all in our power to prevent the continuation of Russian control of Romania and still more of Bulgaria through puppet governments and to encourage the present progress of Hungary towards representative and democratic government. We are publicly committed to this policy by the Yalta Declaration on Liberated Territories and our commercial and political interests will suffer if this policy cannot be carried out.

In a sentence which is important for assessments of whether British objections to spheres of influence in Europe were conditioned by opposition to Soviet interference in domestic affairs (allegedly in contrast to British spheres of influence in the Middle East) the document then pointed out that:

Our strategic position in Greece and the Middle East moreover makes it particularly important to us that Bulgaria should not act simply as an instrument of Soviet foreign policy. Our interest in securing an independent government in that country is indeed greater than that of the United States Government. There should, therefore, be no question of any radical change of policy in this area.[50]

It was an echo of Sir Orme Sargent's view that as Britain was trying to build up 'a kind of Monroe system in the Middle East', it was of 'vital importance that Bulgaria should be an independent buffer state'.

However, the Foreign Office clearly had doubts as to whether the continued insistence on a complete change of Soviet policy as a condition for the conclusion of peace treaties was the best way to realise British aims. In fact, the brief argued that the aims referred to above were not being brought nearer to realisation by policies which were clearly antagonising the Soviet government. The origins of the antagonism were related quite specifically to the change of policy at Yalta and the abandonment of the percentage agreement by the British. The percentage agreement, defined in December 1945 as British acceptance of substantially larger Soviet interests in Romania and Hungary in return for recognition of preponderant British interests in Greece, was seen 'on reflection' as unsatisfactory. 'Nevertheless the British Government set out to interpret them with the greatest possible strictness' which precluded it from taking any initiatives in the political development of Romania, Bulgaria (now included) and Hungary. Precluded that is until Yalta, when, following the Declaration on Liberated Territories, His Majesty's Government assumed that this superseded the Moscow agreement, and this was what the Foreign Office believed had led, in great measure, to the differences between the two governments.

Given this situation, and the fact that the Foreign Office saw no chance of a material reorganisation of the Romanian and Bulgarian governments (free elections had been held in Hungary, although the British believed the composition of the government did not accurately reflect the result) it was argued that the best policy was to work for the gradual creation of conditions which would produce representative governments. The initial step would be securing the withdrawal of the Russian troops which were supporting the puppet regimes in Romania and Bulgaria. Otherwise opposition groups would not be able to take effective action. And as there could be no withdrawal until peace treaties were signed, British interests appeared to require their early conclusion without any radical change in the internal political situation. British policy should therefore be geared simply to the inclusion in the present regimes of representatives of parties and groups in opposition.[51] As on previous occasions this raised the question of whether concessions should or should not be made as a matter of general principle; but in the event the issue was to be decided by American shifts on Romania and Bulgaria.

At the first meeting of the Foreign Ministers on 16 December 1945, Bevin had more pressing matters of imperial concern. The American agenda included items on Japan, Romania, Bulgaria and China as well as UN control of atomic energy, and Molotov immediately requested additional items on the withdrawal of US troops from China and British troops from Greece. Bevin refused to accept that Greece should be included and deprecated bargaining consideration of one country against consideration of another, as he claimed each case was right or wrong and should be considered on its merit.[52]

This initial Soviet challenge to British interests in Greece may have been behind Bevin's outburst at a meeting with Byrnes the following day. The Foreign Secretary claimed that Soviet policy was disturbing as it seemed that the Russians were attempting to undermine the British position in the Middle East. Soviet attitudes towards Greece, Turkey and now Persia, 'the three points where the USSR rubbed with the British Empire', indicated Russian intentions according to the Foreign Secretary. The world to Bevin appeared to be drifting into the position of three Monroes.[53] As has been seen, there were those in the Foreign Office who believed this would be disadvantageous for Britain whereas a British Monroe was desirable; what had to be avoided was the British Monroe being undermined by Soviet encroachments. On the 'Monroe' question Bevin was prepared to run the risk of a spheres of influence deal and, as he put it, to lay British cards on the table, in an attempt to solve the problem of the three points of Anglo-Soviet imperial friction. Thus on 18 December Bevin met Molotov with the object of discussing spheres of influence and the questions of Greece, Turkey and Iran. These, together with the thorny question of Cyrenaica and Tripolitania, formed the heart of the British Monroe and were the key areas for British imperial strategists.[54]

Greece, not surprisingly, was the first issue discussed by the two Foreign Ministers, and Bevin was very much on the defensive and clearly unconvincing. The Foreign Secretary tried to argue that because Greece had been invaded by both Italians and Germans there was nothing left of the army or the civil service, and this therefore justified the presence of British troops. When Molotov pointed out that the Italians and Germans had left a long time ago, Bevin argued that conditions in Greece were the same as in Bulgaria which Molotov did not accept because there had been elections in Bulgaria, and in any case the Soviet Foreign Minister pointed out that Greece, unlike Bulgaria, had been an ally, and people who had fought against the Germans in Greece were now being punished.

Following his brief on the desirability of Soviet troop withdrawals, Bevin stated he would like to see all troops withdrawn from the Balkans, but as he also stated that British troops could not be withdrawn from Greece at present, his point would have carried little weight. Bevin then turned to Iran to remind his Soviet counterpart that there was deep feeling about Iran in the United Kingdom, before attempting to justify the continued presence of British troops in parts of Southeast Asia.

Molotov did not accept the British position on Greece, claiming it was wrong to lump all the Balkan countries together, and pointing out that Soviet troops had withdrawn from Czechoslovakia because no lines of communication lay through that country. His main point was, in essence, that Romania was the only Balkan country where the Soviets were interfering and that the people of Bulgaria, Hungary, Austria, Finland and Iran had been left to settle their own affairs. Molotov may have been rather economical with the truth in this matter, but his approach indicated again that the Soviets were determined to control Poland and Romania. It appeared that in Soviet eyes the clash over Greece, as in the past, could be avoided by a British acceptance of Soviet control over Romania. Unfortunately this simple trade off was not now seen as desirable by the British, nor did it seem possible given American attitudes. Bevin ended his unconvincing performance by protesting that the elections in Romania (where there had been no elections), had not been fair.[55]

On the question of Soviet/British imperial clashes, the implication was, as earlier in the year, that for the Soviets an imperial trade off should apply on the Turkish question: a British base in Egypt in defiance of Egyptian wishes, a Soviet base in the Straits in defiance of Turkish wishes. In the briefs on Turkey, the ultimate Soviet aim was defined by the Foreign Office as breaking the Anglo-Turkish alliance and bringing Turkey into the Soviet sphere of influence, but as the Soviets had made no approach to the Turkish government since Potsdam there was no desire to have the question placed on the Moscow agenda. Bevin, however, took the opportunity to raise the question with Stalin at a meeting on 19 December in order to confirm the nature of Soviet demands. Stalin again claimed Kars, Ardahan and a Soviet base in the Straits, along with a revision of Montreux to prevent Turkey closing the waterway on her own authority. Bevin emphasised his wish not to have Turkey's independent position destroyed and it was agreed that the matter could not be settled at the Moscow Conference.[56]

What was resolved, two days later, were the Asian questions of the Far Eastern Advisory Commission, Korea and the Allied Control Council for Japan, although compromise remained difficult on Romania and Bulgaria. Molotov accused the Americans and the British of taking an attitude towards Greece which was inconsistent with their attitude towards Romania and Bulgaria, with the US government recognising the Greek regime despite the greater instability in Greece. It took a meeting between Byrnes and Stalin before it was agreed that a joint commission to Romania should arrange for the inclusion of additional ministers and for the Big Three to *advise* the Bulgarian government to include some members of the loyal opposition.[57] By the time the Conference ended on 27 December agreement had also been reached on a proposed United Nations Commission on atomic energy and on the resumption of the peace negotiations on a five-power basis.[58]

What had not been settled were the Anglo-Soviet disagreements over the Middle East and the Mediterranean. The last of these to be discussed at Moscow concerned the Soviet claim to the trusteeship of Tripolitania, which Stalin raised again in response to Bevin's request that the Dodecanese be handed over to Greece. The Russian leader had correctly assessed that the British and Americans were afraid of agreeing to a Soviet trusteeship, but Bevin countered by referring to his September acceptance of the US proposal for an international trusteeship, as opposed to individual trustees 'because the Mediterranean was such a trouble-some and dangerous area'. This was precisely Attlee's point about the whole Mediterranean and Middle Eastern region, but Bevin had no desire to apply general principles of international involvement to troublesome and dangerous areas within Britain's Monroe. For the Foreign Secretary, faced with protecting the Empire from Attlee and the Soviets, the need in December was to put forward a joint Anglo-American policy because American support for Britain was being questioned. Word had reached the Embassy in Moscow that the Russians were thinking seriously about the advantages of working through a Big Two rather than a Big Three procedure; there was no sign of American support for Bevin's attempt to get an agreement on Iranian affairs into the Moscow protocol and, assessing the Conference, the Embassy felt that the lack of agreement on Turkey and Iran outweighed any of the Conference's achievements, leaving Britain apparently facing, 'with doubtful American backing, constantly increasing Soviet pressure in the whole zone vital to British security between India and the Dardanelles'. The only glimmer of hope, which was to play an important role in Britain's imperial strategy and in Anglo-American cooperation in the Middle East, was Stalin's attitude to the British position in Egypt. Given the importance attached to the Middle East by Bevin and Conservative politicians, and the attitude of the military, who were now defining the problem in terms of preserving Britain's predominant position in a way compatible with the UN Charter, it must have been reassuring for them to hear Stalin say 'he was not particularly anxious to see the British leave certain territory. That might indeed, be to the disadvantage of everyone. For instance, the presence of the British in Egypt during the war had been of considerable value.' Bevin immediately took this up and asked if Stalin's sympathetic consideration could be counted on when it came to dealing with 'that part of the world' and Britain's responsibilities within it. The Russian leader indicated his assent, perhaps in the hope that sympathetic consideration of Soviet responsibilities in other regions could be counted on in return.[59]

The Moscow Conference had not been a success for the British because agreements on areas in which they had vital imperial interests had not been secured. On the other hand it had not been a complete failure, and there was still the possibility of winning American support for a common policy towards the Soviets in Turkey, Greece and Iran. Moreover Bevin, by refusing to discuss Greece, had avoided any discussion of the Balkans as whole, thereby preserving the position favoured in London of trying to maintain some British influence in Romania and Bulgaria; he had also avoided offending the French by excluding them from discussions on Europe. Bevin had made some changes in British policy towards Romania and Bulgaria in line with American concessions and with the Foreign Office view that this would help preserve British influence and avoid an out-and-out spheres of influence deal. Yet Bevin had still not completely ruled out some form of spheres of influence arrangement if British vital interests could be protected. As earlier it was a question of what spheres should be involved: Greece and Romania; Greece and a Soviet sphere in Romanian Bulgaria and Poland; or Soviet acceptance of its territorial concessions in Europe as the quid pro quo for accepting Britain's sphere of influence in the Middle East. Much would depend on American attitudes and whether a common Anglo-American policy could be developed to prevent any erosion of Britain's imperial position.

In the first two months of 1946 this seemed much more likely following a general hardening of American policies towards the Soviets and the inept way in which Stalin attempted to increase Russian influence in Iran. The precise reasons for the general American shift may have been linked to British policy or more likely to the shifts in US public opinion which became less well disposed to the Soviets in the wake of the concessions made by Byrnes in Moscow. There is no doubt, however, that the crisis in Iran provided the opportunity for the Americans to take a tough line with the Soviets and helped promote Anglo-American unity and the strengthening of Britain's Middle Eastern position.[60]

The Iranian issue developed from complaints made by the government of Iran concerning Soviet interference in their internal affairs at the end of 1945; the impending meeting of the United Nations in 1946 offered the Iranians the chance to present their case to an international audience with a formal protest about the continued Soviet occupation of Azerbaijan. After initial opposition to an Iranian appeal to the UN, the Foreign Office became keen to provide support and encouragement in order to demonstrate to the Americans the British willingness to stand up to the Russians.[61] More importantly Soviet interference reinforced British concerns about the Soviet threat to their Middle Eastern position and probably convinced Bevin that the policy of no concessions should be wholeheartedly adopted as a short-term tactic. In late January the Foreign Secretary tried to convince leading American Republicans of the nature of the Soviet threat and described Soviet aims in terms of the 'two arms of a bear'. In the West one arm was trying to wrap itself around the Straits; the other was to be wrapped around eastern Turkey by obtaining Kars and Ardahan, undermining the Iranian province of Azerbaijan, penetrating east Kurdistan and threatening the Iraqi oil-producing area around Mosul. According to Bevin this demonstrated how vital it was to stand up to the Russians in Iran because their technique was exactly the same as Hitler's and appeasement had to be avoided at all costs; if Russia was rebuffed on Iran then Turkey would be saved. Significantly Bevin also argued that the Russian technique allowed for no give and take because the Soviets had no intention of making concessions and would insist on their point of view at all times.[62]

Bevin's views were very much in line with a despatch from Moscow, two days earlier, in which Frank Roberts attributed the unsatisfactory outcome of the recent Big Three conference to Soviet stubbornness and American reluctance to promote a solution of any Middle Eastern problems. Roberts detected a new Soviet approach which assumed there was no part of the world which was not of direct interest to Moscow. The Russians were also deemed to have a desire for buffer states, (as opposed to countries in the Soviet orbit) but to the south, Britain was barring the way to the Mediterranean and Middle East by a system of Arab client states and the more or less client states of Turkey, Afghanistan and Iran. Thus whereas in Europe and the Far East the Soviet Union can ensure her own security, however exaggerated her conception of this may be, without damaging British or even American interests, this is unfortunately not the case on the southern borders of the Soviet Union. Throughout the Middle East prestige and security considerations are closely intermingled. Even limited Soviet success in Persia and Turkey, and still more concessions to the Soviet Union in Tripolitania would presumably be interpreted as a severe set back to Britain throughout the Arab world and any concession, even to legitimate Soviet aims – as for example in the Straits – must be carefully considered against this background.[63]

It would be hard to find a better illustration of Britain's initial Cold War concerns or of the essential nature of the Anglo-Soviet conflict.

The importance attached by the Foreign Office to an imperial strategy of no concessions to the Soviets, backed by the United States, was emphasised at the official level in February when the problems in Big Three relations were deemed to stem from an Anglo-American failure to confront Russia with a common minimum programme. The Americans, in the Foreign Office view, had to abandon their fear of ganging up with the British Empire against the Soviet Union, because one way of halting the expansionist moves of the Russians was to confront them with a joint Anglo-American aggregate of power.[64] The importance of this was confirmed by the Foreign Secretary himself when, in discussions with Dominion representatives about the Mediterranean, he explained that the first British priority was to get a satisfactory US attitude. This, of course, following Stalin's Moscow pronouncement on Britain's position in Egypt, meant support for the British stance on the Mediterranean and the Middle East rather than direct American involvement in the region. For one official this would be easier said than done because although the US insisted on safeguarding its security interests in the Pacific, when Britain's vital Mediterranean and Red Sea communications came under consideration the US took a purely humanitarian view.[65] However, the Iranian problem was to provide evidence that the Americans were prepared to stand up to the Soviets in an area of vital importance to the British Empire.

In some ways Iran seemed an unlikely place for the cementing of Anglo-American power against the Soviets. Within Iran there had been considerable suspicions between British and US representatives during the war,[66] but the importance of cooperating with the Americans overcame British fears, and the Soviet refusal to withdraw troops in March 1946 led the Americans to urge the Iranians to renew their complaint to the Security Council. The US was now in fact taking the lead in opposition to Soviet imperialism which was precisely what British imperial strategists required, whatever the long-term implication for the future of the British Empire. This was not only evident in the case of Iran, but also in the case of Turkey, which was still regarded in the Foreign Office as important to the British Empire in the early months of 1946. A draft Cabinet Paper argued in January that 'it is of major British interest that Turkey should continue to be a genuinely independent country looking to Britain for support' and that it would be in Britain's interest to try and defend Turkey even without United States support.[67] In January 1946 there were fears in Ankara that at the Moscow Council the Americans had sold Britain out in the Middle East, and with Turkey therefore apparently forced to rely on the British, doubts appeared in the Turkish parliament about the extent of Britain's support for the Turkish alliance.

The situation was dramatically changed by a statement in the House of

Commons in February and by the American announcement in early March that it would send a naval task force to the Eastern Mediterranean. Ostensibly this was to take home the body of the late Ambassador to Turkey but in reality it was to show support for the Turks against Moscow. In particular, it was to strengthen the Turkish hand over the Straits following the Soviet concession to leave frontier questions out of the account, temporarily, in order to discuss the Straits. In Britain, the Chiefs of Staff remained opposed to any Russian involvement in the Straits, even as part of a United Nations base there, and the Foreign Office was still not convinced that Turkey had been 'saved'. There was the possibility, mooted by the Turkish Ambassador, that the Soviets would try and establish a base in the Dodecanese, given their reluctance to cede the islands to Greece. At the Embassy in Ankara the view was that Turkey's future orientation would depend on the outcome of the conflict in Greece and the realisation of Soviet ambitions in the rest of the Mediterranean; if the Russians were allowed to get a foothold south of the Dardanelles it was believed that Turkey would slide inevitably towards the Soviet Union.[68]

The confrontation over Iran in March marked a new phase in the Cold War. Along with Churchill's famous Fulton speech, Stalin's February pronouncement on the incompatibility of communism and capitalism and Kennan's Long Telegram, it embodied the new emphasis on confrontation rather than coop-eration. Further evidence of this appeared to be provided in early April with the establishment of 'The Committee on Policy Towards Russia'. The Russia Committee was created after the circulation of a document suggesting that the Soviets would have realised, in the wake of the showdown over Iran, that their policy had consolidated opposition to them. Britain should therefore, while pre-paring for 'more subtle tactics' on the part of Moscow, also prepare for a renewed Soviet assault against Britain.[69]

The Russia Committee did not, in essence, mark a watershed in British policy towards the Soviets; nor was it established primarily to define what British priorities and vital interests were or the tactics that should be employed to protect them. The Russia Committee was the response to the new situation of greater confrontation, which in part stemmed from the British determination to defend vital imperial interests and to make no concessions to the Soviets. It was therefore set up to deal more with the results of British policy than with its formulation at a time when presentation and propaganda were becoming more important. The essential thrust of British strategy towards the Empire, the Soviet Union and the United States had been in place since the summer of 1945. Various modifications had been proposed and policy towards the Soviets had not been defined absolutely in terms of no concessions and the maintenance of imperial interests. Yet con-cessions, other than these produced by the need to align Britain closely with the United States, had never actually materialised because circumstances and atti-tudes seemed to preclude them. The Russia Committee therefore had to justify British policy, while at the same time planning how to react to possible Russian propaganda against Britain given the confrontational situation in the spring of 1946. The latter requirement was much more important than any reassessment of Soviet intentions which, to officials, had long been evident in those areas of vital concern to Britain from Iran to the Western Mediterranean.[70]

What the Russia Committee indicated was a desire to go on the offensive in the confrontation with the Soviet Union, a policy which Bevin had serious reservations about.[71] For the Foreign Secretary, the policy of confrontation should not prevent future collaboration once the Soviets accepted that such cooperation could not be secured at the expense of concessions by the British Empire. In part this echoed Roberts' views, which Bevin had circulated to the Cabinet, and which warned against sabre rattling that would make it difficult for the Russians to climb down without loss of face.[72] Long-term cooperation was certainly not excluded, but if in the short term the British Empire was to be maintained with American backing, such cooperation could prove difficult and the likelihood of greater Soviet consolidation of a sphere of influence in Europe would be increased.

The third imperial area of vital importance to Britain was Libya, which had already been a source of dispute with the Soviets. More importantly the future of the Italian colonies had provoked a debate within the government about Britain's imperial presence in the Middle East and the strategic importance of the Mediterranean. In January 1946 these questions began to be considered by the Defence Committee with Attlee and Dalton challenging the existing levels of British forces overseas which, over the coming year, were defended staunchly by Bevin and the Chiefs of Staff.[73] By February Attlee had again questioned one of the strategic premises on which Britain's Empire was based, namely the preservation of communications through the Mediterranean; the Prime Minister did not see how, in the age of air power, this could possibly be done, irrespective of the resources Britain could afford to devote to such a task.[74] Such views were to produce a mad scramble, first in the service ministries and then in the Foreign Office, to produce military, economic and foreign policy justifications for the continuation of such a role that was of course deemed necessary to avoid any loss of imperial status as a great world power. By the end of the month the Air Ministry was delving deep into the realms of foreign economic policy to justify a military presence on the grounds that the revenue lost through a reduction in Middle Eastern trade, which a British presence allegedly promoted, would be greater than the military expenditure incurred to maintain it.[75] Needless to say no figures were produced, but it was a ball that Bevin was soon to pick up and run with.

By the time this debate got underway, the Chiefs of Staff and the Foreign Office were beginning to express doubts about the policy on Libya agreed with the Americans in September 1945; the idea of collective trusteeship under the UN auspices that the Foreign Ministers' deputies had been asked to study was now being seen as too disadvantageous for Britain. In essence this was connected to the securing of British strategic requirements in Cyrenaica which increased in importance following the formal Egyptian request at the end of 1945 to renegotiate the 1936 treaty in order to remove British forces from Egypt. Yet the issue was also inextricably linked to Britain's great power status which was deemed so dependent on a dominant imperial position in the Mediterranean and Middle East. In the Foreign Office it was argued that the American plan needed modifying because collective trusteeship would make it difficult to assert Britain's strategic interests in Cyrenaica. The aim now should be to give Cyrenaica independence as soon as possible so that Britain could conclude an alliance with King Idris that would satisfy its military requirements.[76] The draft minutes for the Prime Minister therefore argued that Idris, the leader of the Senussi, should be recognised as the independent ruler of Libya subject to a trusteeship agreement by which he would undertake, for a limited period, to accept advice and assistance on specific subjects from the United Nations. A UN Resident would be installed and the trusteeship agreement would provide for whatever strategic facilities Britain desired in Cyrenaica.[77] The whole idea was justified on the basis that Idris had frequently declared his readiness to conclude an alliance with Britain and to provide any bases or facilities the British might require;[78] these would be primarily for the strategic reserve in the Middle East, the necessity for which was being questioned by Attlee and Dalton.

On 13 February 1946 the Chiefs of Staff pronounced on the unsatisfactory nature of the likely Libyan settlement and asserted that collective trusteeship under the UN did not meet British military requirements. With regard to the alternative, they reemphasised their view that sole Russian trusteeship of any colony was always unacceptable; that a joint trusteeship should only be accepted as a last resort and on condition that the principal administrator would at no time be a Russian; and that if no favourable solution could be agreed it would be in Britain's interest to delay the final settlement.[79] The stakes were then raised even higher by the information that all the Dominions supported Smuts' views on the importance for the Empire of keeping the Russians out of the Mediterranean and on the value of delaying the Italian colonies settlement.[80]

Given the fact that cooperation with the Dominions was so important for the future of Britain's world position it is not surprising that senior officials began to write lengthy minutes on the general importance of the Libyan question; their conclusions were nothing short of apocalyptic. In part this tone was conditioned by the latest developments in the Defence Committee where memoranda on the Italian colonies and the future of the British Empire were being debated in the first half of March. The most notable was a devastating critique by the Prime Minister of the outdated strategic assumptions of the military, described by one historian as 'amongst the most radical produced by a British Prime Minister in Office'.[81] This was something of an understatement, but a fitting tribute to Attlee who stands out amongst post-war British Prime Ministers as perhaps the only one capable of looking forward to the sensible management of decline rather than backwards to the preservation of former greatness. Attlee pointed out that with the advent of air power the Mediterranean sea routes could not be defended, and neither would Britain be able to supply the necessary forces to protect the Middle East oilfields from Soviet attack. Britain should therefore withdraw from the region and not give hostages to fortune for sentimental reasons based on the past. Imperial links could be maintained much more cheaply round the Cape, through the Panama Canal or across Africa, with the strategic reserve located in Kenya.[82]

In most senses the strategic case had been won hands down, although the Chiefs of Staff were opposed to the location of the reserve in Kenya and were later to argue that the Middle East had to be protected to defend Africa (given the ease of moving forces across the Sahara Desert!), and to provide bases to bomb the Soviet Union from, even though British bombers had the range to reach only a very tiny fraction of the Soviet Union if they were to return.[83]

In essence Attlee's case was accepted by Harvey who agreed that maintaining Mediterranean communications was outdated and Britain could reach the Far East just as easily via the Cape or across Africa from Lagos to Mombasa. However, this was not now seen as the issue. Harvey argued that Britain's

Mediterranean position is vital to our position as a great power because it is the area through which we bring influence to bear on the soft underbelly of France, Italy, Yugoslavia, Greece, Turkey and southern Europe. Without our physical presence these states would fall, like Eastern Europe, under the totalitarian yoke. The Mediterranean would become a second Black Sea and Russian influence would spread into Africa. These are far weightier reasons than the route to India argument for making sacrifices to hold the Mediterranean.[84]

Gladwyn Jebb went much further in terms of the dire consequences for Britain and Europe should the Mediterranean be abandoned. Jebb believed that 'Russia would attempt to secure bases in the Mediterranean and set up pro Russian governments in Greece, Italy and Spain. France would then fall, and if so, how could we defend Great Britain?' Britain would have to rely on the deterrent effect of US bombs but the Americans 'might not consider Great Britain sufficiently important to defend and we would become not a client state of the US but a client state of Russia and Social Democracy would be ground between the millstones of capitalism and communism'. Britain therefore had no choice but to safeguard its lines of communications in the hope of American support.[85]

The enormity of the catastrophe looming into view on the back of a British retreat from the Mediterranean was summed up by the recently appointed Permanent Undersecretary, Sir Orme Sargent. Sargent concluded that 'our position as a World Power and therefore as a Great Power depends on maintaining our position in the Mediterranean, and this not for strategic reasons but on political grounds'. This was of course the crux of the matter, whatever the Chiefs of Staff might say about bombing the Soviet Union. The Permanent Under-secretary then put this in context by arguing that

at present there are two realities in Europe: the Eastern bloc created and dominated by Russia and the Mediterranean zone controlled by Britain. We talk a lot about a Western group but shall we be able to bring it into existence or maintain it if ever we abandon our position as *the* Mediterranean Power? I doubt it . . . If we no longer have the political and military strength to maintain our position the world will draw its own conclusions with inevitable consequences. We shall thereafter only be able to play a subordinate part in the affairs of Europe and a still smaller one in the affairs of other continents. We shall not be able to convince either our friends or our enemies that we are merely retreating owing to the changes of modern warfare from an indefensible position to a stronger and shorter line in the politico-strategic front.[86]

The importance of Central and Eastern Europe seemed to have paled into even greater insignificance as Italy, France, Britain, the Empire, Africa and Social Democracy were all allegedly threatened by the Prime Minister's proposals. Meanwhile in the Defence Committee, Bevin toned down the arguments of his officials and used the economic expertise of the Air Ministry to claim that if Britain's political influence in the Mediterranean was vital to its great power status, and if it was abandoned, then essential trade would be lost and serious economic consequences would follow.[87] The idea of using strategic arguments to justify a cheaper and more effective defence line around or across Africa seemed to be ruled out by Bevin and Sargent on political grounds, although ironically it was to remain at the heart of the debate on imperial and Cold War strategy partly because of a new strategic conception.

The source of this new strategic thinking embodying a retreat from the Middle East to a line across Africa from Lagos to Mombasa was none other than Liddell Hart. The Foreign Secretary had, as early as February, been thinking of the development of Mombasa as a major base to compensate for the loss of facilities in Egypt; he had also been thinking of a road across Africa from Lagos to Cairo which would have a branch down to Mombasa and the Chiefs of Staff were asked to give their views on Mombasa as a major base, which they soon deemed unsuitable. Liddell Hart's ideas stemmed from pressure on resources and the need to prevent a confrontation with the Soviet Union. 'So long as we persist in the policy of clinging to strategic positions in the Middle East . . . we obviously weaken the argument against our allies' inclination to maintain similar strategic "occupations" on a greater scale. We also court a clash with Russia over conflicting interests in the Middle East and feed her suspicions.' With British imperial defence based in Black Africa there would be no military presence in striking range of Soviet oil supplies and Britain would be better placed to meet a Soviet threat. This argument centred on Hart's view of the Sahara Desert as a barrier to the Red Army because even if the worst anticipations of those who feared Soviet aggression were realised, the Russians would get no further than Egypt and therefore be no threat to British dispositions 'for these would be covered by the world's widest desert'. It is an interesting reflection on the nature of the imperial strategy debate that an important element of it hinged on whether the Sahara was likely to be a barrier or a channel for Soviet expansion into Black Africa. For Hart, the strategic reorientation would bring benefits in terms of international relations and the management of Britain's decline. 'Strategic policy and peaceful policy would seem to coincide in the suggested reorientation', he noted, as 'in recent times we have been led to disregard the national limits of our strength and to indulge in dangerous dispersion . . . We have paid the penalty in excessive exhaustion and diminished power. We might go far to restore our situation by returning to the principle of concentration.' Hart's argument was to appeal to Attlee, whose ideas were moving in the same direction, because it was based on sound military logic and financial savings that would help avoid the danger of overcommitment, while also avoiding a clash between Soviet and British imperialism. It was to arouse some contempt and hostility in the Foreign Office, for reasons which should now be clear, and which were accurately summed up in Hart's memorandum which stated 'at bottom the main argument against it lies in the risk of losing "face" by any contraction of our imperial sphere'.[88]

The official who recorded his comments on the file accused Hart of thinking only of armies and not of propaganda 'whose success depends on prestige, ours and theirs'. For him the Anglo-Soviet conflict was not between regions but between two ways of life and thought; regions were important only in so much as some of them had a psychological value. Then somewhat inconsistently, it was argued that 'to abandon the Mediterranean as a Russian lake would be to lose Western Europe. We *must* hold a dominating position in the three peninsulas, Iberian, Italian, and Greek. They are as essential to us as the Low Countries used to be, and we cannot hold them if the Middle East is out of control.' In addition, Middle Eastern oil was deemed essential to Britain's recovery, while if the

Russians dominated North Africa they would soon penetrate further south because 'the desert is only a screen behind which to assemble forces'. Finally, if the Middle East was 'abandoned, India would not, perhaps could not, stay in the Commonwealth. Western Europe's frontiers are in the Persian and Turkish hills.'[89]

As the internal battle of the imperial strategists rumbled on through the late spring, the external battle against the Soviets over Tripolitania was scheduled to resume on 25 April. The Council of Foreign Ministers was to reconvene in Paris to prepare for the Peace Conference that would secure the signing of peace treaties with Germany's allies. In preparation for the Council, the Foreign Office, with some Colonial Office input, began to prepare briefs and a Cabinet Paper on the Italian Colonies. At the end of March the Dominions Secretary, conscious of the feelings of Britain's Commonwealth allies, formally requested a delay until after the discussion with the Dominions' leaders.[90] This tactic was not, however, fully extended to the Paris Council because Bevin felt it would be difficult to implement and might not help keep the Russians out of Africa. The Cabinet was told that it was vitally important to be in the Mediterranean to act, in Harvey's phrase, on the soft underbelly of Europe, and that if Britain was not to renounce its Middle Eastern position it had to deny the Italian colonies to any hostile influence and retain certain strategic facilities. If the US plan for collective trusteeship were to be adopted, Advisory Committees would have to be eliminated according to Bevin's recommendations.[91]

Bevin was clearly supporting the ideas opposed by Attlee at the April Defence Committee when the Middle East's importance was defined in relation to keeping the Soviets out of the main support area of Black Africa, and which the Prime Minister rejected because Britain could not provide sufficient forces. The Foreign Secretary was, however, showing enthusiasm for the idea, not only of developing a major base in Kenya, but of a Lagos–East Africa trunk road. This would bring Britain into closer contact with Southern Africa, and the area, according to Bevin, included sources of manpower and raw materials of enormous potential. He therefore proposed a survey by an expert commission to cover the strategic, political and economic implications of developing East and West Africa and a trans-Africa trunk road. One benefit of this shift of emphasis would be to provide the resources necessary for the maintenance of a Middle Eastern presence.[92] In terms of the strategy for Libya, at the Council of Foreign Ministers, the Foreign Office plan, as suggested in the conference brief, was to argue that since the issue involved trusteeship it was not a proper subject for a peace treaty, as other UN powers were involved, and therefore the conference should simply agree to Italy renouncing its colonies;[93] this would then leave the door open for Libya or Cyrenaica to be treated as an independent state in line with earlier Foreign Office recommendations.

The Libyan question was complicated by the debate within the government over Britain's Mediterranean and Middle Eastern role which should have provided some constraints on Bevin in the conduct of the Paris talks, but in fact did not. As in the case of Egypt, Bevin was too forceful a character to meekly accept Cabinet decisions. The Libyan issue was further complicated by the negotiations that were in progress with the Egyptians over the future of the Suez Canal base and the 1936 Anglo-Egyptian treaty. In one sense it was important for the Cyrenaican question to be settled quickly in order to enable the British to decide what facilities were required in Egypt; in another sense it was important for the Egyptian question to be settled in order to determine what facilities would be needed in Cyrenaica. And of course the Cabinet acceptance of Egyptian evacuation in the late spring of 1946 made it more imperative to secure a base in Eastern Libya.[94] Finally, the issue was complicated by the fact that agreements over bases for Britain would only serve as an encouragement for the Soviets to press for bases in the Straits.

Fittingly, given the British concerns over the Mediterranean and the growing rivalry with the Soviets there, the two sessions of the Paris Council of Ministers were dominated by the Italian peace treaty and the Mediterranean issues they involved. As one historian has noted, Byrnes 'seemed to have written off the Balkans' and apparently 'did not consider the uncompleted Balkan treaties'.[95] Moreover, with the German question not being raised until 9 July, three days before the end of the Council, the extent to which the proceedings were dominated by Mediterranean and procedural questions is even more significant than at previous meetings in London and Moscow. The agreements that were produced emerged despite, or because of, the British tactics of no concessions, and followed the significant abandonment of previous Soviet demands. These agreements related to the question of Trieste, the Italian colonies, the Dodecanese and Italian reparations.

The opening meeting produced what Byrnes called a 'striking withdrawal' from the previous Soviet position with an agreement that all four powers should discuss all five treaties; this led Bevin to report to the Commonwealth Prime Ministers' Conference that the Soviet delegation was 'more conciliatory and helpful than at London'. Smuts remained adamant that, whether the Soviets were conciliatory and helpful or not, security in the Mediterranean was more important than any other consideration to the future of the Commonwealth; the British Empire had to define the boundary at which the spread of Russian influence must at all costs be stopped, and both the New Zealand and Australian Prime Ministers agreed that on no account should the Soviets get Tripolitania.[96] The fourth formal meeting in Paris began without a conference agenda because of the lack of agreement on what exactly should be discussed now that the powers had finally agreed on who should be involved in the discussion. It was, however, agreed to address the peace treaties with Germany's allies, starting as in 1945 with Italy. The opening statement on the Italian colonies revealed four different positions now that the British, as planned, were modifying their support of the earlier US proposal for collective trusteeship with an international administrator appointed for 10 years. The French wanted the Italians to be given the trusteeship of their former colonies. The Soviets proposed a 10-year trusteeship based on Italy and an Allied power serving as joint trustees for each territory and assisted by an Advisory Council. Bevin put forward the idea of simply stripping Italy of its colonies and making arrangements that the two parts of Libya should be prepared for rapid independence on similar lines to an 'A' class mandate.[97]

In early May it was decided that more progress at the Council could be made with smaller informal meetings, and the Italian Colonies were raised at the first of these. Molotov wanted to know if Britain would withdraw troops from Libya, and Bevin explained that if the British suggestion was adopted the UN would decide what to do about troops. In any case, he said, the presence of a British base amounted to 'only a small claim' and 'after all the UK was worthy of some consideration which they very seldom got'. Molotov retorted sarcastically that perhaps Britain had too few colonies and wanted some more. Already the issue was becoming one of whether British claims to strengthen the Empire could be met when similar Soviet claims were not going to be conceded apart from the territorial gains in Europe. Molotov concluded that perhaps something could be worked out on the basis of the Franco-Soviet-American proposals but that the British ones were too selfish.[98]

The confrontation was resumed at the second informal meeting four days later, which shed interesting light on Bevin's attitudes to Britain's imperial role because the question of imperialism was directly addressed. The Foreign Secretary claimed that in Britain, nineteenth-century imperialism was dead and Britain was not an expansionist power (except, of course, in Libya), but he sometimes suspected that Britain's place had been taken by others (presumably nineteenth-century imperialist powers). Molotov replied that Bevin had forgotten about twentieth-century imperialism because the facts were that Britain had troops or bases in Palestine, Greece, Egypt, Indonesia, Transjordan (which he claimed was the model for Libya) and Iraq, whereas the Soviet Union only had troops beyond its frontiers in accordance with treaties and for specified periods. Referring to the Egyptian demand for British troop withdrawals, but not mentioning the Soviet desire for bases in the Straits, Molotov enquired what sort of relationship there would be between UN members if one insisted on maintaining troops in the territory of another by force of arms. On the specific issue of Libya, Bevin wanted his recent proposal to be considered first, but was adamant that in view of what the UK had gone through in the desert he could in no circumstances agree to go one inch beyond what had been proposed by the US delegation in London. Two new twists were added to the problem at this discussion of imperialism. First, Byrnes proposed that Italy should renounce sovereignty, which should be invested in the Great Powers for 12 months, and if during this time they could not agree on the future of the territories then the United Nations should decide. Second, Molotov suggested that if the French plan of giving the colonies back to the Italians was accepted that would compensate Italy for the loss of the whole province of Trieste.[99] In other words, through a communist Yugoslav state gaining at the expense of the Italians, Soviet influence in the Mediterranean would be increased. It was a clear hint that the Soviets were prepared to bargain concessions in order to reach agreement on Mediterranean issues, and it may have reflected the fact that the demands made by the Soviets for an increase in their imperial role in the Mediterranean had been greater than those made by the British in Cyrenaica.

However, as has been seen, British policy had either been linked to one of no concessions involving vital interests, or to no concessions until all demands had been tabled, or to no full tabling of demands because of the danger of spheres of influence deals. Therefore Soviet concessions on the trusteeship of Tripolitania were not likely to produce a positive response from Bevin. Moreover, unbeknown to the Soviets, any British concessions on Trieste were even more unlikely. The day before Molotov's hint of a Tripolitania/Trieste trade off, Bevin had told Byrnes that the Soviets wanted Trieste as a shipping, military and naval base because their purpose was to keep Italy under virtual subjugation by projecting overwhelming power into the Adriatic. In addition, he reminded Byrnes of Soviet desires for bases in the Straits and for a Bulgarian port in the Aegean Sea. Then, cleverly, he outlined a possible scenario of concessions to the Soviets involving a UN base in the Dardanelles with a similar base in the Suez Canal Zone; then, stated Bevin, Stalin would raise the question of the Panama Canal.[100] The message quite clearly was that concessions to the Soviets in the Mediterranean could have unfortunate repercussions in the western hemisphere.

At the third informal meeting on 10 May, the Soviets decided to try and break the deadlock on the Italian colonies by giving up their claim to be involved in the trusteeship of Tripolitania and accepting the French proposal for an Italian trusteeship over the two main areas of Libya; the only difference was that the Russians accepted the American idea of a 10-year time limit whereas the French did not. This immediately prompted Bevin to up British demands in defence of its threatened Mediterranean position with a claim for the trusteeship of Cyrenaica if the Italians were to be responsible for Tripolitania. The reasons given were threefold: the British promise not to return the Senussi, who had supported the British during the war, to Italian rule; the British blood shed in North Africa; and the importance of the region for Commonwealth defence. Bevin explained to Byrnes and Molotov the Dominions' leaders' views on North Africa's importance for imperial security and asserted that Britain could not abandon all control over Cyrenaica. Britain had to have this control because it was an essential link in the chain of imperial communications. The country was 'vital from the point of view of the British Empire' and his colleagues must ask themselves whether their intention was to eliminate that Empire or join 'with the UK in helping to safeguard it'.[101] From the British point of view it was a classic statement of the conditions for post-war Allied cooperation.

Bevin's change of position had to be explained to London, not least because it went against the Cabinet's April policy, but also because it was now more out of step with the Americans. The Foreign Office received a despatch on the change but the Prime Minister was sent a secret and personal message by Bevin along broadly similar lines. The crux of the letter was a passage very revealing of imperialist perceptions of the relation of the Soviet threat to the Empire's position and of perceptions of the American attitudes to the Empire. Bevin explained that Byrnes had shown signs of weakening after Molotov's concession, and once the Soviets withdrew their claim to be in Africa it was obvious that United States interest in collective trusteeship would cease. In other words the Americans were only concerned with preventing the spread of communist influence whereas the British also had to be concerned with their imperial position in the region. Bevin believed Byrnes would therefore support the French and the Russians on Italian trusteeship leaving Britain facing a united tripartite front with no prospect of securing the trusteeship of, or bases in, Cyrenaica. In order to prevent this by clouding the issue and encouraging the Americans to retain collective trusteeship as a possible compromise, Bevin felt forced to put in the British claim for Cyrenaica. A key factor, as he told Attlee, was the situation in Egypt and Palestine where Britain was on the retreat and the implication was that the military abandonment of Cyrenaica, as well as Egypt and possibly Palestine, would be too much.[102]

Initially it seemed that Bevin's tactics would not produce the desired results.

The formal memorandum presented by the Americans, the day before the Council adjourned on 16 May, proposed that Italy should cede sovereignty over Libya for the 12-month period when the colonies would be administered by Italy or one or more members of the United Nations acting as trustees. In other words, as the British realised at the meeting the day before, the French, the Americans and the Russians were prepared to see the colonies under Italian trusteeship, and the Russians did not accept that the British pledge to the Senussi precluded Italian trusteeship as opposed to Italian rule. Bevin's best throw now was to try and get the matter referred again to the deputies.[103] On the other hand Molotov was also in some difficulty over a familiar problem. Soviet concessions might have pleased the French, the Americans and presumably the Italians, but not the British; and if Molotov now backed the British he would be less likely to gain Italian concessions over Trieste and could therefore get no quid pro quo for his original concession over Tripolitania. The latter was clearly his goal, as he reminded the Council 'that the Soviet Government had made a big concession concerning the Italian colonies' and that he hoped 'that this concession was correctly understood'.[104] What Molotov seemed to be hoping for were Western concessions on Trieste and Italian reparations and a quick agreement on the date of the peace conference without further discussion on the position of Romania and Bulgaria. In this he was disappointed because the conference adjourned on 16 May with an agreement to reconvene on 15 June, and the British, in private, were adamant that there would be no bargaining Russian concessions on Tripolitania with Trieste.[105]

Soviet concerns about the way things had developed were made known to the British in early June through Sir Maurice Peterson's meetings with Stalin. The real problem, according to the Russian leader, was that France, Britain and the United States all regarded the Soviet Union as the antagonist. More particularly, Bevin was denying the Russians access to the Mediterranean and, according to Molotov, Soviet concessions had not met with due recognition, which meant the British were denying the Russians equality as an ally. The Ambassador was particularly struck by Stalin's unfavourable contrasting of Bevin and Churchill with the latter deemed willing to accept Soviet access to the Mediterranean.[106] Opinion in the Foreign Office tended to see things from the exact opposite perspective. To one official, Soviet tactics were to keep Britain and the United States out of their orbit while insisting on the right to a say in the affairs of the British orbit. The Russians were portrayed as hoping to detach as many colonial territories as possible from foreign control in order to establish Soviet influence there, which was why Molotov was trying to weaken what he called Britain's monopolistic position in the Mediterranean.[107]

If anything, Cyrenaica became more important to Britain's alleged monopolistic position at the end of May. The Chiefs of Staff, examining the progress of the Anglo-Egyptian negotiations, thought it unlikely that all Britain's peacetime military requirements in Egypt would be met, and Cyrenaica therefore assumed an importance parallel to Palestine as an alternative.[108] Whatever happened, according to a Foreign Office brief, it would be necessary to retain strategic facilities in Cyrenaica, and the sooner agreement was reached the better, because negotiations with the Egyptians were being held up due to the uncertainty over Cyrenaica. Under Britain's proposals, its strategic facilities should be secure, but there could be a problem, according to the Foreign Office, if the Italians got the trusteeship of

Tripolitania. The Foreign Office believed this would be unacceptable to local opinion and the military commanders in the Middle East, felt it would cause resentment throughout the Arab world.[109] Fortunately from the British point of view, when the Council reconvened, whether or not as a result of Bevin's tactics, the Americans reviewed their commitment to collective trusteeship, and the Foreign Office believed that any question of restoring the colonies to Italy was now dead. It was expected that the Americans would be satisfied with something like a Class 'A' mandate for Libya and might be prepared to support Britain on bases in Cyrenaica.[110]

When the Paris Council met again on 15 June the British were only too aware of Molotov using Libya as a bargaining counter for Trieste. The British delegation met on the opening day to consider appropriate responses and to discuss tactics in the Mediterranean battle for imperial influence. As has been seen, with Britain preferring collective or international trusteeship for Tripolitania, rather than Italian trusteeship, Bevin indicated he would be prepared to consider internationalising both Tripolitania and Trieste.[111] This however, began to seem unlikely, as an agreement seemed near by 28 June whereby Italy would renounce sovereignty over its colonies and the Great Powers would be given 12 months to find a solution. The points of difference concerned the Soviet desire for an interim advisory council, whereas Bevin insisted on retaining British military administration in the 12-month interim period, and on not investing sovereignty over the colonies in the four Powers.[112]

By 27 June, Mediterranean issues were being discussed along with Balkan issues. The British were keen to preserve economic opportunities, particularly in Romania, as part of maintaining some British influence in the Soviet sphere. Agreement was reached on the Hungarian treaty and a number of minor issues, including the British acceptance of a Soviet proposal for the disposal of Romanian assets in Allied nations. Then, quite unexpectedly, Molotov made another important Mediterranean concession by accepting that Greece should receive the Dodecanese. The British and the Americans were astonished, and Vandenburg wondered if Molotov was 'building up what he will call Russia's cumulative surrenders (on relatively minor issues) in order to make the world think it is our fault if the Council breaks down over final disagreements on the major issues'.[113] In the event the Council did not agree on completed Balkan treaties before the peace conference but it did produce a compromise on Trieste with the city becoming an international zone. All, however, was not sweetness and light because of the niggling Soviet tactics which produced considerable delay in the issuing of invitations to the peace conference.

When the Paris Council finally ended on 12 July Bevin had successfully prevented any erosion of the British position in the Mediterranean, and although there were considerable doubts over the future of Libya and over the British securing military facilities in Cyrenaica, the Soviets had made all the Mediterranean concessions. Not only could the British take satisfaction from keeping the Soviets out of their sphere, there was some confidence that the other policy goal of avoiding exclusion from the Soviet sphere was within their grasp. On the question of Danube navigation the delegation informed the Foreign Office that it 'never expected that we should do as well on this front as we have done; if we get this we get behind the curtain'.[114] The Soviets may have been difficult and they may have been awkward, but they seemed to be making concessions which offered Britain the prospect of imperial security and global status based on influence throughout Europe and an exclusive area of informal Empire in the Mediterranean and the Middle East.

On returning from Paris, Bevin and the imperial strategists were again confronted with the Prime Minister in the Defence Committee, who showed less inclination to concede over the Mediterranean than Molotov. By then the Chiefs of Staff had produced papers on the strategic position of the British Commonwealth and its strategic requirements in the Middle East. Oil, bases to bomb the Soviet Union from, and the protection of Africa figured prominently as justifications for a continued military presence without which the Soviets were deemed certain to fill the vacuum left by the retreating British Empire. Yet the main point of the strategic argument now seemed to be that the defence of the Middle East was vital to the defence of Britain itself because of the need to reduce the weight of the Soviet attack. Attlee still seemed determined to secure a sensible strategic policy which was not geared to preserving status and prestige but to what Britain could afford, and which emphasised cooperation rather than confrontation with the Soviet Union. Having heard the Chiefs of Staffs' arguments, Attlee concluded that the only reason for being in the Middle East appeared to be preparing for war against Russia.[115]

The other problem for the imperial strategists was ensuring that either Britain's allies or the United Nations agreed to Britain gaining military facilities in Cyrenaica. Jebb believed the UN would be unlikely to grant such facilities, and in the Defence Committee Bevin suggested a possible deal with the Soviets; the Russians might accept a British trusteeship in Cyrenaica if Britain agreed to a revision of Montreux allowing the Russians to close the Straits in time of war. In part this was in response to the latest developments in the Straits issue which involved Soviet proposals for joint control with Turkey. Unfortunately when the Soviets explained exactly what this would entail the British found their ideas unacceptable. They involved the Straits always being open to merchant shipping and to the war vessels of the Black Sea powers; no other war vessels would be permitted except in special cases. The establishment of the new regime would be the responsibility of the Black Sea powers and there would be joint defence arrangements between the Turks and the Soviets. The British found the last two proposals unacceptable because in the eyes of the Foreign Office they would mean the end of Turkish independence.[116] Soviet imperialism was not having much success in terms of British acceptance, even though Soviet demands had now reverted to a revision of Montreux and to joint defence arrangements with Turkey. And of course such Soviet demands were likely to rule out a deal over Cyrenaica where the military remained unconvinced that the Paris agreement would exclude all Soviet involvement in Libya and ensure the British obtained the desired base in Cyrenaica.[117] The hope was that an international regime for Tripolitania would be accompanied by a kind of class 'A' mandate over Cyrenaica for Britain during the negotiation of independence. This remained British policy despite objections by Smuts. Smuts wanted to be more sympathetic to the Italians and allow them a role in North Africa in order to fend off possible gains by the communists who might exploit the ending of Italy's African Empire.[118]

The Paris Peace Conference began on 29 July and lasted until 15 October. It was a gruelling two and a half months with continual haggling taking place over procedural details and the minor points of the treaties. Molotov's stubborn and relentless determination to fight every inch of the way proved intensely irritating to the British and American delegations given that few if any vital interests were now at stake. In the Foreign Office these Soviets tactics were attributed to a need to buy time 'to ensure the hold of their puppets in the iron curtain countries and to complete their arrangements for gearing the economies of these countries completely to the Soviet economy'.[119] With the Conference proceedings made public, it became a forum for propaganda, and in order to speed up its work it was agreed to reconvene the Council of Foreign Ministers from 22 September. The aim of the Conference was to get agreement from most of the 21 nations present on recommendations for the peace treaties that would then be finally concluded at the next Council of Foreign Ministers in New York. It was particularly important to sort out the 26 articles which the Paris Council had failed to agree upon, including the nature of the international regime for Trieste and economic issues concerning the Balkans, where freedom of commerce and navigation on the Danube was probably the most significant.[120]

On the latter question Bevin was insisting on freedom of transit and equal commercial opportunities before the Balkan treaties could be signed; it was in effect a question of trying to secure a foothold in the Soviet sphere rather than protect the British sphere.[121] The agreement on the Italian treaty at least secured the latter, if not the military facilities within it, and by the end of the Paris Conference Soviet pressure on Turkey over the Straits had prompted the stationing of a US fleet in the Eastern Mediterranean as well as Anglo-American diplomatic support for the Turks.[122] There was thus little prospect of the Soviets undermining the British sphere of influence.

The New York Council of Foreign Ministers finally produced agreement on the treaties with Germany's allies on 6 December. It had been a long, hard battle conducted with suspicion and hostility on both sides in the wake of the early 1946 confrontation. In the end all four powers made concessions on various clauses of the treaties, but the ill feeling and long drawn out negotiations did not bode well for the important German and Austrian peace treaties. Who was most intransigent and who most eager to reach a settlement have been subjects of debate, with Molotov's tactics usually provoking the most historiographical criticism. At the end of the day it is not so much who conceded most but who got acceptance of their vital interests which is most significant. The question is in some sense academic, given the de facto spheres of influence that emerged by 1948, but it is interesting, given the goals of Britain's imperial strategists, to compare the exclusive consolidation of Britian's informal Empire with that of the Soviets, even though the position of Cyrenaica remained largely uncertain. The conclusions of the British delegation to New York were unequivocal about the results of the treaties, claiming 'it is clear that we have got more in all the treaties than we had, I think, any right to expect, and further that our interests in Romania have been well safeguarded'. For the Foreign Office the agreements were portrayed (as one might expect) as a real achievement that provided the basis for eventual understanding between East and West.[123] If the British were pleased with the protection of their interests in Romania and the maintenance of their position in the Mediterranean, then one can understand the basis for such pleasure given the policies pursued since Potsdam and the Soviet concessions in the Mediterranean that had ensued. On the other hand, one can hardly imagine the Soviets being pleased with their achievements in the Straits, Libya or Iran. Consequently, it is not hard to see how spheres of influence came to be defined, not by cooperation between imperial powers, but by confrontation. And whatever ideas the British might have had about power, status and global influence, the next five years were to reveal both the intractable nature of the growing confrontation and the nature of the power-political realities that would ultimately undermine British imperial strategy.

Meanwhile there was still the battle with Attlee to win, which became more problematic in late 1946 when the rundown of Britain's foreign currency reserves was first noticed.[124] In the event, as Jim Tomlinson has shown,[125] the detailed costs of overseas military expenditure, as they affected Britain's foreign currency holdings, did not figure in the defence debate, but there was clearly concern within the Cabinet about the level of defence expenditure. In this context the importance of Mediterranean communications, as compared to a line of defence across Africa from Lagos to Mombasa, remained an issue. With hopes still high for the development of this new axis, Attlee argued that the Greek game was not worth the candle.[126] In the Foreign Office officials were clearly concerned that the Prime Minister might be winning the argument on withdrawal from the Middle East and the Eastern Mediterranean. Attlee was already keen to abandon Palestine and the Cabinet was prepared to remove combat troops from Egypt. A minute by Dixon therefore spelled out new arguments against a retreat from the Middle East. Bevin's private secretary accepted that the 'points of friction countries of Turkey, Greece, Persia and to a lesser extent Iraq and Africa are the nub of Anglo-Soviet relations', but he discounted any idea of a neutral zone as suggested by Attlee and Liddell Hart. Britain had to be in the Mediterranean to keep others out and to preserve influence in France and Italy; to abandon it would mean the Russians would get into Africa and arrive at the Congo and the Victoria Falls.[127] For Attlee, however, the determination to remain in the Middle East was a policy of despair which had no positive value, and by the Chiefs of Staffs' own criteria would not succeed because Britain did not have the forces to deter the Soviets, and therefore a continued military presence might even precipitate hostilities.[128]

The culmination of the long-running battle was approaching, and the thought of the loss of prestige associated with an imperial scuttle was driving officials to use the most extreme language. Attlee's ideas on retreat were depicted as another Munich, and a neutral zone in the Middle East as Alice in Wonderland. To attempt an agreement with the Soviets would not work, it was claimed, because Britain was bidding from weakness not strength. There would be a bad effect on Anglo-American relations and a disastrous impact on Europe; war and the massacre of British citizens would be likely and the world would be divided into two blocs. It was clearly not easy to convince officials of the benefits of a retreat from Empire. Dixon's memorandum was discussed by Sargent, Howe, Warner and Hayter before Bevin replied to Attlee. The letter which was eventually sent to the Prime Minister was somewhat different in tone and substance from Dixon's statement and referred more explicitly to the basic idea of the imperial strategists, as defined by Sargent in 1945. There would be a bad effect on the Dominions; India would gravitate to Russia; the Russians were like Hitler and should not be given concessions that could encourage them to believe they could achieve their aims without war; and, no doubt, for Attlee's particular benefit, the UN would be weakened.[129]

Bevin's conclusions were that negotiations with the Soviets on Middle Eastern policy should wait until Britain's strength was rebuilt, but the private discussions were to be continued with the Chiefs of Staff present. This meeting must have been the occasion when, according to Montgomery, the Chiefs threatened resignation and thereby won the Prime Minister's acceptance that the Middle East should remain one of the three main pillars in British defence strategy.[130] It was a great victory for the imperial thinkers: the Middle East was to remain more important than Europe; Africa was to be protected; the Mediterranean position was to be upheld because there would be no concessions to or bargaining with the Soviets when British interests were at stake.

In effect it was the successful culmination of the strategy laid down by Bevin, the Foreign Office and the military, and designed to protect Britain's great power status which was deemed to depend on its Mediterranean and Middle Eastern position. Ever since 1944 when this had come under threat, the Foreign Office had been primarily concerned to conduct Anglo-Soviet relations with this in mind. Preventing any expansion of Soviet influence, whether it be through international cooperation or not, if it threatened to undermine British influence in the Middle East or the Mediterranean was a sine qua non for imperial strategists; this in turn influenced attitudes and policies to Greece, Bulgaria, Yugoslavia and to a lesser extent to other areas of Eastern Europe. At the same time policy was influenced by the need to win the Dominions' support and ensure, for the sake of future strategy, that France was restored to a position in the first rank of global powers from which it could cooperate effectively with Britain. The question was how best to achieve these goals within the framework of continued tripartite cooperation. On this there were conflicting ideas within the Foreign Office which were complicated by the need to consider the views of the military strategists, even though it was clear that the problem of Anglo-Soviet imperial rivalry was essentially a political one. The idea of complete non-cooperation that emerged before the Potsdam conference was over did not win general acceptance at the official level.

Yet it is hard to see how Bevin departed from it in order to compromise with the Soviets on any major issue; what concessions there were were designed to produce the Anglo-American front that was increasingly desired by the British. If concessions were not absolutely ruled out, Bevin decided that there could be no piecemeal concessions: the British would have to stand firm until the whole picture of Soviet aims and ambitions was clear. This may have encouraged more Soviet aims and ambitions, but in any case Bevin's attitudes were based on the assumption that Soviet territorial gains in Eastern Europe entitled the British to maintain their exclusive sphere of influence in the Mediterranean and the Middle East (as opposed to international arrangements), but did not entitle the Soviets to an exclusive sphere of influence in any part of Eastern Europe. There cannot be an exact comparison between the situation in Eastern Europe and the Mediterranean or Middle East, or between the nature of the spheres of influence, but the Bevinite imperialist interpretation of Soviet territorial gains and the position of the British and Soviet Empires came to embody a policy of excluding the Soviets from the Mediterranean while securing British involvement in Eastern Europe. If one assumes that the Soviets had an interest in cooperation and compromise this obviously made both more difficult to achieve.

Tripartite cooperation would have had to have been linked either to spheres of influence arrangements or to international cooperation covering all the important strategic areas of the globe. The Foreign Office specifically considered both these options and ruled out the former for reasons linked to Britain's world standing, although American attitudes would have made its realisation virtually impossible. Unfortunately there was also a view in the Foreign Office that waiting until the whole global picture was clear would inevitably result in some kind of spheres of influence arrangement. In other words, any such strategy, although this was never spelled out, was likely either not to succeed or to prove disadvantageous for Britain.

On the other hand, Bevin was prepared to consider the possibility of some kind of arrangement, but not one in which Britain's vital imperial interests might be compromised. It was therefore not surprising that British policy came to represent firm opposition to short-term concessions and compromises in the hope that, backed by the United States, this would win Soviet acceptance of the exclusive British position in the Mediterranean and Middle East. This policy did not change even when Bevin's belief that the Soviets would make no concessions was proved wrong as Molotov backed down over the Mediterranean and left the British well pleased with the outcome of the Romanian treaty. The imperial strategists had won the initial battle to preserve the British Empire from Soviet encroachment, but they may have undermined the chances of future cooperation be it on spheres of influence or through international arrangements. This may have been the negative outcome of an essentially short-term defensive strategy, but imperial policy makers were also faced with the longer-term difficulty of strengthening Britain's international position by more positive policies based on cooperation with the Empire and Western Europe.

Notes

1. A. Bullock *The Life and Times of Ernest Bevin* Vol. 1 (London 1960) pp. 1–2, 198–205.
2. Bullock op. cit. pp. 435, 439–47.
3. Churchill College, Cambridge, Bevin Papers 3/1 Bevin to Cranborne 1.1.44 cited in Rothwell op. cit. (see ch. 1, n. 42) p. 224.
4. Labour Party's 43rd Annual Conference Report 1944 cited in P. Addison *The Road to 1945* (London 1975) p. 254.
5. D. K. Fieldhouse 'The Labour Governments and the Empire-Commonwealth' in R. Ovendale (ed.) *The Foreign Policy of the British Labour Governments 1945–51* (Leicester 1984) p. 89.
6. Adamthwaite op. cit. (see Preface, n. 3).
7. CAB 104/176 record of meeting 5.9.45.
8. FO371/47883 Clark Kerr to Bevin 6.9.45 reproduced in Ross op. cit. (see Ch. 1, n. 36) doc 42.
9. FO371/53289 General Political Review of 1945 by HM Ambassador in Cairo 15.3.46.
10. CAB 79/38 COS (45) 216th 6.9.45.

11. Ibid. COS (45) 220th 11.9.45.
12. CAB 129/2 CP (45) 162 10.9.45 reproduced *DBPO* Series I Vol. II doc. 33.
13. CAB 128/1 CM (45) 30th 11.9.45.
14. *DBPO* Series I Vol. II doc. 37 10.9.45.
15. The text of the protocol can be found in CAB 21/870 and is reprinted in Ross op. cit. doc. 43.
16. FO371/50915 record of 1st meeting of Council of Foreign Ministers 11.9.45. The relevant British records of the London Council meeting referred to are contained in FO371/50915–50922 and reproduced in *DBPO* Series I Vol. II. The American records are in *FRUS 1945* Vol. II.
17. FO371/50916 record of 4th meeting CFM 14.9.45, *DBPO* Series I Vol. II doc 53, 55.
18. CAB 84/75 JP (45) 251 *aide mémoire* on 'Future of Italian Colonies' 14.9.45.
19. CAB 84/75 JP (45) 251 14.9.45; CAB 79/39 COS (45) 225th 15.9.45.
20. CAB 128/3 CM (45) 32nd 15.9.45.
21. Presumably Bevin meant the Yalta agreement which gave the Russians South Sakalin and the Kurile Islands. *DBPO* Series I Vol. II doc 57. The Cabinet meeting of 15.9.45 clearly forced Bevin to modify his position on the US proposals.
22. FO371/50916 record of 5th meeting CFM 15.9.45; *DBPO* Series I Vol. II Doc. 57; FO800/464 note of conversation at Chequers 16.9.45.
23. FO371/50916 record of 13th meeting CFM 20.9.45; FO371/50917 record of 14th meeting CFM 20.9.45; *DBPO* Series I Vol. II doc. 42, 86, 87.
24. FO371/50917 record of 15th and 16th meetings CFM 21.9.45. *DBPO* Series I Vol. II doc. 94, 95.
25. FO371/47861 minute by Sir O. Sargent 23.9.45; *DBPO*, Series I Vol. II doc. 107.
26. FO371/50917 note of meeting in Molotov's room 22.9.45; *DBPO* Series I Vol. II doc. 97.
27. Ibid. Bevin to Attlee 22.9.45. doc. 105. The Cabinet Office believed that Molotov was right in contending that the Council of Foreign Ministers' decision to extend participation went beyond its terms of reference. FO800/475 note by Norman Brook 6.10.45.
28. This is the argument put forward in R. L. Messer (see n. 60 below).
29. FO371/47861 minute by Sir O. Sargent 23.9.45; *DBPO* Series I Vol. II doc. 107.
30. J. L. Gormly *The Collapse of the Grand Alliance* (Baton Rouge 1987) p. 73
31. This is the argument put forward in M. M. Bull *Cold War in the Balkans: American Foreign Policy and the Emergence of Communist Bulgaria 1943–47* (Kentucky 1984) p. 154.
32. FO371/47861 minute by Sir O. Sargent 23.9.45, *DBPO* Series I Vol. II doc. 107.
33. Ibid. minute by P. Dixon 24.9.45; Rothwell op. cit. p. 239 citing P. Dixon's diary.
34. FO371/47861 minutes by Sir O. Sargent and Sir A. Cadogan; *DBPO* Series I Vol. II docs 107, 109. Bevin to Roberts enc. Attlee message 23.9.45. The State Department representative believed the chief Russian aim was recognition of the Romanian and Bulgarian governments: FO371/50917 minute by Sir R. Campbell 20.9.45.
35. *DBPO* Series I Vol. II doc. 108 record of Bevin/Molotov conversation 23.9.45. It would of course be difficult to find anything more that had been mentioned to the Chiefs of Staff.
36. FO371/50784 minute by Sir N. Charles 20.9.45; FO371/50920 record of Bevin/Molotov conversation 1.10.45. *DBPO* Series I Vol. II doc. 105.
37. FO371/47856 Moscow (F. K. Roberts) to FO 28.9.45; minute by P. Dixon 2.10.45 reprinted in Ross op. cit. doc. 44; FO371/50922 record of conversation between Bevin and Molotov 23.9.45.
38. FO371/47856 Moscow (F. K. Roberts) to FO 28.9.45; minute by C. F. A. Warner

6.10.45 reprinted in Ross op. cit. doc. 44.

39. *DBPO* Series I Vol. II doc. 108 23.9.45.

40. FO371/50920 draft letter to Halifax Oct. 1945; FO371/47856 minute by C. F. A. Warner 6.10.45.

41. FO371/50920 minute by J. G. Ward 18.10.45 recording Dixon's account of a conversation with Bevin.

42. FO371/50795 Heaton Nicholls to FO 6.10.45; Secretary of State to Heaton Nicholls 11.10.45; Secretary of State to Earl Halifax 17.10.45.

43. *DPBO* Series I Vol. II note to doc. 168; minute by Sir O. Sargent, 6.10.45.

44. Ibid. doc. 177 F. Roberts to Bevin 8.10.45 and note referring to telegram to Washington in which Bevin expressed support for Roberts' views on concessions and the Soviets meeting the Anglo-Saxons halfway.

45. FO371/50921 F. Roberts to Sir O. Sargent 27.10.45 reproduced in *DBPO* Series I Vol. II doc. 182.

46. Gormly op. cit. pp. 101, 105.

47. FO800/475 Moscow to FO 29.11.45.

48. *DBPO* Series I Vol. II doc. 265 Moscow to FO 8.12.45.

49. Ibid. doc. 266 FO brief 8.12.45.

50. Ibid. doc. 281 brief for UK Delegation at Moscow 12.12.45; *DBPO* Series I Vol. VI doc. 63 Sir Orme Sargent to Houston Boswall (Sofia) 26.11.45.

51. Ibid. and annex.

52. FO371/57102 record of 1st formal meeting of Moscow Council of Foreign Ministers 16.12.45 reproduced in *DPBO* Series I Vol. II doc. 289.

53. Ibid. record of conversation between Bevin and Byrnes 17.12.45 reproduced in *DBPO* Series I Vol. II doc. 294.

54. Ibid. record of conversation between Bevin and Molotov 18.12.45 reproduced in *DBPO* Series I Vol. II doc. 300. The reference to spheres of influence comes from the US record of the Bevin/Molotov conversation cited by Gormly op. cit. p. 117.

55. Ibid.

56. *DBPO* Series I Vol. II doc. 308 record of meeting between Bevin, Stalin and Molotov 19.12.45.

57. Ibid. doc. 325 record of 8th meeting of Foreign Secretaries 22.12.45; Gormly op. cit. pp. 122–3; P. Dawson Ward *The Threat of Peace* (Kent, Ohio, 1979) pp. 64–5.

58. Harbutt op.cit. (see Ch. 1, no. 29) p. 140.

59. *DBPO* Series I Vol. II doc. 340 record of meeting between Bevin, Stalin and Molotov 24.12.45; doc. 328 minute from F. Roberts to Sir A Clark Kerr 22.12.45; Gormly op. cit. p. 133; FO800/475 minute by P. Dixon 5.12.45; CAB 84/76 JP (45) 276 6.11.45.

60. On the reasons for the American change see T. H. Anderson *The US, Britain and the Cold War 1944–47* (Columbia, Mo., 1981) pp. 103–7; R. L. Messer *The End of an Alliance; Byrnes, Truman and the Origins of the Cold War* (N. Carolina 1982) pp. 31–155; Harbutt op. cit. pp. 152–9.

61. Gormly op. cit. pp. 141–2.

62. FO800/513 record of talk between Bevin, Dulles and Vandenberg 26.1.46.

63. FO371/52327 F. K. Roberts to Bevin 16.1.46.

64. Ibid. note to Foreign Office on memorandum by J. Davies 18.2.46.

65. FO371/57172 note of meeting with Dominion representatives 15.2.46.

66. Louis L'Estrange Fawcett 'Invitation to the Cold War: British Policy in Iran 1941–47' in Deighton op. cit. (see Ch. 2, n. 86) p. 188. See also on the internal situation in Iran Kuniholm op. cit. (see Ch. 2, n. 24) and M. Lyttle *The Origins of the Iranian–American Alliance* (New York 1987); Louis L'Estrange Fawcett *Iran and the Cold War: The Azerbaijan Crisis of 1946* (Cambridge 1992).

67. FO371/59240 draft Cabinet Paper 14.1.46.

68. FO371/59241 A. K. Helm to Bevin 21.3.46; Anderson op. cit. p. 119; FO371/59240 Angora to Foreign Office 27.2.46; minute by Sir Orme Sargent 6.2.46.
69. Harbutt op. cit. pp. 260–1.
70. The idea of a reassessment of Soviet intentions linked to the Russia Committee's establishment is put forward in Smith op. cit. (see Ch. 2, n. 86) p. 37. On the Russia Committee see also R. Merrick 'The Russia Committee of the British Foreign Office and the Cold War 1946–7' *Journal of Contemporary History* 20 (1985). H. Thomas *Armed Truce: the Beginnings of the Cold War 1945–6* (London 1986) p. 734 argues that British policy was produced by Roberts' despatches from Moscow. Thomas accepts that Soviet policy in the Middle East was more disturbing to the British than in Eastern Europe but dates Roberts' first telegram to March. Soviet refusal to withdraw troops from Iran could then be pointed to in order to explain how the British were reacting to Soviet 'behaviour'. This of course is not the whole story and there is no reference to Roberts' January telegram about the clash between Soviet and British imperialism which confirms earlier British attitudes and came before the culmination of bad Soviet 'behaviour' in Iran. For an analysis of Roberts' 'reassessment' despatches see S. Greenwood 'Frank Roberts and the "Other" Long Telegram' *Journal of Contemporary History* 25 (1990).
71. Smith op. cit. p. 38.
72. Greenwood op. cit. pp. 113, 117.
73. For the links between strategic thinking, overseas expenditure and Britain's balance of payments position, see J. Tomlinson 'The Attlee Government and the Balance of Payments, 1945–51' *Twentieth Century British History* 2, 1 (1991) which provides an excellent summary of the 1946 debates in the Defence Committee.
74. CAB 131/1 DO (46) 5th 15.2.46.
75. AIR9/267 memorandum by ACAS (P) 24.2.46 which became an appendix to DO (46) 40 of 13.3.46.
76. FO371/57170 minute by C. Cope 8.2.46.
77. FO371/57171 draft minute for the Prime Minister 9.2.46.
78. FO371/57170 minute by C. Cope 14.2.46.
79. CAB 80/99 COS (46) 43 13.2.46.
80. FO371/57171 minute by Lord Hood 15.2.46; FO371/57172 minute by C. Cope 26.2.46.
81. A. Bullock *Ernest Bevin: Foreign Secretary 1945–51* (London 1983) p. 242.
82. CAB 131/2 DO (46) 27 2.3.46.
83. CAB 79/46 COS (46) 39th 13.3.46; CAB 131/2 DO (46) 47 2.4.46. On the bombers, see Aldrich and Coleman op. cit. (see Ch. 1, n. 46).
84. FO371/57173 minute by O. Harvey 11.3.46.
85. Ibid. minute by G. Jebb 8.3.46.
86. Ibid. minute by Sir Orme Sargent 12.3.46 (emphasis in original).
87. CAB 131/2 DO (46) 40 13.3.46; CAB 131/1 DO (46) 8th 15.3.46.
88. FO371/52346 memorandum by B. M. Liddell Hart 20.3.46.
89. Ibid. minute by J. T. Henderson 29.6.46.
90. FO371/57175 Addison to Bevin 27.3.46.
91. CAB 129/9 CP (46) 165 18.4.46.
92. CAB 131/1 DO (46) 10th 5.4.46.
93. FO371/57176 draft brief for Paris Conference 18.4.46.
94. CAB 128/5 CM (46) 37th 24.4.46.
95. Ward op. cit. p. 126.
96. Ibid. p. 90; FO371/57177 record of 6th Commonwealth Prime Ministers' meeting 28.4.46.
97. FO371/57278 record of 4th meeting of CFM 29.4.46.

98. FO371/57269 record of 8th meeting (1st informal) of CFM 2.5.46.
99. FO371/57270 record of 10th meeting (2nd informal) of CFM 6.5.46.
100. FO800/513 record of talk between Bevin and Byrnes 5.5.46.
101. FO371/57278 record of 3rd informal meeting 10.5.46.
102. FO371/57179 Paris to FO 11.5.46; CAB 120/204 Paris to FO 11.5.46 enc. Bevin to Attlee (secret and personal).
103. FO371/57278 memo by US delegation 15.5.46; record of 17th Meeting of CFM 14.5.46.
104. *FRUS 1946* Vol. II pp. 362–6 record of informal meeting 13.5.46 cited in Ward op. cit. p. 98.
105. FO800/475 Paris to FO British Delegation to Sir O. Sargent 11.5.46.
106. FO371/59242 Moscow to FO 28.5.46; Sir M. Peterson to Bevin 4.6.46; FO371/57273 Sir M. Peterson to FO 27.5.46.
107. FO371/57273 minute by T. Brimelow 31.5.46.
108. CAB 79/48 COS (46) 82nd 24.5.46; FO371/57181 brief for the Secretary of State n.d. June 1946.
109. FO371/57174 FO memorandum on Libya March 1946; FO371/53517 copy of telegram from C in C Middle East to WO April 1946.
110. FO371/57277 record of British delegation (Paris) meeting 19.6.46.
111. FO371/57180 minute by D. M. H. Riches 27.5.46; FO371/57276 record of British delegation (Paris) meeting 15.6.46.
112. FO371/57279 record of 29th Meeting CFM 28.6.46; FO371/57280 record of 33rd meeting CFM 3.7.46.
113. Ward op. cit. pp. 110–11.
114. FO371/57279 Paris to FO 30.6.46.
115. CAB 131/2 DO (46) 47 2.4.46; CAB 131/3 DO (46) 80 18.6.46; CAB 131/1 DO (46) 22nd 19.7.46.
116. FO371/59225 minute by W. Henniker 7.8.46; FO371/57181 minute by G. Jebb 25.5.46; FO371/59226 M. Koukin (Soviet Embassy) to Bevin 8.8.46; FO371/59227 minute by C. F. A. Warner n.d. See also J. Knight 'American Statecraft and the Black Sea Straits Controversy' *Political Science Quarterly* 90, 3 (1975).
117. CAB 128/6 CM (46) 63rd 1.7.46.
118. CAB 129/13 CP (46) 354 23.9.46; CAB 128/6 CM (46) 83rd 26.9.46; FO371/53518 minute by D. Scott-Fox 14.9.46.
119. FO371/57349 minute by C. F. A. Warner 20.8.46.
120. Ward op. cit. pp. 127–46.
121. FO371/57355 record of US delegation (Paris) meeting 2.9.46.
122. FO371/67286A brief for Moscow CFM 28.2.47.
123. FO371/57407 New York to FO 6.12.46. For a more detailed outline of why the Italian and Balkan treaties were regarded as successful see FO371/57414 New York to FO 22.12.46.
124. For details on this see Chs 4 and 5.
125. Tomlinson op. cit. pp. 55–8.
126. FO800/475 Attlee to Bevin 1.12.46; record of Bevin/Attlee conversation 27.12.46.
127. Ibid. minute by P. Dixon 9.12.46; record of Bevin/Attlee meeting 27.12.46.
128. FO800/476 memorandum by Attlee 5.1.47.
129. Ibid. minute by P. Dixon 8.1.47; Bevin to Attlee 9.1.47.
130. On this issue see R. Smith and J. Zametica 'The Cold Warrior: Clement Attlee Reconsidered 1945–47' *International Affairs* 61, 2 (1985).

Chapter 4
Empire and global strategy 1944–46: Implementing an imperial strategy: the Empire and the pursuit of European cooperation 1945–46

The battle within the government over the Middle East and policy towards the Soviets was linked to preserving Britain's imperial position and maintaining its influence in Europe; it was an exercise in holding the imperial line. Yet if Britain's future role as a Great Power was to be strengthened in more positive ways new initiatives would be required, as Sargent had realised in the summer of 1945. In terms of high policy the Middle Eastern conference was one such initiative. In terms of colonial policy there was a sense of confidence and expectation which was to produce many new ideas and initiatives[1] particularly before the imperial crisis of 1947 influenced colonial development and subordinated some aspects of colonial policy to the requirements of the imperial state. The focus for colonial policy makers throughout the period of the Labour government was on Black Africa where it was expected there would be time to implement new policies geared to self-government without undue interference from the international and nationalist pressures that were undermining Britain's freedom of action in South and Southeast Asia. Africa would be the theatre in which the new dramas of constitutional change and economic and social development would be enacted. The attention of British policy makers was undoubtedly focused on the Middle East and Africa rather than on Asia where promises of Indian independence and the inadequacy of British defence provisions were two of the main legacies of the Second World War. In the Colonial Office the expectation was that, as in the immediate pre-war years, the strengthening of Britain's imperial position would involve the pursuit of liberal, progressive colonial policies[2] including the eventual transfer of power which was regarded in the Colonial Office as 'not a sign of weakness or of liquidation of the Empire', but as 'a sign and source of strength'.[3]

In power-political terms Britain's future world position was seen to depend neither on progressive colonial policies nor simply on the preservation of a military presence in the Middle East but on the cultivation of new relations between the Empire and the states of Western Europe. Bevin's and the Foreign Office's rejection of the Churchillian contempt for the post-war weakness of France and the lesser West European states was evident as early as 1945 when the new Secretary of State explained his long-term policy of establishing close relations with the countries of the Mediterranean and Atlantic fringes of Europe as much in commercial and economic matters as in political questions. Bevin's view was that the cultivation of close relations with France would have to be the first step,[4] but in the view of one junior official if Britain could become the leader of a West European Union it would restore its former status of top dog.[5] This link between commercial and other economic ties between Britain, France and Western Europe and the preservation of Britain's great power status had already been made at the official level in July 1945 when policy towards the Soviets was being considered in terms of the same overriding consideration of British world power. It was inspired by Duff Cooper who was to become a key figure in the push for the closer European and African ties between Britain and France that were to form a central element in British imperial strategy. Believing that the French were keen on an Anglo-French customs union, an interdepartmental meeting considered Duff Cooper's request that economic policy should be based on the fact that Western Europe was an area where it was vital for the success of British foreign policy that there should be strong economic ties between Britain and France. The Board of Trade was opposed to a customs union as too ambitious and difficult to reconcile with imperial trading links, but Sir Edmund Hall Patch, the key figure in the formation of Foreign Office economic policy, pointed out that Britain, France, Holland and Belgium, together with their overseas territories, would form a large potential market and a source of many key raw materials. If the World Security organisation broke down it could provide a possible alternative framework for cooperation and if the Dominions joined it would be a very powerful combination. Referring again to the alleged scant consideration given to Britain by the Soviets and the tendency in the US to consider the UK an exhausted and second-rate power, Hall Patch argued that 'if we became the recognised and vigorous leader of a group of Western powers with large dependent territories we would gain that weight in the counsels of the Big Three the need of which has been stressed'. The result was an agreement at the official level on the desirability of a Western European group to secure political and strategic advantages and on economic measures to promote a multilateral commercial system stopping short of a customs union.[6]

Even before the Second World War had ended British officials were thinking of a Western bloc based on economic cooperation which would bring power-political advantages and would be linked to the resources of the colonial Empire. Bevin was more specific in September 1945 when he told one of France's leading politicians, Léon Blum, that he hoped to work for closer collaboration between the British and French Empires involving a common policy for raising the standard of living of the natives. The Secretary of State hoped to arrange for meetings of experts to help solve the various colonial problems and to perhaps build up a kind of joint economic organisation similar to the combined Allied military organisations that had been established during the war.[7] The idea of Anglo-French economic planning was thus, from the start, tied up with the goals of colonial development. Similar developmental ideas were laid down for the Middle East[8] where one role of the newly established British Middle Eastern Office was to offer technical and economic advice and assistance to the countries of the region. Yet the nature of economic development within Europe and the Empire could not fail to be affected by the process of reshaping the post-war international economy in which the United States would inevitably play the leading role.

That post-war American assistance for Britain would be desirable was fully realised in 1945; just as it was also realised that the United States was unequivocally committed to a multilateral trading system in which any discrimination against US exports or imports by imperial trading blocs would be unacceptable. Anti-British imperialists the Americans might be, but their short-term support for Britain's financial position was paradoxically seen as necessary for Britain's long-term economic recovery. Unfortunately American ideas on the post-war economic order were casting a shadow over Colonial Office plans for economic development as early as March 1945. With the aim of bringing greater benefits to African producers the Colonial Office was considering the extension of government sponsored purchasing organisations in West Africa which disturbed the Foreign Office because any unilateral gestures on future marketing organisations would arouse American suspicion and 'create a very bad atmosphere for the Article VII talks' and the possible extension of Lend Lease.[9] When Keynes went to Washington to ask for American financial assistance in the autumn of 1945 Lend Lease had been terminated by the Americans and Britain was faced with a balance of payments deficit of some £2000 million. The subsequent talks in Washington were to last nearly three months because not only did the Americans refuse to consider an outright gift, they were keen to use the talks to remove imperial preferences, dismantle sterling area controls and gain a British commitment to the elimination of other barriers to multilateral trade. Bevin 'felt the most profound reluctance to agree to any settlement which would leave us subject to economic direction from the US'.[10] And Dalton later recorded the existence of dissatisfaction within the government over the loan and its conditions.[11] This resentment at American treatment, and more importantly the dependence it embodied, was to be a crucial factor in the future development of imperial strategy. Paradoxically, at the time it appeared that while there was an urgent need to regain economic independence from the Americans, the imperial options open to the British were at best severely curtailed and at worst ruled out altogether. Thus attention was directed more firmly onto the idea of Western European economic cooperation.

In the Foreign Office the reaction of officials to the Moscow Conference and the conclusion of the loan negotiations in December 1945 was to stress the importance of 'clearing our minds as to where we stand on the Western bloc idea'. Bevin was still nervous, given the American position in particular, of abandoning tripartite cooperation and accepting the idea of the three Monroes; a Western bloc might well antagonise the Soviets and help produce such a situation.[12] Concentration on an Anglo-French treaty and the avoidance of any formal association with other European powers would not create such difficulties. However, the short-term prospects of even an Anglo-French treaty seemed remote given the current political problems in Britain's relations with France over the future of the Ruhr and the Rhineland, and the ill feeling engendered by the crisis in the Levant in the early summer of 1945.[13] Economic links, in particular an increase in British purchases of French exports, would avoid these political difficulties. In January 1946 Anglo-French conversations began on the arrangements to replace the wartime financial agreements which terminated at the end of

February. Despite attempts by the Foreign Office, the Treasury and the Board of Trade refused to grant the French further credits with the result that the British could only stress their willingness to establish the closest possible economic cooperation based on the development of trade between the franc and sterling areas and express a willingness to grant further sterling facilities without requiring payment in gold.[14] This was of course a reflection of Britain's desperate post-war economic circumstances which had produced a Cabinet Paper, written by Keynes, and put forward by Dalton, arguing that Britain's overseas political and military expenditure had already gone far beyond the figure which could, on any hypothesis, be sustained.[15] As has been seen, in 1946 the Foreign Office was not prepared to accept this would require a retreat from the Middle East and expressed general reservations about the thrust of Keynes' paper given Britain's 'inescapable responsibilities' as a Great Power.[16] It was, however, clear that economic expenditure to help the French, for political reasons, was not likely to be acceptable.

As the same time as thought was being given to helping the French, in the spring of 1946 an interdepartmental working party was set up to consider ways of helping Britain's colonial subjects by examining the possibilities of price stabilisation to provide support for colonial producers. The Treasury was in favour of developing colonial production for export and home consumption, subject to any International Trade Organisation proposals, and providing stabilisation was not confused with subsidy and was linked to a general development plan; the Treasury had even been considering a customs union with the colonies in January 1946.[17] Unfortunately the working party broke up in disagreement and the report that was produced only reflected the ideas of the Colonial Office which, in 1946, was committed to a developmental approach that gave priority to the needs of producers. Just as British agricultural policy was designed to provide stability for farmers so the Colonial Office wanted to give colonial producers security of income. It therefore argued for price stabilisation funds, cooperative marketing organisations, initially under government sponsorship, and long-term British government contracts with producers' representatives. Such an approach was rejected in the Treasury because of its potential cost and in the Board of Trade and the Foreign Office because it would produce an immediate conflict with the Americans.[18] Already, British weakness and dependence on the Americans were conditioning colonial economic policy. By the middle of 1947 the Colonial Office approach was to be completely jettisoned in favour of a completely new set of priorities geared to the rather different constraints inherent in greater British weakness and continued economic dependence on the Americans.

In the meantime attention focused squarely on Anglo-French economic relations, partly because of French pressure for greater cooperation and partly because of the continuing confrontation with the Soviets which made it more important to strengthen Western Europe. In May, Bevin mentioned the possibility of using African resources to Bidault, the French Foreign Minister. In July, as Duff Cooper was arguing that only a Europe of states sinking their old differences and linking their policies could restore the balance between the Americans and the Soviets, Hervé Alphand, head of economic affairs in the Quai d'Orsay, was suggesting the economic integration of the British and French economies. Such a far-reaching proposal was instantly rejected by the British whose economic departments were no more committed to far-reaching economic cooperation than they had been in the summer of 1945. In the Foreign Office, as Bidault appealed to Attlee in August for the economic coordination of the two economies, Bevin sat down with officials of the Western Department to consider ways of breathing new life into Anglo-French relations which were still bedevilled by differences over Germany. One way forward appeared to lie in a study of a customs union, another in improving the short-term aid Britain was giving to France.[19] At the same time Bevin wanted a paper put to the Cabinet on the economic possibilities of a Western bloc which drew attention to the *political* need for economic cooperation.[20] The draft paper emphasised the dangers inherent in the division of Europe into two blocs should there be no agreement on the future economic unity of Germany. Its essential point was that if such a division occurred the Soviets would seek to extend their political and economic influence into Western Europe which could only be prevented by economic ties binding the West European countries closer to Britain and centred on Anglo-French cooperation. Such ties would be even more important if the US sponsored plans for a post-war multilateral trading economy broke down because then the importance of Western Europe as a potential market would be increased. Significantly the draft also argued that a deepening of Anglo-European cooperation by ever-increasing mutual concessions would be in breach of the 1945 American loan agreement and therefore if European economic cooperation was to be firmly secured, Britain might well have to opt for a full customs union which would be permitted under the American proposals on commercial policy.[21]

Against this background Bevin met his French counterpart, Georges Bidault, on 5 September 1946 to discuss Anglo-French economic relations. It was agreed that an Anglo-French Committee of Experts should be established to discuss trade problems and to focus on the issues arising from the French reconstruction plan, the French balance of payments problem and French gold payments to Britain. At the meeting Bevin emphasised his desire to have the closest possible economic association with the French, not only with metropolitan France but also with the French Empire.[22]

The imperial element in foreign economic policy had always been part of Bevin's thinking since his inter-war days in a Trade Union movement which had investigated the possibilities of the Empire being used to alleviate Britain's economic difficulties. Bevin had not only been involved with the first Colonial Development Act of 1929 but was the key member of the TUC's Economic Committee which produced a report on Imperial Economic Groups in 1930. In his conference speech which introduced the report, Bevin analysed the First World War and any future conflict in terms of a struggle for spheres of influence and the control of raw materials. Referring particularly to oil, he argued that if this resource was developed in the colonies and mandates Britain would have most of the world's output. Going on to emphasise the general importance of colonial development, Bevin stressed that such development should be carried out through the establishment of an organisation to control the raw materials of the colonial Empire rather than leave them to the tender mercies of private companies. The TUC should therefore aim to put before the Labour Party a proposal for a definite economic organisation within the British Empire and a call for regular imperial economic conferences in order to prevent competition between British products and products from the rest of the Empire. Interestingly, Bevin, as early as 1930, could not discuss imperial economic matters without a political reference to what was to dominate his post-war thinking: the fact that in the crisis of 1930 the British race was not down and out or finished;[23] the Empire would provide a means therefore for the demonstration of British strength and greatness.

As part of the work on its imperial group's paper the TUC's Economic Committee considered Britain's economic relations with the United States and Europe, in an almost exact parallel of the situation confronting Bevin as Foreign Secretary in 1945. A United States of Europe was considered and its advantages compared with a European and a Commonwealth economic grouping and an Anglo-American economic bloc. The conclusion was that the most practical was the economic development of the Commonwealth, although it was made clear that this did not rule out cooperation with the United States or Europe. The latter would have been particularly important for Bevin given his support for a United States of Europe in 1927.[24]

The tendency, in Bevin's thinking, for European links to be supplemented by imperial economic ties was undoubtedly reinforced by the post-war attitude of the Board of Trade to European economic cooperation. As the Foreign Office began to suggest the need for a European customs union, especially if a multilateral trading system foundered, the Board of Trade opposed the idea 'of a purely European body' tackling Britain's long-term economic and industrial problems. It wanted the issue addressed on a global basis because Britain had more important trading links with the rest of the world, especially the Empire, than with Europe. In addition, it believed that the extent of private industry throughout Europe was too great for detailed coordination and that because British economic reconstruction was geared to its export trade it was vital to avoid commitments that would cut across its general export policies.[25] This was to a large extent a restatement of the Board of Trade's view which gave priority to Empire trade and therefore opposed European economic integration because of its impact on economic relations with the Dominions in particular. In a sense the issue for the Cabinet to pronounce upon was whether the political importance of European cooperation could be reconciled with the economic importance of the Empire and if not whether the former should be allowed to override the latter. In the meantime the Foreign Office had to consider ways of reconciling the two, while searching for some positive economic advantages that would accrue from economic cooperation with Western Europe and continuing to emphasise the political requirements of cooperation with the West Europeans.

The Foreign Office paper presented to the Cabinet was completed on 18 October and was largely based on Stevens' draft. It emphasised the importance of close economic ties as a means of preventing the spread of Soviet influence and pointed out that because of the loan agreement forbidding commercial discrimination against US suppliers, European economic ties might have to be a full customs union or Common Market. Bevin therefore wanted Cabinet sanction for an investigation into a full European customs union, an economic regime falling short of a customs union between Britain and metropolitan France, between Britain and the French Union and between Britain and Western Europe including West Germany. In addition, and reflecting Foreign Office priorities in late 1946, the Secretary of State suggested an examination of the colonial dependencies and the

Dominions in a customs union or special regime.[26] The Board of Trade was opposing the proposed study on the grounds of pressure of work stemming from the negotiations for a future International Trade Organisation and the Copenhagen Conference on Food and Agriculture. The Foreign Office therefore suggested farming out part of the study to a number of university economists, but by October there was another economic issue emerging which was bound to impinge upon the proposed customs union investigation. The day before the Cabinet met to consider the latter, Sir Edmund Hall Patch referred to a paper that was being prepared on Britain's balance of payments problems and which would show that Britain was too dependent on North America for supplies. As a consequence, Britain's dollar reserves were being depleted too rapidly and Hall Patch suggested that the remedy may be to draw on the rest of the world more extensively and that perhaps this problem should be considered before examining a European customs union.[27] In line with this, the official meeting to study future Anglo-French economic coordination agreed that the balance of payments working party should examine dollar imports on a product-by-product basis with a view to obtaining alternative sources of supply. In the meantime the Cabinet decided to postpone the customs union investigation until after the French elections, which, if they led to a Communist victory or greater instability, would rule out close Anglo-French economic ties.[28]

Bevin's political requirements in Europe, linked of course to Britain's future position as a Great Power, were not easy to reconcile with the economic requirements of Britain's recovery. At the same time his requirements in the Middle East, again linked to the needs of Britain's world position, were also encountering difficulties. As has been seen, the battle with Attlee was soon to be won, the dispute over Cyrenaica was in abeyance while the Anglo-Russian dispute over the Straits appeared to be going in Britain's favour. In August 1946 when Stalin finally revived the latter issue with a note to the Turks outlining five Russian proposals, the British and the Americans sent messages to the Turks to encourage them to resist such suggestions. The United States also sent more naval units to the Eastern Mediterranean as a further indication of American resolve to support the British and the Turks in resisting Soviet efforts to control the Straits.[29] However, the issue of Russian bases and Russian control over the Straits was intimately linked to the issue of the British base in Egypt and British control over the Suez Canal. With the Egyptians determined to renegotiate the 1936 treaty Bevin and the Cabinet had to devote a considerable amount of time to devising an approach which would be acceptable to the Chiefs of Staff and the Egyptians and ensure that British use of facilities in the Suez Canal Zone was seen to be in accordance with Egyptian wishes and not with the 'security' requirements of an imperial power (as Stalin argued should be the case in the Straits). Given the importance of Britain's Middle Eastern position it was in some ways surprising that the Chiefs of Staff were prepared to accept the principle of evacuation. This was reluctantly conceded in the spring of 1946[30] and combined with the developmental rhetoric of the Foreign Secretary, who waxed lyrical on the subject of a Middle Eastern partnership that would benefit the peasants rather than the pashas.

Some historians have therefore detected a new British approach to informal Empire in the Middle East. Such an approach was allegedly based on a retreat from power linked to the demands of Arab nationalists and to the British desire to treat them on an equal footing.[31] In fact the concessions made by the Chiefs of Staff were reluctant ones justified in terms of the disadvantages of an acceptance of evacuation being less than a commitment to stand firm; this military largesse only arose when it was believed that Palestine would be available and Cyrenaica was likely to be available, and was soon to be reversed in favour of retaining a peacetime military presence in Egypt.[32] In the meantime Bevin, in defiance of the Embassy, the Chief British negotiator and even of the Cabinet, conducted negotiations with the Egyptians in a protracted and stubborn manner with the aim of securing precise British requirements over the reoccupation of the base in times of war and its maintenance in peace.[33] Given the lack of any British operational plans (except to bomb the Soviet Union with bombers that could not return carrying nuclear bombs Britain did not possess) and no precise definition of the base's role in wartime, these demands reflected the political requirement of avoiding anything that could be portrayed as embodying a British retreat from the Middle East and the associated loss of influence in the region. By the winter of 1946 Bevin was faced with the unpalatable fact that these political requirements could not be reconciled with Egyptian demands and concessions would have to be made if agreement was to be reached.[34] In Europe at the end of 1946 it appeared difficult to win acceptance of economic policies that would meet political requirements; in the Middle East it appeared difficult to gain acceptance of strategic requirements that would not bring political disadvantages. These were just the early signs of difficulties that would plague British imperial strategists, however deeply they buried their heads in the sands of decline, as long as they gave priority to preserving and strengthening Britain's position in the first rank of global powers.

The importance of Britain's dollar position in late 1946 was emphasised when Dalton raised it in Cabinet in early November, although he did not refer to all aspects of the growing problem. The Chancellor did however stress that Britain now had to practise a strict economy of imports from hard currency areas and requested an interdepartmental study on increasing exports to these areas and on acquiring alternative sources of imports in Europe and the sterling area. The Ministerial Committee on Economic Policy immediately saw in this an important role for Western Europe which, provided it could recover economically, would furnish supplies for Britain and earn hard currency with which to pay for British exports.[35] Such thinking did not address the problem of what to do *before* Europe recovered if Britain's economic difficulties became acute. Should Britain divert goods and credits to assist European recovery at the expense of exports to the rest of the world? How could Europe recover and pay for British exports if it continued to run a deficit both with the dollar zone and with Britain unless the British or the Americans directly or indirectly paid for West Europe's recovery? This dilemma was to play a central role in conditioning British attitudes to European cooperation. Economic sacrifices might be justified if European recovery could be guaranteed, provided the short-term disadvantages were not too great or if there were continued voices in the Foreign Office emphasising the political advantages that would accrue. If these conditions did not apply then it was difficult to see how Britain could justify closer economic ties with Europe.

The political importance of European cooperation remained joined with the idea of a Western grouping that had originally been linked more to security requirements than to European economic recovery. The issue was considered again within the Foreign Office in December 1946 in terms of the original wartime ideas and on the basis of a paper produced by Assistant Undersecretary Nigel Ronald. The discussion made reference to the importance of linking any such group to the new United Nations Organisation, although the need to maintain international cooperation and avoid alienating the Russians was decreasing in importance as time passed and was to almost disappear by the end of 1947. The crucial question regarding Britain's commitment to a Western bloc, the meeting agreed, was whether the United Kingdom could continue to be one of the principal second-class powers in the world, or must it sink to the status of 'a colonial appendage of an American Empire'.[36] In the event the Foreign Secretary, believing of course that the British race was far from finished, would not even accept the idea of second-class status in 1947 or 1948. The whole question related to the role of the United States in relation to a proposed West European grouping. Should the Americans be involved in or associated with such a grouping that might encourage isolationist sentiments in the United States by giving the impression that the Europeans could manage without American support? In the wake of the French elections that produced a constitutionally appointed government, the Foreign Office considered American reactions to any British attempt to formalise an Anglo-French alliance which would be the first stage of a Western bloc. The Permanent Undersecretary was aware of the danger of reducing American interest in European affairs but argued that if Britain made all its diplomatic moves dependent on US approval it would lose the chance of giving a lead to West Europe 'and we shall never attain what must be our primary objective, viz by close association with our neighbours to create a European group which will enable us to deal on a footing of equality with our two gigantic colleagues'.[37]

At the end of 1946 the question was whether Britain should attempt to give an economic lead to European recovery and the extent to which this should be linked to or preceded by imperial economic initiatives. The concern of the Board of Trade for imperial trading links has been noted; the Treasury's main concern was with the position of sterling that was being threatened by balance of payments difficulties and the dollar shortage. In theory the British could help the French and the West Europeans by purchasing more of their exports thereby reducing the sterling deficit that was causing concern in Paris. Unfortunately there was little that Britain actually needed from the French: wine and silk, two leading French exports, were very much luxury items that were distinctly unhelpful as contributions to Britain's economic recovery. In short the Treasury saw little prospect of making any satisfactory complementary links between British production and that of the West Europeans. The Foreign Office was informed that French officials were 'singularly costive' in informal talks on cooperation. The Treasury's view was that increased trade with Latin America was likely to be more beneficial than increased trade with West Europe.[38] Again it was a question of looking more to non-European areas, and those in the Treasury who were prepared to consider a European customs union were adamant that it should succeed rather than precede similar arrangements with the colonies and Dominions because 'one of the big things in any cooperation with France is the integration of the colonial Empires'. Similar views were later expressed by the economic section of the Cabinet

Secretariat which saw no advantages to be gained from a European customs union as the colonies, the Dominions and the United States offered more valuable export markets. Should the ITO fail, as indeed proved to be the case, the Secretariat favoured a close economic relationship with the United States as Britain could not defend Western Europe and should therefore avoid dependence on it.[39]

The colonial question was of particular importance to a Treasury preoccupied with the position of sterling because of the large sterling balances accumulated by the colonies as a result of the war.[40] Although India was by far the largest holder, the colonies, including Southern Rhodesia, held £800m which was roughly one quarter of the total. The Treasury hoped to 'raid' such balances for Britain's benefit which aroused opposition in the Colonial Office because it ran directly counter to the developmental ethos founded on British assistance for the colonies rather than the other way round. Caine was at pains to point out that the sterling balances had not been acquired as a result of profiteering at Britain's expense because over the 1939–45 period the terms of trade had moved against the colonies, and particularly sharply in West Africa. In the Gold Coast, taking a base of 100 in 1939, exports had risen to 109 by the end of the war, but imports to 209. To cancel the balances acquired in the face of such sacrifices would look extremely odd in terms of development and welfare.[41]

Treasury interest was also directed to a colonial customs union given that under the Bretton Woods agreement Britain and the colonies were accepted as a single monetary area, and the Colonial Office in 1946 was certainly not averse to the idea. Caine pointed out to the Treasury that the loss of customs revenue would require an increase in grants in aid as nearly half of some colonies' income came from customs duties, but revenue could be raised within the colonies from consumption taxes.[42] On the question of involving the colonies in a European customs union (which interested the Foreign Office rather than the Treasury), Caine's view was that, if excluded, the colonies would desire the present preferential treatment to continue; but they would prefer to be included if the customs union enabled them to enjoy the same degree of preference as the French colonies currently enjoyed in metropolitan France. Caine, however, was aware of the likely difficulty that the French territories would not be keen to see the existing favourable situation threatened by British colonial competition.[43] But not everyone in the Treasury was favourably inclined towards an imperial customs union. Sir David Waley was convinced the colonies could not afford such arrangements, and the implication was that the Treasury would not be willing to foot the bill, while the Dominions would be opposed as their priority was to build up their own industry and not serve as the agricultural providers for British economic recovery. As a result some form of economic cooperation, short of a customs union, seemed preferable.[44]

In late 1946 it looked as if, out of all the various combinations of increased and reduced exports and imports to and from the various corners of the globe, the Treasury was favouring increased exports to the dollar zone, particularly Latin America, as the most promising way forward; the Board of Trade simply desired to keep the focus on the Empire as the fulcrum of British trade and had doubts about the short-term prospects of increasing exports to the dollar zone without drastic cuts in exports to Europe and the Empire; while the Foreign Office could only hope that increased trade with Latin America would come from an absolute increase in total trade rather than from the reduction of exports to Europe which were 'vital for political reasons'.[45]

From the Foreign Office's point of view the only positive sign was Cabinet agreement to set up in January 1947 a study of the customs union options by a group of university economists under Sir Denis Robertson.[46] With closer Anglo-French economic cooperation the Foreign Office could make no progress, despite continued French pressure, because of the attitude of the Board of Trade. When Massigli, the French Ambassador, proposed an informal meeting of experts to discuss harmonising the French and British economies in the light of Monnet's centralised reconstruction plan, the Board of Trade resisted, on the somewhat spurious grounds that the customs union inquiry should first be completed and because of the lack of a British equivalent to the Monnet Plan.[47]

The reality was that the Board of Trade was averse to any kind of cooperation which threatened to undermine links with the Empire and expose important sections of British industry to European competition. Its hand was strengthened by the emerging dollar shortage because increased trade with Western Europe ran counter to proposals to increase exports to the hard currency areas unless it was a question of replacing dollar imports by imports from Europe. This seemed to be out of the question because in terms of recovery needs the European economies seemed to be competitors of Britain's, and complementary trading relations seemed more likely to be found within the Empire.

The Foreign Office was not primarily concerned with economic requirements in Europe any more than it was concerned with strategic requirements in the Middle East. Its priority was with policies which preserved or enhanced Britain's world position – cost – benefit analysis did not therefore form part of its imperial strategy which was based on avoiding any appearance that Britain's position in the Mediterranean and the Middle East was being undermined, and strengthening Britain's position in Western Europe with a view to attracting new European collaborators with the British Empire. In both areas the portrayal of the Soviet threat had formed part of the strategy, but whereas the Foreign Office had the 'imperialists' on its side in the Middle Eastern struggle, the two were in opposition over economic links with Europe. In addition it was always easier to invent strategic rationales for maintaining a power-political position than it was to invent economic ones to support foreign policy goals, because economic policies were invariably much more in contact with the realities of British strengths and weaknesses. The strategic rationale for the political requirements of great power status in the Middle East and the economic rationale for the political requirements of European leadership and a Western bloc were not however the only elements of an imperial strategy which had to be reconciled with Britain's post-war economic and military weakness. There were the questions of Middle Eastern and colonial development both of which were designed to enhance Britain's reputation as an imperial power but both of which required the input of economic resources if the political dividends were to be obtained. Whether Britain could produce economic policies that would fulfil the political requirements of formal and informal Empire while also strengthening ties with Europe was clearly open to question by the end of 1946, not least because different government departments had different priorities within Britain's imperial strategy.

Notes

1. For a fuller development of this point see Ronald Hyam's introduction in R. Hyam (ed.) *British Documents on the End of Empire: the Labour Government 1945–51* Vol. I (London 1992).
2. J. Kent *The Internationalization of Colonialism: Britain, France and Black Africa 1939–56* (Oxford 1992) pp. 2–6.
3. Hyam op. cit. p. xxv and doc. 72 CO537/5698 pp. 334–66.
4. FO371/49069 record of meeting to discuss policy towards France 13.8.45.
5. Ibid. minute by S. Hebblethwaite 16.8.45.
6. T236/779 record of interdepartmental meeting 25.7.45.
7. FO371/49069 Bevin to Duff Cooper 21.9.45 giving an account of his meeting with Blum.
8. See Hyam op. cit. p. xxviii and doc. 2 CAB 128/1 CM (45) 38 4.10.45 pp. 2–4 and doc. 7 CAB 128/5 CM (46) 57 6.6.46 pp. 10–14 for ideas on Middle Eastern development.
9. FO371/45886 Sir E. Hall Patch to S. Caine 24.3.45.
10. Bullock *Ernest Bevin* (see Ch. 3, n. 81) pp. 121–3.
11. H. Dalton *High Tide and After, Memoirs 1945–64* (London 1962) pp 74–5.
12. FO371/59951 minutes by F. Hoyer Millar 1.1.46 and Sir O. Sargent 4.1.46.
13. On the Levant and differences over Germany see John W. Young *Britain, France and the Unity of Europe* (Leicester 1984) pp. 3–4, 14–6, 19.
14. FO371/53012 Treasury Overseas Finance Progress Report Feb. 1946. The actual agreement in April 1946 did not, however, do away with French obligations in this respect.
15. FO371/53011 CP (46) 58 8.2.46.
16. Ibid. FO memorandum for the Treasury (approved by Bevin) March 1946.
17. On Treasury views see FO371/53012 and T236/685.
18. FO371/58428 memorandum relating to Working Party on Prices of Colonial Products n.d.; minute by Crowe 30.7.46; minute by Nicholls 30.7.46. One FO official did admit to sympathy for the Colonial Office view and noted that 'objections to giving practical effect in our colonies to the four freedoms came particularly badly from the USA'. minute by Troutbeck 30.7.46.
19. FO371/59963 Duff Cooper to FO 29.7.46; Young op. cit. pp. 71–3.
20. FO371/53007 minute by R. B. Stevens 31.8.46.
21. Ibid. draft Cabinet Paper by R. B. Stevens n.d. The loan agreement stipulated there should be no discrimination against imports from the US.
22. T236/1975 record of Anglo-French meeting 5.9.46; Young op. cit. pp. 40–1.
23. CAB 21/1802 FO note 16.9.47.
24. Ibid.
25. T236/1975 draft note by the Board of Trade 14.10.46.
26. PREM 8/498 CP (46) 386 18.10.46.
27. FO371/53007 Helmore to R. B. Stevens 18.9.46; minute by Sir E. Hall Patch 24.10.46. The 1946 deficit was £298m and the dollar/gold drain £226m Cmd 9585 cited in K. O. Morgan *Labour in Power* (Oxford 1984) p. 511.
28. PREM 8/498 CC (46) 91st 15.10.46.
29. FO371/67286A brief for the Moscow Council of Foreign Ministers 28.2.47. On the Straits issue in 1946 see Knight op. cit. (see Ch. 3, n. 116).
30. CAB 79/47 COS (46) 64th 24.4.46.
31. Wm Roger Louis *The British Empire in the Middle East* (Oxford 1984) p. 8.
32. In March 1947 Bevin decided to stand on the 1946 treaty which meant the peacetime presence of up to 10,000 British troops and the Chiefs of Staff began to argue that a peacetime presence was increasingly important until by July 1948 it was deemed essential. DEFE 5/3 COS (47) 57 17.3.47. FO letter of 2.3.47; DEFE 4/3 COS (47)

53rd 16.4.47; DEFE 4/14 COS (48) 14th 7.7.48, JP (47) 72 1.7.48. See Ch. 5 for more details.

33. On the advice of Stansgate on 1 August 1946 when Bevin was not present, Attlee and the Cabinet agreed to accept the Egyptian draft of Article 2 of the proposed treaty (CAB 128/6 CM (46) 76th 1.8.46), but Bevin refused to go along with this and wrote to Attlee to obtain his support for overturning the Cabinet decision (FO371/53309 Bevin to Attlee 4.8.46) even though Attlee believed Britain would not gain any material benefits from refusing to accept the Egyptian draft. Bevin argued for no more concessions to the Egyptians when the Cabinet met on 7 August and Stansgate had to prolong the talks over Article 2 (CAB 128/6 CM (46) 77th 7.8.46).

34. The final draft was no better from the British point of view than the draft offered by the Egyptians in July. For an indictment of Bevin's policy see FO371/62942 Stansgate to Bevin 8.2.47.

35. FO371/53085 CC (46) 94th 4.11.46 and MEP (46) 10.

36. FO371/59951 N. Ronald to F. Roberts (Moscow) 9.12.46; record of FO meeting 5.12.46.

37. FO371/67670 minute by Sir O. Sargent for Secretary of State 21.12.46.

38. FO371/53085 Sir W. Eady to Sir O. Sargent 20.11.46.

39. T236/779 minute by R. W. D. Clarke 4.10.46; PREM 8/498 note by the economic section of the Cabinet Secretariat January 1947.

40. On the question of sterling balances see A. Hinds 'Sterling and Imperial Policy 1945–51' *Journal of Imperial and Commonwealth History* Vol. 15 no. 2 (1987) and 'Imperial Policy and Colonial Sterling Balances 1943–56' *Journal of Imperial and Commonwealth History* Vol. 19 no. 1 (1991).

41. CO537/1378 S. Caine to Sir D. Waley 2.3.46; note for Creech Jones 1.7.46.

42. T236/685 S. Caine to E. Rowe-Dutton 28.8.46.

43. FO371/53007 S. Caine to J. Troutbeck 2.10.46.

44. T236/779 minute by Sir D. Waley 23.10.46.

45. FO371/53085 Sir O. Sargent to Sir W. Eady 3.12.46.

46. Alan S. Milward *The Reconstruction of Western Europe 1945–51* (London 1984) p. 241.

47. FO371/67686 minutes by Sir O. Sargent 23.12.46 and 5.1.47.

Chapter 5
Drowning Europeans clutch at African straws, 1947

The attempt to reconcile the conflicting elements of imperial strategy with its various geographical regions and its economic, strategic and political requirements was to produce in 1947 an enormous but short-lived interest in the African continent. British elites seemed mesmerised by the prospects it appeared to offer of providing for British military and economic needs while also serving to strengthen links between Britain and Europe. In short, it provided an imperial dimension to a European economic policy which was making little progress towards meeting British economic needs but was deemed essential for political reasons if the Europeans were going to be installed as collaborators with the British Empire. Africa thus came to be seen as vital for British recovery and for preventing Britain being overshadowed by the United States and the Soviet Union.

The alleged strategic and economic potential of Africa had been vaunted in the Defence Committee during 1946 when the idea of a Lagos to Mombasa trunk road, or rail link, had been mooted. For Attlee the idea was to use such an axis to form a new line of defence across Africa and on to the Persian Gulf and the Indian Ocean; for Bevin the idea was to facilitate African development, which could perhaps provide the resources to support Britain's continued large-scale presence in the Middle East, and to provide strategic benefits as a back up to the forward defence position in the latter region. The development of such an axis, based on land communications, was studied by an ad hoc Cabinet Committee whose proceedings are not only still closed but the records of such a study's existence have, along with many other named and withheld files, been deleted from the Public Record Office indexes. The Committee received information from intelligence sources, the Joint Administrative Planning Staff and the Colonial Office. Five possible routes were examined starting from different points in West and Central Africa. The four most northern routes would require large-scale road construction and some would also be dependent on river transport; it appeared that the costs of manpower and the movement of stores along the route would be out of all proportion to the results obtained as some 17,000 drivers and maintenance personnel would be required to deal with 10,000 lorries transporting stores and equipment. The southern routes would start at Benguela and use the existing railway so that a single-track line could be provided, but the conclusion was that the strategic benefits would not justify the costs. Therefore unless there were significant commercial advantages to be obtained the routes would be deemed unsuitable.[1] Yet military eyes were to remain on the Empire because the CIGS, Field Marshal Bernard Montgomery, was, at the end of 1946, convinced that his first requirement as the head of the army was a strong, well prepared Commonwealth which would display a strong and resolute national character. Technical and scientific research would also be important for the military along with small, regular forces and the sending of troops to the Continent was deemed virtually useless by Montgomery (but favoured by Ismay) against a Soviet enemy with unlimited manpower.[2] The CIGS was later to change his mind about Europe, at a time when he was also attaching greater significance to Africa; it was to be an interesting shift, which, while linking Africa to Europe, came to focus more on European military cooperation as the economic focus of imperial strategy was increasingly on Africa.

At the beginning of 1947, Duff Cooper was becoming increasingly frustrated by the apparent failure of his efforts to consolidate Anglo-French links and produce a formal Anglo-French treaty of alliance. The Ambassador in Paris had received a memorandum from the Consul General in Lyons, Robert Parr, who during the war had been Consul General in Brazzaville. Parr's eccentric habits and his wartime determination to support Free French views had not made him popular in the Colonial Office or Nigeria because his ideas on colonial policy and cooperation with the French in Africa were somewhat at odds with official thinking.[3] His African experiences convinced Parr that Europe's future lay in cooperating to develop the resources of Africa, and he believed this would require a fundamentally different approach from that of the Colonial Office. Territorial changes would be necessary to create a single administrative unit covering the whole of Black Africa from Dakar to Mombasa and from the Tropic of Cancer to the Zambezi. The British and French Colonial Offices had resumed their efforts to cooperate in African policy at the end of the war but cooperation had been limited to technical aspects of development; Parr saw this as merely the beginning of a grandiose scheme which would provide much needed political and administrative lessons for those eager to pursue cooperation in Europe and bring enormous economic benefits for Africa.[4] Duff Cooper, almost certainly inspired by Parr's ideas, wrote to Bevin in order to emphasise the advantages of pursuing a policy of European cooperation in Africa. He argued that cooperation with the French would be easier outside the 'narrow divisions and traditional animosities' of Europe, and that in Africa both Belgium and Portugal would be eager to play a role. 'If the Western democracies working in harmony together developed Africa as it might be developed, integrated the now divided territories in an African union under European guidance, a political unit would emerge which would not fear comparison either in transport or in agricultural and mineral resources with either the United States or the Soviet Union . . . It is more feasible and presents fewer difficulties than does the idea of a United States of Europe.'[5]

The Foreign Office, as a result of the 1946 conflict with the Treasury and the Board of Trade, was preparing to urge British exporters to devote the highest priority to Latin American trade but in the hope that as far as possible exports to hard currency areas should not be at the expense of those to soft ones; it was also looking to Middle Eastern oil output as a possible future solution to the balance of payments problem rather than to colonial development in Africa. Bevin, however, was already keen to discover what raw materials the colonies contained which were needed by the United States.[6] Concerned by Britain's dependency on the United States, which had been so apparent in 1945, the Foreign Secretary was searching for some sign of American dependency on Britain. As problems with European economic cooperation grew through 1947 and finding ways to eliminate Britain's dependency on the United States (that the dollar deficit embodied) became more urgent, Bevin's support for some kind of Euro-African cooperation increased. He was soon to show a much greater interest in the details of Anglo-French imperial ties than that indicated by his general comment to Blum, that close cooperation between the British and French Empires formed one of the three main pillars of British foreign policy.[7]

In the early months of 1947 the Anglo-French Economic Committee's meetings had been added to by a meeting of colonial officials to discuss economic development and price and marketing questions in Africa.[8] British ideas in both areas centred on the exchange of ideas and information, rather than moves towards integration or common policies. Consequently there was little prospect of having combined programmes for either the colonies or Europe – let alone both. The Colonial Office was to continue with the bulk purchasing schemes at fixed prices in West Africa which had begun during the Second World War and which were in no way compatible with French ideas on pricing and marketing policy.[9] However, it is unlikely that knowledge of such practical difficulties became available to the Foreign Secretary who discussed African cooperation with the French President, Vincent Auriol, in the spring of 1947. The latter mentioned the importance of African development in response to Bevin's proposed Western union based on bank, currency and other economic arrangements.[10]

There was, however, a problem with overseas development which the Treasury made clear in March 1947. Its memorandum spelled out British priorities in terms of the resources that could be made available following a disastrously harsh winter in the first three months of the year. The abnormally cold spell had brought industrial production grinding to a halt because of fuel shortages in the wake of large demands on coal production. In such circumstances the Treasury pointed out the needs of the home market for capital and consumer goods and the importance of giving priority to paying for imported food and raw materials. Britain's limited financial resources should then be diverted to liquidating some of the country's overseas liabilities vis-à-vis the sterling area. Treasury concern for the position of sterling made it particularly averse to any expenditure on Middle Eastern development, an attitude no doubt encouraged by the significant sterling balances held by countries there which were technically independent. Pointing out the other pressing claims of the armed forces and colonial development, the Treasury memorandum stated that 'until 1951 it must be assumed that there would be no additional help for the Middle East beyond those limited resources released out of sterling balances; and even these could only be used for development if import controls were employed to make sure that sterling releases did not finance an adverse balance of payments account'.[11] Here was the appearance of one of the main constraints on British policy overseas in the post-war period – the need to prevent the sterling area as a whole producing a deficit with hard currency areas that could affect international confidence in the pound.

The winter of 1947 had a more immediate effect on Britain's balance of payments by contributing to a loss of approximately £200m of exports in the run up to the April budget.[12] As the American loan was then rapidly being used up on the balance of payments deficit, British exports to the United States barely exceeded in value Britain's consumption of Virginia tobacco.[13] Already the colonies were appearing as a possible source of assistance if not salvation. In March the Colonial Secretary wrote to the Prime Minister outlining the idea of a Colonial Development Corporation which was being considered by the Colonial Economic and Development Council. The Corporation should 'promote in every possible way increased colonial production on an economic and self-supporting basis with an eye to the production of foodstuffs, raw materials and manufactures whose supply to the UK or sale overseas will assist our balance of payments'.[14] The colonial territories, unlike the Middle Eastern states, had the great advantage that imports could easily be controlled by the British and increased colonial exports would not therefore produce a sterling area deficit by sucking in imports. Just as Bevin's ideas of working with the masses rather than the privileged classes fell foul of Britain's old fashioned strategic and power-political requirements in the Middle East, so the idea of Middle Eastern development met the same fate because old fashioned economic imperialism, based on the increased extraction of foodstuffs and raw materials in colonial territories with import restrictions, was more suited to Britain's economic needs in the spring of 1947.

The process by which this imperial strategy gained acceptance in the Labour government was extremely ironic, and illustrative of a decision-making process that was not based on full Cabinet deliberations nor even on discussions in key committees where all the relevant facts were presented to ministers; it also involved a great deal of lobbying, persuasion and even bullying on the part of Bevin and leading officials who had contact with the Prime Minister on an ad hoc basis. Thus in the key January 1947 meetings about the fundamental nature of Britain's Middle Eastern role, Bevin argued with Attlee for an exclusive and expensive British presence as the region would be commercially vital, and not just because of oil but because of the development of the Middle East as an export market and as a replacement for the food supplies which had formerly been obtained from India.[15] Yet Middle Eastern development was ruled out because Britain did not possess adequate resources; and one of the reasons for this was the large diversion of financial, material and other productive resources into defence expenditure centred on Britain's Middle Eastern role.

The financial aspects of defence expenditure had been a source of controversy in the Defence Committee throughout 1946 where the crux of the issue was whether Britain's 'responsibilities' and great power role should be maintained in the wake of the financial difficulties that made the maintenance of large forces extremely problematical. Those opposed to radical cutbacks, led by Bevin, always argued that economic recovery could be achieved provided Britain's world role was maintained; if it were to be abandoned then this would make it difficult if not impossible to revive Britain's economic fortunes. Those in favour of cuts had to argue that the country simply could not afford to spend such amounts because it would prevent the desired economic recovery. Or as Dalton put it, what good would it do to spend nearly £1000 million on an army of over a million if 'we come an economic and financial cropper' within two years?[16]

By April 1946 Attlee, having initially insisted that by the end of 1947 the armed services must be reduced to 1.1 million men, was protesting that he could not see how the country could afford more than a million service personnel. Defence expenditure of £1736m in 1946 represented 20 per cent of GNP, and although this would fall substantially as a result of demobilisation in 1947, Dalton wanted peacetime expenditure reduced to £500m not the £750m being proposed. On the other hand, there was the danger, of which Attlee was no doubt aware, of repeating the Labour errors of the 1930s when resistance to high levels of defence expenditure produced all sorts of allegations. The Prime Minister did not want Britain to abandon all its responsibilities and therefore did not support Dalton's more radical cuts in 1946. At the end of that year, however, with his belief that the Middle East was an 'outpost', Attlee was opposed to the commitment of forces to Greece. It was part of his attempt to use Britain's resources more sparingly and only to secure what were essential British interests. Yet after his January conversion to an imperial defence strategy centred on the Middle East, at the Cabinet Defence Committee meetings in January Attlee gave Dalton no support for his proposed 10 per cent cut when the 1947–48 Defence estimates were considered. The Chancellor argued that Britain could not afford the defence expenditure proposed and claimed the 10 per cent cut was an essential measure if the balance of payments deficit was to be reduced.[17]

The decisions taken in early 1947 were a milestone in terms of Britain's future economic and military strategy linked to the presence in the Middle East of British forces and the preservation of great power status. Of course Britain also had substantial military commitments in other areas of the world, notably in the occupation of Germany and in Trieste, which was still a source of great power conflict. Yet in 1947–48 Middle Eastern expenditure, as a percentage of the War Office budget was seen to rise from one third to one half.[18] It has often been suggested that in the face of the constraints produced by the economic crisis of 1947 Britain began to cut its imperial coat according to its post-war cloth. The decision to leave India was formally announced in February 1947, in the same month that Britain announced the referral of the Palestine problem to the UN and while the transfer of the major responsibility for Greece and Turkey to the United States was taking place. In fact, these decisions were taken before the extent of the financial crisis became fully known in 1947, and the decisions to adopt a Middle Eastern based defence strategy and *not* to make radical defence cuts were more important for Britain's imperial strategy and more indicative of the attitude of the Labour government to its future development. Such attitudes of holding on whatever the short-term cost were reinforced by events in Egypt.

At the end of 1946, after a protracted wrangle which undermined the domestic position of the Egyptian leader, Sidky Pasha, who was portrayed as too weak to stand up to the British, agreement was finally reached on the conditions that were to be attached to the British withdrawal from Egypt, the maintenance of the base in peacetime and its reactivation in war. The agreement on the new treaty to replace that of 1936 also contained a protocol recognising 'the framework of the unity between the Sudan and Egypt under the Common Crown of Egypt', but asserting the right of the Sudanese to determine the future status of the Sudan.[19] In order to strengthen his domestic position, Sidky publicly portrayed the agreement as enabling Egypt to acquire the Sudan. Fearing disturbances in Khartoum which could threaten British influence there, the Labour government felt obliged to make a statement rejecting Sidky's deliberate misinterpretation of the protocol's meaning. This sealed Sidky's political fate and with him in December 1946 went the immediate prospects of an Anglo-Egyptian defence agreement.[20]

In March 1947, at the end of the harsh winter, Bevin decided to stand on the 1936 treaty which gave Britain the right to maintain forces in Egypt in peacetime.[21] Thus while the initial acceptance of withdrawal from Egypt in 1946 had been linked to the British belief that alternative facilities in Palestine and probably Cyrenaica would be available, the withdrawal from Palestine became acceptable in 1947 because Britain intended to remain in Egypt and to secure facilities in Cyrenaica. Furthermore, not only did the Chiefs of Staff reverse their previous decision about the withdrawal of British forces from Egypt, they then insisted that revised assessments of the nature of a Soviet attack on the Middle East required the deployment of a peacetime garrison. By 1948 the size of the proposed garrison was still far in excess of the numbers permitted under the 1936 treaty.[22] Therefore although Attlee had managed to defeat the 'imperialists' over India, in that crucial area of concern to the defenders of the Empire, the Prime Minister had been forced to abandon his customary realism. It was not a retreat but a redeployment of British strength involving a decision not only to defy the Egyptians who were opposed to the British presence, but also military requests that the terms of an international treaty should be ignored by the British government. Moreover, the logic of Britain's strategy, which was to underpin the management of decline for at least the next decade, had been revealed: British economic resources would be used in the Middle East to create a market and a source of raw materials that would be of economic significance for the future, yet Britain did not have the resources to do this. However, because the development of economic links with the region was deemed so important, Britain had to retain its influence, and therefore its military presence in the Middle East. Thus the arguments of the cost reducers were defeated on the grounds that the military expenditure had to be incurred to ensure the economic benefits of development produced by resources Britain did not have, and was unlikely to acquire while high levels of military expenditure were maintained. To accept this, however, would have been to accept the loss of great power status.

All this was of course connected not to the realistic management of decline but to the fending off of decline, and in 1947, as in the immediate post-war years, to the reestablishment of British influence. In this context, the lack of realism in British policy makers is often excused on the grounds that British leaders could not have been expected to abandon the traditional assumptions about the value of a great power role especially in the wake of the victories of 1945. In addition British leaders, driven by the logic of their own and the nation's position, had what amounted to a duty to find ways of maximising British influence and to avoid the humiliating acceptance of second-class status. In short it was beyond the capacity of the governing elite to throw off the weight of British history and come to terms with the enormity of the post-war changes that, in retrospect, clearly constrained the fulfilment of great power aspirations. Yet there were voices in the wind which not only understood the nature of the British position but were prepared to advocate radical new approaches, indicating that it was not a question of being able to grasp the idea of a rapid retreat from great power status, but of finding it unacceptable for reasons which are essential to an understanding of Britain's post-war imperial role.

In May 1947 a Treasury official argued along the following lines:

> My basic thesis, which I do not think you accept is that any foreign policy of a great power type is at present a very doubtful luxury for the UK. Any such policy requires examination on strict Treasury lines. All activities of foreign policy should at present be concentrated on saving us from bankruptcy and improving our economic position . . . Strategic responsibilities should be off-loaded onto the US or where this cannot be done re-examined to make sure they are really necessary . . . Assertion of political predominance seems positively dangerous'.[23]

Such radical views were emerging when the British economic departments were having to consider relations with Europe and the Empire in the context of the developing crisis of 1947 which posed more acute problems for the Foreign Office strategy of using economic policy to help gain political influence.

Relations with the French had improved dramatically in political terms with the signing of a defence treaty in March 1947 (Treaty of Dunkirk), but new economic problems were appearing. In the wake of the 1946 discussions which resulted in the French having to pay on normal commercial terms for goods purchased within the sterling area, French exports to the UK had, out of necessity, increased, in order to fund sterling imports. The result was that France's visible trade with the UK was approaching a surplus. Not only were the French selling goods which by and large were luxury items, but if the trend continued the French surplus could be exchanged for dollars as soon as convertibility was restored in the summer of 1947 when Britain would have a greater need for hard currency. This was precisely what happened, and by July 1947 the French surplus with Britain was £65 million despite a predicted deficit with the rest of the sterling area. Such problems were bound to focus more attention on non-European areas as a remedy for Britain's economic difficulties. If both Britain and France were seeking to improve their balance of payments problems, ways had to be found which would prevent this being done at the other's expense; this was certainly what the Board of Trade was insisting on discussing *before* any attempts were made to move towards closer economic integration. Otherwise, in its view, Britain would continue selling the French goods, which could have been made available against dollars, in return for imports which were over-priced and dominated by non-essential items.[24]

The question of European integration was being considered with greater urgency in the spring of 1947 because the Council of Foreign Ministers was finally concentrating on the German peace treaty; if agreement could not be reached then Germany and Europe would effectively be divided. The Moscow Council began on 10 March and lasted until 25 April, provoking in some sections of the Foreign Office a number of thoughts on the implications of the division of Germany for Britain's approach to European cooperation. For one official it reinforced the need to consider the political advantages of supporting France economically; this would provide encouragement for the resistance of communism by the French which would be more important if no agreement was reached on Germany.[25] At the same time, while Britain was still committed to the idea of achieving tripartite cooperation (albeit on Britain's terms), Bevin did not want to take too many steps towards a West European bloc because of the danger of the Russians perceiving such an organisation as essentially anti-Soviet. Yet some Europeans were expressing greater interest in closer links with Britain. Spaak, the Belgian leader and committed Europeanist, enquired in March if Belgium could be associated with the Anglo-French treaty.[26] The Foreign Office was of course keen on the principle of such a West European grouping, but not keen on the timing. The need to avoid antagonising the Soviets by a Western bloc while efforts were being made to secure agreement on a German peace treaty was accompanied by the old fear that such a grouping might encourage American isolationism by giving the impression that the Europeans could fend for themselves and would not need US assistance in dealing with the German situation;[27] this would be doubly dangerous if it coincided with the antagonism of the Soviet Union. As long as the Moscow Council of Foreign Ministers was in session the British could easily put off the Belgian enquiries; after that date it would be more difficult.[28]

One interesting aspect of British policy at this time concerned the Foreign Office argument that a divided Germany would make West European economic, and indeed other, links more vital. Yet British policy towards Germany was definitely one of endorsing its division because 'the achievement of economic unity on other than our own terms will be extremely dangerous and costly'. Britain, however, needed to produce a reasonable plan for economic unity to ensure the onus for dividing Germany was placed on the Russians.[29] Another interesting development was that Stalin, in response to Bevin 'making it clear' that Britain was going to retain its presence in Egypt in accordance with the 1936 treaty and that the whole of the Middle East was a British sphere of influence, repeated his December 1945 assertion that the Soviet Union had no intention of interfering with British policy there.[30] It was another example of how the British were determined to secure their own sphere of influence which could only have contributed to, or reinforced, Stalin's eventual strengthening and extension of his own area of control east of the Western zones in Germany. At the Council sessions, the Soviets, according to the British, moderated their position by accepting a greater degree of decentralisation in their constitutional proposals for Germany and a higher level of steel production on the understanding that it would allow for reparations from current production;[31] this was not, however, easily reconcilable with the British determination to ensure export proceeds should be used first to cover German import costs, which in the British zone, constituted a considerable drain on dollar resources. The Soviets were also insisting on four-power control of the Ruhr[32] and it appeared that no agreement on British terms could be achieved; the economic costs and political dangers of a united Germany falling prey to Soviet influence were far too great for any compromise to be acceptable. This failure to agree on Germany's future was to have an impact on British policy towards Western Europe and its links with the rest of the world when the next Council of Foreign Ministers in December also failed to break the deadlock and no date for a future meeting was set.

Bevin's thinking on Western Europe in the spring of 1947 reflected a determination to avoid the surrender of sovereignty that would be necessary if a United States of Europe was to be established. The Foreign Office was interested in a regional grouping of West European states for general cooperation in social, political and military matters with what was referred to as a European Economic Commission for reconstruction and development and the closer integration of the European economies.[33] In April there was still uncertainty about the future of Germany and the customs union study group had yet to report. After the Moscow Council it seemed almost inevitable that Germany would be divided and the need, always at the back of British and American minds, successfully to incorporate the Western zone of Germany into Western Europe would assume greater significance. As part of this growing trend the US Secretary of State, George Marshall, made his famous announcement in June 1947 which offered the prospect of American financial aid for Europe's economic recovery and which had enormous implications for Britain's European policy which would clearly require consideration.

By the summer of 1947 there were several more signs, apart from the problematic nature of economic links with Europe, that the Empire, and Africa in particular, would have to be involved with European cooperation. The Belgians were now involved in the programme of technical cooperation in Africa[34] and the Foreign Office were also keen to involve the Portuguese.[35] Duff Cooper had reinforced his earlier call for African cooperation which would not only improve conditions in the colonies and consolidate Britain's position there, but provide 'among the countries of Western Europe a new community of interest' that would reinforce 'the closer association of those countries which it is our aim to achieve'. The Ambassador saw the African cooperation in technical matters as an excellent foundation on which to build.[36] Then there was the vital importance of uranium from the Belgian Congo (70 per cent of world supplies), which the British had managed to get a share of before the McMahon Act,[37] and which became more important after the January 1947 decision to create a British atom bomb 'with the bloody Union Jack flying on top of it'.[38] In the wake of the Moscow Conference, when the Belgians could no longer be fobbed off, Bevin wanted discussions with the French on a Belgian treaty and proposals put to the Cabinet. Before that, however, the Chiefs of Staff should be asked to consider such a treaty, not just from the point of view of its European implications, but from the point of view of Africa's strategic importance and the raw materials it contained.[39] Bevin was now becoming more and more convinced that the United States lacked many raw materials, like uranium, which could be found in colonial Africa.

One day after Marshall's speech the Colonial Secretary was submitting a Cabinet Paper on the basis that colleagues were already aware of the importance of increasing production in the colonies. The balance of payments deficit had transformed Colonial Office priorities from benefiting producers through price and marketing arrangements to increasing production for the alleged mutual benefit of Britain and the colonies. The Colonial Development Corporation was awaiting approval, and a Colonial Primary Products Committee had been established to review commodity by commodity the possibilities of increasing colonial production with regard to the interests of the Empire and of the foreign exchange position. The Colonial Office was also proposing an interdepartmental committee 'to provide for regular consultation with the Ministry of Food, the Board of Trade, the Ministry of Supply and the Treasury, so that full account can be taken of the needs of this country for physical supplies and of the possibilities of improving the balance of payments position'. This committee would keep in touch with the operations of the Colonial Development Corporation and give it guidance on major matters of policy. The Colonial Secretary did point out that the Colonial Development Corporation would not be limited to expanding supplies of food-stuffs and raw materials, but would have the opportunity of developing other industries where these showed promise of being remunerative and of benefiting the colonies or the UK.[40] Nevertheless these developments were bound to build up hopes that the colonies, particularly in Africa, could provide a solution to Britain's difficulties, and it was in the summer of 1947 that Parr's memorandum was passed to the Colonial Office.

As the convertibility deadline of 15 July approached, Bevin took further steps to find a solution to the problem which he defined as meeting loans without endangering Britain's foreign exchange position or cutting living standards. He set up a Foreign Office investigation into all the essential raw materials in the colonies which the Americans were short of, with the aim of 'having a policy to feed our industries and produce raw materials in short supply in the United States in order that instead of being supplicants we can develop a position independent of the United States'. Emphasising raw materials avoided any competition with American manufacturers. Moreover Bevin feared that by pushing manufactured goods into the hard currency areas Britain might risk 'another form of collapse' because the home market and the soft currency areas would not be consuming British goods and the hard currency nations might become a bottleneck.[41] In other words the balance of payments problem would be solved through raw materials from the Empire and not solely from the exports of British industry. The minute received the general agreement of the Prime Minister and also of the Colonial Secretary. The latter accepted the importance of paying for British imports through colonial currency earnings and of meeting the supply needs of the home market, but did not want to confine development to areas which met British requirements. It was part of the Colonial Office's policy of accepting the essential thrust of economic strategy while endeavouring to broaden it so that the benefits to the colonies would be maximised as the push for increased production gathered pace.[42]

As attention began to focus more and more on the anticipated economic benefits from colonial Africa, the strategic and power-political importance of the Middle East was also being reinforced in the minds of imperial strategists. Not only was it defined as one of the three pillars of British defence policy, but as the area where Russian expansion would be easiest and would hurt Britain most. The defence of the Middle East would therefore be the army's primary task in war and more important than defending Britain from an airborne attack because retaliation from Middle Eastern bases against the Soviets (particularly nuclear weapons and long range bombers were acquired) would be essential if the weight of the Soviet assault on the West was to be reduced and the defence of Britain thereby ensured.[43] Meanwhile, at the Labour Party Conference Bevin was endeavouring to impress on the party what he had told Stalin the previous month and what had been central to his and to the Tory imperialists' thinking since 1945. Referring to the sugges-tion of one comrade that the Middle East should become an international responsibility Bevin replied that 'I am not going to be a party to voluntarily putting British interests in a pool and everybody else sticking to his own. The standard of life and the wages of the workmen of this country are dependent upon these things.' (Here was a good indication of how in one respect the Labour imperialists differed from their Tory counterparts.) 'Why should Great Britain be the only country to hand over?' Bevin demanded. 'Many of these other countries have great resources internally. Is everything to be put into an international concern or is it this one place because part of it belongs to Britain?' (Here was an indication of Bevin's concern about Britain's lack of resources compared to the United States and the Soviet Union.) Bevin also referred to the strategic value of Egypt and its treaty links with Britain which he claimed had prevented Hitler and the Japanese from joining up in the Second World War. Then there was the oil which could save Britain dollars, and later on there would be (presumably as a result of Middle Eastern development schemes which the Treasury was refusing to finance) 'great schemes of irrigation which will help provide great opportunities for people'.[44]

Bevin's flights of imperial fancy, or as one imperial historian has put it, his 'neo Palmerstonian cosmoplastic schemes', seemed at odds with the ideas of officials dealing with practical problems, but of course fully in tune with the Foreign Office conception of regaining British status and influence. The Treasury was already averse to the idea of even attempting Middle Eastern development and with regard to African development, which was much more acceptable, even as the ideas were being enunciated the difficulties that would rapidly prove their undoing were being spelled out. The Treasury official who challenged the fundamental premise of an imperial strategy geared to great power status also produced criticism of the means suggested to secure the latter goal. In the Middle East, Playfair pointed out that the currency argument worked against sending exports to the region, and any improvement in the region's standard of living would produce demands for capital goods that would have to be supplied through the release of sterling balances. Moreover, the emphasis on British know how and technical advice supplied through the Middle East Office would, in Playfair's view, only lead to development projects which Britain would be unable to supply the materials for.[45] Such arguments tended not to surface outside the corridors of junior officials and, like the Colonial Office memorandum by J. S. Bennett arguing for a rapid and radical approach to the transfer of power, were put to one side without full consideration and therefore remained outside the mainstream of post-war thinking.[46]

The Colonial Office, while generally swept along by the tide of development for greater production had, from an African perspective, serious reservations about the likely impact of production drives. In a memorandum to the Cabinet the Secretary of State explained that in most of tropical Africa the land was generally infertile and that native labour was in short supply and often inefficient. There was a shortage of technical personnel and inadequate capital equipment in the colonies while great difficulties were being experienced, because of British shortages, in getting deliveries of new equipment. Shortages of consumer goods, necessary to provide incentives for producers, were also in evidence, while immediate results would be impossible, for most colonial products were tree crops which took from three to eight years after planting before producing fruit.[47] Thus, when the real crisis came the following month, British leaders should have been well aware that no instant African solutions were likely.

At the end of June, by which time the dollar drain over the first six months had reached $1890 million,[48] British efforts to deal with the crisis were complicated by the Marshall proposals and the resultant meetings with European leaders to discuss the combined response that was desired by the Americans. The proposals reflected the United States' determination in 1947 to promote European economic integration which it was believed could produce the kind of free trade and large-scale market that would take American goods. These would initially be purchased through dollar loans, but the prevailing view in Washington was that the ending of trade controls, combined with sound budgets and production programmes, would get Western Europe back on its feet. The main differences within the Truman administration were not initially over whether European economic integration was desirable but whether a formal customs union and payments scheme were necessary to achieve it.[49] Thus the old question of a customs union reappeared at the end of June, when the study group had still not reported, because of American and French support for the idea.[50] More generally, the political aspects of Western union, as represented by treaty arrangements, had to take a back seat to economic issues again, and the Foreign Office draft treaty with Belgium was mothballed because Bevin 'was trying to keep everything on an economic plane'.[51]

The Board of Trade was quick to try and keep a European customs union at arm's length, pointing out that Britain would have to persuade the Dominions of the desirability of European goods entering Britain free of duty, while produce from the Dominions faced tariffs. Later, and more forthrightly, it argued that a European customs union in the foreseeable future was quite impractical. Even more disturbing from the perspective of the pro-integrationists was the Board of Trade's view that there was very little possibility of reducing Anglo-French tariffs to the mutual benefit of both countries.[52] The Foreign Office, unsurprisingly, saw the Marshall Plan and European economic difficulties as a golden opportunity: the financial position of Europe was believed to be so desperate that there was a 'chance to break down barriers which will never recur'. Moreover, if there was no integration of the European economies comparable to the vast industrial integration of the United States, which the Soviet Union was trying to emulate, then Europe would gradually decline in the face of American and Soviet pressure.[53]

The Commonwealth Relations Office was convinced that a European customs union would be unacceptable to the Dominions, and the Colonial Office preferred some kind of preferential arrangement between the colonies and Britain or the colonies and a European customs union rather than full membership of any such union. Caine believed a customs union would benefit the colonies by giving them a wider market, but in some respects might hardly benefit them at all.[54] In the Treasury, the main European worry was that the Marshall Plan might put British reserves at the disposal of Europeans. On the customs union scheme, there was a clear Treasury rejection of British involvement in a European one, with preferences expressed for an 'Empire, West European and Argentinean group which would discriminate against the United States or a customs union between Britain and the colonies'.[55] A customs union with the colonies would be fundamentally different from one with the Dominions because the former needed protection against other tropical produce while the latter needed protection against European manufactures; this was one of the key problems of reconciling any form of imperial customs union with a European one. However, throughout 1947, as has been seen, pressure was building from one source or another to link the colonies in some way with Europe.

The Marshall Plan customs union debate intensified when it became clear that the international conference held in Paris to consider the European reconstruction programme desired by the Americans was in favour of a customs union.[56] Ministers decided that the British attitude to a customs union should be one of reserve, largely because of the pro-Empire orientation of the Board of Trade and to a lesser extent the Treasury. On 8 August, again before the study group had reported, the Cabinet accepted participation in talks on a customs union without giving any prior commitments, no doubt because the Foreign Office's pro-Europe strategy would be damaged by a completely negative response, and later in the month the British suggested a CEEC Study Group should meet in Brussels, where it would be less vulnerable to French and American pressures for a customs union.[57]

By the end of August the committee of outside experts had produced its report on a customs union. Regarding a union between Britain, Benelux, France and West Germany the four members saw several disadvantages. The UK would have more difficulty disposing of exports and of obtaining primary produce. In particular the customs union would bring a great increase in the availability of goods already manufactured in Britain. The report argued that a customs union with primary producing countries would, however, be likely to benefit Britain. Also if a European customs union were set up without Britain, again there would be disadvantages.[58] These kinds of argument were in fact to be repeated in similar guise over the next decade. The balance of views within the government was fairly accurately represented by a draft despatch to the Dominions in August 1947. A European customs union was not practical because it could not easily be reconciled with imperial preference, and Commonwealth trade was twice as important as European trade. Even a European free trade area was deemed undesirable because it would divert into European consumption British exports to hard currency areas. Any system including the Commonwealth and Europe was deemed unacceptable to the Americans, although the difficulties with Washington would no doubt have been less awkward to resolve than the differences with the Dominions and the Europeans over the nature of a combined customs union.[59]

These developments which helped define Britain's approach to a European customs union in particular, and the nature of Britain's economic relations with the industrialised and primary producing nations in general, took place at precisely the same time as the dollar drain crisis which culminated on 17 August with the Cabinet decision to suspend convertibility and seek the understanding and support of the Americans;[60] it was another humiliation for those, like Bevin, who had set their sights on Britain's great power status. In the mind of the Foreign Secretary the customs union idea was still very much alive precisely because of the dollar crisis, the true intensity of which had finally been revealed when £542 million was lost in the first four weeks of convertibility.[61] It now became much more urgent to restore Britain's balance of payments position and gain economic independence from the Americans. In a sense, unless Bevin was to abandon his European strategy and the regaining of a position of equality with the Americans, the European powers, to paraphrase Sir Orme Sargent's important stocktaking memorandum, *had* to be enrolled as collaborators with the British Empire, whatever the practical difficulties which were evident to some before the financial débâcle of August 1947. When the Cabinet decided to set up an interdepartmental body to handle balance of payments questions, Bevin protested that its terms of reference did not provide for coordinated consideration for *earning* Britain's balance of payments income other than through manufactured goods. In other words it did not take into consideration the development of imperial resources which could contribute to the easing of Britain's balance of payments problems. Bevin wanted to establish priorities for the quick development of these facilities, despite what Creech Jones had told the Cabinet before the true extent of the crisis was fully appreciated, and to coordinate colonial development with the development of British industry.[62]

On 3 September the Foreign Secretary addressed the Trade Union Congress, and advocated a customs union which would embrace the Empire and perhaps other states as well.[63] He followed this up by a letter to the Prime Minister urging a high level study group to consider a customs union for the colonies, the Dominions, Europe, the colonies and the Dominions, and the relation of an Empire customs union to a European one.[64] Bevin's thinking emerged more clearly in yet another letter to Attlee in which he argued that we

must free ourselves from financial dependence on the United States as soon as possible. We shall never be able to pull our weight in foreign affairs until we do. I fear however we shall not achieve this purpose solely by selling manufactured goods to a world which is becoming increasingly industrialised and that multilateral trade may not suffice . . . We must have something in the way of raw materials with which to buy our food and other requirements in other countries. Hence the importance of closer trade relations with the Commonwealth and Empire and for an intensified effort for development within them.[65]

The question remained of how best to secure this. By August the Foreign Office investigation into raw materials which the US was short of had produced a list which included mercury, platinum, antimony, nickel, chromite, tin, and industrial diamonds. The development of such minerals was not, however, something which the Colonial Office believed could be secured in the short term and would certainly require an additional call on capital goods. Both in the long term and the short term the lack of British resources for African development formed the crux of the problem. In the short term the colonies could send more materials to the dollar zone by restricting sales to the UK, but this was likely to cause as many problems as it solved; there were, according to the Colonial Office, with very few exceptions, 'no commodities of which we could quickly produce more'.[66] Yet the August crisis led to expectations that the colonies *would* produce more of the things the UK was importing from dollar countries, more goods which could be sold for dollars *and* more of the things they needed for themselves because of the need for the sterling area to cut back on imports from the dollar zone.[67] In fact the Secretary of State instructed that because of the 'changes in policy required by the present dollar crisis' and after a total suspension of all colonial import licences on 30 August, 'a regime of wartime austerity as regards imports must, I fear, be reconstituted and rigid standards of essentiality adhered to . . . and the cutting down of imports from *all* sources must be regarded as of paramount importance'. It was not just a question of limiting imports from the dollar zone, but of imposing wartime restrictions on colonial territories at precisely the same time as officials and ministers in London were clamouring for increased colonial production. 'It will be necessary to revert to an import licensing system at least as strict as that obtaining at the height of the last war' with the result that licences would be issued in restricted quantities even for essential imports.[68] Such exploitation, and the short-term contradiction between the Colonial Office's ideas on development and welfare and the desperate need to solve Britain's economic problems, was bound to have an effect on the colonies. Although the British would try to argue that Britain and the colonies had a mutual interest in increasing production, the fact was that while this was at least possible in the long term, in the short term the balance of sacrifices and benefits was weighted firmly against the colonies and in favour of Britain. Thus colonial policy in 1947 became subordinated to, and at odds with, the broader more exploitative thrust of imperial economic strategy.

A possible way out of the problem presented by Britain's lack of resources for long-term development lay in using American resources for colonial development which would be similar to, or perhaps part of, the Marshall Aid programme for Europe. Indeed the relationship between European reconstruction and aid for the colonies was to pose some interesting questions for imperial strategists. The initial approach by Bevin to the general issues of Britain's role in European reconstruction was to try and carve out a special British position between the United States and Western Europe. Given the existence of the Empire and, as we have seen, Bevin's wish not to merge British sovereignty with that of the Europeans, the Foreign Secretary hoped that the 'United States would not treat Britain as just another European country'. For the British to be reduced to a relationship with the United States similar to that between 'the USSR and Yugoslavia' was seen as highly undesirable. Given the aim of reestablishing a position of equality with the Russians and the Americans, Bevin had to try and argue that Britain could also play an important role in European recovery. If the British could act as a channel for US aid to Europe, and combine this with the resources of the Empire, then Britain would not have to be lumped together with the other recipients of Marshall Aid.[69]

And at the conference with the Europeans Bevin tried to create the impression that Britain had a special role in which the resources of the Commonwealth would be directed as far as possible to the rehabilitation of Europe.[70] This posed one great difficulty, which formed another contradiction within an imperial strategy based on attempts to use the Empire's resources to regain economic strength when the economic and military strength necessary to sustain imperial commitments was lacking. If the British were going to argue the case for the Empire's resources being used to help Europe, it would be distinctly difficult to ask the Americans for the resources to develop the Empire. On 15 August the Foreign Office did, however, contact the Colonial Office to ascertain its views on United States financial participation in African development plans. The Colonial Office was prepared to consider it but intimated that for political reasons it would be undesirable to make arrangements that would necessitate or imply American control over particular developments.[71] Here was an old wartime concern that United States money would turn Africans away from their British masters and make it more difficult for the Colonial Office to carry out its post-war mission and retain the respect and admiration of colonial subjects being prepared for self-government. Unfortunately with the British having to go back to the Americans on the suspension of convertibility yet another separate approach to Washington for British economic assistance for African development was certain to be embarrassing and unlikely to be welcomed, although Bevin, in August, was still 'taking colonial needs into account in the discussions on the Marshall Plan'.[72]

This idea was not to last very long for there were several difficulties in associating colonial development with European reconstruction. The situation was that Britain had a deficit with the dollar zone; the rest of the sterling area, excluding the colonies, also had a deficit, but the colonies had a surplus. Even if the US agreed to the colonies' inclusion in the Marshall Plan it was likely that their dollar surplus would have to be offset against the deficit of the rest of the sterling area. In order to maximise US aid the simplest thing would be to exclude the colonies' requirements and supplies. This was to be an issue throughout the early months of the European Recovery Programme, as the British attempted to have their cake and eat it by allowing the colonies to get a share of allocated Marshall Aid exports from the United States while preventing the colonial dollar surplus being offset against British needs.[73] Furthermore, as it became more important to aim for independence from the Americans and to avoid any appearance of being just another European power, the African Empire in particular offered a way out which might well be closed if the Americans were involved in both European recovery *and* African development; there would then certainly be a significant reduction in the appearance of an independent Empire providing a source of economic strength.

By October, when, as will be seen, the efforts for European cooperation in the development of Africa were gathering pace, Bevin was suggesting that the government 'should go very slow on linking colonial development with Marshall's proposals. We must keep our hands free and not whet US appetites in the colonial Empire.'[74] It was all part of a consistent post-war British approach to the involvement of the Americans with the British Empire. Wartime suspicions of the anti-imperial sentiments of many Americans may have been overcome but American power and wealth, even used in a spirit of cooperation, remained a danger to British influence in the world until economic recovery was assured. Consequently, as with the political support of the United States for excluding Soviet influence from Britain's imperial sphere of influence, the economic support of the Americans was desirable but only if it was given in ways which did not undermine British influence in the colonies and did not appear as capitalist exploitation. An interesting example occurred at a meeting at Chequers in October 1947 when ministers discussed the need for 'imaginative plans for colonial development', and it was suggested that American capital should be encouraged in government controlled companies for African development to the extent of 10 to 15 per cent. Socialist ministers would then control the exploitative tendencies of capitalist firms and the American role would be kept to a minimum.[75]

Another example of how the British hoped to enlist American support for their vital imperial interests, but in carefully managed ways, concerned the talks that also took place in the autumn of 1947 on the Middle East. Bevin desired the talks because he wanted to move towards a better understanding between the British and the American militaries and because of the Anglo-American differences over

Palestine.[76] The Foreign Office defined the main objective of the discussions as enlightening the Americans on the importance of the Middle East to the United States as well as to Britain, and to explain British achievements and present policies in the region; but there was also a view in the Office that the talks should cover the strategic importance and economic development of Africa.[77] There was now renewed interest in a Middle Eastern defence pact prompted by the difficulties with an Anglo-Egyptian defence agreement and the opposition in Iraq to the Anglo-Iraqi treaty. Bevin took up the idea of a regional pact and typically produced another grandiose scheme linking Egypt to Pakistan which, if Jinnah (the leader of the Muslim League who became the head of the new state of Pakistan) took the initiative with the Muslim world, would enable Pakistan to succeed Egypt as the dominant Muslim power. Crucially Bevin also desired to keep the Middle East a predominantly British sphere and exclude the United States militarily from the area; he was opposed to American military missions but hoped the United States might be prepared to provide financial backing.[78] In other words American economic power would underwrite the exclusively British defence commitments to the region which were necessary to ensure that the Middle East was viewed as a British sphere.

While American support was becoming more and more necessary for maintaining Britain's military and economic position, it was also more important to develop a strategy that would promote British independence and ensure that at some point in the not too distant future American support would be given on the basis of equality rather than dependence. If there were difficulties over British colonial development and American participation, then it would be all the more important to secure European cooperation in Africa which might also make the whole issue of European economic cooperation more palatable to the Board of Trade and the Treasury. In the immediate aftermath of the August crisis Bevin was to have a series of meetings with French leaders in which both sides agreed on the importance of cooperation in the development of Africa and on the extension of the present collaboration between the Colonial Ministries which was limited to the technical field. The first meeting was with the French President of the Council, Ramadier, when Bevin, referring to the colonial cooperation in Africa, suggested extending it to commercial matters and urged a general tightening of Franco-British links in order that together the two powers would occupy a place equivalent to the United States and the Soviet Union. Bevin and Ramadier also agreed that 'recent Russian moves' made it appear inevitable that Europe would be divided into two blocs and therefore it would be necessary to try and organise Western Europe into a coherent unity, perhaps through the customs union which some American officials favoured as part of the Marshall Plan.[79] Two weeks later an article in L'Aube, which the British Embassy believed to have been inspired by the French Foreign Minister, Georges Bidault, discussed the idea of an Anglo-French Union.[80] Bidault was now also convinced that the world would be divided into two blocs,[81] and both French and British were beginning to take more seriously the question of how to organise Western Europe. In the British case it was inspired partly by the acceptance of the division of Europe, which therefore removed much of the need to avoid alienating the Russians, and partly by the need to find some way of linking Europe to the Empire to avoid complete economic dependence on the Americans. However the British did not want to move towards a political union and the Embassy in Paris was told that 'for the present we are tackling the economic and colonial aspects without prejudice to other studies later'.[82]

By 8 October, after a meeting with the Secretary of State, officials from the Foreign Office were spelling out Bevin's ideas on European cooperation to their colleagues from the Paris Embassy, the Colonial Office, the Treasury, the Commonwealth Relations Office, the Board of Trade, the Ministry of Fuel and the Bank of England. Bevin had spoken of creating 'vested interests' in other Western European states by which a union would be built up with 'natural cohesion' that would be more independent of the Americans and capable of exercising a strong influence on Eastern Europe. The Secretary of State wanted closer integration with France, the joint use of African resources and finally the building of a stable group between Russia and the United States containing Belgium, Holland, Portugal, Italy and Eire. The Board of Trade representative immediately indicated that a customs union could not be justified and that if resources were pooled Britain would be the loser. The Foreign Office representative agreed that a customs union was not 'practical politics', but claimed Bevin was thinking in terms of an economic association for political reasons such as combating communism. He might well have added some remarks on the dollar gap and British weakness as elements in Bevin's thinking, but here was an indication of how the need to combat communism could be used to justify policies that were being considered for other reasons. After mentioning the political dimension, Oliver Harvey then urged the creation of an African development plan by the Europeans which had cold water poured on it by the Colonial Office representative because of the similarities between French and British Africa. There was not much that Britain could get from the French colonies that was not available in the British territories, so coordination on African development would mean little more than switching investment. Again the shortage of skilled technical manpower as an important constraint on development was mentioned.[83]

The following day saw the first meeting of the post-balance of payments crisis Committee on Economic Policy at which Bevin found himself alongside all four of his senior ministerial colleagues. The Foreign Secretary now had an important ally in Stafford Cripps, and while the new Minister of Economic Affairs urged the exploration of all possible means of stimulating trade between the countries of Western Europe and the sterling area in order to reduce the dollar gap, he asserted that the colonial Empire must in future be developed as an economic unity with the UK. At the ministerial level there was a firm acceptance of the idea of greater imperial cohesion which was to be combined with European economic cooperation despite all the obstacles that had been pointed out at the official level. Cripps, with his experience in the Board of Trade, was intent on solving Britain's economic problems within an imperial framework; Bevin, with his Foreign Office experience, combined with his penchant for 'cosmoplastic schemes' was intent on using a European economic framework combined with an imperial one to end Britain's weakness and its dependence on the Americans. The two ministers were able to agree quite readily on a new approach to Anglo-French cooperation beginning with an examination of Britain's colonial resources in order to ease the dollar position and then, before France and Belgium were approached, an examination of how far these two countries could make a similar contribution. What Bevin and Cripps were looking for was an area in Western Europe and Africa which would become self-supporting and prevent more dollar difficulties; these were the ideas Bevin put to his next meeting with the French on 20 October.[84] By then his stance would have been encouraged by Duff Cooper's farewell despatch from Paris. The importance of Britain's West European policy was portrayed in stark terms by the Ambassador who claimed that the time had come to decide whether Britain will 'place herself at the head of a confederation of European democracies or whether she will become a satellite of the United States. She can no longer, relying upon her own resources and upon those of the Empire, be one of the greatest powers in the world, but she can be the leader of a group which by its population, its overseas possessions and its high standard of intelligence, can be the equal of if not the superior of either of its great competitors'.[85]

In October Bevin learned that the Quai was in favour of an ad hoc Franco-British Committee to deal with political, administrative and economic questions concerning Africa and other overseas areas; and that it wanted the existing colonial cooperation to be formalised in a rather grandiose way through the establishment of a joint Colonial Commission.[86] The convergence of views on the advantages of imperial economic cooperation and its importance for British great power aspirations undoubtedly led to a conversation between Bevin and Bidault which drew attention to the great resources which were available in Africa, if properly developed, and which were lacking in the United States. Bevin told the French of encouraging contacts with Portugal on cooperation in Africa, and both ministers agreed that such matters should be taken beyond the range of technical discussions and dealt with by ministers; the ways and means should be discussed between Sir Oliver Harvey and the French Ambassador, René Massigli.[87]

The greater importance of Anglo-French economic cooperation in Africa produced a set of proposals by the joint Anglo-French Economic Committee and prompted Creech Jones to write to Cripps urging, 'in view of the importance of colonial development', the establishment of an interdepartmental working party to consider priorities in the supply of goods for development projects. This was a crucial issue given the disappointing reports on the likely short-term benefits of production drives in the colonies. Moreover, the interim report of the Colonial Primary Products Committee became available at the end of October and referred to some increase in exports of certain foodstuffs and raw materials over wartime levels while pointing to the necessity of 'bearing in mind the doctrine of trusteeship'.[88] From the Colonial Office point of view the inputs from Britain into colonial development needed to be greater if Africans were to benefit and if the whole thing were to work now that it had assumed such significance. What was needed were consumer goods as incentives for producers, more technical assistance and perhaps financial aid from the United States: precisely the things Britain would have difficulty in organising because of its financial weakness and the short-term need to direct resources to solving the dollar gap and becoming independent of the United States.

The ideas on African development had in Britain's case been put forward most strongly by those with least knowledge of the obstacles; and despite the discouraging reports and comments that appeared throughout 1947. They were inspired, not by official reports and studies emanating from within the bureaucracy, but by the ideas of ministers like Bevin who were determined to find ways of rebuilding British power and influence. The fact that there was an economic crisis forced the

Colonial Office to change tack and go along with the attempts to use the colonies to alleviate Britain's short-term plight; they could only endeavour to apply a heavy dose of realism and to ensure that the longer-term goals of producing benefits for the colonies were not lost sight of. Thus the machinery of government had to continue operating with renewed vigour over Anglo-French cooperation in colonial development, just as it was continuing to investigate the customs union in the autumn of 1947, despite the disadvantages that had been noted. When Bevin supported Creech Jones's idea of a working party on development this went ahead under Lord Plowden. There was also an interdepartmental meeting in December on how to respond to French suggestions for renewed discussion on colonial economic cooperation; and the issue of African development had resurfaced in the Defence Committee.

The French approach on colonial economic cooperation initially produced an informal meeting between Alphand and Hall Patch where the former suggested four subjects on which cooperation would be useful: the coordination of production plans; marketing; communications; and inter-colonial trade. When the British interdepartmental committee met it was then agreed that a Colonial Office working party should be established to produce papers on each of these subjects, although there would clearly be some repetition of the work already done for the Anglo-French colonial officials' meeting earlier in the year.[89] The reference to African development in the Defence Committee arose out of a paper which urged large-scale British emigration to the Dominions. Bevin saw some difficulties in this, and favoured instead a new approach to the development of the African colonies. Significantly he also wanted to see a much closer union of the West European powers which he believed would be much stronger if the African territories of those participating in it were integrated with their respective mother countries.[90] The defence committee's interest in the issue of emigration had arisen from the growing belief that in an atomic war it would be impossible to defend the civilian population in Britain. Emigration, particularly to Africa and Australasia, would reduce the numbers who required protection and be a source of strength in war. After the discussion on these matters the Defence Secretary, A. V. Alexander, wrote to the Prime Minister suggesting that there would be economic advantages too, because Britain would be more easily self-sufficient in food and British industry could be spread more widely through the Empire.[91] Such suggestions provide an interesting example of the extent to which 'salvation by the Empire' had penetrated the Labour government by the end of 1947.

Another example was provided by the visit of the Chief of the Imperial General Staff, Bernard Montgomery, to a large number of African countries in November and December 1947. Montgomery had been thinking of changing the make-up of the British army, no doubt with a view to compensating for the loss of the Indian army. He believed that Britain must consolidate its position in Africa and he wanted to explore the possibility of using East and West African manpower. Montgomery was looking for an imperial reserve which could be drawn upon in a crisis and which would be used in conjunction with British Middle Eastern forces. African manpower would also be buttressed by forces based in Iraq, Greece and Turkey as Montgomery believed these were the countries that would fight for the British Empire and so British garrisons overseas could be kept to a minimum during peacetime. With this in mind Montgomery visited the Gambia, the Gold

Coast, Nigeria, South Africa, Southern Rhodesia and Kenya as well as some non-British territories. Bevin was told of the visit only in strict confidence because the CIGS did not want the nature of the visit to be discussed by ministers.[92] Montgomery returned to present Bevin with an extraordinary impression of Africa. He claimed it had immense possibilities for development because it contained everything Britain needed in terms of minerals, labour, food and raw materials; but there was no grand design or master plan in any of the colonies which would enable Britain to use these resources and maintain its standard of living. (The African was termed 'a complete savage . . . quite incapable of developing the country himself'.)

Montgomery called for a policy of development laid down by a central authority, and his ideas on what this should be put Robert Parr's earlier effort very much in the shade. Existing colonial barriers had to be broken down in order to create a power grouping, the first stage of which would be a federal system in Central, East and West Africa. The territories would then be part of combinations which would be economically and politically strong and ideally run by 'go-getters' 'who would adventure courageously as Cecil Rhodes', and not by lethargic colonial administrators who had spent too long in hot climates and disliked anything that disturbed their routine. The second stage of Montgomery's plan would be to link South Africa to the Central African federation and the third stage closer cooperation between the British territories and the colonies of the other European powers.[93] Such fantasies are easily dismissed, with the benefit of hindsight, as outrageous nonsense completely out of tune with post-1945 realities, yet at the time they were very much in tune with some of the thinking in Whitehall and certainly in line with the general thrust of the proposals that were being put forward about development, cooperation and great power status. Indeed, Bevin was so impressed he wrote to the Prime Minister to say that the issues raised by Montgomery which concerned African development required serious and urgent study. The Foreign Secretary invited Cripps, Creech Jones, Alexander and the Commonwealth Relations Secretary, Philip Noel-Baker, to be sent the report after which a meeting would be held to consider how best to get on with the study of Montgomery's ideas on African development.[94]

By this time, another of the government's studies which appeared to have very little impact on Bevin's thinking, had produced an interim report on the customs union idea. The draft report drawn up in the Board of Trade was based on the conclusions of the academics' August report. It referred to the disadvantages if Britain was left out of a European customs union, but the interim report to the Economic Policy Committee argued that membership would not make any significant contribution to solving Britain's immediate problems. It then went on to list the long-term advantages of membership as benefits from increased product specialisation and expanded markets, an improvement in Britain's trade balance with Western Europe, benefits to particular industries and being better placed with regard to American competitors. The disadvantages would be that substantial short-term adjustments in the British economy would be needed, that stable prices and assured markets for British farmers would be difficult to secure, that the iron and steel industries would suffer, that the maintenance of exchange controls would be doubtful (and if ended would undermine the sterling area connection), that increased exports to Europe would strain yet further the gold and dollar reserves and finally that Commonwealth preferences would have to end.[95] Bevin found this rather disappointing as he felt it was essential for West Europe to attain some measure of economic unity if it were to maintain its independence against Russia and the United States.[96]

Regarding the customs union with the Commonwealth or colonies, or a combined European/colonial union, as might have been expected, the work of the interdepartmental group was not very encouraging. The Board of Trade believed that the most serious objection to bringing the colonies into a European customs union was that British manufacturers would lose the benefit of preferences in colonial markets and therefore be faced with European competition under duty-free entry conditions; it was believed that the opportunities offered to British manufacturers in the colonies of the other European powers would be a small offset against the preferential advantages they enjoyed in the British colonies. The Board of Trade, as part of building its case against bringing the colonies into a European customs union, also noted that the colonies would lose revenue through having to admit European goods free of charge.[97] If there were to be just a British customs union with the colonies, as favoured by Cripps, it was believed the British would gain from free access to the colonial markets because it would increase the preference in the colonies for British goods. On the other hand the benefits would be one sided as there was no real margin for preferential increases for colonial produce; not only therefore would the colonies lose customs revenue, they would lose protection for their industries without any corresponding gains.[98] In addition the Colonial Office pointed out that at the recent Conference of African Governors held in November, all Governors had stated that their territories would not voluntarily enter a customs union with the UK.[99] The combined paper drawn up by the customs union group also drew attention to the disadvantages the Dominions would suffer in colonial markets, and with a keen eye on one of the guiding principles of the time, noted that a colonial customs union would not help with the balance of payments problem.[100] The political difficulties of a British customs union with the colonies would clearly outweigh the economic advantages. Some kind of less formal arrangement would therefore be needed to develop Africa and tie it more closely to Britain and Europe in ways which would assist Britain's recovery in both economic and power-political terms. No wonder that Creech Jones in referring to the recently established working party on Anglo-French colonial economic collaboration asked to be kept informed of its work 'as all this is now part of major foreign policy and frequently the subject of ministerial discussions'.[101]

As has been indicated the problems of some kind of Euro-African colonial development scheme were not limited to a customs union. In Europe, the British were still unhappy about the kind of goods they were receiving from the French, although France's sterling surplus on British trade had been offset by a deficit with the rest of the sterling area. In Africa the problems of poor soil, labour shortages and lack of technical personnel had already been noted by officials, if ignored by ministers. Where imported materials and equipment were required these were generally in short supply in the UK, and the Colonial Development Corporation was already complaining about the availability of equipment.[103] Therefore some criteria for deciding upon priorities would have to be agreed upon. There could be few incentives to African producers because of the shortage of consumer goods resulting from the limitations on colonial imports. So even if massive funds were available under the Colonial Development and Welfare Act (which they were not) the chances of them being effectively employed were rather remote. At the same time the prospect of the colonies of the other European powers providing for British needs was even more remote given the economic weaknesses of Western Europe and the fact that the French African colonies produced similar foodstuffs and raw materials to the British ones.

In terms of trade and finance there were also doubts raised over the value of an imperial bloc. The Board of Trade was keenest to sell goods in imperial markets and was under pressure from British exporters whose desire to sell goods in colonial markets was being thwarted by colonial import restrictions.[104] Yet if colonial imports were increased these were likely to run down the sterling balances as well as reduce the volume of British exports to the dollar zone. As the Treasury noted, Britain's dollar deficit was accompanied by a surplus with the rest of the world and this balance had to be corrected by sending more goods to the dollar zone and reducing exports to non-dollar sources; the sterling balances, if released, would only encourage the imbalance the British needed, in the short term, to correct. Thus the Treasury view was that the restrictions on exports to colonial and other soft currency destinations had to be maintained. If the colonies were to receive more imports they would have to be paid for by increasing colonial exports[105]; and so the vicious circle of British weakness and demands on the colonies continued with short-term exploitation looming larger than any long-term benefits for the colonies. As such the strains of a customs union with the colonies and the idea of Europe developing Africa were unlikely to avert continued economic problems whatever the rhetorical exuberance of Montgomery and Bevin.

It is an interesting reflection on the British policy making process that the official voices who warned of the problems of an African, European or imperial economic strategy did not reach the attention of ministers or could not be listened to while the overriding goal of British policy overseas was to maintain great power status and avoid becoming a satellite dependent on the United States. Therefore at the end of 1947 after reports and studies the European customs union idea was still alive and the British were participating in a CEEC study of its feasibility; ministers were involved in discussions on African development inspired by a remarkably obtuse memorandum from Montgomery; a colonial development working party had been established; working parties were investigating the prospect of Anglo-French economic cooperation in Africa; and Cripps was urging a British Colonial customs union as the first step towards greater multilateral trade between the European powers.[106] There was no doubt about the importance the Cabinet attached to the economic value of the African Empire, and the consensus view was clearly expressed in a memorandum by Cripps which stated that 'our only real hope of permanent improvement in our balance of payments must lie in the expansion of sterling Area resources in foodstuffs and raw materials. The development of our African resources in particular is, therefore, of prime importance and must be a major consideration in planning and economic activities.' Most ministers would also have shared Dalton's view that the principal value of any arrangement made with the Europeans would lie in the colonial resources that would be made available.[107] No wonder that the Cabinet Secretary, Norman Brook, advised his socialist Prime Minister that the policy fell within the normal definition of 'imperialism'.[108]

Unfortunately the British lacked the strength to be traditional or any other kind of 'imperialists' and were locked into a developmental bind in Africa which they were unlikely to break free from, even if the problems of African soil and climate could easily be solved. The equipment and consumer goods which may have helped the developmental process were often needed for home use or for export to the dollar zone and their supply would add to rather than alleviate the short-term problem. In Europe it was clear by the end of 1947 that Britain was running a surplus, rather than its pre-war deficit, with its West European partners due to the lack of German competition and the comparative weakness of its other European competitors; and this surplus was unlikely to be offset by goods that the British needed to help their own recovery programme. The Marshall Aid programme might have an impact, but the deficit of the rest of the sterling area would not be fully covered by American aid, and the shortfall would be greater if the colonial dollar surplus was offset against the British deficit. What was needed was for the United States to provide for colonial development which would avoid the drain on British goods and offer the prospect of increased colonial production. Moreover if the Americans were not to be involved it would be better in the short term for the Europeans to take the lead in providing resources for Africa and thus enable Britain to sell more goods to the dollar zones. Yet the likelihood was, as the Treasury noted, that neither the Americans nor the British and the Europeans would be able to accelerate economic development in the colonies[109] and there would be an economic and political price to pay for non-British supplies entering British territories in Africa. What could be said with certainty about British thinking on their links with the Europeans and the Americans was that stronger economic ties with the former were unlikely to bring material benefits but were highly desirable for political reasons, while economic ties with the Americans were likely to bring benefits but were undesirable for political reasons. Faced with this dilemma that had to be resolved to secure great power status, by the end of 1947 British imperial strategists were clutching at the hope that by involving the Empire, and particularly the African colonies, with Western Europe, political and economic benefits would accrue that would resolve the dollar crisis. While the implementation of such an unlikely strategy was being attempted, further problems and contradictions emerged out of important developments in the Cold War.

Notes

1. CAB 80/55 COS (46) 271 report by ad hoc committee 13.12.46; DEFE 4/2 COS (47) 28th 19.2.47; CSA/P (47) 21 13.2.47.
2. CAB 79/54 COS (46) 127th 23.12.46.
3. Kent 'Anglo-French Cooperation' (see ch. 2, n. 33) p. 60.
4. FO371/67697 memorandum by R. Parr Jan. 1947.
5. Ibid. Duff Cooper to Bevin 20.1.47.
6. FO371/62420 draft circular Jan. 1947.
7. FO371/67686 minute by O. Harvey 14.1.47, recording meeting between Bevin and Blum. The other two pillars were the Middle East and the navy and air force.
8. For the colonial meeting on 19 Feb. see FO371/67697. The early meetings of the Anglo-French Economic Committee are in FO371/67686.

9. FO371/67697 CO memorandum Feb. 1947.
10. FO800/465 note by O. Harvey on meeting between Auriol and Bevin 17.4.47.
11. T236/1274 memorandum 'Economic Policy in the Middle East' March 1947.
12. Morgan op. cit. (see Ch. 4, n. 27) p. 340.
13. H. Pelling *The Labour Governments 1945–51* (London 1984) p. 171.
14. PREM 8/457 Creech Jones to Attlee 26.3.47.
15. DEFE 32/1 COS (47) 6th 7.1.47.
16. H. Dalton *Memoirs: High Tide and After 1945–60* (London 1962) p. 197.
17. A. Bullock, *Ernest Bevin: Foreign Secretary 1945–51* (London 1983) pp. 240, 244–5, 323, 339–40, 354.
18. T236/1640 minute by R. W. B. Clarke 15.5.46.
19. FO371/53317 draft Anglo-Egyptian Treaty 25.10.46.
20. FO371/53318 Cairo to FO 18.11.86; FO371/53320 New York to FO 5.12.46 and 6.12.46.
21. FO391/62965 minute by R. G. Howe 6.3.47.
22. DEFE 6/3 JP (47) 105 6.8.47; DEFE 4/16 COS (48) 140th 1.10.48.
23. T236/1274 minute by E. W. Playfair 19.5.47.
24. FO371/67687 minute by J. Wilson 17.5.47; Ellis-Rees (Treasury) to H. Lintott (Board of Trade) 18.7.47; FO371/67686 H. Lintott to Holmes (British representative at the Geneva international trade negotiations) 19.5.47; T236/1975 record of inter-departmental meeting 8.5.47; H. Lintott to F. Hoyer Millar 17.5.47.
25. FO371/67687 minute by J. Wilson 17.5.47.
26. FO371/67663 minute by F. Hoyer Millar 10.3.47.
27. FO371/67224 record of FO meeting March 1947.
28. Ibid. record of FO meeting with Secretary of State 7.5.47.
29. FO371/64181 minute by P. Dean 23.1.47. For more details on British policy towards Germany see A. Deighton *The Impossible Peace: Britain, the Division of Germany and the Origins of the Cold War* (Oxford 1990).
30. FO371/64195 Moscow to FO 29.3.47.
31. FO371/64201 minute by B. A. B. Burrows 28.3.47.
32. FO371/64197 record of 18th meeting of Moscow Council of Foreign Ministers 31.3.47.
33. FO371/67686 FO circular by Bevin 10.4.47.
34. For the technical cooperation programme see Kent *Internationalization of Colonialism* (see Ch. 4, n. 2) p. 202.
35. FO371/67862 minutes by J. N. O. Curle and J. W. Blanch 18.4.47 and 21.4.47.
36. FO371/67697 Duff Cooper to Sir O. Sargent 8.3.47.
37. Bullock p. 246.
38. The quotation from Sir M. Perrin was obtained by Peter Hennessey for a 'Time-watch' programme in 1982 and cited in Bullock p. 352.
39. FO371/67724 record of FO meeting with the Secretary of State 7.5.47.
40. D. J. Morgan *The Official History of Colonial Development* Vol. II *Developing British Colonial Resources 1945–51* (London 1980) pp. 271–5; CAB 129/19 CP (47) 175 6.6.47.
41. FO371/62557 minute by Bevin for the Prime Minister 7.7.47.
42. Ibid. minute by Attlee for the Foreign Secretary 8.7.47; Creech Jones to Bevin 17.7.47.
43. CAB 131/4 DO (47) 23 7.3.47.
44. FO371/61545 extract from Bevin's Labour Conference speech, Margate 29.5.47.
45. R. Hyam 'Africa and the Labour Government 1945–51' *Journal of Imperial and Commonwealth History* 16, 3 (1988); T236/1274 minute by E. W. Playfair 19.5.47.
46. Bennett's memorandum of 30.4.47, calling for a rapid withdrawal from North Africa,

Southeast Asia and the Middle East, leaving a colonial Empire of effectively the strategic islands, Black Africa, the Pacific and the Caribbean is in CO537/2057 and reproduced in Hyam *British Documents* (see Ch. 4, n. 1) Vol. II doc. 174 pp. 409–21.

47. CAB 129/19 CP (47) 177 8.6.47.
48. K. O. Morgan op. cit. p. 340.
49. M. J. Hogan *The Marshall Plan: America, Britain and the Reconstruction of Western Europe 1947–52* (Cambridge 1987) pp. 69–76.
50. The French believed that something was needed to catch the American imagination in order to speed up the process of granting European aid. See FO371/62552 minute by B. C. A. Cook 5.8.47.
51. FO371/67724 minute by Bevin July 1947.
52. FO371/62552 note by the Board of Trade 30.6.47. Milward op. cit. (see Ch. 4, n. 46) p. 240 citing FO371/62565 8.8.47.
53. FO371/62552 brief for the Secretary of State by Sir E. Hall Patch 7.8.47.
54. Ibid, minute by R. Makins 23.8.47; Sir S. Caine to R. W. B. Clarke 14.8.47; FO371/62553 minute by C. T. Crowe 11.9.47.
55. T236/794 minutes by R. W. B. Clarke 16.7.47 and E. Rowe-Dutton 21.7.47.
56. The Paris Conference met on 12 July 1947 and agreed to establish the Committee on European Economic Cooperation (CEEC) to supervise four technical committees to investigate food and agriculture, coal and steel, power and transportation, Hogan op. cit. pp. 60–1.
57. FO371/62552 minute by B. C. A. Cook 16.8.47; Milward op. cit. p. 240.
58. FO371/62554 skeleton draft by R. J. Shackle (Board of Trade) on European customs union 8.10.47; Milward op. cit. p. 240.
59. FO371/62552 draft telegram to Dominion governments, August 1947.
60. Bullock pp. 451–2; Pelling p. 176.
61. K. O. Morgan op. cit. p. 344.
62. CO537/3047 Bevin to Attlee 13.9.47.
63. Milward op. cit. p. 241.
64. FO371/62553 Bevin to Attlee 5.9.47.
65. FO800/444 Bevin to Attlee 6.9.47.
66. FO371/62557 report of Economic Intelligence Dept on raw materials in short supply in the US 16.7.47; CAB 129/20 CP (47) 242 23.8.47; FO371/62571 Sir S. Caine to R. B. Stevens 12.7.47.
67. CO537/3047 I. Thomas (Parl. Undersecretary) to Creech Jones 17.9.47.
68. CO537/2984 Secretary of State to all Colonial Governors 5.9.47.
69. *FRUS 1947* Vol. III meetings of W. Clayton with members of the British Cabinet pp. 271, 281; Hogan op. cit. p. 49.
70. FO371/62571 minute by B. C. A. Cook 24.7.47.
71. FO371/62658 R. Makins to Sir S. Caine 15.8.47; Sir S. Caine to R. Makins 18.8.47.
72. FO371/62557 Bevin to Creech Jones 20.8.47.
73. T236/822 FO to Washington 3.12.47.
74. FO800/444 FO to Washington personal for Minister of State from Secretary of State 17.10.47.
75. FO371/62559 note by R. Makins 30.10.47.
76. FO371/61557 C. F. A. Warner to Sir L. Hollis (Secretary Chiefs of Staff Committee) 17.9.47.
77. FO371/61558 brief for Washington talks 23–30 Oct. 1947; FO371/61557 FO memorandum 11.9.47.
78. FO371/61558 record of FO meeting with Secretary of State 8.10.47.
79. FO800/465 note of conversation with Ramadier 22.9.47; FO371/67673 record of FO meeting with Secretary of State to discuss the talks with Ramadier 26.9.47.

80. FO371/67673 Paris to FO 6.10.47.
81. Ibid. record of conversation between Bidault, Couve de Murville, Jebb and the Minister of State 7.10.47.
82. Ibid. FO to Paris 8.10.47.
83. Ibid. record of FO meeting with Secretary of State to discuss the talks with Ramadier 26.9.47; record of interdepartmental meeting 8.10.47.
84. PREM 8/494 record of first meeting of Economic Policy Committee 9.10.47; FO371/67673 note of Bevin and Cripps' meeting 20.10.47; FO800/465 note of conversation with M. Chauvel (Secretary General of French Ministry for Foreign Affairs) 20.10.47.
85. FO371/67674 Duff Cooper to Bevin 16.10.47.
86. FO800/465 translation of memorandum left by Chauvel at the Foreign Office during his October 1974 visit; FO371/67674 Sir S. Caine to Sir E. Hall Patch 16.10.47.
87. FO800/465 note of discussions between Bevin, Bidault, Creech Jones, Couve de Murville, Harvey and Dixon Oct. 1947.
88. FO371/67674 note on November meeting of Anglo-French Joint Economic Committee; FO371/62559 Creech Jones to Cripps 22.11.47; FO371/62558 interim report of Colonial Primary Products Committee 30.10.47.
89. CO537/3151 minute by D. G. Pirie 7.1.48; CO537/3544 record of meeting between French and British officials 19.2.47.
90. CAB 131/5 DO (47) 24th 14.11.47.
91. FO 800/444 Alexander to Attlee 25.11.47.
92. FO800/451 Montgomery to Bevin 25.9.47.
93. FO800/435 report by Montgomery on his African tour 19.12.47.
94. Ibid. Bevin to Attlee 22.12.47.
95. PREM 8/1146 EPC (47) 11 6.11.47.
96. FO371/62740 record of EPC 6th meeting 7.1.47; Hogan op. cit. p. 110.
97. FO371/62554 skeleton draft by R. J. Shackle on European customs union 8.10.47.
98. FO371/67623 report on Ch. V on customs union between UK and colonies 3.11.47.
99. T236/787 Meeting of UK Group on customs union 21.11.47.
100. FO371/67624 CP (47) 39 24.11.47.
101. CO537/3151 minute by Creech Jones n.d.
102. T236/1977 record of second meeting of 6th Session of Anglo-French Economic Committee 5.12.47.
103. FO371/62546 memorandum by Lord Trefgarne n.d.
104. T236/1814 minute by A. T. K. Grant 3.12.47.
105. Ibid. unsigned minute 10.12.47.
106. PREM 8/1146 EPC (47) 6th 7.11.47.
107. CAB 134/217 memorandum by the Chancellor of the Exchequer 3.1.48; PREM 8/1146 EPC (47) 6th 7.11.47.
108. PREM 8/923 Norman Brook to Attlee 14.1.48.
109. T236/822 Treasury to Sir G. Munro (UK Treasury Delegation Washington) 8.12.47.

Chapter 6
'There's no success like failure':[1]
The collapse of an imperial strategy 1948–49

The development of the Cold War in 1947 followed a relentless path which culminated at the second London Council of Foreign Ministers. In session since 25 November the Council broke up on 15 December without agreement on Germany and without fixing a date for its next meeting. The tensions over Germany had been evident even before the Moscow Council had failed to provide for the future of a united Germany. The division of Europe that this implied was undoubtedly strengthened by Marshall's offer of American aid which Stalin regarded as a more serious threat to Soviet interests than the rhetoric of the Truman Doctrine. The establishment of the Cominform in September 1947 amidst denunciations of Western imperialism signified that conflict rather than cooperation was to be the order of the day and that the propaganda war and the tightening of controls over the Soviet sphere of influence would continue with renewed vigour. The Council of Foreign Ministers' break up merely formalised the end of cooperation and the division of Europe. Bevin's initial hope that cooperation would not be ruled out once Britain's interests had been resolutely defended in both Europe and the Middle East seemed unrealisable in the immediate future.

This had several implications for British imperial strategists. Bevin's fears about alienating the Soviets at the time the Russia Committee was established had now been overtaken by the events which had effectively divided Europe into two opposing camps. More importantly the whole Western bloc policy was not only free from the constraints of alienating the Soviets, but had to be pursued with greater urgency; the more firmly Europe was divided the more important it was to organise the Western half and to ensure that the Western zones of Germany were fully integrated into it. As with the dollar crisis and the earlier efforts to confront the Soviets over exclusive and non-exclusive spheres of influence, the British had a short-term problem to overcome in Western Europe, for which they needed American support and backing, while the long-term goal was to ensure that their position was strengthened in order to pursue an independent world role. From the

British perspective, the *organisation* of Western Europe, whether under the auspices of Marshall Aid or a Western bloc, should only be done by Britain even though United States support was necessary. The Cold War's intensification in one sense simply added a new reason to follow an old strategy, but in another it altered the priorities of some British and European policy makers.

Bevin, always in the forefront when it came to producing vague initiatives or unrealistic ideas, responded quickly to the December 1947 termination of tripartite cooperation. In a talk with the Canadian High Commissioner on 17 December Bevin spoke of working towards an informal Western federation with no written constitution which would involve the whole of Western civilisation including the United States.[2] Bevin also met both Bidault and Marshall after the break up of the London Council and was slightly more specific about his federation of Western civilisation, speaking of a 'spiritual federation' of the West to Marshall and of a West European federation of a formal or informal character to Bidault.[3] The Foreign Office could not be sure of exactly what was in Bevin's mind, but the seeds of European economic cooperation, which had been cast about liberally since 1945, had certainly given it a good working knowledge of the kind of stony ground it faced when concrete proposals had to gain approval within Whitehall.

As a result of the 1947 breakdown, the practical aspect of British cooperation with Western Europe had also been given an important military dimension because of the altered international situation, and this figured prominently in the talks between Bevin and Bidault. The French were particularly keen to get the British involved in the military aspects of European cooperation. Always nervous of a German revival, which had long been seen by the British as essential for a successful West European grouping, the private French acceptance of the importance of West Germany for the West had not removed this concern. The issue was now the speed of German recovery which was linked in French eyes to the Soviet threat; the more the Soviets became alarmed about the rehabilitation of the Western zones, the more likely they were in French eyes to take action to prevent it. In other words it could provoke Soviet aggression against the West.[4] Anticipating the results of the London Council, the French had indicated their fears about the military implications of this to the British in October 1947. Chauvel explained that if the talks on Germany failed, and if the Western zones were fused, then the result would be a new frontier against Russia in Germany. Therefore in considering their position on this the French wanted to know what military support they could count on against Russia.[5] This was the start of French pressure to secure staff talks with the British that would provide them with such answers, and in particular to send their army Chief of Staff, General Revers, on a visit to his British counterparts.[6]

The Foreign Office's response to the French proposals had been extremely cool. Neither it nor the military felt that the Soviets were likely to deliberately start a major war in 1948. Exhausted by the Second World War and faced with the American atomic bomb, the Russians were busy tearing up railway lines in Eastern Europe as part of their internal reconstruction.[7] A conflict in 1948 would have been far from their minds in the view of the British, who felt the French were too concerned with the short-term military threat presented by the Russians. Sargent believed that it would be unwise to frighten people by staging Anglo-French military talks prematurely; he was also concerned that if the French were told the true extent of Britain's weakness they would be disheartened, and, with the French communists so strong, the information might reach the Russians.[8] The Permanent Undersecretary had, however, to rethink his views in the light of the new situation in December, and because Bevin had virtually committed the British to staff talks in his conversation with Bidault. The Foreign Secretary had expressed a desire for military talks to begin soon, and stated that France and Britain should agree on the best line of defence. In another remark significant for a full understanding of Bevin's aims at the turn of the year, he referred to bringing in the Americans later; remembering that the United States would never agree to alliances or treaties, Bevin maintained that there were ways of bringing the US Chiefs of Staff to collaborate.[9]

Bevin's remarks reflected little understanding of the implications of this for British military strategy. The Middle Eastern emphasis of British strategy combined with the pressure on British resources to rule out in most military minds any thought of supporting the French; the latter would certainly have been unimpressed to learn that while the three pillars of British defence strategy included the defence of the Middle East and the protection of sea communications, the defence of Western Europe had no such importance. Indeed what thoughts had been given to British military planning for Western Europe centred on the evacuation of the British forces in Germany in what would have been a 'Dunkirk' operation coordinated with the Americans.[10] As in the Second World War, the Continent would have to be abandoned to its military fate and British salvation sought through military cooperation with the United States. This was the dominant view in British military circles and it was bound to be a source of difficulty in any staff talks with the West Europeans. Bevin, however, clearly felt these were necessary, and when the Chiefs of Staff complained that Britain was in no position to assist the French in the event of an attack and needed to discuss the whole question of military assistance with the Americans, the Foreign Office replied that it had 'now become a matter of urgent necessity to draw closer to France in the political and military field'.[11] The issue was now the establishment of what became known as Western union, a phenomenon which the Foreign Office had to define in relation to Bevin's ideas on the spiritual federations of the West that appeared so necessary with the breakdown of tripartite cooperation.

Officials considered Western union in the light of the developments that had occurred since Sargent's memorandum on enrolling the West European powers as collaborators with the British Empire: the problems of economic cooperation and the customs union; the resources of the Empire as opportunities for European cooperation; and the importance of regaining independence from the Americans. With these considerations in mind officials from a number of interested Foreign Office departments expressed views on the desirability of a Western union in which Britain would accept unprecedented commitments to Europe. The minutes touch on a central issue of British policy overseas and of Britain's future world role, and are worth quoting in some detail. R. B. Stevens initiated the debate by suggesting that a customs union would be bound to develop towards a full economic union, meaning at least the coordination of fiscal and monetary systems; Britain would therefore have to intervene politically, militarily and economically in Europe to a degree hitherto uncontemplated. Stevens then pointed out what was to prove a decisive consideration: if Europe prospered then British power and British responsibilities would be great; but if Europe foundered then it would be difficult for Britain to disentangle itself from the economic wreckage. On balance Stevens considered that the political risks were worth taking.[12]

P. M. Crosthwaite, the head of the Western Department, touched again on the old theme of the awful fate awaiting Britain if Western union was not implemented. In his view individual European states could only survive as 'pygmies between two giants' dependent on one for military protection from the other and 'living in constant expectation of being trampled underfoot when they quarrel'. Only by proceeding by stages to the unification of Western Europe could Britain hope to play an important role in world affairs and thus restore world equilibrium. Crosthwaite maintained that European economic unification would seem to be an indispensable part of the process.[13] R. M. A. Hankey (head of the Northern Department) returned to the linkage between European cooperation and the future of the Empire. Britain could not 'sponge on the United States' indefinitely and had to keep the Soviet Union in check, which in the long term could only be done if Western Europe was able and willing to defend itself. This situation could only be dealt with, in Hankey's view, if the potential of the Empire was built up and the economic and political reconstruction of Europe carried out. Britain should therefore go for European unification but strive to keep the leadership in British hands.[14] Hayter, of the Services Liaison Department, and Rundall, of the North American Department, both agreed, with the latter pointing out that the United States expected Britain to take the leading role in Europe.[15] An even more explicit pro-European statement was made by Gladwyn Jebb, who maintained a customs union should be the precursor of an eventual economic and political union which he referred to as a federal entity comprising all European states west of the Iron Curtain and their colonies. Jebb believed that if such a federal entity was created it would restore a balance of power and raise British living standards to American levels; it would also maintain those spiritual and cultural values which many believed were lacking in the United States and the Soviet Union 'without which industrial civilisation would be like a tale told by an idiot, signifying nothing'. Yet, if the future of civilisation now hinged on the success of the European elements of the Foreign Office's great power global strategy, Jebb also foresaw some dangers. First the emphasis on Europe would lead to the white members of the Commonwealth, except South Africa, coming under American influence; this was another indication of the centrality of a Euro-African bloc in Foreign Office thinking. Second, and not surprisingly, there was the possibility of German domination of Western union, which Jebb saw as a real danger if Germany was reunited, and he even suggested that Britain would thereby have achieved the European *Neuordnung* (including Britain) which Hitler had been denied. This fear was accompanied by Jebb's pessimistic assessment of the likely establishment of a customs union, even though he was in favour of going ahead with one. 'For what are the alternatives? Frankly I believe, and I believe that the rulers of the Soviet Union believe, that if we don't or can't constitute some middle power we shall eventually have to make the dismal choice between becoming a Soviet satellite state or the poor dependant of an American pluto-democracy. Or more probably we shall have no choice, hard fate will force us into one position or the other.'[16]

The final word came from Hoyer Millar who expressed his agreement with the idea of a customs union entailing close economic and political ties which, if it included the European colonies, would constitute a very strong bloc economically and politically. Hoyer-Millar believed Britain might have to make some economic sacrifices, but a West European grouping would eventually attract East Germany to the Western camp. If it was not established with Britain taking the lead or playing a very prominent part then Britain would become a third-rate power.[17]

Undoubtedly the latter concern, as it had been since 1945, was the main driving force behind the Foreign Office ideas on Britain's links with Europe; for officials, the detailed economic arguments were much less significant than the broad need to regain the first rank of world powers and avoid dependence on the Americans. Thus the political advantages of a customs union continued, in the eyes of the Foreign Office, to outweigh the disadvantages, and to such an extent that the abandonment of sovereignty was definitely acceptable. For the Foreign Secretary, the detailed arguments were also less important than the need to act quickly in the wake of the failed Council of Foreign Ministers to establish Britain's leadership of Europe and thus secure its future great power status. Indeed Bevin submitted his memorandum 'The First Aim of British Foreign Policy' to the Cabinet before all his officials had outlined their views on the desirability of cooperation between Britain, the Western European powers and their respective Empires. The memorandum referred to the need for material assistance from the United States – the embodiment of the dependency inherent in the 1945 Loan Agreement, the Marshall Plan and the suspension of convertibility – but argued that 'provided we can organise a Western European system . . . backed by the resources of the Commonwealth and the Americans, it should be possible to develop our own power and influence to equal that of the United States of America and the USSR'. This first aim of British foreign policy was therefore dependent on Britain organising a Western European system but also on two other strands of Bevin's thinking. The first went back to the idea of a 'spiritual' union because 'the countries of Western Europe . . . despise the spiritual values of America' and 'by giving a spiritual lead' Britain would 'be able to carry out our task in a way which will show clearly that we are not subservient to the United States or to the Soviet Union'. The second concerned colonial development because Britain 'had the material resources in the Colonial Empire', and as Bevin told the Cabinet on 8 January 'it would be necessary to mobilise the resources of Africa in support of West European Union' in order that in terms of population and productive capacity the new organisation could be equal to the Western Hemisphere and Soviet blocs.[18]

The day after the Cabinet discussion on the 'First Aim of British Foreign Policy' ministers met to discuss Montgomery's ideas on African development. By then the Colonial Secretary was able to present a paper, almost certainly drafted by Andrew Cohen, which endorsed the importance of African development for both Britain and Europe in economic and political terms, but which disagreed with Montgomery's proposed means for achieving it. The Colonial Secretary accepted that rapid and vigorous African development was essential not just for Britain but for Europe as a whole. However, Montgomery was criticised for being over-optimistic about the material resources of Africa and underestimating the limitations on directions from London; the best results could not be achieved by directing African development centrally but by devolving it to the component parts of the Empire where the cooperation of local people could be secured. Indeed from the Colonial Office's point of view, in both the economic and political fields, future policy could not be geared to uniformity or federation because it would undermine Britain's existing friendly relations with African people; and if progress was going to be made in the field of development more British resources would be needed. The memorandum pointed out that vast areas of Africa were barely self-supporting in food and there was a need for water supplies, bush clearance and fertilisers. To develop exports of raw materials railway construction would be required, which in turn would require steel and other capital goods in short supply in Britain. There would also be a need for many other things which would be difficult to obtain in the post-war years, including technical staff, labour and consumer goods.[19] In some ways it was beginning to look as if African development would have to wait until after Britain's recovery rather than make an important contribution to it. Bevin, however, was not one to be easily discouraged, and while acknowledging that Montgomery's proposals were over-simplified, he claimed that the general feeling of the meeting was that an overall plan should be prepared for the development of Africa.[20]

This was of course essential for the success of the overall strategy to secure economic recovery and European cooperation in ways which would ensure great power status. The details of economic development were not the prime concern of the Foreign Office officials for whom the idea of a British-led power bloc independent of the Americans was the main goal. Interestingly those parts of the 'First Aim of British Foreign Policy' referring to this ultimate goal were excluded from the draft sent to Washington for approval by the Truman administration.[21] The commitment to this idea of what would in effect be a Third Force, although initially requiring American backing, was so strong that the Foreign Office was prepared to accept limitations on sovereignty to establish it. At the same time, imperial connections in both the formal Empire in Africa and the informal Empire in the Middle East had to be incorporated into the new power bloc involving the Western Europeans.

This was to be an important consideration when the next steps towards closer defence ties were contemplated by Bevin and his officials in January 1948. Bevin did not want simply to sign an Anglo-Belgian and an Anglo-Dutch treaty similar to that already signed by Britain and France in 1947, neither did he want the French to do so, as he believed the French would not then want to go on to a Mediterranean arrangement. The Foreign Secretary feared 'putting this thing into watertight compartments with no grand scheme or objective that we shall be working to'. He was happy with an Anglo French Belgian Dutch core bound by economic, political and defence arrangements which would help with the Middle East and then with colonial development, but it would only be when that was done that the system would be brought to a coordinated whole.[22] Thus, far from seeing Western European arrangements as designed to secure an American commitment to Western Europe – a sprat to catch a mackerel as has been alleged[23] – Bevin initially wanted to design a European system that would extend to Africa and the Middle East rather than across the Atlantic.

On the other hand the defence aspects of European cooperation were likely to be problematic given the British military's preference for Anglo-American collaboration; it was a preference grounded in the experiences of the Second World War when the forces of the West European powers had not distinguished themselves.

Moreover, with the strength of the Communist Party in France, the British military were even less willing to cooperate with their French counterparts. Yet the French, who were increasingly concerned by the East-West breakdown and the rebuilding of West Germany, desired cooperation with both the British and the Americans.[24] Bevin, unlike the majority of military leaders, was keen to get defence cooperation started once tripartite cooperation had broken down, and this brought him into conflict with the Chiefs of Staff committee. The problem was not simply the British military's distrust of the French and their reluctance to act without the involvement of the Americans, but the fact that what planning there had been over Britain's role in West Europe involved the US navy in an operation, code named 'Dunkirk'; this aimed at a rapid evacuation from the Continent of the German occupation forces.[25] Such plans, if revealed, were hardly likely to provide a good atmosphere for Anglo-French staff talks or to make a positive contribution to the general goal of closer Anglo-French cooperation. In short there were going to be the same kind of difficulties reconciling foreign policy and military strategy as there had been with foreign policy and the needs of the British economy. With the British military seeking to withdraw troops from Western Europe rather than despatch more, Ivone Kirkpatrick concluded that Britain would have to admit this to the Europeans or refuse to reveal its military plans; either way the West European powers would be discouraged from associating themselves with Britain. He therefore concluded that the only course would be to involve the Americans in the defence of Western Europe; if, as seemed likely, the Americans were to refuse to commit any forces then a general commitment to go to war with an aggressor might provide some reassurance to the Europeans.[26] This was a significant early assessment of the problems that were later to emerge and of their eventual solution.

The political strategy in January was soon defined in terms of first making a joint Anglo-French offer of a treaty to Belgium, Holland and Luxembourg and then considering the association of Italy, other Mediterranean states and Scandinavia. In this way the non-communist countries of Western Europe and the Middle East could be linked. It would also be necessary to supplement European economic integration with a planned development of Africa and to make provisions for security in Western Europe, the latter of which could only be done with American cooperation. To achieve this, the military stressed it would be necessary to decide on a specific British strategy in the event of a war with Russia and discuss the defence of Western Europe with the Americans. In short to get agreement with the United States on political and military questions.[27] All this could well prove difficult. On the European side the snag was that the French were not in favour of grand designs in early 1948 and preferred bilateral treaties on Dunkirk lines. The Benelux countries felt that only a multilateral treaty would provide them with sufficient security while avoiding French domination. The importance of French cooperation ensured that on 20 January the British and French governments informed the Benelux countries that they would jointly offer a treaty to them, although the French were insisting that any military arrangements would have to wait until Anglo-French military discussions were completed.[28] In the meantime Marshall was to be informed of the West European treaties, Britain's overall aim, 'which should not be subject to his approval', and how the whole idea was linked to what Britain was doing in the Middle East.[29] On 20 January Marshall gave his support for the proposals, although the State Department expressed the view that a treaty modelled on the Rio agreement would be better than one modelled on Dunkirk,[30] and two days later Bevin went public on the idea of Western union with a speech in the House of Commons.[31]

As the Foreign Office was grappling with the kind of arrangements that would be finalised with the Western Europeans, the important issue of military coop- eration, within whatever framework was decided upon, came before the Defence Committee. Decisions on the future size of the armed forces would obviously affect whether or not Britain was in a position to provide assistance to the Europeans. When discussions were held on the old question of sending ground forces to the Continent, the Foreign Secretary 'pointed out the embarrassment that would be likely to arise with our potential European allies if our plans were based on the assumption that we did not intend to do this'. Several ministers were, however, inclined to agree with the Chief of the Air Staff that the 'maintenance of a first-class Navy and a first class Air Force, together with an army on a continental basis was beyond our resources'.[32] The only support for Bevin's idea of linking military strategy to foreign policy came, surprisingly, from the CIGS, Montgomery, who had now completely changed his mind on the value of a continental commitment, and who suggested that Territorial units could be expanded to fight in Western Europe. The opposition of the other Chiefs, however, ensured that the drafting of a White Paper went forward on the basis of no provision for a continental army.[33]

Montgomery's change of heart may have been connected to the hope he shared with Bevin of developing European and African resources, although, unlike the Foreign Secretary, the CIGS saw the Empire as a potential source of military manpower. For whatever reason, when the Joint Planners concluded that a land defence of Western Europe would require 30 to 40 Anglo-American divisions, and therefore was impractical until Western Europe revived economically and militar- ily or Germany was rearmed, Montgomery began a determined campaign against such ideas and in favour of committing British forces to fight on the Continent.[34] The campaign was to be based on the close consultation already established with Bevin on the basis of a shared interest in grandiose schemes for Europe and Africa, because the Foreign Secretary somehow had to integrate West European defence cooperation into his overall plan for the Third Force backed initially by the Americans. Montgomery's reply to the idea of the Joint Planners focused on the inevitability of the struggle between the free world and the communist bloc over Germany, and the need to have a united Germany looking west. Control of adequate resources was behind the idea of German reunification, but European resources alone were not deemed enough; Europe's future would depend on developing a non-dollar economy in Africa and linking it to Europe, and then preparing for the inevitable military conflict with the Soviets which Montgomery deemed likely by 1957. In order to build up a Western union which would have the necessary resources to deal with that threat, Montgomery argued it would be necessary to provide the psychological reassurance inherent in a British commit- ment to fight on the Rhine.[35] The Chief of the Naval Staff believed such ideas were nonsensical, and argued it would be pointless to try and defend the Rhine unless it could actually be done; it would be impossible in 1948 to prevent the Russians marching westwards and therefore Britain should not commit its forces to any continental scheme until the West European countries had sufficiently recovered to make a military campaign feasible. In contrast Montgomery was suggesting that Western Europe would lack the resolve to regain its military and economic strength unless Britain committed itself to a military strategy which, while completely unrealistic, would provide the necessary encouragement. The question was whether such assurances should be given in view of the damaging effect on Western union if they were not.[36]

Two days later, in light of the important implications the military debate had for the 'First Aim of British Foreign Policy', ministers became involved in the discussions. Montgomery suggested that with American equipment and two British divisions properly organised and well led, European forces should eventually be able to keep the Russians out; in other words making a commitment to the Continent now would not produce a massive increase in Britain's defence burden. The Prime Minister was, in his words, 'disturbed', because, as has been seen, he had been led to believe that the whole purpose of British defence strategy was to hold the Middle East and launch a counter offensive from it as the most effective way of dealing with a Soviet assault on Western Europe; nor did he think that the West Europeans would get much comfort from a British commitment to supply one or two divisions. Bevin, not surprisingly, disagreed, arguing that the West Europeans did have sufficient forces, and if Britain had ground troops to spare there should be no objection to sending them to the Continent. The Foreign Secretary did, however, make two key points which illustrated his attitude to the whole question of continental defence and Western union. He was clearly concerned that defence issues were dominating the Western union debate when in fact they were only one facet of it; it was therefore also important, he argued, to arrange for close links between the countries concerned in banking, financial and currency matters and to establish economic links with Africa and the Commonwealth. Moreover, the crucial factor affecting force provision was the United States, and no decision had been made in Washington on American policy.[37]

In fact there were some differences within the State Department over the exact form of Western union, with Hickerson (head of the Office of European Affairs) and Kennan (head of the Policy Planning Staff) in favour of a Third Force that would resist communism and be friendly to the United States, but be independent enough not to make excessive demands on American resources. Yet while Hickerson felt the United States should be prepared to enter a defence arrangement in support of this Third Force 'strong enough to say "no" to both the United States and the Soviet Union', Kennan was wary of becoming involved in military talks. Both were, however, convinced that Western union should be a European creation, and that while the United States might be prepared to give the kind of backing Bevin envisaged, some form of European organisation would have to be established before Washington was involved.[38] Bevin, on the other hand, partly because of the problems of persuading the British military to cooperate with the Europeans without the Americans, and in line with Kirkpatrick's ideas, formally sought, on 27 January, an Anglo-American commitment to go to war with an aggressor in order to reinforce the defence treaties envisaged for Europe. Undersecretary Bob Lovett replied to this suggestion in line with Kennan's and Hickerson's views, and the Embassy recorded on 2 February that when there was 'evidence of unity with a firm determination to effect an arrangement under which European countries were prepared to act in concert to defend themselves, the United States would carefully consider the role it might play in support of Western union'. This led Bevin to refer to the idea of a 'vicious circle'. Western union would have to be established before the United States would make a commitment to support it, yet in terms of the defence arrangements necessary to make it work, there were difficulties in the way of further progress without American involvement.[39]

In the Chiefs of Staff Committee Bevin asserted that he would impress upon the Americans that, unlike in previous wars, the Europeans could not be expected to act as a mercenary army or a defensive outpost of the United States; the Americans would have to be involved militarily from the beginning of any future conflict. In the ensuing discussion the importance of the imperial dimension again emerged. It was pointed out that Western union defence arrangements should not be confined to a campaign in Western Europe, but should incorporate the Middle East from where ultimately the offensive should be launched. The plans already announced for Western union were deemed to have probably turned the tide of American opinion in favour of approving Marshall Aid, and so it was agreed that without further study no decisions could be taken on the question of sending land forces to the Continent.[40]

Foreign Office concern that too much attention was being paid to the defence aspects of Western union was again expressed in a telegram to Paris, indicating that, far from being primarily an attempt to drag the United States into a military alliance with Europe, the whole idea was conceived for other reasons connected to the Empire, a Third Force and Britain's global position. The Ambassador in Paris was told that Western union should not be bogged down in an examination of defence problems and discussions should be lifted to a higher plane which would permit the examination of economic (including the colonies), spiritual and cultural problems.[41] (The 'spiritual' idea was one going back to December 1947 and one official had already recorded a query over whether it meant a United States of Europe, a customs union or a regional defence arrangement.)[42]

A further defence snag had appeared following the Benelux suggestion at the beginning of February for a regional pact in accordance with Article 52 of the UN Charter. Interestingly, the Foreign Office was 'at this stage' *against* a military pact not only because it would not provide security against Russia but because it would encourage those 'isolationists' in the United States who believed West European security could be assured without the American involvement that the British military and the Foreign Secretary believed to be either necessary or desirable.[43] Similar views were expressed by the French who wanted to defer discussions on security until the US government could be associated with them.[44] Thus it appeared that the British were well and truly in a vicious circle. It has been argued in the literature, which generally acclaims Bevin's achievement in breaking this circle and producing the Atlantic Alliance, that the vicious circle represented the West European refusal to make progress towards Western union without security assurances from the Americans and the United States' insistence that the West Europeans set up a security organisation before it became involved.[45] However, it should not be assumed that the idea of Western union, stemming from the breakdown of tripartite cooperation, was, in its 'spiritual' or general aspects, dominated by the quest for a security arrangement. In fact Bevin was seeking to play down the defence aspects in the first two months of 1948 because the real goal of Western union was the eventual establishment of a Third Force. The real vicious circle was finding ways to make this essentially imperial strategy produce a European organisation under British leadership when it was so difficult to get any military arrangements between Britain and Western Europe without the Americans becoming involved and playing the leading role.

Another problem is that defence arrangements, treaties, and guarantees, which fall under the general umbrella of 'security', involve political issues of alliances and treaties and military issues of strategy, pooling of resources, battle plans and command structures. It is important to distinguish precisely what is meant when 'security' questions were being discussed by military and political leaders. For instance, in February 1948 when the French were pressing for security guarantees and the Benelux countries were referring to regional arrangements compatible with the UN Charter, it transpired that the latter did not necessarily mean territorial guarantees but effective joint military planning.[46] Given the British military's attitude to fighting on the Continent, and the decisions taken in January 1948, this was unlikely to prove a fruitful source of cooperation. As things stood on the political aspects of a treaty, the British and the French submitted a draft on 19 February based on the Dunkirk model, while Bevin pressed for a five-power meeting to iron out the differences between a bilateral and a multilateral approach; this was initially opposed by the French who did not want to hold a ministerial meeting until agreement was certain.[47]

It almost looked as if the Foreign Office's emphasis once again would have to be on economic cooperation, despite all the opposition this had produced from other government departments. A working group within the office of Stevens, Kirkpatrick and Hall Patch produced a paper in mid-February entitled 'Economic Aspects of Western union'. The paper argued that defence arrangements should be supplemented by an integrated European economic system that would end Western Europe's financial dependence on the United States. The system would include a customs union and eventually a full-scale economic Union of France, West Germany, Italy, Benelux and the United Kingdom. In institutional terms the draft distinguished between Western union and the CEEC because the latter was linked to the United States which therefore made the ultimate goal of independence from the Americans more difficult to achieve. Creating this new organisation would mean the abandonment of unqualified multilateralism, some sacrificing of self-interest and sovereignty, the disruption of imperial preferences and of the government's attempts to regulate competition in the home market. Yet in the long run the memorandum claimed that such radical solutions would guarantee security in Western Europe and, most importantly, ensure Britain's survival as a world power.[48] Two days later in a conversation with the French Ambassador, Bevin made sure to remind Massigli that the customs union had to be separated from the European Recovery Programme and that important work had to be done with regard to the overseas territories of France and Britain.[49]

One argument that the Foreign Office could continue to use was the American predisposition for a customs union. In early 1948 the Treasury suggested that a possible way of avoiding a customs union would be to make a declaration in favour of a less far reaching European arrangement which might be achieved by, for instance, negotiating a series of preferences in direct association with the CEEC.[50] On 23 February, however, Bevin presented a paper to the Cabinet which proposed a Western union bank as a mechanism for dealing with the problems of France's post-convertibility crisis deficit with the sterling area as a whole and with Belgium's European trade surplus which produced a greater Belgian demand for gold or dollars. The Treasury was opposed to the idea of a central European bank just as it had always been opposed to a customs union. What was supported was 'transnational economic planning on an ad hoc, project-by-project basis with a view to intergovernmental and interindustrial agreements aimed at maximising dollar earnings and savings in the ERP area as a whole'. This was the kind of policy that was to emerge at the official level, through an interdepartmental group, before being approved by the Economic Policy Committee and then by the Cabinet on 8 March.[51]

By then greater Cold War tensions had produced new fears in the West which led to fresh initiatives over Western union and to a multilateral treaty which was a step towards implementing some of Bevin's ideas on cooperation, but not exactly one which many in the Foreign Office would have liked. In the last week of February an internal coup in Czechoslovakia brought to power a communist regime and eliminated the last remaining democratic regime in Eastern Europe. The fear grew that with strong and rebellious communist parties in Italy and France the hand of Moscow would be extended to Western Europe. In Paris the immediate reaction was to send what the British later termed an hysterical message to Washington urging immediate consultations on security matters. What was causing concern was not primarily a military invasion by the Soviet Union (although the French feared German recovery might produce one), but internal communist subversion which could be better deterred and dealt with if the Western powers, and especially the United States, joined in taking measures which would signal their determination to prevent the spread of communism.[52] At the same time the coup in Prague brought the French round to accepting a multilateral defence treaty and therefore helped prepare the way for the signing of the Brussels Pact on 17 March.

In Britain the Soviet actions brought forth a Cabinet memorandum on the 'Threat to Western Civilisation', while the Embassy in Washington urged that the prospects of ultimately securing US support for closer European defence ties would be greater if Britain showed boldness rather than hesitating to move without American concurrence.[53] The result was a Cabinet meeting on 5 March which agreed on the urgency of completing negotiations for economic, cultural and defence pacts between Britain, France, Holland, Belgium and Luxembourg and enlisting the cooperation of the Commonwealth and other friendly countries, including those in the Western Hemisphere, in defence of Western civilisation.[54] The result of this decision was a directive to the Chiefs of Staff to examine what was required, short of war, to support diplomatic action to prevent the spread of communism (and military measures if all else failed); the Chiefs were also asked to look at the possibility of British military involvement on the Continent in any future war and to examine the size and shape of the armed forces within a total budget of £600m.[55]

Western union was now rapidly approaching the moment when some steps would have to be taken to give concrete form to Bevin's vague ideas, and it was not easy to see what could be achieved given the problems of economic and defence cooperation. In the wake of the Czech coup the priority was clearly to produce something which would remove the fear in Western Europe of falling prey to communist takeovers. On the other hand a simple defence treaty without the Americans might not fit the bill in terms of security; nor might it incorporate the other elements that Bevin deemed so essential for Western union. Indeed as late as 10 March Bevin was still pointing out that, contrary to some views, his plan for Western union was very much more than a defensive military agreement.[56] In other words there was a danger that the whole idea of Western union would be boiled down to a defence treaty.

In the wake of the Prague coup this danger understandably increased, and the Cabinet meeting in early March which produced the instructions to the Chiefs of Staff to review a European commitment threatened to undermine the emphasis on the Middle Eastern region, which, as we have seen, was the area deemed most important by the British military. It also meant that defence policy would have to be geared much more to the requirements of diplomacy in encouraging a feeling of confidence and solidarity amongst the West Europeans. While it was necessary, as part of the broader global strategy, to prevent Western union simply becoming a defence treaty, the Foreign Office also had to ensure that military cooperation helped to strengthen the ties between Britain and the West Europeans in order that British goals could be achieved.

As far as the first of these requirements was concerned, the signing of the Brussels Treaty was to some extent a source of disappointment for the Foreign Office, who had of course hoped to use this step towards Western union as a means of promoting economic ties between Europe and Africa. Article 1 of the Brussels Treaty referred to the importance of economic cooperation and stated that the Consultative Council would organise and coordinate economic activities and produce the best possible results by the 'elimination of conflict in economic policies, the coordination of production and the development of commercial exchanges'.[57] The talks which produced the treaty also covered colonial questions which, particularly in Africa, were such an important part of Britain's imperial strategy. The original Foreign Office draft for Article 1 in fact stated that the five powers 'will make every effort to associate the overseas territories for whose foreign relations they are respectively responsible in the attainment of these aims'. Unfortunately the Benelux countries suggested that the Brussels Treaty Organisation was not an appropriate body to deal with colonial cooperation between the West European powers because Portugal was concerned with African cooperation while the Dutch were not involved to the same extent as the British and French. The Foreign Office position, as expressed to the British negotiating team, was that it accepted this view but 'attached great importance to colonial cooperation'.[58]

This disappointment over the scope of the Brussels Treaty Organisation was accompanied by more awkward problems over defence cooperation. By March 1948 it was clear that for the French and the Belgians the main rationale for moving towards defence cooperation was not the security associated with treaties or declarations but the development of a common strategy for the defence of Western Europe and the provision of military assistance. It was the need for military assistance and the adoption of a joint strategy which prompted the visits to

London of senior French officers in early 1948.[59] Yet, as has been seen, British strategy had been based on a major commitment to the Middle East and a withdrawal from Western Europe. With the exception of Montgomery, senior military figures did not want to get involved with talks on the defence of Western Europe and the provision of military assistance to carry out such a strategy. Cunningham still argued that it made no sense to talk about military support for Europe until sufficient military forces existed. In addition there was the general distrust of the French by the British military which was made worse by the strength of the communists within France, even though by 1948 they were no longer members of the government. The military argued it would be foolish to reveal to the French the weakness of British forces and distinctly counterproductive politically to explain the need to repeat the 1940 scenario where France would be abandoned while British forces were sent to prosecute the war in the Middle East. Moreover there was no real reason to risk compromising British security or damaging Anglo-French relations because the British military did not believe the Soviets would deliberately start a major war until the mid-1950s when their recovery from the devastation of the Second World War had been achieved. There was of course always the possibility of war breaking out by accident or miscalculation, but in that case Cunningham felt that Soviet forces would draw back rather than get involved in a total war, while Tedder believed the Russians were thinking of withdrawing east in any conflict rather than attacking west.[60]

This, however, did not rule out a need to make preparations in 1948 for the time when conflict with the Soviet Union was deemed likely as a result of deliberate communist aggression; this, it was believed, would first require the building of confidence through cooperation in Western Europe. Military alliances would also help convince the Russians of the determination of the West to resist the spread of communism and therefore discourage them from internal subversion through indigenous communist parties in France and Italy. In the eyes of the Joint Planners the British had to make Soviet leaders realise that war *would* be the result if communism spread further west through the means employed in Czechoslovakia. Britain also had to use security pacts to encourage anti-communist forces to take action against their opponents in certain countries without feeling that such actions would produce a Soviet response.[61] However, Montgomery, with Bevin's support, was claiming that the sought after confidence and encouragement could not be provided without an alliance based on a military strategy to defend Western Europe by fighting on the Rhine.[62] This was the kind of military commitment which, while desirable on grounds of foreign policy and long-term defence needs, could not, in the short term, be reconciled with Britain's resources or with British strategic thinking.

For the military, if any form of commitment to or cooperation with the West Europeans was going to be made then the role of the United States was vital. The British Chiefs of Staff, faced by their own military weakness and by overwhelming American strength, could all accept that transatlantic cooperation was the most important consideration; Britain's role in Europe had therefore to be considered from the perspective of what if any resources the United States might provide.[63] Once the British knew this then they would be more able to determine what if any commitments they could make on the Continent of Europe.

In March 1948 the Americans had not of course decided on what actions to take in support of Bevin's Western union idea or in response to the creation of the Brussels Treaty Organisation. Bevin wanted, as the first step, to secure American backing for the newly signed Brussels pact, although he did not specify whether this backing should take the form of a presidential declaration, the provision of military aid or the association of the United States with the Organisation.[64] Then, in line with his power-political conceptions of Britain organising the middle of the planet, it would be necessary to have treaties with the other European powers on the Atlantic fringes of the Continent and also with the Mediterranean or Middle Eastern states; these were vital as part of securing the broader aim of Western union and preventing it becoming merely a treaty of military assistance as the Foreign Office believed the French desired.[65] From the strategic point of view Tedder argued it made no difference whether the United States initially backed Western union, an Atlantic pact or a Mediterranean security system, because there was no difference in the degree of priority between them.[66]

Securing the backing of the Americans for the various pacts led to General Hollis, Chief Staff Officer to the Ministry of Defence, being sent to head a team engaged in secret talks at the Pentagon between 22 March and 1 April which also involved the Canadians.[67] By the time Hollis left, the Soviet threat to Norway inherent in rumours of an approach from Moscow for a treaty with the Norwegians, had led Bevin to conclude that an Atlantic system 'should be studied without delay'.[68] Hollis returned with a belief that the United States would be willing to come in on any security arrangements made by the European powers; it was therefore a question of deciding exactly what form these 'security arrangements' would take.[69]

On receiving this report from Hollis, Bevin wrote to Attlee emphasising that he was still thinking in terms of a triple system in which the Brussels Treaty would be accompanied by Atlantic and Mediterranean security systems.[70] The importance of this linkage to the Mediterranean had increased because of the need for military cooperation in Western Europe which might threaten the British ability to provide forces for the Middle East. Indeed the Chiefs of Staff, following the 5 March Cabinet meeting that gave added importance to the European situation, had been obliged to define a 'stop line' for the defence of Europe to be drawn as far east as possible, although it was argued that no actual decision could be taken to defend such a line until American support was guaranteed.[71] Hollis had therefore to try and secure American acceptance of the 'stop line' and of the importance of defending the Middle East, but obtained only an acceptance in principle of the 'stop line', although in 1948 there was an Anglo-American agreement on the general military importance of the Middle East.[72] Unfortunately, the kind of tripartite security system Bevin had in mind was more difficult for the Americans to accept, and they wanted the Mediterranean system abandoned and Italy brought into an Atlantic security scheme. Bevin told Attlee a Middle Eastern system could replace the Mediterranean one, but given Britain's difficulties with Egypt and Iraq, such a system was not politically practical in the immediate future.[73] Thus there seemed to be significant obstacles to the construction of defence arrangements, backed by the United States, which would link Europe and Britain's informal Empire in the Mediterranean and Middle East.

Moreover the difficulties of providing defence arrangements which could encourage closer European ties with Britain were also becoming increasingly apparent in the spring of 1948. At the same time as the Pentagon talks were being held on American support for the Brussels Treaty, involvement in an Atlantic pact and support for the defence of the Middle East, members of the British Planning Staff were asked to go to Washington for discussions with their United States counterparts. The talks were to reflect the nature of Anglo-American cooperation over strategic planning for the next decade inasmuch as they provided for a significant pooling of information before the drawing up of *separate* plans. In other words the talks would cover force deployment in particular areas and overall strategy (but not the targeting plans of the Strategic Air Command) in order that each side could support the other as much as possible. The idea in 1948 was to prepare plans for global war in the three periods of 1948–50, 1954–56 and after 1956.[74] It soon became clear that the Americans, with memories of Pearl Harbor, gave priority to plans for dealing with a global conflict with the resources available on 1 July 1948; this emergency planning would essentially provide for the most effective response to a Soviet attack before 1950. Hollis, who remained in Washington, also reported an American fear that Britain was too weak to mean business, which in turn strengthened the US Service Chiefs' resolve to secure British involvement with emergency planning before turning to long-term cooperation. Such planning would of course be significant in terms of relating military cooperation to any new security pacts. Unfortunately the British military were only too aware that the American ideas on evacuating their German forces from Western Europe had not changed. At the Pentagon talks, General Gruenther had emphasised that any American commitment to aid a victim of Soviet attack should *not* require that such aid would be delivered locally.[75] The British planners, like Tedder and Cunningham, were willing to go along with this refusal to commit land forces to the defence of Europe, leaving the politicians with the problem of explaining to the Europeans the importance of signing defence treaties with Britain and the United States when neither country was actually willing to defend them.[76] As long as this remained the case it was difficult to see how the building up of French and Belgian morale was likely to be achieved.

The signing of the Brussels Treaty had of course taken place by the middle of March, which could be interpreted as providing the evidence of West European cooperation which those in the State Department had seen as necessary if an American commitment to West European defence was to be secured. In fact the State Department defined such cooperation not in terms of pacts or declarations, but in terms of concrete measures to ensure the collective defence of Western Europe. Indeed, on 10 April 1948 the Washington Embassy reported Assistant Secretary Lovett's views that the Brussels Pact would remain a piece of paper until its signatories got to work on active plans for their own defence. In effect the State Department was looking for an emergency plan for the defence of Western Europe when the Pentagon was geared to evacuating American troops from the Continent. In Europe not only did the British military largely share that view, but they were also reluctant to start military talks with the French and the West Europeans.[77] In fact on 15 April when the American Ambassador in London explained to Bevin that the integration of the defence plans of the Brussels Treaty powers would impress the authorities in Washington and enable the Europeans to decide what they needed in terms of United States support, no steps had been taken towards serious military talks by the five European powers.[78] In fact the British, and particularly the French, were approaching things radically differently from the State Department. Bidault's reaction to the signing of the Brussels Treaty had been to urge immediate work on obtaining US support for the treaty. Bevin agreed, stating that 'immediate consideration should be given to security'. Clearly the two Foreign Secretaries saw the Brussels Pact as a political device to get American military support rather than something which embodied military cooperation as a prerequisite for American military assistance.

However, there was one fundamental difference between Bevin's and Bidault's approach. The French position was that it was pointless to make any defence plans without the Americans who alone had the resources to provide for the effective defence of Western Europe.[79] Bevin, because of his Western union plans and the consequent need to build the Third Force, saw things in a rather different light. The Foreign Secretary explained to Bidault that he did not want the Americans involved 'from the beginning' because they would 'tell us what we should do'.[80] It was an attitude consistent with 'The First Aim of British Foreign Policy' which sought independence from the Americans through short-term United States support in economic and security matters.

On 16 April the British learned of a State Department questionnaire to be sent to the Brussels Pact signatories requesting information on such issues as the pooling and standardising of equipment, the structure of a future military organisation and, most crucially, on what forces the five powers would assemble and what plan they would follow before American help arrived.[81] The first problem was to persuade the French that there was some value in military preparations without the involvement of the Americans. The second problem was going to be the nature of the future defence organisation, given that the State Department initially seemed keen to bring Italy and the Scandinavian countries into the Brussels Treaty. This was opposed by the British for three reasons: because they were aware of the reluctance of the West Europeans to make commitments to the Scandinavians; because they wanted a separate Mediterranean pact; and because the Brussels Treaty powers could more readily form the hard core of Western union with links to Africa.[82] The third problem was persuading the military that emergency planning had to be geared to the defence of Western Europe.

The nature of Anglo-American emergency planning had become clearer as a result of the talks held in Washington by the planning staffs in April 1948. Two emergency plans emerged, and the British plan 'Doublequick' was the first attempt to define in detail a response to a Soviet attack and was, unsurprisingly, based initially on the evacuation from Europe of British forces in Germany.[83] The original draft, produced in early May, seemed to highlight the problems and contradictions which the British had become entangled in. 'Doublequick' had emerged because the Chiefs of Staff believed it was *militarily* essential to cooperate with the United States; Western union was conceived as part of a power-political determination to secure independence from the Americans which made it *politically* essential to cooperate with the West Europeans. The Europeans saw such cooperation, in the tense atmosphere of early 1948, as involving military collaboration, but the British, hoping to build confidence, could not afford to let the Europeans know the nature of their essential military cooperation with the Americans; this would have to be revealed if the answers to the State Department questionnaire were to be a true reflection of British military thinking. Bevin may not have fully grasped the nature of the difficulty because he proposed that answers be provided as part of what he felt was psychological reassurance for the West Europeans. The fact was that precisely the opposite was likely to occur; but in any case the Chiefs of Staff insisted that they could not provide top secret information until they were satisfied with Western union security arrangements.[84] In addition there was the fact that the State Department wanted some evidence of combined military planning before making any commitments to European defence, whereas the French were arguing for American assistance first, a position reflected in the Brussels Treaty powers' response to the questionnaire which stated that, while they were ready to make arrangements for military talks, they would 'simultaneously require the assistance of the United States in order to organise the effective defence of West Europe'.[85] In this context a Military Staff Committee of the Brussels Treaty Organisation was then formed on 30 April and charged with 'preparing jointly the building up and the eventual use in the field of the forces of the Five Powers for the defence of West Europe'.[86] If the French had their way and involved the Americans in military planning there was bound to be some political embarrassment, and it would prevent Bevin from creating a well-organised European grouping which, while backed by the Americans, would eventually emerge as a powerful and independent world force.

In April 1948 Bevin was still firmly committed to this strategy and explained to Bidault that 'we should prepare our own plans' while also securing United States support, whereas Bidault argued that the Americans should decide what support they would give to the Europeans in order that the latter could then decide what they should provide. The following day Bevin returned to the charge, arguing that the West Europeans should not begin discussions with the Americans without having made some progress together as they had to 'maintain some element of independence' and then obtain United States assistance in so far as this was required; in defence terms, therefore, it was a question of seeing what each nation could provide for the defence of West Europe.[87]

The problems of promoting European defence cooperation independently from the Americans were increasingly matched in the economic sphere. In April 1948 the CEEC gave way to a formal body known as the Organisation for European Economic Cooperation (OEEC) with its headquarters in Paris. The OEEC was to work with the American European Cooperation Administration (ECA) and, of course, to be geared to balancing Europe's dollar account by 1952–53. Bevin had initially hoped to distinguish between the building of Western union and the organisation for distributing Marshall Aid, in order to achieve more readily economic independence from the Americans by linking the European powers and their colonial territories whose dollar earnings might not be offset against Europe's deficit. The failure to take steps towards this through the Brussels Treaty Organisation was to help link the OEEC more firmly with the overseas territories of its member states and to emphasise the importance of the OEEC for the economic goals of Western union. Indeed, the failure to provide for or encourage economic links between the Europeans and their African colonies under the Brussels Treaty meant that British imperial strategy became much more firmly focused on the OEEC. The idea of a standing organisation of the Brussels Treaty powers to deal with economic matters was resisted by the Economic Policy Committee for fear of prejudicing the work of the OEEC which contained all the

European colonial powers and which was to offer the best prospect of linking Europe with the economic development of Africa.

The role of the OEEC was also strengthened by the attitude of the Colonial Office to the involvement of the Europeans in the kind of African development envisaged by the Foreign Office. In the first third of 1948 the whole question of European cooperation in Africa as part of reducing the dollar shortage came to a head when, despite the obvious difficulties over a customs union, the Cabinet agreed 'there was no alternative to a policy of full support for close cooperation in West Europe . . . even at the cost of considerable changes in the structure of the United Kingdom and some loss of the advantages which we now enjoy over other European countries'.[88] However the Committee on European Economic Cooperation was considering the implications of European integration, not only in terms of structural changes in Britain, but in terms of Marshall Aid and dollar saving. The customs union idea had been attacked within Whitehall because of its implications for the British domestic economy, but increasingly its acceptability, or lack of it, was to be seen in terms of bridging the dollar gap. The Committee's predictions of the impact of Marshall Aid in early 1948 made gloomy reading. By the end of 1952 Europe was deemed likely to meet a mere two-thirds of its deficit with the Western Hemisphere, and therefore without an increase in Marshall Aid there would be an acute standard of living crisis; to avoid this and to direct efforts to overcoming the deficit the UK would have to make adjustments to its basic economic structure. Yet if European unification was to become the inevitable result of the kind of European cooperation embarked upon, great changes would be required. The memorandum also pointed out that while Marshall Aid committed Britain to European economic cooperation, the concentration on specific dollar savings and earnings presented the least difficulty if done in conjunction with the sterling area Dominions (Australia, New Zealand and South Africa).[89] Here was another analysis of the conflict between meeting the dollar deficit and European economic cooperation, which was deemed acute if European unification occurred, and which was likely to have disastrous consequences if, as predicted, the dollar deficit of Western Europe as a whole was not overcome by 1952. The clear implication was that Britain was not going to achieve recovery by cooperation between Europe and the Empire, but by concentrating on the Empire instead of Europe in order to avoid the difficulties and upheaval of restructuring *and* an acute standard of living crisis. Consequently, despite the Cabinet rhetoric on the costs Britain should be prepared to pay for European economic cooperation, by the time Bevin met Bidault in April he was explaining his preference for a free trade area rather than a customs union.[90] It was another indication of how, even when the defence questions were looming so large, Bevin was concerned that European cooperation should not be limited to security matters despite the likely drawbacks to close economic cooperation with the West Europeans.

The promotion of European cooperation in Africa, which was what Bevin hoped to use to overcome the dollar gap, was facing further obstacles in 1948. In late 1947 the French proposed a formal colonial commission to examine development projects in Africa. The Colonial Office was extremely alarmed by such an idea, as with its attempt to promote greater African involvement with the affairs of the colonies, it feared such a body would be resented by Africans as embodying continued European exploitation. Such resentment would be all the more likely to occur if such a body was composed exclusively of colonial powers. Partly for this reason the Colonial Office suggested that the CEEC, as it then was, should establish a body which would be concerned with the economic position of the colonies in relation to the Marshall Aid programme; this would have the advantage of not being composed exclusively of colonial powers and would therefore avoid the accusations of 'ganging up' which were likely to come from the anti-colonial elements within the United Nations. Such considerations were deemed important, and by linking the OEEC to the African development question the Colonial Office would score another political point; if non-colonial powers were involved it would strengthen the argument that the problems of non-self-governing territories should not be treated as colonial issues but looked at in the same way as the problems of independent states at a similar stage of development. The Colonial Office, somewhat surprisingly, was able to avoid the appearance of 'ganging up', when later in the year an Overseas Territories Sub-committee of the OEEC containing the representatives of the colonial powers was established under the chairmanship of the head of the Economic Bureau in the Ministry of Overseas France, Georges Peter. Its terms of reference defined its objectives as the promotion of the social and economic development of the overseas territories and the definition of their role in European recovery. The committee contained a member of the ECA and thus the United States was to some extent directly involved with the linking of African development to European economic cooperation which was certainly not the outcome Bevin would have preferred.[91]

In February 1948, the working party on Anglo-French economic cooperation in West Africa, headed by Kenneth Robinson, completed its work with the presentation of papers on communications, commodity price policy, inter-colonial trade and the coordination of development plans. The papers saw little prospect of any significant progress in these areas: what was possible in communications was being catered for by the existing conferences on technical cooperation while progress in other areas was handicapped by the reluctance of the French to delegate responsibility to the men on the spot and to share information with the British. In addition there were the inevitable difficulties arising from exchange controls, fluctuating exchange rates and the implications for the franc and sterling zones of radical proposals on inter-colonial trade. Robinson did not believe that there was any likelihood in the next few years of 'substantial results either in raising the standard of living of colonial peoples or in increased supplies to metropolitan countries'. However, talks with the French went ahead, which merely confirmed the differences in developmental and price policies with the result that while there was a friendly exchange of information there was no coordination of policies. Bevin, having read the conclusions of the talks, called for a progress report on action taken and an assessment of the results in terms of colonial living standards and the British balance of payments.[92]

In terms of the dollar gap the interesting thing was that the colonies of the other European colonial powers all had a dollar deficit except the Belgian Congo, and the Treasury envisaged other difficulties about Euro-African development. The French now had a sizeable sterling deficit and therefore Britain would be under pressure to provide loans; then there was the difficulty with the sterling area balances which were increasing in the first quarter of 1948 because of the success of efforts to reduce the sterling area's net deficit with the dollar zone.[93] If the balances were to be allowed to be run down (an obvious possibility given the political implications of their rise) what could or should the money be spent on? These financial issues were accompanied by other dilemmas in terms of trade and finance related to the British colonial surplus with the dollar zone and to Britain's trade surplus with the rest of Western Europe; this was complicated by the fact that the Rest of the Sterling Area (RSA) had an even bigger surplus with Europe. Such facts would become more pertinent when the question of a European payments agreement, linked to Marshall Aid, was discussed later in the year and provide further contradictions between an imperial/sterling area strategy and a strategy which required linking Europe to the Empire.

In the meantime, the problems centred on colonial development. In April 1948 the interim report of the Colonial Development Working Party under Sir Edwin Plowden was completed. It referred to the shortage of goods and services and predicted that development would also be held up because of a shortage of administrators and technical staff. The report recommended that priority be given to the repair and improvement of the existing colonial infrastructure, with transport and communications receiving special attention, and emphasised the practical difficulties in the way of reaping short-term benefits from African development.[94] Such conclusions could not be easily reconciled with Creech Jones' March statement to the Colonial Economic and Development Council that 'to integrate the economy of the colonies more closely with the economy of the United Kingdom, should give the colonies opportunities which they might not otherwise have to raise the standards of living and develop social welfare'.[95]

Colonial officials were also keen to emphasise the benefits to the colonies of West European Union, arguing that the primary object of European cooperation was the promotion of the interests of the colonial territories themselves, which just happened to fit in with Bevin's suggestions.[96] In order to give some meaning to this rhetoric the Colonial Office contacted the Treasury to argue that as colonial development had to be implemented to reduce dollar expenditure, financial restrictions should be removed to enable the colonies to get access to the London money market and to the sterling balances. The Treasury found this attitude 'rather tiresome', and informed the Colonial Office that the colonies should live within their income except in so far as large-scale measures of development and investment called for the running down of sterling balances. There were clearly fears that the balances would be reduced to permit capital development in the colonies which existed alongside Treasury concerns that the Board of Trade wanted the balances to be used to purchase British exports when it was important to gear trade and finance to dollar earning.[97] In the event the colonies were informed that 'the control of imports must continue to be an essential feature of colonial policy'.[98] Thus, despite the rhetoric of colonial development, and despite the determination of Bevin to link European economic cooperation to African development, the practical difficulties of supplying goods and equipment were accompanied by the financial constraints inherent in Treasury desires to ensure the sterling area as a whole came to terms with the dollar deficit whatever the needs of British exporters or colonial consumers. This kind of imperial strategy was not reconcilable with European cooperation in African development, especially as most of the non-British territories were running a dollar deficit. It looked therefore that, as with the earlier focus on European economic cooperation, the

Foreign Office's idea of using economic policy to serve the goals of foreign policy and great power status was heading into another cul-de-sac.

Bevin was not, however, going to abandon such goals in the spring of 1948, even though he appeared to have accepted the undesirability of a European customs union (which had aroused his interest for so long) and the subsequent moves to economic integration which were likely to follow. At the end of April, speaking to a luncheon of the City Livery Club, Bevin lamented the fact that money had been sent to other parts of the world rather than developing British industry or putting resources into colonial development. Then, with an acknowledgement of Britain's post-war weakness, Bevin underlined the overall aims of British imperial strategy when referring to 'the great task' of restoring 'one of these invisible assets . . . our position in leadership of the world; our prestige and our determination to recover'.

In fact Bevin was already looking further afield than the French, the Belgians and the Portuguese by seeking to involve the Italians in his plans for the development of tropical African resources. In part this new idea was not only an element of Western union but a requirement of British policy towards Italy's North African colonies which had caused so many problems in 1945 and 1946. With the failure of the Council of Ministers to agree on the future of the Italian Colonies within the 12-month deadline, the issue was placed in the hands of the United Nations. Consequently there would be a need to get Arab support for the British policy on Cyrenaica as the strategic facilities there were still regarded as vital. In order to get the trusteeship with Arab backing the Foreign Office believed that the trusteeship of the whole of Libya would have to be secured because of the desire in the Arab world to preserve the unity of Libya. Unfortunately the French and the Russians were encouraging the Italians to believe they would obtain the trusteeship of Tripolitania. Faced with British opposition to such a plan, there was a fear in London that this might turn the Italians away from involvement in Western union.

Such fears were heightened by Bevin's conversation with the Italian Ambassador in January 1948. The Ambassador pointed out that if Italy was to enter into Western union it must have its 'dignity and moral force restored' and Italian public opinion satisfied, and therefore the Italian colonial question should be considered against that background especially as the collaboration of the European powers in African development had been mentioned as an essential feature of Western union. The issue was given added significance by the Italian elections of April 1948 which threatened to produce a victory for the communists, especially if the Western powers provided them with an issue to exploit. Given these circumstances, the Foreign Office suggested that Italy would have to be compensated elsewhere for the loss of Tripolitania. Several proposals were made for this compensation of Italy: supporting its claims for the trusteeship of its East African colonies; safeguarding its interests in Tripolitania; and maximising Italian cooperation with Britain and the other European powers in African development. As regards the third element in the Foreign Office scheme, it was suggested that Italy could take part in the programmes for technical cooperation and join with the British and French in economic cooperation which could be extended to East Africa; such schemes would allow for limited numbers of artisans to go to East Africa and help alleviate Italy's unemployment problem.[99]

While a limited amount of Italian involvement in Africa could be accepted by the Colonial Office, problems arose as it became clear that Bevin was thinking in more grandiose terms. When Bevin met Sforza he talked of the importance of Africa's raw materials for Europeans and Americans, which meant that Britain would have a programme of African development extending over at least 20 years and there would be a place in it for Italy. This pronouncement was followed by a flattering portrayal by the British Foreign Secretary of the contribution already made by Italian technicians and labour to developing great areas of the world. Cohen immediately sensed that the Italians were being led to expect something that would be difficult to reconcile with British ideas on self-government and 'partnership', and therefore unacceptable to African opinion. Italy, in his view, could be brought into the technical cooperation programme after regaining some African possessions and a limited number of artisans admitted on a strictly repatriation basis, but West African opinion would be 'extremely touchy' about involving Italians in Africa in any capacity. Sir Sidney Caine did not agree, and attached importance to the help skilled Italian labour and more highly trained personnel could give to the pace of development; the political and psychological objections should therefore be seen as difficulties to be overcome rather than absolute barriers to action. With Cohen supported by Hilton Poynton, Sir Thomas Lloyd decided that Italian and other outside help should be involved 'to the fullest extent which local opinion permits'.[100]

Unfortunately the Foreign Office, as Cohen feared, intended to use the issue of Italian involvement to change the character of African development and the nature of the low profile technical cooperation conducted by the British, the French and the Belgians. A Foreign Office meeting in April 1948 proposed the establishment of an African Development Council comprising Britain, South Africa, France, Belgium, Portugal and Italy, the promotion of colonial development with Italian participation under the aegis of the OEEC, the permanent settlement of Italians in British Africa and the launching of large scale development schemes in which Italian engineering and building contractors could have a role. Particular emphasis was placed on the employment of European labour without which it was believed that African development would be retarded. At a meeting with the Foreign Office, Colonial Office officials challenged some of these assumptions. They were not well disposed to any additional machinery which would detract from the existing provisions for technical cooperation in Africa, and Cohen explained that the aim of the Colonial Office was to train Africans to participate in development schemes and that the expansion of agricultural and industrial activities should mean increased technical education for Africans not opportunities for Italian artisans. Foreign Office officials accepted the Colonial Office presentation and asked for a memorandum which could be submitted to Bevin.

In the summer of 1948 Bevin was still committed to the idea of African development in tandem with the Italians and told the President of the Italian Senate, how, with the unemployment problem in Italy, he was in favour of using Italian labour in Africa. Perhaps because of his position as a protégé of the Foreign Secretary, Creech Jones was somewhat equivocal about his officials' memorandum opposing such plans. He thought it might be possible to use 'judiciously' some Italian labour without prejudicing the training and advancement of Africans. Accepting that it could have a bad effect on African and Indian opinion, the Colonial Secretary pointed to the European problem which might make it advantageous to have a small Italian contribution in Africa. However, in the end Creech

Jones did not insist on any alterations in the memorandum which was to be sent to Bevin.

The Foreign Secretary found the memorandum 'disappointing' and demanded a personal meeting with Creech Jones at which he complained about the lack of encouragement given by colonial governors to European workers. The Colonial Secretary felt Bevin was somewhat anti-Indian and saw Europeans and Africans as more deserving of opportunities in Britain's colonies, and of course he was treated to another lecture on the importance of African development and how Bevin was anxious to ensure everything feasible (i.e. the employment of Italians) was done to make it possible. The issue was kept alive by the Ministry of Labour's request for a brief prospectus of development schemes and the manpower used, and by the possible Italian membership of the Overseas Territories Sub-Committee (OTC) of the OEEC. The Colonial Office was more nervous by the end of the summer as it expected an announcement of the return of Somalia to Italy which would undoubtedly have a bad impact within Black Africa. In such circumstances it was felt that any involvement of Italy with the OTC would be resented by Africans and give the impression that Italy was now to be a partner in the exploitation of Africa for purely European ends; what the Colonial Office proposed was a statement welcoming Italian participation in the measures Britain was seeking to concert between the various African administrations for the solution of common scientific and technical problems. The Colonial Office was more vehemently opposed to the employment of Italian labour which it did not view as an economic issue but as a political one. In repeating the arguments of the memorandum already sent to Bevin one official remarked that they should 'take the opportunity of once again rubbing it into the Foreign Office that the question of the non-employment of Europeans as artisans, etc. in Africa is not a matter in which the Colonial Office or colonial governors are free to decide on policy. Within very narrow limits we have to do what the Africans will accept, and this cannot be put too strongly to the Foreign Office, who seem to me to live in the middle of the nineteenth century on this, as indeed on other matters'.[101]

It may well have been an accurate perception of Foreign Office attitudes both to the kind of global power it expected Britain would be able to wield and to the feasibility of those policies which Bevin and his officials expected to implement in order to achieve such a powerful world position. However unrealistic the ultimate aim of creating a Third Force out of Britain's European and imperial strategies, clearly the policies advocated to achieve such a goal were running into ever greater difficulties. In general terms this reflected the fundamental fact that the spectacular relative decline of Britain's military and economic strength during the Second World War had taken away the means to regain the kind of status and position that the Foreign Office so desired. More specifically the policies suggested to achieve this were, by 1948, either being accepted as unworkable, or meeting opposition from other government departments, or even producing conflicts and contradictions with other elements of the overall imperial strategy. The desire for European economic cooperation through increased intra-European trade involving Britain was seen to be damaging to Britain's economic interests with or without a customs union; the latter was also seen as having adverse short-term implications for the domestic structure of the economy particularly in terms of agricultural prices. The idea of colonial development in Africa to meet the dollar gap was increasingly being portrayed as impractical in terms of dramatic short-term benefits to Britain let alone the colonies, and had been since the summer of 1947, albeit with little apparent effect on certain key ministers by the summer of 1948. Moreover measures likely to make it more realisable were meeting Treasury opposition because of their likely impact on sterling area finance. Cooperation with Europeans in African development was not seen as likely to bring immediate benefits, and by 1948 likely to have disadvantages for Britain's own position in terms of financial sacrifices and the failure to contribute to the narrowing of the dollar gap.

Also the Foreign Office's desire to emphasise the importance of European cooperation in the implementation of African policy was producing a clash with the Colonial Office because it effectively undermined the essential basis of colonial policy which increasingly depended on working closely with indigenous representatives to meet African rather than European requirements. In the Middle East there were difficulties with the Egyptians; development schemes had been largely killed off by the Treasury because of the relative importance of colonial development; and with the abandonment of Palestine in May 1948 and the troubles in Iraq which prevented the ratification of the Anglo-Iraqi treaty in January 1948, there was little prospect of creating the kind of political or military links with Middle Eastern states that were necessary to strengthen Britain's informal influence. Western union had been launched, but because of Cold War concerns, was being bogged down in defence issues which were creating more problems than they solved because the political requirements of foreign policy were completely at odds with the mainstream of military thinking on defence strategy. Ironically, the British stance on cooperation with the Soviets may have contributed to the tensions which had produced the concerns in Europe about security and communist subversion and thereby created a conflict between defence requirements in the Middle East, and Foreign Office desires to gear military strategy to the requirements of foreign policy in Europe.

By May 1948 this conflict had become so acute that efforts had to be made to mitigate its impact. As far as Western union was concerned the Foreign Office could point yet again to the undesirability of focusing exclusively on its military aspects,[102] but something would have to be done to gear military strategy more to the requirements of Western union if Britain were to establish the Third Force. Faced with this need ministers decided to make a commitment to fight as 'far east in Germany as possible', although where that should be would have to be decided by the military. On 5 May the Chiefs of Staff began to discuss it, which re-opened earlier arguments on the desirability of adopting a military strategy which was not feasible. Montgomery argued that British troops in Germany should stay and fight on the Rhine, and on this occasion he got support from Air Marshal Tedder. Admiral Cunningham continued to argue that as this was not possible it would be better to continue with the strategy of evacuation being incorporated into 'Double-quick'. Montgomery again opposed such hard-headed realism, despite conceding that in Western union Britain was linked to something which 'militarily was a nonsense'; but he argued that this was unimportant as, with the Russians unlikely to start a war in the near future, an examination of the practicality of fighting on the Rhine was not required. What was needed was to encourage the West Europeans to resist aggression and to reorganise their forces on the correct lines in preparation for the post-1957 period when war would be likely. All that was needed in the short term was a paper commitment to stay and fight on the Rhine, not a military plan to do so, let alone the forces required to successfully implement such a plan. In other words there would be no question of actually sending reinforcements to the Continent in order to defend the territory west of the Rhine. Such attitudes rather naively assumed that the French would be satisfied by this British commitment without enquiring further into what forces would be available; and they also assumed that without the combined military planning desired by the French and the Belgians the psychological reassurance of the West Europeans would be secured.[103]

After the Chiefs of Staff meeting the issue was discussed at Downing Street by Montgomery, Bevin, Attlee and the Minister of Defence, A. V. Alexander. Bevin was now arguing that it was vital for the Americans to give effective support to Western union and that what was required from the Europeans was an agreement that all parties would commit their military forces from the outset; it would then be necessary to determine the strength of the forces available before discussions on whether to defend the Rhine. Attlee agreed and emphasised that the Europeans could be best employed proving that what they could provide for Western union was insufficient and therefore the United States would have to furnish assistance. It seemed to be a question of a European stocktaking designed to reveal how essential American support was if Western union was to succeed. There was a distinct aversion to making a public commitment to defend any particular 'stop line', and Alexander wanted to ensure that the total military forces available would be sufficient before any strategy was openly endorsed.

Montgomery's argument had clearly not been fully accepted by ministers, but in order to help alleviate some of the problems stemming from the existing military plans it was agreed to revise 'Doublequick' in order to remove references to the evacuation of British forces from Europe. The revised plan was then sent to the Americans in the hope that this would convince them to do likewise, although the published version of 'Halfmoon' contains, under the heading of 'Evacuation', a statement that the initial withdrawal of United States forces would be to the Rhine, with a further retreat either to the Channel coast or to the Pyrenees. In addition the Chiefs of Staff decided on a very tentative and essentially meaningless commitment to keep British forces fighting on the Rhine 'unless and until pushed out'.[104] Finally, as part of sending the right signals and avoiding the kind of military cooperation with the French that would have damaging political implications and present a security risk, the military governors in Germany were to attempt to concert plans to meet a sudden emergency stemming from a Soviet attack.[105] This situation may have developed from the fact that early in the year (sometime before March) Bevin and Montgomery, without Cabinet approval, had instructed General Robertson to talk with Generals Clay and Koenig on holding the threat from the East. Only the Commanders in Chief and the Chiefs of Staff were to work on it and neither the Royal Navy nor the Royal Air Force were kept informed.[106]

By mid-May the Military Committee of the Brussels Treaty Organisation had had time to consider the State Department's questionnaire of mid-April, and the replies reflected the moves towards full military cooperation by the Brussels powers which avoided any pooling of resources or developing a common strategy for the defence of Western Europe. The State Department was informed that the five powers were preparing an inventory of the total military resources 'mobilisable in the near future' and of the 'potential military forces' that might be available. The aim was to fight 'as far east in Germany as possible', and to hold the Russians on the best position, covering the territory of the five powers, to enable American military power to intervene.[107] The reply reflected British reticence about joint planning with the Europeans and the general desire to persuade the United States of a willingness to prepare to fight. It was also in line with Bevin's idea to discover what forces would be available so as to decide on the feasibility of fighting on the Rhine.

Yet that kind of approach to the problem indicated the failure of Bevin to come to terms with the difficulties of reconciling the idea of world power status through European cooperation with the defence of the Empire based on the Middle East. What forces would be available for the defence of Western Europe would depend on what forces were allocated by the British to other theatres; as it stood in 1948, not only was the main theatre for ground forces the Middle East, but reinforcements were designated for that theatre rather than Western Europe. As General Hollis noted, the British could not reveal to the Western Europeans any plans drawn up by them or the Americans which did not cater for the despatch of reinforcements to the Continent.[108]

In order to gain any form of reassurance the French would need to be convinced that the British were serious in terms of their commitment to Western union; this would certainly require the dispatch of continental reinforcements, but the French were also likely to want information on the relative importance the British attached to European as opposed to imperial defence. Indeed, later in the year, as part of the attempt to prepare an inventory of the forces likely to be available to the Brussels Treaty powers, the French were to insist on the British providing full details of their military resources on a global basis, rather than those which Britain intended to commit to a European theatre. This was to meet with a blunt refusal by the British military on the grounds that 'it would at once lead to arguments about our strategy which was no concern of the French'.[109] The idea appeared to be that the likely confrontation with the French could be avoided by keeping short-term emergency planning on an Anglo-American basis, while gearing long-term planning to Western union and the United States. This ignored the fundamental fact that above all else the French were interested in the provision of reinforcements for the Continent which the British had ruled out in terms of both land and air forces. It also reemphasised the dependence on the United States to make Western union work through the provision of British and American forces for the defence of the Continent.

Another potential conflict was created by this, especially in view of the increasingly difficult circumstances the British were facing in the Middle East. The drawing up of the first global emergency war plan ('Doublequick') had also led to the first emergency plan for the defence of the Middle East – Plan 'Sandown'. 'Sandown' was based on deployment from the main base in Egypt to defend a line across what was then South Palestine (but by the summer of 1948 was the new state of Israel), running from Tel Aviv through Ramallah.[110] The predicted speed of the Soviet advance dictated the abandonment of most of the Levant and all the other parts of the Middle East. This strategy reinforced the need for the immediate deployment of troops and, more importantly, aeroplanes for the air defence of Egypt; thus the 1946 strategy of withdrawing combat forces from Egypt was now, according to the military, much more dangerous because it could allow the Soviets time to neutralise the Canal Zone base. 'Sandown' reinforced fears that without American assistance, even the peacetime presence of British forces in Egypt might not be enough to hold the line.[111] Bevin and the British military had, since 1947, been keen to get an American commitment to defend the Middle East. The well-documented talks held in October and November 1947 had secured agreement on the importance of Middle Eastern defence reiterated in the spring of the following year.[112] Then, sometime in 1948, the United States agreed to provide three divisions plus 350 tactical aircraft at D-Day.[113] Yet while this agreement was being given in line with the main thrust of British defence strategy, for political reasons both Britain and the United States were being required to consider the defence of Western Europe in the face of massive Soviet superiority in ground forces, and to help create an Atlantic pact as the second stage of the new security arrangements. In the midst of all this in June 1948 came the Russian blockade of West Berlin which made war 'by accident' seem more likely.

When the blockade began the British had withdrawn their European evacuation plans for any such war, but had not persuaded the Americans to do likewise. Templer, Vice Chief of the Imperial General Staff (VCIGS); was therefore opposed to integrating the latter into a future Western union command organisation until their attitudes were 'sorted out', which presumably meant being prepared to pay lip service to the intention to fight on the Rhine for as long (or as short) as possible.[114] As Templer later explained, any exchanges in operational planning would sooner or later lead to the disclosure of US intentions to retreat from Europe in war, and this would produce a situation where Britain was faced with the breakdown of Western union or the virtual cessation of defence collaboration with the United States.[115] Yet the Berlin crisis made emergency planning all the more necessary; it also made it more important for the Western powers to do something positive in terms of the future of their occupation zones in West Germany. The commitment to retreat to and fight on the Rhine was not likely to have much appeal to nervous and beleaguered West Germans. In such a tense situation the British military were even more concerned about lax French security because of the danger of the Russians or the Germans finding out about British weakness and intentions.

In such circumstances the Washington talks on security scheduled for 9 July assumed major significance. There was the question of American support for the Brussels Pact (initially the first British priority) which the French and the State Department wanted to see in the form of short-term emergency planning, and in a plan to provide American equipment and forces for Western Europe, but which the British and the Pentagon wanted to avoid given the nature of their military planning; and there was the question of an Atlantic pact which since March Bevin had wanted to see established without delay. The latter had the advantage that even if it was 'militarily a nonsense' like the Brussels Treaty, it would at least offer the prospect of papering over the divisions likely to be opened by attempts to coordinate practical measures to meet a Soviet attack, and would therefore be a more effective contribution to the British goal of Western union than the kind of military cooperation desired by the French.

As Kirkpatrick had predicted in January, an Atlantic pact solution was to emerge as the only way out of the conflicting priorities of the various European powers, largely because it was favoured by the United States and because the Western Europeans were prepared, with encouragement from Bevin, to accept it as the most likely way of securing future military aid from the Americans. This had always been the French priority and became even more important in Bidault's eyes following the signature of the Brussels Treaty, and the French Foreign Minister was initially in favour of US accession to that pact. American reluctance to join was one of the reasons why an Atlantic pact figured so prominently in the Washington talks that were held in early July 1948. The French were not then impressed by American support for the idea of an Atlantic pact, and felt it should not be encouraged because it ran contrary to the idea of supporting the Brussels Treaty. The French were clearly concerned that an additional and much larger organisation based on the Atlantic powers would shift 'the security axis in a contrary sense to the direction of the actual menace', and suspected that the United States was trying to save its conscience by something that involved no real obligations. Bidault believed the proposed pact would confuse the issue and add nothing to existing guarantees. Finally, of course, a larger organisation would mean the spreading of American resources more thinly even if the United States were disposed to provide any.[116] As Bonnet, French Ambassador in Washington, told the British, unless the Americans entered into an arrangement with the Brussels Treaty powers, there was no value in doing anything.

Such negative attitudes on the part of the French were bound to have a detrimental effect on Western union which Bevin, at the time of the Washington talks had 'in no sense lost interest in'.[117] Unfortunately unless the Americans and the French could be reconciled there would be no prospect of any further developments. In an effort to keep Western union alive, and of course to avoid as far as possible the clash between military strategy and the political requirements of defence cooperation with the Europeans, Bevin attempted to persuade the French that going ahead with an Atlantic pact would not weaken American support for the Brussels Treaty powers. Bevin told the French it was a question of leading the Americans so they eventually came into line on support for the Western Europeans but without disappointing them by rejecting the Atlantic pact. The British Foreign Secretary suggested that the Americans might well give a guarantee to the Brussels Treaty powers if they entered an Atlantic pact; the latter, which appealed primarily to the Americans, could thus be reconciled with the Brussels Pact and Western union which appealed primarily to the British and the Europeans.[118]

NATO was thus very much part of Bevin's attempt to keep Western union alive by successfully persuading the French that their best hope of receiving actual military assistance instead of 'hollow words' lay in going ahead with the Atlantic pact idea. Yet this still left the difficulty of military planning which was advancing in the wake of the Brussels Treaty's creation. Moreover, by the beginning of July the British Chiefs of Staff had received a message from Washington proposing that Western union defence talks should begin with the British, the French and the Canadians. As the Joint Planners produced the old argument about a strong bomber force operating with weapons of mass destruction from bases in the Middle East being an essential strategic requirement of the Western powers, the Chiefs of Staff were instructed to plan for a withdrawal from Germany to a defensive line on the Rhine.[119] From a military standpoint the requirements of imperial defence in the Middle East were being undermined by political requirements in Europe geared to a strategy that made no military sense. At the same time the work of the Military Committee and discussions on a Western union supreme commander also threatened to shift attention away from the Middle East to Western Europe with detrimental military effects, unless more resources were available, and detrimental political effects so long as Anglo-American global strategy continued to ignore the political requirements of Western union.[120]

By September 1948 not only were the British military refusing to discuss with the French their global allocation of forces and declining to provide additional land forces for the Continent, the air force was committed to the reinforcement of the Middle East, should war break out, rather than Western Europe. It was in September 1948 that the NATO talks which had commenced in July were adjourned after a tentative blueprint had been drawn up for a North Atlantic Treaty. Agreement had not been easy because Bidault had not readily accepted Bevin's suggestion of a trade off between accepting a North Atlantic Treaty and concrete American support in the form of military assistance for the Brussels Treaty Organisation. The French Foreign Minister was determined to get American support organised before accepting an Atlantic pact; he therefore wanted agreement on assistance for the rearming of Western European ground forces and an understanding between the United States and the Europeans on the manner and place in which a military emergency involving the Soviets would be met. This was precisely what the British and the American military, as opposed to the State Department, were keen to avoid. In short the more the French took this attitude the more necessary it was to have an Atlantic pact to keep Western union alive. Fortunately the British were able to postpone the issues of European and American military cooperation till after the agreement on a North Atlantic treaty by arguing that everything that could be done to meet the present danger in Europe was being done by the Military Committee of the Brussels Treaty Organisation and by the military commanders in Europe who were engaged on planning for the withdrawal to the Rhine; this could appease the French because one of the commanders was an American and because it gave the impression that the Anglo-Saxons were serious about planning to defend the Rhine. At the same time the Americans were telling the French that work should be done on a long-term programme of assistance and cooperation rather than on short-term emergency planning to deal with a Soviet attack.[121] Such an approach might reconcile the contradiction between the political and military elements of Western European cooperation, but ultimately it would undermine the military commitments of both Britain and the United States to the vital imperial region of the Middle East.

Almost on the same day that the preliminary agreement on an Atlantic pact was secured, the British Joint Planners presented their study of a withdrawal from Germany in order to defend a line on the Rhine to the Chiefs of Staff. They accepted the short-term strategic aim of defending the Rhine, but pointed out quite unequivocally that if war should occur Allied resources would be totally inadequate to fight successfully on the Rhine. At the same time they were aware that the 'strategic aim must be rigidly adhered to if we are to achieve any unity and efficiency in Western union'.[122]

By October the Military Committee had belatedly arrived at the obvious conclusion that the proportion of forces available for Western Europe could not be decided upon until the commitments of France, Britain and Holland outside Europe had been examined.[123] Tedder, unlike Templer, was prepared to face the possible breakdown of Western union by accepting that the Western union Chiefs of Staff should be involved in strategy outside Europe because the defence of the Continent was linked to the defence of areas outside it.[124] The Foreign Office, unsurprisingly, took a different view on the idea of attempting to reconcile the requirements of an imperial strategy with military cooperation in Western Europe. Its suggestion was for the Western union Chiefs of Staff to produce a report concentrating on the allocation of 'all possible reserves to meet threats considered to be most immediate and most likely in Western Europe'. By this they meant making the best use of forces allocated to Western Europe as global strategy was reserved for the British and the Americans.[125] In the middle of the Berlin crisis both the military and the Foreign Office were agreed that the most immediate threat to world peace lay in Europe. Therefore the question was likely to be raised of diverting reinforcements from the Middle East to Europe; this, Templer felt, would be very dangerous.[126]

At exactly the same time Templer was reflecting on the danger of diverting forces from the Middle East to Europe, Bevin was lecturing the Consultative Council of the Brussels Treaty on the value of an Atlantic pact because the five-power pact was not enough. However, Bevin wanted European defence to be approached in the same spirit as the Marshall Plan; the United States would provide the means to enable the Europeans to help themselves. More specifically the Brussels powers should mobilise the wealth and productive capacity of the North American continent for the defence of Western Europe, but by organising a European group in some form of coherent defence system the five powers would 'stand on their own feet militarily and maintain their independence and prestige'.[127] Thus as the French had more vigorously argued, the Atlantic pact should complement the Brussels Treaty and Western union rather than act as a substitute for them.

The question of how American military support for Western Europe could help produce its independence and prestige was more difficult to answer than the question of how Marshall Aid would produce the economic independence of Western Europe within whatever framework Western union would assume. There was clearly an element of wishful thinking on Bevin's part in both of these ideas of using short term American backing to produce long-term independence for a European grouping in which Britain would play the leading role. That this was still Bevin's goal when the details of a North Atlantic treaty were being discussed by a working party between September and December was illustrated by a speech in parliament. The Foreign Secretary spoke of an association of nations comprising Western Europe and their colonies running through the 'middle of the planet' with its great potential and wealth. Its importance was clearly linked to what Bevin termed the first object of foreign policy, namely the achievement of independence from any other Great Power. As Britain alone could not achieve this the aim was to build up a self-reliant, independent and rejuvenated Europe.[128]

In a Foreign Office brief in the same month the stages in this process were defined and linked to Britain's relations with 'three main groups'; these were the American democracies, Western Europe and the Commonwealth.[129] Later, in

December, Bevin referring in the Commons to his Western union speech of January 1948 which emphasised looking beyond Europe, spoke of the Commonwealth, the European colonies and the United States of America in order to point out that 'it is in this order of ideas that the government is striving to advance the Western union cause . . . In the end it is the combination of Western union with these great countries of the Commonwealth which, as I said in a previous speech, is bound to be the stabilising influence in the world'.[130] As far as creating Western union went, the first stage had been achieved with the hard core created by the Brussels Treaty Organisation; the second stage would be achieved by reinforcing this through an American guarantee, and this was deemed achievable through the Atlantic pact; the final stage was the extension of the system to other European powers.[131]

Unfortunately, in disregard of this timetable, and in the Foreign Office view prematurely, the French had put a spanner in the works by raising the question of a European Assembly on 20 July which the British had to agree should be considered by the Brussels powers. Then on 18 August, without further consultation, the French announced their support for the convening of a preparatory European Assembly. According to Ramadier the French public's interests in European unity needed reviving by vigorous means; the practical work of European cooperation, he claimed, would eventually come to a stop in front of the barrier of national sovereignty. The French were clearly prepared to take the initiative in pursuing Western union, which in itself was bad for the fundamental British aim of linking Western Europe with the Empire through the organisation of the 'middle of the planet'. Bevin immediately wrote to Attlee lamenting that a European Assembly would wreck all prospects of closer association between the nations of Western Europe, and later complained to Maurice Schumann, Chairman of the Mouvement Républican Populaire, that if an Assembly were representative of the European parties it would be introducing a Trojan horse into Europe in the form of the communists.[132] The inescapable fact that communists were being elected in Western Europe was to prove a considerable disincentive for the British to become involved in European cooperation. However, in the autumn of 1948 the French attempt to seize the initiative was to lead to counter-proposals from the British for a Council of Europe in which power was exclusively retained in the hands of European governments. The British were in fact losing the initiative because their proposals for defence cooperation had not produced the results favoured by the French and the Belgians, and because European economic cooperation was making little progress. This state of affairs reflected the vague and well-known fact that Britain had an Empire to consider, but it also reflected Britain's weak position in military and economic terms which meant it had little to offer the Europeans and, consequently, what progress could be made depended on the Americans. Moreover, this progress was limited by the British need to prevent anything occurring that would hinder what Bevin and many officials saw as the revival of British power and influence. Thus the type of military cooperation favoured by the French and the Belgians had to be discouraged while the moves towards a customs union under the auspices of the OEEC could not be endorsed in principle because of British fears about their short term economic implications.

The formal establishment of the OEEC in April 1948 came when several of the Western European powers were experiencing financial crises linked to the problems of intra-European trade. The fact that some countries were running an unsustainable deficit or surplus as a result of trade disequilibrium was to produce several balance of payments difficulties and to focus attention on the need to examine the system of payments within Europe. Ironically, in the month after the signing of the Brussels Treaty with its Article 1 centring on economic cooperation, it was clear that the European trade disequilibrium was greatest amongst the Brussels Treaty powers. The Belgians, partly because they insisted that purchasers of essential goods should also buy some non-essentials, had accumulated a sizeable surplus and were reluctant to extend credits. The French, in the wake of their dollar crisis in September 1947, had been forced to dramatically curtail dollar purchases and replace them by purchases from the sterling area. The result was that British concerns in 1947 about a French sterling surplus were replaced in the spring of 1948 by serious concerns over the French sterling deficit which was predicted to be £72 million for 1948. The granting of sterling credits thus became an issue which was defined in terms of gaining time for the development of Western union cooperation. And the Economic Policy Committee and the Cabinet had accepted that if Britain was to achieve its aim of Western union it would have to be prepared to make some financial sacrifices even though one Treasury paper favoured concentrating on the Empire rather than Europe.[133] Without these sacrifices the problems of intra-European trade would increase, as each country would endeavour to have payments not covered by bilateral commodity exchanges made in dollars. When the ECA began to function there was the possibility of payments being made in dollars to European nations in credit who could then release equivalent sums for intra-European trade credits. This was the idea put forward by Hubert Ansiaux of the National Bank of Belgium which was undermined by the American decision to provide most of the dollars in the form of loans rather than grants. An alternative system would be to provide dollar aid equivalent to the amount of a country's dollar deficit less the European surplus; this would then encourage European creditors to buy more in Europe in the knowledge that dollar finance would be available.[134] For the British the situation was complicated by the large RSA surplus with the countries of Western Europe which would have to be covered in order to release sterling credits to cover French purchases.

As Michael Hogan has pointed out, 'the British were caught between the demands of the OEEC countries for the sterling credits they needed to cover essential imports from the sterling bloc, and the demands of the RSA countries for the dollars they required to finance purchases in the Western Hemisphere'.[135] It was another illustration of the practical difficulties inherent in enrolling the European powers as collaborators with the British Empire. The Americans agreed in August to finance the RSA deficit, but on condition that the RSA countries agreed to fund their accumulated sterling balances and to curtail non-essential imports from the Western Hemisphere.[136] Here were the kind of political difficulties that were to prove impossible for the British to face up to in dealings with the white Dominions which were members of the sterling area. In the event the 1948 agreement on European payments, the Intra-European Payments and Compensations Scheme, was made along different lines and was to prove far from satisfactory. It was based on estimates of bilateral surpluses and deficits by the participating countries; prospective debtors would receive drawing rights from prospective creditors who would then receive the same amount of 'conditional aid' from the ECA which could be used to pay for dollar imports.[137]

This agreement in October 1948 followed the September agreement on a North Atlantic Pact, the French initiatives on a European Assembly, and the OEEC's appointment of a Committee of Nine, formed of European ministers chaired by Spaak, to study organisational questions. With Spaak's reputation as a supporter of European integration the Americans at least hoped that the new Committee would recognise the need for the 'dynamic high level direction of OEEC'.[138] In the light of these developments it was clearly time for the British to take some firm decisions about what kind of European institutions and organisations would be reconcilable with their economic interests and the goals of the Third Force. As ever such decisions had to be taken in the context of the need for Britain, Western Europe and the Empire to establish the ties and the cooperation that would be economically beneficial and politically productive.

Also in the autumn of 1948 the long-running customs union saga was finally drawing to a close. On 7 September the Chancellor submitted to the Economic Policy Committee a memorandum which was designed to kill off the idea. The disadvantages could hardly by then have been something with which ministers were completely unfamiliar; the loss of freedom to pursue budgetary and exchange policies; the modification of sterling area arrangements with political effects on the Commonwealth; limitations on the government's programme of agricultural development; and the short-term dislocation of agriculture and some manufacturing industry. The advantages were equally familiar: the long-term likelihood of improvements in the productive wealth and standard of living of the United Kingdom; the increased opportunities for certain industries; and the heartening political and psychological effect which was important for Western union. All these had to be considered in the face of what were seen as the long-term dangers for Britain if it was not involved in a successful European customs union, and in the face of the short-term problems of payments which a common market could not solve as long as import restrictions were necessary to avoid unacceptable balance of payment deficits.

The paper also considered the international political aspects which centred on the increased influence European cooperation would enable Britain to exert over the Western Europeans and the advantages of convincing the Americans that Britain was in earnest about making the European Recovery Programme a success. If Britain refused to go along with OEEC ideas on economic cooperation it would indicate it did not mean business over Western union, which would be particularly damaging as the British were resisting the French proposals for a European Assembly.[139]

The conclusions of the report, as outlined by Cripps at the meeting, were that future studies of European economic cooperation should be carried out in a wider context than a simple customs union. In economic terms this was undoubtedly a reflection of the fact that the European payments problem could not be solved by the customs union and was intimately linked to American dollar aid which would best be approached through the OEEC. As with NATO, British interests appeared best served by the involvement of the Americans. The result of this important meeting was that Bevin reinforced his April views on a customs union by stating that anything in the nature of a formal customs union or a federation of European states was out of the question. The whole question of Britain's role in

Europe was now at issue inasmuch as decisions were impossible to postpone. And the problem with these decisions was that as long as the economic linkages between the European states and their Empires were not being strengthened by colonial development, it appeared more a question of deciding between two competing interests (the European and the imperial) rather than of reconciling them under the umbrella of the Third Force; this had implications for the development of a British imperial strategy that was still deemed vital to secure independence from the Americans.

There was of course much more at stake than colonial development: the future position of the Empire as a power bloc also rested on political collaboration with the Dominions and economic cooperation with the sterling area countries. Nevertheless Bevin, in that vital autumn of 1948, still saw some kind of salvation through the development of the African colonies. He believed that Britain had the strategic raw materials in Africa – in Sierra Leone there were mountains of manganese – and if these were developed Britain would have the Americans eating out of its hand in a few years' time.[140] It was an astonishing conclusion, even allowing for the fact that the colonies were net dollar earners. Yet Bevin was not the only minister to harbour such thoughts, as Harold Wilson, the President of the Board of Trade, had referred in August to successful colonial development, especially in Africa, possibly reversing the existing situation between Western Europe and the United States.[141]

As has been seen, the initial assumptions that African development would provide the solution to Britain's dollar difficulties had not been universally shared within Whitehall. While pressure mounted for measures to be taken with the other European powers, the Colonial Office, in early 1948, remained fearful of the political consequences within Africa, and sceptical of the economic benefits to Europe. The former concern had been particularly acute over the question of involving Italians in the development of Africa to meet the political requirements of the Foreign Office; but this was not the only problem facing Colonial Office policy makers as a result of Bevin's African schemes. In April Bevin was proposing an East African Development Council on which all the European colonial powers and the South Africans would be represented.[142] One role for such a Council was seen by the Foreign Office as the linking of African and Middle Eastern development schemes. The question was discussed at an interdepartmental meeting in July 1948 when the Foreign Office attempted to collect information on development schemes in order to assess their political implications and establish supply priorities where there was a shortage of raw materials. The Colonial Office attempted once more to pour what it saw as much needed cold water on virtually every aspect of the Foreign Office intentions to develop the 'middle of the planet'. K. E. Robinson saw no merit in associating the African territories with the Middle East and questioned the fundamental premise of grandiose African development projects. He pointed out that both the Colonial Development Working Party and the Sterling Area Working Party had concluded that the first essential was not new projects but the maintenance of existing production and the upkeep of capital equipment, particularly in transport, which had been heavily overstrained during the war. Therefore, undue concentration on 'development projects' might well lead to the neglect of existing productive resources. Moreover, Robinson believed that excessive concentration on Africa could be dangerous if it was given priority over the tin and rubber in Malaya which were important for the balance of payments. Michael Wright, the supervising undersecretary for the Egyptian Department, emphasised the importance Bevin continued to attach to cooperation between the Western European powers in making the best possible use of resources in Europe and overseas; he disagreed with the Colonial Office view on linking the Middle East and Africa and pointed to two particular projects Bevin was in favour of, namely flood control and irrigation in Iraq and the Nile Waters project involving Egypt, the Sudan and the East African territories.[143]

These interdepartmental discussions at the official level occurred in the summer of 1948 when the issue of linking Europe and its overseas possessions made an impact within the OEEC and led to the establishment of the Overseas Territories Sub-Committee to study the question, along with a Special Strategic Materials and Stockpiling Sub-Committee.[144] These committees may well have been why Bevin was still confident of the eventual reestablishment of Britain's independence from the Americans. They also prompted the Foreign Office to keep its options open on the employment of Italian technicians and capital in African development.[145] At the same time the question of European cooperation in South East Asia was put on to the agenda of Western union by the Dutch. The Dutch, who had been opposed to the furthering of colonial cooperation under the auspices of the Brussels Treaty Organisation because of its emphasis on Africa, became attracted to the idea of winning the support of their European allies for their efforts to reestablish a position in Indonesia. Not surprisingly, the French saw advantages in extending colonial cooperation to Southeast Asia with the aim, like the Dutch, of demonstrating to the world the idea of Western union solidarity in the region. The Eastern Department of the Colonial Office was surprisingly encouraging, but others saw the dangers. As in Africa it was important to focus exclusively on technical questions, and the agreed Office view was that the Commissioner General, Malcolm Macdonald, should be allowed to go as far as he thought safe, provided he was guided by the merits of the case in Southeast Asia and not by the fact that the Brussels Treaty and the concept of Western union obliged the British to cooperate openly with the French and the Dutch.[146] This was another example of the difficulties in linking Western European cooperation with non-European areas that illustrated the conflicting priorities of two government departments. For the men on the spot and the Colonial Office, Western union and the requirements of a broad imperial strategy had to be subordinated to the requirements of particular territories or regions.

Such views, however did not accurately reflect the economic realities associated with the dollar saving aspects of the European Recovery Programme and the commitment to colonial development which was also geared to the short-term requirements of Britain's economic recovery. The reality was that the needs of Britain and Europe were overriding the needs of the colonies through import restrictions, rather than colonial development taking precedence over Britain and Europe by receiving priority in terms of aid and equipment.

To a limited extent it could be argued that the importance of colonial development for the Empire's recovery in 1948 had produced some concessions to colonial needs by, for example, the allocation of steel being doubled as a result of the Colonial Development Working Party's intervention. However colonial import ceilings were imposed by the Colonial Dollar Drain Committee, albeit linked to estimates made by the colonies in the light of the Secretary of State's circulars on import restrictions. A Colonial Office paper urged that much more needed to be done in order to 'take colonial development seriously'. Some colonies, because of staffing shortages or costs, did not have an economic or planning secretariat and therefore would be unlikely to be able to complete even a rudimentary development survey; and then there was the old problem of colonial supply requirements which the Colonial Office felt was much more important than any new bodies or institutions linked to colonial development.

As Colonial Office officials pointed out in a meeting with their Treasury counterparts, when colonial requirements came up against British requirements or those of the Dominions and foreign countries they tended to suffer; the colonies, it was felt, tended to get what was left over from bilateral commitments. Consequently, if colonial development was not taken seriously there would be continual trouble in the dollar earning colonies, where a state of emergency had been declared in June 1948 in Malaya and serious riots had taken place in the capital of the Gold Coast in February 1948. Britain would then be left only with those colonies that cost dollars. Taking colonial development seriously in the eyes of the Colonial Office meant Britain or Europe paying for it through exports to the colonies.[147] Taking European recovery seriously in the eyes of the Foreign Office meant the colonies paying for it through exports to Britain and the dollar zone. Thus, far from colonial development providing opportunities for impoverished colonies through the European recovery programme, another interpretation, noted by the Colonial Office, was that associating the Brussels Treaty Organisation in particular with the colonies was in fact linking a bankrupt Europe with the overseas territories in order to promote the former's recovery (unless of course colonial development was taken seriously by countries whose economic capacity may have precluded the provision of the necessary resources even if the political will existed).

This conflict was never openly acknowledged outside the walls of Whitehall where, however disingenuously, it was glossed over by the linking of colonial needs with imperial requirements in mutually beneficial ways. The Governors were told in 1948 of the two main considerations in developing colonial resources: the first was raising the standard of living of the colonial peoples; the second was the possibility of a triangular trade opening up by which it would be possible in the long term to bring the balance of payments of the sterling area into equilibrium. Governors were told that it 'was fully realised' that increased production must be based on improvements in social, health and educational services.[148] These ideas were also expounded by the British representative on the OTC of the OEEC, E. E. Melville, who followed up Georges Peter's opening address calling for the interests of the overseas territories to be taken into account, by speaking of the harmonisation of overseas investment, production and trade with a corresponding social and political development. The ECA representative, Milton Katz, not fully realising how this could be done, wanted to know how such goals could be reconciled with the immediate objectives of the OEEC which were to balance European payments and stockpile certain raw materials in short supply.[149]

The report of the OTC working party would have made it more difficult to see how the goals that interested Mr Katz could be reconciled with Colonial Office objectives. It referred to the low volume of exports of 18 selected foodstuffs and raw materials including cocoa, tea and rubber, which, along with many others, were lower in 1946–48 than they had been in 1936–38. This was partly due to difficulties created by the war and such factors as disease and bad harvests, but the most important cause was found to be the running down of capital equipment and the continued post-war scarcity of capital and consumer goods. Consequently, although it was agreed that long-term development should not be slowed down by short-term needs, in practice the shortage of equipment meant priority would have to be given to those projects likely to produce immediate results, rather than to those in basic services.

If that was likely to undermine the Colonial Office's strategy the report also had implications for what Bevin and the Foreign Office hoped to achieve. The capital shortages would inevitably mean, so the report claimed, concentration on production by peasant farmers and established industries rather than new, large-scale development plans which could be undertaken before the end of the European Recovery Programme in 1952. This was very much in line with the conclusions of the Colonial Development Working Party which produced its final report on 1 November 1948. The report drew attention to the financial commitment to domestic investment programmes which restricted the possibility of quickly raising the amount of UK investment in the colonies. For that reason the working party recommended the use of dollar funds and other non-British finance for colonial development, which would of course undermine the idea of using African resources independently of the Americans and reduce the political gains the Colonial Office hoped would accrue from the British involvement in social and economic progress in Africa. The report emphasised that colonial development should be chiefly concerned with multiplying over a wide area a number of small improvements, and should not commit too large a proportion of resources to large schemes. Yet eight months later Bevin and the Foreign Office were pressing for a large-scale development scheme, the development of the Nile Valley, involving Middle Eastern and East African territories.

The prospects of European cooperation in the overseas territories also seemed very limited according to the report, which stated that 'the most speedy advance in practical cooperation between the overseas territories is likely to result from the five metropolitan powers working together, and within the framework of their long-term programmes, to employ the means most appropriate to their own circumstances for reaching the essential objectives of development policy in the overseas territories for which they have responsibility'.[150] In short the Colonial Office policy of avoiding large-scale projects on an inter-territorial basis and of carrying out what limited programmes there were on a territorial basis seemed to be vindicated. As such it was hardly surprising that the report was criticised by the Italians for seeing European colonial development as amounting to the sum of the existing national programmes. Their view, like Bevin's, was that European economic cooperation overseas required more than the increased production of certain raw materials, and that there was excessive concentration on improving the existing links between the metropolitan countries and their dependent territories. Understandably the Italians wanted the colonies open to all to ensure that the necessary flow of capital and manpower from Europe could take place.[151]

The report of the OTC working party came at the same time as decisions were being taken on the future of the British Empire's relations with Europe and the

United States and on the way the European colonial powers could cooperate within key imperial regions. In defence policy, final decisions were being taken about the precise form of an Atlantic pact. The question of economic cooperation in Europe had been resolved to the extent that Britain had ruled out a customs union or federal bodies, and this appeared to coincide with British attitudes to political cooperation in late 1948; attitudes which by May 1949 were to result in a Council of Europe whose power depended on inter-governmental cooperation rather than on the decisions of European bodies. All these developments have been portrayed in terms of a successful post-war definition of Britain's world role in relation to Europe, the Empire and the United States, and as the culmination of a logical and well thought out strategy linked to Britain's geostrategic position which reinforced its connections to Europe, North America and the Empire.[152] In fact, the long-term goals had been to strengthen links between Europe and the Empire in order to remove the crucial short term ties to the United States which reflected British dependence in a very unequal partnership. Unfortunately because the long-term goals were defined in vague, general terms by the Foreign Office, with the emphasis on status, influence and prestige, when practical measures to achieve them had to be proposed opposition developed within Whitehall from those departments more concerned with specific British interests and with a more realistic understanding of the difficulties Britain faced. In essence, the Foreign Office was attempting to recreate those conditions which produced the kind of status which it believed was Britain's right, rather than adapting to the new power-political conditions existing at the end of the Second World War. As this was attempted through European and imperial policies not only did opposition develop, but Britain, because of its inherent lack of real political, economic and military power was forced back into the kind of dependent relationship with the United States that the Foreign Office had initially been so keen to avoid.

Other departments were more prepared to confront the problems of adaptation and decline. Thus, the Colonial Office was well aware of the political need to meet the wishes of its African subjects as well as the difficulties of economic development because of the constraints of Britain's economic position. The Foreign Office, because of its perceived need to achieve African development in order to have an impact on Britain's imperial standing, was less concerned with, and necessarily less aware of, the political and economic constraints. The Colonial Office continually pointed to the problems of an imperial strategy, implemented by a power with inadequate resources, which was based on the successful economic development of those overseas areas in need of a massive injection of external resources. Development, the Treasury was informed, involved the putting of money into circulation in the form of wages for local labour which produced a demand for consumer goods; such demand could not be adequately satisfied as long as import restrictions were imposed and as long as UK suppliers were unable to meet colonial demands.[153] In June 1949, a conference on colonial supplies produced a paper to make it clear that the sole purpose of restrictive import licensing was, as the Treasury was so keen to make clear, to protect the gold and hard currency reserves of the sterling area; restrictions were not intended to protect UK exporters. The question then arose of whether those OEEC countries which had a deficit with the sterling area should be encouraged to sell goods to the colonies.[154] Unfortunately, this would have undermined British exporters and would not have been conducive to the Colonial Office's ideas of 'partnership' in Africa. In addition it would have caused problems with the Dominions who were also keen to gain greater access to colonial markets. Here were yet more problems of linking Europe to Africa.

In 1949 the Foreign Office still seemed reluctant to accept the fundamental practical obstacles to linking colonial development to its European and imperial strategies, and even to accept the advice that small-scale development projects based on existing schemes would be the best way forward. In July, as part of the aim of jointly developing the Nile territories, Bevin proposed an International Advisory Board with members from Egypt, the Sudan, Uganda and the Belgian Congo. Cohen drew a distinction between a technical council to supervise the administration of the Nile Waters and a board concerned with social and economic development; the latter would get the blessing of the Africa Committee 'over my practically moribund body'.[155] Again Cohen drew attention to the fundamental fact that colonial development would not be brought about by international boards linking Uganda to the Middle East and other parts of Africa, but by helping Uganda secure finance, supplies and staff to implement its own development programmes. The Colonial Office was still trying to prevent the subordination of individual colonies to the broader requirements of imperial strategy and international politics. Hilton Poynton described the whole idea as a characteristic piece of Foreign Office nonsense which should be vigorously opposed.[156] Creech Jones also commented, expressing doubts on the practicality of Bevin's proposal, which might in fact hinder colonial development and which would involve the colonies in international bodies when they did not have sufficient 'political responsibility'.[157]

One of the reasons for the continued Foreign Office advocacy of such schemes was the importance attached to creating a good impression in the Middle East in general and the Sudan in particular. Another was the continuing disillusionment with economic cooperation in Europe. From the autumn of 1948 until the balance of payments crisis and sterling devaluation in 1949, the British, and even the Foreign Office, became more and more sceptical about the advantages of European economic cooperation and began to see salvation not in a combination of European and imperial collaboration but in cooperation between Britain and the United States. In a sense the particular economic disadvantages were finally overriding the general Third Force goals in the eyes of Foreign Office officials.

For Bevin himself, given his reluctance to put pen to paper, it is more difficult to determine how his perceptions of Britain's economic relations with Europe, the Empire and the United States changed. He never committed himself in writing, as his officials did, to a policy of European economic union, and while he began to shy away from a customs union in the spring of 1948, it was never clear precisely what arrangements the Foreign Secretary saw as giving concrete form to his ideas of Western union. As concern grew about Britain's position in a European economic organisation that required some form of irreversible integration, Bevin may have turned more to the Empire in 1948 as a means of achieving independence from the Americans. Yet what was also clear in 1948 was that the difficulties facing European recovery came to be seen as far greater, which tended to focus British attention on the importance of American economic support at precisely the same time as the needs of defence cooperation also emphasised Britain's reliance on the Americans. The economic difficulties did not essentially concern the probable disadvantages of a common market or economic union; nor did they simply focus on the dollar gap, as they involved the dollar shortage and the related question of European payments upon which increased trade, and therefore recovery, were seen to depend.

As early as June 1948 the Economic Policy Committee was considering a rather gloomy analysis of Britain's trade prospects. Given the existing trade relations and economic policies, the projection was that Britain could not be confident of earning by 1952 (when Marshall Aid would end) the means to obtain more than about 75 per cent of its 1938 volume of imports; it was a reflection of the difficulties of expanding trade within Europe as well as between Europe and the dollar zone. Interestingly, however, in July 1948 there was still a commitment to strengthening European links along with those of the Empire, as it was stated that any economic or political strengthening of Europe would be a strengthening of the Commonwealth and that Western union was not an alternative to the Commonwealth but a means of strengthening it.[158] This would of course depend on future economic developments affecting European and Commonwealth trade in relation to the dollar gap. A more accurate assessment, not based on political requirements, would have defined the strengthening of the Empire and Europe in terms of whether either area would help or hinder Britain's commitment to protecting the sterling area and balancing its trade with the dollar zone.

In July 1948, the Economic Policy Committee was informed of the necessity to shift £100 million per annum of purchases from the dollar area to soft currency sources in order to overcome the projected dollar deficit. At the same time the importance of increasing agricultural output in Britain was emphasised, which of course could not be achieved within a common market, and the sterling area development working party focused on the need to reduce imports of foodstuffs and raw materials from the dollar zone in line with the £100 million shift that was required.[159] These were the key elements in the British strategy for recovery which tended to differ from those supported by the Americans and the West Europeans. The British were keen to reduce imports from the dollar zone and to replace them by purchases from the Empire and Europe, although there were clearly major barriers to colonial development. In the European cases, as recovery proceeded, it could be expected that more goods would be available for Britain to purchase, and the deficit Britain would then have with Western Europe would be compensated by the surplus earned by the Rest of the sterling Area from its European trade.[160] The British strategy, as defined for the Cabinet's Economic Policy Committee, was to reduce dollar imports and to replace them from other sources in Europe and other soft currency areas; it was a Treasury strategy geared essentially to the sterling area rather than, in the case of European trade, to gaining access to important goods to satisfy particular British needs. The Europeans, on the other hand, placed more emphasis in the short term on expanding multilateral trade through new payments arrangements. This approach was not so attractive to the British who, despite their enthusiasm for the eventual goal of multilateral trade, did not want to move towards it at the cost of undermining the sterling area.

The issue became crucial in relation to the allocation of Marshall Aid and the significant trade imbalance within Europe. The British were allocated $1263 million of aid in 1948 on condition they made $312 million available in sterling grants, while receiving $30 million in Belgian francs, and on condition they allowed the OEEC countries to draw $209 million from balances in sterling which would count as unrequited exports to Europe.[161] In effect, rather than tending to encourage exports to Britain to relieve British dollar needs, most of the Europeans were receiving goods from Britain without having to sell goods in return and could thus gear exports more to the dollar zone. They were also inclined to favour preserving a trade deficit within Europe, financed by the British and the Belgians, to concentrate on exports to dollar countries, whereas Britain argued that if the Europeans could not export more to the European market they must purchase less rather than rely on Britain using the resources of the sterling area to fund their deficit. The initial payments agreement in October 1948 did not, from the British point of view, alleviate the problem, because there was no incentive to increase exports within Europe if deficits gave the debtor nations drawing rights.[162]

By the beginning of 1949 the British were becoming increasingly concerned about the payments difficulties facing the OEEC countries. There was a belief that to solve the problems of trade and payments the Europeans would need to make drastic changes in their financial and commercial methods. If not there would be a need to forego dollar imports and to isolate Europe more from the United States economically which, given the development in the security field, would be some-what contradictory.[163] Cripps and the Treasury did not want to make British financial resources available to the Europeans even if this were compensated to some extent by access to dollars, because the amount of dollars available was not believed to be sufficient, even in 1948, to end the imbalance; this also tended to undermine the whole idea of *European* development in Africa because if Foreign Office schemes were to be implemented it was likely that sterling finance would be important. In short the Treasury, because of the payments problem, did not want to put the resources of the sterling area at the disposal of the Europeans.

Bevin, following the French proposals for a European Assembly, had become quite firm in his belief that progress towards European union should be carefully considered and should not be hurried or, unlike African development, linked to grandiose ideas.[164] The Foreign Secretary's European policy has thus been labelled 'pragmatic' and 'empirical', again in contrast to his somewhat neglected interest in the Empire in general and Africa in particular, which centred on grandiose schemes that were far from being pragmatic.[165] A more accurate assessment of Bevin's European policy, and of his approach to the Empire, lies in the conflicts between broad goals, like Western union, and important, concrete British interests like the preservation of sterling area reserves. Grandiose and ill defined aims could be supported, even though they were likely to be unrealisable, as long as their promotion did not threaten to be disadvantageous. In the case of European economic cooperation the payments issue was important in identifying particular disadvantages for the British while there were doubts about European recovery.

Consequently the memorandum submitted to the Economic Policy Committee by Cripps and Bevin in January 1949 was very different from their ideas 12 months earlier. Gone was the enthusiasm for European help in developing an independent trading bloc drawing on the resources of Africa and the other overseas territories. In its place was a fear that the OEEC, which was believed to be at a crucial stage of its development, would break down unless new initiatives were forthcoming. Cripps and Bevin argued that only Britain could provide them but such policies would entail both risks and sacrifices. If the latter were to be made by Britain, and Europe failed to recover, then the British would have deprived themselves of the things necessary for their own economic survival. Thus it was decided that Britain should not involve itself in the economic affairs of Europe beyond the point from which it could withdraw. In case of a European economic collapse it was clearly implied that Britain, as in the war, would need to disentangle itself from the Continent and seek salvation through American help.[166]

This early 1949 British decision could only have been reinforced by the dramatic events of the spring and summer which produced more serious doubts about European recovery and culminated with the devaluation of the pound in September. The crisis really began in April 1949 when the start of the drain on British reserves coincided with an OEEC interim report that predicted a European dollar gap of $3 billion when Marshall Aid ended in 1952.[167] Equally alarmingly, despite the post-war recovery of production in Western Europe, the dollar gap actually widened in the first six months of 1949. Thus the key official in the making of foreign economic policy warned against 'putting all your eggs in the European basket. It is a pretty shoddy contraption and there are no signs yet that the essential repairs are going to be made'.[168] Somewhat ironically it was the depression in the United States which was at the heart of the problem because it reduced the demand for European goods, and in Britain produced a dollar drain of $149 million in April and $230 million in May. There was forestalling of payments because of devaluation fears and the colonial dollar surplus disappeared despite the commitment to colonial development as a means of easing Britain's plight.[169] By the middle of June Britain's reserves had fallen well below the $2 billion considered necessary to protect the value of the pound,[170] and it was therefore more important to prevent further pressure being exerted on sterling.

By the spring the Americans were eager to find ways to increase European exports to the dollar zone and liberalise trade within Europe as possible solutions to the dollar gap. If drawing rights and the conditional dollar grants that supported them were made transferable amongst the OEEC countries debtors could be given incentives to shop for imports in all markets. And if there was convertibility into dollars for some or all of the funds available as drawing rights this would provide incentives to debtors to improve their position in Europe.[171] In the case of Britain this introduction of a dollar element into the European payments system could put further strains on sterling because while Britain was an overall European creditor it was in debt to the Belgians whose accumulation of unusable sterling would be reduced by greater access to dollars. From the British point of view the solution lay in cutting European dollar imports or providing some special treatment for the Belgians as part of a special arrangement between the sterling Area and the dollar zone.[172] The latter was in fact what the British sought to achieve from talks with American and Canadian officials in July 1949, and the talks led to an OEEC agreement on the principles of a new payments plan. Only 25 per cent of drawing rights and conditional aid would be convertible, and, to limit the gold and dollar demands on the British Treasury, Belgium was to receive more Marshall Aid and to put a ceiling on its acceptance of sterling transfers while the French agreed to spend their sterling rights within the sterling area.[173]

In 1949 the British were still trapped between Europe and the sterling area, with the latter providing a large surplus on European trade, while Britain's trade surplus with most of Europe was significantly affected by the deficit with Belgium. The RSA had to be considered in the Marshall Aid programme otherwise its dollar needs could not be met and there would be fewer advantages in staying in the sterling area for the Dominions. This RSA surplus with Europe produced a situation where Britain had to provide unrequited exports and sterling drawing rights to Europeans in the face of a deficit with Belgium as part of the dollar aid programme. In a multilateral system British debts and sterling area credits could produce strains on British reserves unless some arrangements were made between the sterling and dollar zones.

These economic problems had, along with the military need for American support that became clear in 1948, significant implications for the future of the third World Force policy based on eventual independence from the United States. In July 1949 Cripps was to produce a paper on these economic questions, but from the spring of 1949, the newly created Permanent Undersecretaries' Committee had been considering the broader aspects of Britain's links to Europe, the Empire and the United States. Established to define longterm foreign policy and global strategy, the committee initially concerned itself with two questions of supreme importance for British imperial strategists: first whether Britain should aim to create a third World Power of Western Europe and the Commonwealth or aim to associate the United States with Western Europe; and second once an Atlantic pact was in force what security arrangements should be made for the Eastern Mediterranean and Middle East.[174]

The first question was considered in terms of its political, economic and military aspects, and a paper produced by May 1949. Politically Western Europe was seen by the committee as lacking cohesion and concerned with local or regional interests. Moreover there appeared to be little prospect of welding Western Europe into a prosperous and secure entity without American help because of the existing political and military situation. To be independent of the Soviet Union and the United States would require developing the economic and military potential of Germany which the Committee deemed unacceptable to the Soviets and to the Western European democracies. Economically the committee was equally gloomy about the prospects of a Third Force: there was little sign that the Dominions would accept the same kind of OEEC planning and it was believed that dollar assistance would be required for industrial development there. As far as Western Europe was concerned it was seen as likely to depend, for a reasonable standard of living, on exchanges between the Eastern bloc, the United States and the Commonwealth. More importantly there was the danger of 'centrifugal tendencies' increasing as Western Europe became stronger and a possibility that when Marshall Aid ended, the present degree of European economic cooperation would not survive. Most significant of all from the British point of view, economic integration was seen as involving great risks which would be worth taking 'only if economic integration would create a unit economically and militarily strong enough to resist aggression'. As there appeared to be little prospect of this, Europe could be overrun and the British segment of the economy unable to function on its own. Militarily the problem was defined in terms of Britain's inability to defend the Dominions without American support, and the inability of Britain and the West Europeans to prevent the Russians occupying the entire Atlantic coast even if the Americans provided some assistance. It was believed that by 1959 the West

Europeans might be able to hold out until full American support was brought to bear, but even then the burden might be too heavy to support. Unless there was a lowering of British living standards or the rearmament of Germany, any possibility of a Third Force providing military resistance to the Soviets would have to be ruled out.[175]

The rejection of the Third Force idea by officials in the Foreign Office in the spring of 1949, one month after the signing of NATO, was clearly linked to the economic and military weakness of Europe as conceived both in the short and the long term. It was reinforced by the view from the Dominions Office that a third Power independent of the United States would impose a serious strain on relations with the Commonwealth,[176] and by the conjunction of the dollar crisis in 1949 with the realisation that European cooperation could impose yet more strains on Britain's reserves and as a result threaten the value of the pound and the cohesion of the sterling area. In July 1949 Sir Stafford Cripps produced a memorandum outlining possible British strategies for dealing with the renewed dollar drain. The first strategy was the one, initially considered favourably by Cripps and Bevin in 1948, of joining the Empire and Western Europe in a soft currency bloc protected against the dollar zone; this was now deemed unrealistic because it would drive Canada and the other Dominions from the Commonwealth and spell the demise of Britain as a world power while cutting 'across the essential political and strategic requirements of the country as represented by the North Atlantic pact, Western union and Commonwealth solidarity'. The second strategy was full-blown multilateralism with free convertibility which was clearly out of the question unless the government was to face up to high unemployment and other dislocations including the undermining of the sterling area. The third strategy was what Cripps termed a 'constructive compromise' with the United States. This would involve maintaining government expenditures while redirecting exports to the dollar zone, and the possibility of some kind of convertibility of sterling with the dollar as part of a comprehensive settlement. For their part the Americans would have to sustain a high level of imports, reduce tariffs, continue aid programmes, stimulate private investment in the sterling area and help the British reduce the sterling balances.[177]

The talks with the Americans in July 1949 did not produce agreement on such major issues of substance and had to be resumed in September after the government had decided on devaluation in August. They did, however, set the pattern for the redefinition of Britain's imperial strategy which had been developing since late 1948; Britain would have to depend on cooperation with the Americans and distance itself from European cooperation if the Empire, and particularly the sterling area, were to be maintained and the projection of British power and influence made as effective as possible. The pattern was further defined by two more papers from the Permanent Undersecretarys' Committee which were finalised in August. The first referred to West European Organisations and the second to present and future Anglo-American relations. On the European question the old issue of a customs union was again discussed and dismissed, with the now extremely important warning that a customs union implied a fiscal or currency union which would involve the pooling of the reserves of the sterling area; this was opposed, with studied altruism, as it would weaken the ties between Britain, the Commonwealth and the sterling area, which in the new Cold War world, would not be in the interests of the general consolidation of the West. In short, a third World Force in economic terms would weaken rather than strengthen Britain because it would involve making sacrifices for the Europeans which would be bad for the West because of the Cold War. In October Bevin and Cripps came out against Britain sacrificing opportunities to earn dollars in order to help the Europeans save them, as this would undermine the unity of the Commonwealth and the sterling area. Politically, the policy which was being implemented through the Council of Europe and the avoidance of supra-national bodies was justified not in terms of pragmatism but in terms of the danger of communism. The communist penetration of key European organisations could not be disregarded and thus the surrender of power to a central, federal authority would be a dangerous undertaking.[178]

As far as Anglo-American relations were concerned, despite the wartime rivalries and post-war British fears of dependency and becoming a pygmy, it was now argued that there was no fundamental conflict of interests provided Britain was independent enough to be able to influence American policy. On the other hand, if there was a sharp contraction of British influence and a reduction of British responsibilities to the extent that it became clear Britain was no longer a world power then there would be a risk of major divergences between Britain and the United States. At the same time, if Britain proved unwilling to maintain its position in the world, the United States might seek a modus vivendi with the Russians and Western Europe be exposed to Soviet pressure as a result. It was a fascinating example of British official thinking within the Foreign Office on Britain's global imperial role, on the Cold War and on British relations with Europe and the United States defined in terms of maximising British power and influence. Or, perhaps more precisely, it was an example of how policy makers sought to justify Britain's world role and the need to maintain the appearance of power even though the real power to maintain a world role, and particularly the role sought by Bevin and the Foreign Office between 1945 and 1948, was clearly lacking. On the specific point of economic cooperation, the Permanent Under-secretaries' Committee defined Britain's best option as 'equilibrium between the dollar and sterling areas at a high level of trade' with the next best a 'closer financial union between the United States and Britain'.[179] Independence from the United States was now less preferable than an Anglo-American union.

Why this change occurred is central to an understanding of Britain's Cold War policies and the reasons for an imperial strategy. The idea that between 1945 and 1948 Britain worked for the kind of American alliance that the Labour government favoured from 1949 onwards is not sustainable; it neglects the imperial dimension by locating the reasons for such policies in the emergence of the Cold War. Similarly the idea that Britain found itself at 'the nodal point of three systems, the Commonwealth, Western Europe and the Atlantic community'[180] was the ex post-facto rationalisation for a policy initially based on a very different geo-strategic perception of Britain's global position; the idea of 'three systems' was eventually adopted because of the failures of previous policies not their successes. Far from a grand design based on the links between Britain, Western Europe and the United States in order to maintain a position as 'the balance wheel in a Western consolidation',[181] Britain had pursued an imperial strategy which would strengthen the Empire and Britain's world position through collaboration with

Western Europe; if in the short term United States backing was necessary, the long-term goal was to break free from any dependence on the Americans. In a sense the resources of the Empire, and the colonies in particular, were seen as vital to preserve future British independence; yet by 1949 a special relationship with the United States was seen as vital to preserve the Empire. An imperial bloc, with or without firm ties to Western Europe, would impose 'an intolerable strain' on the resources and cohesion of the Empire.[182] Over the period as a whole the key influence on British policy was not a grand design based on pragmatism and special relationships; nor was it the impact of the Cold War and the concern for security. What was vital for the Foreign Office was the preservation of Britain's prestige and status as a world power. If that could not be done through independence from the Americans and a Third Force it would have to be done through dependence on the United States once it became clear that the quest for independence would be more damaging to Britain's world standing.

The arguments developed by Foreign Office and Treasury officials during 1949 formed the basis of a Cabinet Paper submitted by Bevin in October after the devaluation of the pound and after the explosion of an atomic bomb by the Soviet Union. It was a paper which assessed the viability of the Third Force idea in the circumstances that by 1949 had produced the NATO alliance, the Council of Europe, devaluation and growing British fears about the chances of European recovery and the future of the sterling area. The Commonwealth was deemed unlikely to be consolidated into an effective unit or to accept the same kind of economic planning arrangements as the Western Europeans: the attraction of the pound and the Royal Navy was deemed to be less strong than that of the dollar and the atom bomb. Faced with a choice, Commonwealth members were likely to choose Washington rather than London, with the implication that complete British independence from the Americans was likely to lead to the break up of the Commonwealth. The links with Europe involved rather different risks, which would not, according to Bevin, be worth taking unless Europe was likely to be economically and militarily strong enough to resist aggression. As there was little prospect of this it meant that, were Western Europe to be overrun, the British segment of an integrated European economy would be unable to function on its own. The conclusion was that no combination of world powers was likely to amount to a unit capable of 'pursuing a policy independent of the Soviet Union and the United States. Therefore it was in Britain's interest to work for a special place within an American-dominated alliance'. This did not mean that Britain would have to abandon its policy of working to strengthen West European links within a Western or Atlantic system since the consolidation of the Western Alliance would, so it was argued, be helped by cooperation between Britain and Western Europe as long as the goal was not what Britain had previously aspired to, namely independence from the Americans.[183] Hence the idea of the nodal point and the commitment to Atlanticism in the expectation that the United States would consider Britain its 'principal partner in world affairs' and thus 'as a good deal more than a European power'.[184]

However, the lack of a contradiction between European, imperial interests and the American alliance did not apply when it came to the question of military cooperation and imperial defence in the Middle East which was the other issue the PUSC was initially requested to examine. When it came down to defining what security arrangements should be made for the Middle East and Mediterranean once the Atlantic pact was in force, the PUSC was faced with serious problems. These stemmed from the old difficulties of convincing the Europeans about Britain's desire to cooperate with them when they were not willing to contribute forces for their defence. One issue was the nature of the command arrangements for Western Europe and the Mediterranean and their relationship to the military organisation within NATO and Western union; this was to drag on for several years and cause problems for Anglo-American relations as well as for Britain's relations with Western Europeans. More important were the implications for the Middle East of a military strategy that had to focus increasingly on Europe for political reasons. With the American support for NATO, the new Chief of the Imperial General Staff, Field Marshal Slim, emphasised the importance of not dividing American forces between the Middle East and Western Europe. In other words the Americans, like the British, should continue to attach more importance to the defence of the Middle East, at least as far as emergency planning was concerned, and act in conformity with British strategic planning.[185]

In the general sense that meant keeping strategic planning on an Anglo-American basis as much as possible, with the emphasis on global planning as opposed to considering just the European theatre which was clearly the main concern of the Western union Chiefs of Staff. With this in mind the ideal British arrangement was an Anglo-American steering committee for an overall Atlantic pact military organisation within which regional organisations would cover the various theatres. In other words the French would not gain the same kind of status as the British and Americans who would in effect continue the wartime Combined Chiefs of Staff arrangements under the guise of an Atlantic pact steering committee; this would prevent the French from becoming involved in global strategic planning and avoid the Americans becoming preoccupied with the European theatre at the expense of Britain's imperial commitments to the defence of the Middle East.[186]

With the signing of the North Atlantic Pact in April 1949 the Western Europeans were keen to start work on the next emergency plan, and therefore the British representative on the Military Committee of the Brussels Treaty Organisation needed information about the extent of the British commitment to the defence of the Continent. Slim explained the precise nature of the British problem in terms of political influence in Europe which could only be maintained by undermining one of the three pillars in British defence strategy – defending the Middle East. If Britain did not increase its contribution of land forces to the defence of Western Europe it would be impossible to retain influence there, and Britain's refusal to commit itself to a major war on the Continent would have a serious effect on West European solidarity. On the other hand it would be impossible, in Slim's view, to defend the Rhine for at least four years and a major campaign in Europe would have obvious repercussions on the Middle East.[187]

Lord Fraser suggested that if Britain promised to send an armoured brigade and the first two divisions of reinforcements to Europe, rather than the Middle East, then the Americans might provide additional forces for the defence of the latter region. Tedder was now opposed to making such military judgements on political grounds and felt British policy should not be influenced by the French who were failing to understand the general importance of the British Empire's contribution to the defence of the West. In any case, General Templer, quite rightly as it turned out, argued that the Americans were not likely to provide a rapid build-up of Middle Eastern land forces; and if the two divisions and armoured brigade earmarked for the Middle East were not despatched at once plan 'Sandown' could not be implemented.[188] This of course did not provide any solutions to the British dilemma, and by August the Chiefs of Staff were pinning their faith in the idea put forward by Fraser that if Britain increased its contribution to Western Europe the United States would have to take up more of the burden in the Middle East. As far as the French were concerned the idea was to promise to supply additional divisions for European defence but only when the continental ones were fully equipped. In the meantime it would be vital to find out what the Americans were going to do.[189] One likely outcome was of course that the British, with their overstretched resources, would have to provide forces for Europe and the Middle East with the United States being called upon to do the same. The decisions could not be postponed indefinitely, and in September 1949 Ramadier made it clear to the British that he expected a resolution of the question of Britain's contribution to the defence of Western Europe very soon after the ratification of the Atlantic Pact.[190] The British military having emphasised the importance of the Middle East now found themselves forced to commit forces to the Continent for political reasons, and it appeared unlikely that the Americans would help get them out of the strategic mess they were embroiled in as a result of the overall British aim to maintain influence and status with inadequate economic and military resources.

In fact American attitudes to supplying land forces for European defence were partly influenced by the British predicament. The view from Washington was that the Americans were unlikely to participate fully in a Western European regional organisation because they might find themselves called upon to give some definite military commitment to provide land forces for the Continent. The American Chiefs of Staff were believed to be 'anxious to avoid the kind of situation recently faced by the British Chiefs of Staff regarding the provision of British forces'.[191] Worse news was to follow regarding the Pentagon's attitude to the defence of the Middle East. In the late summer of 1949, no doubt influenced by the creation of NATO, the American Chiefs of Staff put forward a whole new strategic concept which they were to persist with despite British objections. Given the impossibility of defending the Rhine the Americans were thinking of defending a bridgehead in Europe, either in southern Spain or in the Pyrenees, which they now deemed more important than the defence of the Middle East. The Americans were primarily concerned to avoid another 'Overlord' by keeping a foothold on the Continent of Europe, and intended to build up a strategic reserve in Morocco. The United States therefore intended to withdraw from defending the Middle East, which would become an exclusively British responsibility, and to provide no reinforcements for the defence of the Rhine. They visualised an operational axis running from their base in Morocco through Spain into France which would require naval operations in the Mediterranean to be geared to the land campaign in Southern Europe rather than to the defence of the Middle East or to British imperial communications through the Mediterranean.

To cap it all, the new American strategic concept meant that United States forces would be unlikely to be engaged against Soviet forces during the first vital six months of war, and the British military did not believe that NATO members would regard this as genuine support for the alliance.[192] The Joint Planners therefore pondered what to tell the French. Should they be told the truth that there would be no short-term reinforcements for Western Europe, or should they be told a lie that Britain intended to reinforce the Rhine? Alternatively should they be given a strategic concept which was militarily poor but which might just be feasible in five or six years?

This was the sorry state of affairs that British military cooperation with Europe had arrived at by the end of 1949. It also meant that one of the three pillars of British defence strategy had been fatally undermined because the Americans had withdrawn their support for it. Thus the whole basis of defence strategy, as defined in 1947 after Attlee's defeat, had now to be reconsidered largely because of Western union and NATO and the importance of American cooperation. It was not the critique of the Prime Minister that was to bring this about and produce a Cabinet decision in March 1950 to give priority to reinforcing Western Europe rather than the Middle East; nor was it because of a change of thinking by the military about what was strategically important. What had changed were the requirements stemming from the political need to retain influence in Western Europe whether to meet the goals of the Third Force or to retain British influence and 'special' status within the American-dominated Atlantic Alliance. It was an imperial strategy that geared military planning to the political requirements of influence and status rather than one which identified military needs. It was also an imperial strategy, which in both military and economic terms, was fundamentally unrealisable because of Britain's inadequate resources and therefore produced a number of contradictions. In the military sense these could only be resolved by adopting impractical plans for the defence of Western Europe at the cost of making the difficult task of defending the Middle East into an impossible one.

The irony is that the strategy Attlee fought so hard against in 1945–46 was undermined in 1950 because of the need to enrol the Western European powers as collaborators with the British Empire in order to retain influence in Europe, and Attlee's own strategy of a Lagos – Kenyan – Persian Gulf axis was adopted in 1957 after the Suez fiasco which was the final British attempt to retain paramount influence in the Middle East. All this has nevertheless been portrayed as a well-planned adaptation to the problems created by Soviet imperialism to which the British reacted with pragmatism, foresight and wisdom. Such are the human powers of rationalising emotive behaviour that the story of the Empire's decline and the onset of the Cold War has not been told in terms of imperial rivalries or of conflicting and impractical attempts to preserve great power status, but in terms of Soviet 'behaviour' in Europe and well-planned British efforts to save Western civilisation from the Soviet threat. In the process the failure to avoid dependence on the Americans has become the most successful achievement of British global strategy.

Notes

1. The quotation is from 'Love Minus Zero/No Limits' on the album 'Bringing it all Back Home' by Bob Dylan which continues 'and failure's no success at all'.
2. FO800/444 note on Bevin's meeting with the Canadian High Commissioner 17.12.47.

3. *FRUS 1948* Vol. III (Washington 1974) p. 1 record of conversation between Bevin and Marshall 22.12.47; FO371/67674 record of conversation between Bevin and Bidault 17.12.47.
4. J. W. Young *France, the Cold War and the Western Alliance 1944–49* (Leicester 1990) pp. 225–4.
5. FO371/67674 minute by O. Harvey 21.10.47.
6. J. Kent and J. W. Young 'The Western union Concept and British Defence Planning 1947–48' in R. Aldrich (ed) *British Intelligence, Strategy and the Cold War* (London 1992) pp. 171–2.
7. FO371/72979 note of meeting with Massigli (French Ambassador) 5.1.48.
8. Kent and Young op. cit., p. 169.
9. WO216/674 record of Bevin–Bidault meeting 17.12.47.
10. DEFE 4/10 JP (48) 4 6.1.48.
11. FO371/67674 Sec COS Committee to FO 30.12.47; Sir O. Sargent to Sec COS Committee 1.1.48.
12. FO371/62555 minute by R. B. Stevens 22.12.47.
13. Ibid. minute by P. M. Crosthwaite 31.12.47.
14. Ibid. minute by R. M. A. Hankey 3.1.48.
15. Ibid. minutes by W. G. Hoyter 5.1.48 and F. B. A. Rundall 6.1.48.
16. Ibid. minute by G. Jebb 8.1.48.
17. Ibid. minute by F. Hoyar Millar 10.1.48.
18. CAB 129/23 CP (48) 6 4.1.48; CAB 128/12 CM (48) 2nd 8.1.48.
19. FO800/435 memorandum by Creech Jones (n.d) Jan. 1948.
20. Ibid. minute by F. K. Roberts 10.1.48.
21. *FRUS 1948* Vol. III pp. 4–6. I am grateful to John Milloy, a postgraduate student at the LSE, for analysing the differences between the Cabinet Paper and the despatch to Washington.
22. FO371/73045 minute by Bevin 12.1.48.
23. E. Barker *Britain between the Superpowers 1945–50* (1983) p. 127.
24. Kent and Young op. cit.
25. DEFE 4/10 JP (48) 4 6.1.48.
26. FO371/73045 memorandum by I. Kirkpatrick 9.1.48.
27. DEFE 4/10 JP (48) 4 6.1.48 and COS (48) 14th 28.1.48.
28. Kent and Young op. cit.
29. FO371/73045 minute by Bevin 12.1.48.
30. Ibid. Washington to FO 20.1.48.
31. *Hansard House of Commons Debates* Vol. 446 cols 387–409.
32. CAB 131/5 DO (48) 2nd 3.1.48 and 3rd 14.1.48.
33. Ibid.
34. DEFE 4/10 COS (48) 15th 30.1.48; JP (48) 16 27.1.48. For Bevin's links to Montgomery see FO800/452 for Jan. 1948.
35. DEFE 5/10 COS (48) 26 30.1.48.
36. DEFE 4/10 COS (48) 16th 2.2.48.
37. Ibid. COS (48) 18th 4.2.48.
38. *FRUS 1948* Vol. III pp. 7–12.
39. FO371/73046 Washington to FO 2.2.48; *FRUS 1948* Vol. III pp. 19–20.
40. DEFE 4/10 COS (48) 18th 4.2.48.
41. FO371/73048 FO to Paris 16.2.48.
42. FO371/73045 minute by R. Makins 21.2.48.
43. FO371/73046 minute by I. Kirkpatrick 7.2.48.
44. FO371/73048 Paris to FO 16.2.48.
45. M. H. Folly, 'Breaking the Vicious Circle; Britain, the United States and the Genesis of the North Atlantic Treaty' *Diplomatic History* 12 (1988) p. 63.

46. FO371/73047 minute by W. N. M. Hogg 12.2.48.
47. FO371/73049 FO note Feb. 1948.
48. Hogan op. cit. (see Ch. 5, n. 49) pp. 114–5 citing FO371/71766 memo by R. B. Stevens n.d.
49. FO371/73047 draft despatch to Paris 13.2.48.
50. T236/804 draft Treasury note n.d.
51. Hogan op cit. pp. 115–16.
52. FO371/68067 Washington to FO 17.3.48.
53. FO371/73050 Sir O. Harvey to FO 1.3.48.
54. CAB 128/12 CM (48) 19th 5.3.48.
55. DEFE 4/11 COS (48) 34th 9.3.48.
56. FO371/73051 Bevin to W. N. Warbey 10.3.48.
57. The text of the Treaty is in Cmd 7367.
58. T236/1884 R. Makins to R. W. B. Clarke 8.3.48; CO537/3548 minute by A. B. Cohen 10.3.48.
59. For these visits see Kent and Young op. cit. and Young *France* p. 181.
60. DEFE 4/11 COS (48) 39th 17.3.48.
61. Ibid. COS (48) 37th 15.3.48.
62. DEFE 5/10 COS (48) 26 30.1.48.
63. FO800/452 COS (48) 58 17.3.48.
64. DEFE 4/11 COS (48) 37th 15.3.48.
65. Ibid., FO371/73054 minute by Sir O. Sargent 5.3.48.
66. DEFE 4/11 COS (48) 41st 18.3.48.
67. On the talks see *FRUS 1948* Vol. III pp. 59–67, 69–75.
68. DEFE 4/11 COS (48) 37th 15.3.48.
69. DEFE 5/10 COS (48) 75 7.4.48 annex: copy of telegram from Gen. Hollis 6.4.48.
70. FO800/452 Bevin to Attlee 6.4.48.
71. DEFE 5/10 COS (48) 58 17.3.48.
72. P. L. Hahn *The United States, Great Britain and Egypt 1945–56* (Chapel Hill 1991) pp. 58–62.
73. FO800/452 Bevin to Attlee 6.4.48.
74. DEFE 4/12 COS (48) 46th annex 31.3.48.
75. *FRUS 1948* Vol. III minutes of 4th meeting of US–UK–Canadian talks 29.3.48 p. 70.
76. DEFE 4/12 COS (48) 46th annex 31.3.48.
77. FO371/68068A Washignton to FO 10.4.48.
78. Ibid. Bevin to Lord Inverchapel 15.4.58.
79. PREM 8/1431 record of 2nd meeting of five Foreign Ministers 17.3.48; *FRUS 1948* Vol. III Caffery (Paris) to Marshall 13.4.48 pp. 84–5.
80. FO371/73057 record of Bevin/Bidault conversation 16.4.48.
81. FO371/68068A Lord Inverchapel to FO 16.4.48 and *FRUS 1948* Vol. III Douglas (London) to Marshall 14.3.48 pp. 123–6.
82. FO371/68067 Washington to FO 22.3.48; Paris to Secretary of State 15.3.48; FO371/68068A minute by G. Jebb 30.3.48.
83. The details of 'Doublequick' are still withheld but the American equivalent finalised in July 1948 and called 'Halfmoon' is printed in T. Etzold and J. L. Gaddis (eds) *Containment: Documents on US Policy and Strategy 1945–50* (New York 1978) pp. 315–23.
84. DEFE 4/13 COS (48) 56th 23.4.48; COS (48) 57th 26.4.48.
85. *FRUS 1948* Vol. III Bevin and Bidault to Marshall 17.3.48 p. 91.
86. Ibid. p. 147. The full directive is in DEFE 4/13.
87. FO371/73057 record of Bevin/Bidault conversation 16.4.48 and 17.4.48.
88. T236/1884 EPC (48) 16th 26.4.48. CAB 128/12 CM (48) 20th 8.3.48.

89. T236/1920 GEN 188/138 2.3.48.
90. FO371/73057 record of Bevin/Bidault conversation 17.4.48.
91. T236/1920 GEN 188/163 note by the Colonial Office 18.3.48; Kent *Internationalization* (see Ch. 4, n. 2) pp. 180–3.
92. CO537/3153 conclusions of CO working party on Anglo-French economic cooperation Feb. 1948; minute by K. E. Robinson 5.2.48; FO371/68997 minute by Bevin March 1948; Kent *Internationalization* pp. 176–8.
93. T236/1920 GEN 188/48th 9.2.48; T236/1757 DD (48) 11 30.4.48.
94. CAB 134/217 EPC (48) 35 interim report of Colonial Development Working Party 27.4.48.
95. D. J. Morgan op. cit. (see Ch. 5, n. 40) p. 69.
96. CO852/868/2 CEDC (48) 3 22.4.48 note by Colonial Office on international colonial cooperation.
97. T236/1815 W. L. Gorrell Barnes to A. T. K. Grant 30.6.68; minute by A. T. K. Grant 1.5.48; draft letter to W. L. Gorrell Barnes May 1948.
98. Ibid. despatch to Colonial Governors 20.5.48.
99. FO371/70258 text of Bevin's speech to the City Livery Club 30.4.48; CO537/3316 record of conversation between Bevin and the Italian Ambassador 24.1.48; CAB 129/24 CP (48) 43 4.2.48.
100. CO537/3316 note of conversation between Bevin and Sforza 15.3.48; minutes by A. B. Cohen 1.4.48, Sir S. Caine 2.4.48, A. H. Poynton 1.4.48 and Sir T. Lloyd 5.4.48.
101. Ibid. note on FO meeting on the association of Italy with African development 13.4.48; note on meeting between CO and FO officials 6.7.48; note of conversation between Bevin and the President of the Italian Senate 23.7.48; minute by Creech Jones 16.7.48; G. L. Clutton to A. B. Cohen 7.9.48; minute by Creech Jones 9.8. 48; J. M. Martin to G. L. Clutton 11.9.48; minute by K. E. Robinson 17.9.48.
102. FO371/68068A FO to Washington 22.4.48.
103. DEFE 4/13 COS (48) 64th 10.5.48; CAB 127/341 record of Downing Street meeting 7.5.48.
104. CAB 127/341 record of Downing Street meeting 7.5.48; DEFE 4/13 COS (48) 66th 12.5.48.
105. DEFE 4/13 COS (48) 70th 24.5.48.
106. FO800/452 Montgomery to Gen. Omar Bradley (US army) 8.3.48.
107. *FRUS 1948* Vol. III p. 125 Douglas (London) to Secretary of State 14.5.48.
108. DEFE 4/13 COS (48) 72nd annex 2 Gen. Hollis to Minister of Defence 25.5.48.
109. DEFE 4/15 COS (48) 122nd 3.9.48.
110. DEFE 4/16 has details of 'Sandown' and see DEFE 5/8 COS (48) 12 16.10.48 for discussion of whether a defensive line further north would be preferable.
111. DEFE 4/18 COS (48) 180th 16.12.48 annex.
112. See for example Louis *British Empire* (see Ch. 4, n. 31) pp. 109–12.
113. DEFE 4/50 COS (51) 204th 17.12.51 JP (51) 211 13.12.51.
114. DEFE 4/13 COS (48) 83rd annex 18.6.84.
115. DEFE 4/17 COS (48) 153rd 29.10.48.
116. PREM 8/1431 record of 2nd restricted meeting of the Foreign Ministers of the Brussels powers on 19.7.48.
117. FO371/73060 minute by F. K. Roberts 8.7.48; Sir O. Harvey (Paris) to FO 15.7.48.
118. PREM 8/1431 record of 2nd restricted meeting of the Foreign Ministers of the Brussels powers on 19.7.48.
119. DEFE 4/14 COS (48) 90th 30.6.48.
120. The arguments over Western union command arrangements are not covered in detail here but they reflect the British military's determination to confine global/imperial concerns to an Anglo-American basis while securing much-needed US involvement

in Western European defence.
121. FO371/73077 record of 6th meeting of Washington Exploratory Talks 3.9.48; brief for Secretary of State for Cabinet 9.9.48.
122. DEFE 4/16 COS (48) 124th JP (48) 91 1.9.48.
123. Ibid. record of 1st meeting of Western union Chiefs of Staff 8.10.48.
124. DEFE 4/17 CO (48) 151st 25.10.48.
125. FO371/73079 minute by P. M. Crosthwaite 18.11.48.
126. DEFE 4/17 COS (48) 153rd 29.10.48.
127. FO371/73099 record of consultative council meeting 25.10.48.
128. *Hansard House of Commons Debates* Vol. 456 cols 91–106 15.9.48.
129. FO371/73062 brief for Sir S. Cripps n.d. Sept. 1948.
130. *Hansard House of Commons debates* Vol. 459 cols 528–86 9.12.48.
131. FO371/73062 brief for Sir S. Cripps n.d. Sept. 1948.
132. FO371/73063 record of Ramadier/Bevin conversation 25.9.48; Bevin to Attlee 26.9.48.
133. T236/1884 note by UK delegation, Brussels n.d. April 1948; EPC (48) 16th 26.4.48; record of interdeparmental meeting to prepare for five power conference 13.4.48. See p. 174
134. Hogan op. cit. p. 165.
135. Ibid. p. 170.
136. Ibid. p. 172.
137. J. J. Kaplan and G. Schleiminger *The European Payments Union* (Oxford 1989) pp. 24–5.
138. Hogan op. cit. p. 160.
139. PREM 8/1146 Pt I EPC (48) 78 7.9.48; EPC (48) 37 8.5.48.
140. B. Pimlott (ed.) *The Political Diary of Hugh Dalton 1945–60* (1986) p. 443. entry for 15.10.48.
141. FO371/72975 Sir O. Harvey to FO recounting a conversation between Reynaud and Wilson 12.8.48.
142. FO371/73150 minute by P. M. Crosthwaite 1.4.48.
143. FO371/71822 note of a FO, CO, CRO meeting 29.7.48.
144. CO852/885/1 UK delegation OEEC to FO 7.8.48.
145. CO537/3316 G. L. Clutton to A. N. Galsworthy 18.11.48.
146. CO537/3550 minutes by J. B. Williams 3.9.48 and 17.8.48.
147. T236/694 CO memorandum on 'Economic Planning in the Colonies', n.d.; record of Treasury meeting 13.8.48.
148. CO852/870/2 memorandum on the 'Colonial Empire and the Economic Crisis' sent to Colonial Governors 26.7.48.
149. CO537/3172 compte rendu de la 1ère séance de L'OTC 12.10.48 and compte rendu de la 2ème séance 12.10.48.
150. Ibid. draft report of Working Party for the Overseas Territories 4.11.84; T234/219 Report by Colonial Development Working Party 1.11.48.
151. CO852/885/1 record of Italian criticism of Working Party Report 25.11.48.
152. For example, Ch. 17 of Alan Bullock's biography is entitled 'The Plan Realised . . .' Bullock (see Ch. 3, n. 81).
153. T236/1816 CO memorandum May 1949.
154. Ibid. CSC (49) 15 June 1949.
155. CO537/4736 FO memorandum 'The Economic Development of the Nile Valley'; mintue by A. B. Cohen 4.7.49.
156. Ibid. minute by A. H. Poynton 5.7.49.
157. Ibid. minute by Creech Jones 7.7.49.
158. CAB 134/218 EPC (48) 53 18.6.48 annexes A and B.
159. Ibid. EPC (48) 66 9.7.48; CAB 134/219 EPC (48) 71 15.7.48.

160. CAB 134/219 EPC (48) 81 14.9.48.
161. Ibid. ECP (48) 85 15.9.48.
162. Hogan op. cit. p. 222.
163. CAB 134/219 EPC (48) 110 7.12.48.
164. CAB 129/30 CP (48) 249 2.11.48; Hogan op. cit. p. 215.
165. See CAB 128/13 CM (48) 68th 4.11.48 and Bullock op. cit. pp. 641–2.
166. CAB 134/221 EPC (49) 6 25.1.49; CAB 129/37/Pt ICP (49) 203 25.10.49.
167. Hogan op. cit. p. 208.
168. Ibid. pp. 191, 212 citing FO371/77999 Sir E. Hall Patch to Berthoud 4 and 16 April 1949.
169. CAB 134/222 EPC (49) 61 11.6.49.
170. Hogan op. cit. p. 228.
171. Ibid. pp. 222–30; CAB 134/222 EPC (59) 67 24.6.49.
172. Ibid. p. 233.
173. Ibid. p. 235.
174. FO371/76384 minute by W. Strang 23.3.49.
175. Ibid. PUSC (23) Final 'Third World Power or Western Consolidation' 9.5.49.
176. Ibid. Noel-Baker to Bevin 18.6.49.
177. Hogan op. cit. pp. 239–41 citing PREM 8/1412 Pt II EPC (49) 73 4.7.49.
178. FO371/76385 PSUC (48) 17.8.49; CAB 129/37 Pt I CP (49) 205 25.10.49.
179. Ibid. PUSC 64 (51) 24.8.49.
180. Hogan op. cit. p. 250 citing FO371/75594 memorandum by R. Makins 26.8.49.
181. Hogan ibid. p. 251.
182. Ibid. citing FO371/75594 memorandum by R. Makins 26.8.49.
183. CAB 129/37 Pt 1 CP (49) 208 18.10.49.
184. Hogan op. cit. p. 250 citing FO371/75594 memorandum by R. Makins 26.8.49.
185. DEFE 4/17 COS (48) 160th annex 10.11.48.
186. DEFE 4/20 JP (49) 32 31.3.49; COS (49) 38th 7.3.49.
187. DEFE 4/21 COS (49) 57th 20.4.49; COS (49) 75th 20.5.49; DEFE 4/19 COS (49) 2nd 5.1.49.
188. DEFE 4/22 COS (49) 86th 10.6.47.
189. DEFE 4/23 COS (49) 112th 2.8.49.
190. DEFE 5/16 COS (49) 298 12.9.49.
191. DFE 4/23 COS (49) 123rd 24.8.49.
192. DEFE 4/24 COS (49) 131st 8.9.49; JP (49) 93 5.9.49.

Conclusion

Historians can all agree that the Second World War dramatically undermined the British Empire. One historian, focusing primarily on the internal threats to the Empire has suggested it was the most important of the many factors that ultimately produced British decolonisation.[1] If anything the war's impact on Britain's global position which was linked to the maintenance of the Empire/Commonwealth as a major force was even more dramatic because of the exposure of Britain's over-stretched imperial position and the changes in the global balance of power. The former was most evident in the Far East, and in the immediate aftermath of the fall of Singapore the abandonment of exclusive British responsibilities in Hong Kong and Malaya was considered in order to gain an American commitment to defend British territories against a renewed Japanese attack. Such policies soon ran foul of the dominant wartime and post-war determination in Whitehall to preserve Britain's global role in the first rank of world powers. If any signs of weakness were demonstrated then the effect on Britain's prestige and great power pretensions would, in the eyes of British imperial strategists, be fatally damaging. In the 1940s this was to be a constant consideration of the British in their assessments of vital interests and enemy threats.

Fears in 1942 of Germany and Japan came to be replaced in 1944 by fears of the Soviet Union which was at best defined as a potential ally but *the* potential enemy. Yet at the start of that year the Soviet Union did not pose the same direct threat to the British Empire as the United States. Despite the dislike of colonialism in Washington and the American determination to prevent the sterling area becoming an integrated trading bloc discriminating against the dollar zone, there was always an assumption in London and parts of Whitehall that the Americans could and should be willing partners and supporters of the British Empire. Such attitudes were typified by that of the Prime Minister who was one of the most enthusiastic supporters of the Empire and of the idea of a transatlantic partnership between the two powerful Anglo-Saxon allies. The fact that there was a potential conflict of economic interests between the United States and the British Empire was one indication of the fact that more was at stake for imperial strategists than the definition and protection of particular imperial requirements. Challenges to the British Empire were also defined in terms of their overall impact on Britain's global standing. Imperial concessions to the Americans in return for supporting other imperial interests were not as damaging as concessions to the Soviets because the latter were not essentially perceived as natural allies of Britain.

That the key issue for men like Churchill was the global position of the British Empire emerges from his attitude to Britain's relations with Nazi Germany and the Soviet Union. Indeed for Churchill, Bevin and the Foreign Office, imperial concerns related to Britain's vital interests and its general global position were the most important element of Anglo-Soviet relations as the Cold War began to develop. In 1938 Churchill told Soviet Ambassador, Maisky, that

twenty years ago I strove with all the energy in my power against Communism because at that time I considered Communism, with its idea of world revolution, the greatest danger to the British Empire. Now Communism does not present such a danger to the Empire. On the contrary, nowadays German Nazism, with its idea of the world hegemony of Berlin, constitutes the greatest danger for the British Empire. Therefore, at the present time I strive against Hitler with all the energy in my power. If the danger for the British Empire from the side of fascism were to disappear and the danger from the side of Communism were to rise again, I – I say this absolutely frankly – would begin to strive against you again. But for the immediate future, and certainly until the end of my life, I do not foresee such a situation. For this period of time we and you share the same path. This is the reason why I am in favour of close cooperation between England, France and the USSR.[2]

In 1938 the threat to the Empire was a concrete military one which was to appear in the Far East, the Middle East and the Mediterranean. Chamberlain was right to perceive that a global conflict would irreparably damage the British Empire, but Churchill was even more right to believe that the Empire could not survive as part of a German dominated world. By the end of the war the threat to the Empire was of a very different nature, unless it is assumed, as many have done since, that the Soviet Union presented an immediate military threat or aimed at world domination. Whatever the truth of such suppositions, which cannot be fully tested in Soviet archives, these were not the assumptions made by British policy makers who, at the beginning of 1945, expected cooperation from the Soviets, and who never saw them as a short-term military threat. The immediate danger was no longer a military one from an enemy state but the nature of the cooperation between allies upon which Britain's vital imperial interests and general world position were seen to hinge. The crucial factors for imperial strategists, and therefore for an understanding of the breakdown of Anglo-Soviet relations, were the specific terms the British required from cooperation.

In 1944 and 1945 Britain's vital interests were in the Eastern Mediterranean and the Middle East which formed the key imperial region and was the focus of Britain's military strategy. European policy was significant primarily because of its impact on that key region. Thus the British were concerned with the future governments of Italy and Greece and determined to prevent left-wing elements seizing power in the latter country. Churchill was much more concerned with controlling the situation in Greece than preventing Russian control in most areas of Europe east of Germany, and until Yalta the general view in the Foreign Office was that, with the possible exception of Bulgaria, the rest of Eastern Europe was likely to be a Soviet sphere of influence. This was acceptable to officials because, unlike the politicians, they would not have to face parliamentary hostility over the fate of Poland, which, like the other areas of Eastern Europe north of the Balkans, did not threaten any of Britain's vital interests. Then Stalin's astonishing behaviour at Yalta in agreeing to immediate free elections in Poland and to the Declaration on Liberated Europe combined with Allied military successes in the West to produce a major shift in British policy. It was based on the idea that the original policy of dealing with the Soviets in terms of vital interests and their related areas of influence was no longer acceptable. In other words Britain's exclusive imperial interests in the Mediterranean and the Middle East could not be reconciled with exclusive Soviet influence over its areas of vital interest because to abandon British rights to be concerned with all areas of Europe would not be compatible with great power status.

In the early summer of 1945 this concern with great power status was then compounded by concerns that the Soviet Union was threatening the British Empire through its imperialistic ambitions in Turkey and the Straits. By the time of the Potsdam Conference when the Soviets expressed a wish for the trusteeship of Tripolitania, one view within the Foreign Office was that no concessions could be made to the Soviets because of the impact on Britain's Mediterranean and Middle Eastern position and because of the consequent effect on Britain's great power status. Undoubtedly the imperialist aims of British policy makers could only be fulfilled if the Soviets were kept out of the Middle East. An exclusive sphere of influence for Britain was seen as a matter of life or death, and therefore any Soviet or international presence in Libya or the Suez Canal Zone could not be accepted. By the same token it was likely that the Soviets would find it equally unacceptable to have any external involvement in the affairs of Poland, Romania and perhaps other areas east of the German border. The British considered a spheres of influence deal on such lines as being unacceptable to the Americans and incompatible with British ambitions to regain equality with its two wartime allies.

Stalin's apparent abandonment of the spheres of influence approach at Yalta also allowed the Foreign Office to give up that strategy and eventually adopt a policy which essentially involved the preservation of an exclusive Middle Eastern and Mediterranean sphere of influence while refusing to agree to the one the Soviets were determined to impose on parts of Eastern Europe. It also strengthened the Foreign Office view that the standard by which the Soviets were to be judged was that of the Declaration of Liberated Europe. If this was not met then Soviet 'behaviour' could be deemed unacceptable, even though the British Foreign Office acknowledged it had no specific vital interests in Eastern Europe north of the Balkans, and that Soviet claims for bases in the Straits and for a trusteeship over Tripolitania may have been produced by the British abandonment of their pre-Yalta spheres of influence policy. In effect, the British were judging the Soviets by their acceptance of British imperialism in the Middle East and their renunciation of Soviet imperialism in the Straits and Eastern Europe, and cooperation had to be based on this. Even the renunciation of exclusive areas of influence could not be accepted by the British because it would weaken their position in the Middle East. For Bevin the continuation of Britain's exclusive position in the Mediterranean and Middle East could be justified on the grounds that the Soviets had made territorial gains in Europe. Cooperation with the Soviets was dictated by the desire to avoid any concessions damaging to Britain's imperial prestige and status rather than by a new world order reflecting the changed balance of military and economic power.

The determination to adopt such a view of post-war cooperation and of the protection of British imperial interests was not simply the consequence of particular economic and military concerns. Even in the vital Mediterranean and Middle Eastern regions both the military and the Foreign Office saw things in general power-political terms. The strategic or economic damage that might occur if the Soviets had bases in the Straits was deemed less important than the effect on British prestige and influence. And the latter had to be preserved otherwise there would be little chance of overcoming the economic and military weakness which was generally believed in 1945 to be only a temporary phenomena.

It was this need to regain great power status that led imperial strategists to devise particular economic and military policies, rather than economic and military requirements dictating imperial strategy. In the Foreign Office the idea of enrolling the European powers as collaborators with the British Empire was seen initially to depend on economic cooperation with the Europeans. At the same time it would remove the short-term economic dependence on the Americans that was embodied in the loan negotiated in the autumn of 1945. Yet it soon became clear that there would be an economic price to be paid by the British if the foreign policy requirements of European economic cooperation were to be met. At this point cooperation began to focus more on economic collaboration involving the European powers and their respective Empires.

Interest in Africa really developed when in 1947 Europe's need for American economic assistance in the face of the dollar gap produced more short-term dependence on the United States. The British aim of getting the Americans to provide short-term political support for Britain's global position, which was seen to be threatened by the Soviets, had been accompanied by the expected short-term economic dependence embodied in the 1945 loan; the Marshall Plan and the dollar gap increased the importance of ending this dependence. With some colonies earning dollars and the perceived need to bolster dollar earnings from manufactured goods by increasing the production of raw materials and foodstuffs, African development loomed large in the minds of imperial strategists. If the Europeans were involved in this then they would become collaborators with the British Empire and European economic cooperation would be extended in ways which would help solve the dollar problem. If this were not achieved then the consensus in the Foreign Office was that Britain would become a second-rate power, a colonial appendage of the United States or a satellite of one or other of Britain's wartime allies.

In the Foreign Office the goals of policy were set in terms of great power status and equality with the United States and Soviet Union, and there was no proper examination or understanding of the obstacles to achieving them. In part this reflected a refusal not so much to face up to Britain's post-war weakness but a refusal to accept that it could not be overcome; this in turn required prestige and influence to be maintained in the peace settlement and in the key regions forming the middle of the planet. These Foreign Office attitudes led to clashes between ministers and between departments as well as to a confrontational stance against the Soviets which almost certainly contributed to the Cold War tensions that were evident by 1947.

These tensions then produced greater insecurity in Britain and Europe particularly about communist takeovers; thus the fear of communism was added to the fear of failing to bring about post-war recovery and the fear of losing imperial influence and great power status. In Europe the fears of Soviet communism meant that the idea of Western union which was designed to enrol the Western European powers as Britain's imperial collaborators had to have a military dimension to at least provide greater confidence in the British commitment to Europe. As Britain could not provide the kind of military assistance the Europeans desired, and as the British military refused to consider European cooperation without the Americans, the idea of Western union ran into difficulties after the Brussels Treaty had been signed. Bevin's idea of getting American backing for Western union and the creation of a Third Force centred on the middle of the planet was replaced by European and American involvement in an Atlantic Pact, even though the Foreign Secretary was nervous about the Americans taking over. For without the NATO treaty, which was portrayed to the French as a paper sprat to catch the mackerel of real American military aid, the whole idea of Western union was likely to have collapsed.

Inevitably, however, Western union and the Third Force were weakened by the involvement of the Americans in a European treaty rather than having them provide support and backing for it. Also in 1948 the French took the initiative as far as the political evolution of Western European union was concerned, and it was an initiative aimed at creating common European institutions. By then, Bevin and the Foreign Office had changed their position and accepted the economic disadvantages of anything likely to lead to European economic union. The ruling out of a European customs union did not, however, rule out other forms of economic cooperation or lessen the Foreign Office's interest in imperial collaboration by the European colonial powers. If Britain was going to regain economic independence from the Americans the Empire's resources and European cooperation were still important. Thus, Bevin's grandiose imperial schemes were not killed off in the autumn of 1948 and they provided a contrast with his more cautious approach to Europe. What has been termed 'pragmatism' and 'realism' in policy towards the latter was not in fact a feature of Bevin's general approach to foreign policy; he was simply concerned with what kind of economic cooperation would be advantageous to Britain within Europe and within the European Empires.

The rejection of a European customs union and opposition to the kind of political cooperation favoured by the French were further blows to the chances of Western union being established under British auspices. The final blow, which was behind the abandonment of the Third Force idea, came with the acceptance of economic dependence on the Americans for the medium-term future and the preference for economic cooperation with the dollar zone rather than Western Europe. By then, however, the military dimension of imperial strategy which had produced the great debate between 1945 and 1947 had been undermined by the importance of convincing the Europeans of Britain's desire for cooperation. The reasons for this dramatic change in policy were obviously linked to the political, economic and military difficulties in the way of the Third Force. However, the most important British consideration was the problem of linking American aid to a

European payments system in ways which would prevent a threat to sterling and avoid the resources of the sterling area being used at Britain's expense for the promotion of European recovery. In fact this issue revealed the fundamental incompatibility of reconciling European and imperial interests in ways which would benefit Britain.

It is true that there were also great difficulties in establishing any kind of European cooperation in African development even if the resources had been available. Here, however, the difficulties simply amounted to no positive gains for the British rather than actual losses. Even in the case of European economic union there were clearly perceived long-term advantages as well as the short-term disadvantages. In terms of bridging the dollar gap and ensuring Britain's economic recovery, by the end of 1948 only disadvantages appeared likely if the resources of the sterling area had to be made available as part of an independent third World Force in competition with the dollar zone. If, as was predicted, Europe failed to recover and became more vulnerable to communism the British would not be facing disadvantages but catastrophe. As 1949 wore on economic weaknesses and inadequate resources undermined the idea of using colonial development as a lifeline for the British. In 1948 there had been disturbances in dollar earning colonies experiencing import controls. In 1949 the colonial dollar surplus disappeared and not only were the hopes of Commonwealth countries unfulfilled but the continued British economic difficulties were likely to make the Dominions turn to the United States. A Third Force could mean the fatal weakening of ties to the white Commonwealth if the latter were presented with a choice between the pound and the navy on the one hand and the dollar and the atom bomb on the other. In these circumstances a need to maintain firm ties with the Americans was essential and a sleight of hand was needed by imperial strategists to justify this change from the goal of independence to the acceptance of a special but dependent relationship with the United States. If the Empire had initially been seen as a form of economic salvation that would produce independence from the Americans, by 1949 dependence on the Americans was seen as necessary if the Empire was to be saved.

Thus the abandonment of the Third Force did not mean the acceptance of hard choices or a general realisation that Britain's imperial role on the world stage would have to be drastically curtailed. There was no abandonment of major defence commitments but the taking up of new ones for political reasons. There was no abandonment of the attempt to maintain a predominant position in the Middle East and no abandonment of European links. All these had to be maintained for the sake of world power and influence within the American-dominated Alliance that was deemed necessary to protect Western civilisation after post-war tensions had emerged partly because of the failure to reconcile the competing British and Soviet imperialisms.

When this rivalry initially developed against the background of British concerns about becoming a junior partner in the grand alliance, American support for Britain was deemed important, not least because of the need to prevent Soviet–American cooperation undermining British interests. The British Empire had to be preserved and therefore Soviet–American collaboration was not deemed desirable, which produced some short-term benefits for the imperialists who could justify the Empire in Cold War terms. In the medium term the Empire in 1945 was also needed to regain independence from the Americans and here the Cold War proved disadvantageous because it encouraged the United States to assume responsibilities which, while they may have been necessary and beneficial, undermined the Third Force.

By 1949 the Empire and links with Europe were no longer seen in terms of avoiding dependence on the United States which was then accepted as desirable. Yet they were still regarded as necessary to retain the influence over the Americans that would ensure there were no disagreements between Washington and London by forcing the United States to go along with British policies; if this was not secured then disagreements could appear and a Soviet–American rapprochement, as in 1945, was deemed likely to occur. These were the links between Cold War issues and an imperial strategy geared to the maintenance of British status and prestige as a Great Power.

In 1945 Soviet–American cooperation had to be avoided to preserve British imperial interests and to ensure British weakness could eventually be overcome; but confrontation with the Soviets could only be justified in terms of 'liberalism' and the concern for freedom and democracy in Eastern Europe. The confrontation then became one element undermining Britain's imperial strategy and the unrealistic and often contradictory attempts to implement it, rather than the essential reason for some British policies. By 1949, because of the Cold War, attempts to preserve power, status and links with the Empire could be justified in terms of Western interests. Thus the Cold War was partly caused by and then helped maintain an imperial strategy that avoided acceptance of the permanent nature of the post-Second World War shift in the global balance of power and a radical reassessment of the costs and desirability of maintaining a global role.

Notes

1. J. Darwin *The End of Empire* (London 1991).
2. R. Edmonds *The Big Three, Churchill, Roosevelt and Stalin in Peace and War* (London 1991) p. 87 citing Soviet sources.

INDEX

Gold Coast, 125, 148, 192; US influence in, 5–6
Gousev, Fedor, 24–5, 27
Greece, 14–15, 18, 20, 23–33, 37–42, 45–8, 54–7, 61–3, 68, 70, 77, 80, 82–4, 88, 90–4, 96, 99, 103, 106, 109–10, 133, 148, 213
Greek Communist Party, 25, 37
Grigg, Sir Edward, 50
Gruenther, General Alfred, 171

'Halfmoon', 172
Hall, George, 65
Hall-Patch, Sir Edmund, 122, 148, 166; on Western bloc, 117
Hankey, Robin, 159
Harriman, Averell, 31, 44, 88
Harvey, Sir Oliver, 54, 98, 146–7
Hayter, William, 104, 159
Hickerson, J., 164
Holland, 117, 146, 162, 167, 185
Hollis, General Leslie, 170–1, 182
Hong Kong, 3, 211
Hood, Lord, 15, 66
Hopkins, Harry, 53
Howe, R.G., 109
Hoyer-Millar, Frederick, 159–60
Hull, Cordell, 4–8
Hungary, 12, 15, 18–19, 24, 26, 30, 38–9, 49, 55–7, 90–2

Imperial strategy, nature of, vii-viii
India, 93, 110, 125, 132, 133
Indian Ocean, 50, 129
Indonesia, 103, 191
International Bank for Reconstruction and Development, 9
International Monetary Fund, 9
Intra-European Payments and Compensation Scheme, 188, 197
Iran, see Persia
Iraq, 50, 56, 86, 94, 103, 109, 145, 168, 170, 180, 191
Italian colonies, 78, 80–2, 97–8, 101–7, 177; trusteeship of, 59, 79, 101, 102. See also Libya, Cyrenaica, Tripolitania
Italy, 15, 24–5, 29, 31–2, 44–5, 49, 54, 56, 64, 69, 80–1, 85, 89, 99, 103, 106, 109, 146, 162, 166, 169, 172, 178, 179, 213; and African development, 178–9; and Western Union, 177; treaty with, 82, 102, 108

Jinnah, Mahomed Ali, 145
Japan, 79–80, 84, 88–9, 91–2, 211
Jebb, Sir Gladwyn, 107; and European economic and political union, 159; and policy of no concessions to the Soviets, 61; and post-war reconstruction, 2, 3; and security arrangements, 3, 19; and Soviet domination

in Eastern Europe, 39, 55; and Soviet policy in the Mediterranean and the Middle East, 55, 61, 99
Johnson, Louis, 5
Joint Intelligence Committee, 38–9
Joint Staff Mission (Washington), 52

Kars, 54, 92, 94
Katz, Milton, 192
Kennan, George, 164; and Long Telegram, 96
Kenya, 98, 101, 149, 205
Keynes, John Maynard, 118–9
Khartoum, 134
Killearn, Lord, 34
Kirkpatrick, Ivone, 162, 164, 166
Koenig, General Pierre, 181

Lagos, 98, 100–1, 109, 129, 205
Law Committee, see Committee on American Opinion and the British Empire
Leathers, Lord, 33
Lebanon, 58
Leeper, Sir Reginald, 25
Lend-Lease, 118; Article VII of, 10, 118
Levant, the, 54, 58, 182; 1945 crisis in, 67, 85, 118
Libya, 59, 63–4, 70, 80–2, 85, 97–8, 101–3, 105–7, 109, 177, 213
Liddell Hart, Basil, 100, 109
Linlithgow, Lord, 5
Lloyd, Sir Thomas, 178
Lockhart, Bruce, 52
Lovett, Robert, 164, 171
Lublin Committee, 23, 43–7, 53
Luxembourg, 162, 167

Macdonald, Malcolm, 191
MacLean, Sir William, 8
Macmillan, Harold, 26, 29
Macedonia, 28
Maishy, Ivan, 212
Malaya, 3–4, 56, 191–2, 211
Marshall Aid, 143–4, 152, 165, 173–6, 196, 199
Marshall, George, 137, 157, 162
Marshall Plan, 140–1
Massigli, Rene, 126, 147, 166
Melville, E.E., 192
Michael, King of Romania, 27
Middle East, see British policy toward
Middle East Development, 117, 122, 131–2, 134, 139
Middle East Office, 117, 139
Middle East Supply Centre, 5
Middle Eastern Conference of British Representatives, 65, 77
Military Sub-Committee, 12
Molotov, Vyacheslav, 31, 44, 89, 108; at London Council of Foreign Ministers, 80,